D0321668

POPULATION STRUCTURES AND MODELS

POPULATION STRUCTURES AND MODELS

Developments in spatial demography

Edited by
ROBERT WOODS and PHILIP REES

London
ALLEN & UNWIN
Boston   Sydney

George Allen & Unwin (Publishers) Ltd,
40 Museum Street, London WC1A 1LU, UK

George Allen & Unwin (Publishers) Ltd,
Park Lane, Hemel Hempstead, Herts HP2 4TE, UK

Allen & Unwin Inc.,
8 Winchester Place, Winchester, Mass. 01890, USA

George Allen & Unwin (Australia) Ltd,
8 Napier Street, North Sydney, NSW 2060, Australia

First published in 1986

British Library Cataloguing in Publication Data

Population structures and models:
developments in spatial demography.
1. Population geography
I. Woods, Robert.   II. Rees, Philip,
1944–
304.6   HB1951
ISBN 0-04-301200-0

Library of Congress Cataloging in Publication Data

Population structures and models.
Bibliography: p. 390
Includes index.
1. Population geography – Addresses, essays, lectures.
2. Population – Addresses, essays, lectures. I. Woods,
Robert. II. Rees, P. H. (Philip H.) 1944–
III. Title: Spatial demography.
HB1951.P67 1986   304.6   85–30642
ISBN 0-04-301200-0 (alk. paper)

Set in 10 on 12 point Times by
Mathematical Composition Setters Limited, Salisbury, UK
and printed in Great Britain by
Butler and Tanner Ltd, Frome and London

To Alison, Rachel, Gavin, Laura, Gareth and Chloe

Preface

This is a book with a message. It argues the case for viewing demographic patterns, structures and systems from a spatial perspective. For by so doing new insights will be gained on the complex forms of human populations and more effective methods will be advanced to monitor and forecast – even change – the growth and distribution of future populations. Spatial demography is not seen as an end in itself or as an alternative to population geography; rather it represents an aspect of population studies in which recent developments have been considerable and new advances promise to be spectacular in this and the next century.

In attempting to convey their message the editors have incurred many debts of gratitude. The Economic and Social Research Council, the Nuffield Foundation, the Wellcome Trust, and the University of Sheffield Research Fund have provided financial assistance to one or more contributors. The contributors have been especially indulgent in allowing us to use their exemplary work to form part of our wider scheme. Anita Fletcher, Paul Coles, Tim Hadwin and Marjie Salisbury have helped us to create a final manuscript. To all those mentioned we express our thanks.

ROBERT WOODS and PHILIP REES
Sheffield and Leeds
January 1985

Contents

Preface   page   ix

List of tables   xv

List of contributors   xxi

1 *Spatial demography: themes, issues and progress*   1
   ROBERT WOODS AND PHILIP REES

Part I *SPATIAL VARIATIONS IN DEMOGRAPHIC*
       STRUCTURES   5

2 *Spatial and temporal patterns*   7
   ROBERT WOODS

   2.1 Demographic relationships   7
   2.2 Methods   9
   2.3 Limitations   18

3 *The spatial dynamics of the demographic transition in
   the West*   21
   ROBERT WOODS

   3.1 Introduction   21
   3.2 The transition described   23
   3.3 Spatial variations   29
   3.4 Transition theory   36
   3.5 Can the transition be explained?   39

4 *The analysis of regional fertility patterns*   45
   JOHN COWARD

   4.1 Introduction   45
   4.2 Divergence and convergence   47
   4.3 The fertility transition in Trinidad and Tobago   54
   4.4 Contemporary fertility variations in England and Wales   58
   4.5 Conclusion   64

5 *Rising fertility in developing countries*   68
TIM DYSON AND MIKE MURPHY

     5.1   Introduction   68
     5.2   The evidence   68
     5.3   Describing common fertility trends: analytic approaches   82
     5.4   Summary and discussion   92

Part II   *MODELLING AND FORECASTING*   95

6 *Developments in the modelling of spatial populations*   97
PHILIP REES

     6.1   What are the Part II chapters about?   97
     6.2   Movement, transition and last residence data   99
     6.3   How are the components of change formulated?   101
     6.4   The measurement of rates   105
     6.5   The use of rates in population models   111
     6.6   Should observed rates or models of rates be used?   115
     6.7   The individual and the household   116
     6.8   The modelling of spatial populations within wider
           systems   123
     6.9   Conclusion   124

7 *Choices in the construction of regional population
   projections*   126
PHILIP REES

     7.1   Introduction   126
     7.2   Sources of variation in population projection   129
     7.3   Accounting frameworks for population projection   133
     7.4   Accounts based models: the ways in which the data are
           assembled   143
     7.5   The ways in which the population system is closed   146
     7.6   Research design   148
     7.7   A demographic information sytem for 20 UK zones   149
     7.8   The projection experiments   154
     7.9   Conclusions   159

8 *The analysis and projection of interregional migration
   in the United Kingdom*   160
JOHN STILLWELL

     8.1   Introduction   160
     8.2   Study area zones, data sources and estimation methods   161
     8.3   Characteristics of internal migration in the UK   169
     8.4   A modelling system   192
     8.5   Conclusions   201

9 *Forecasting place-to-place migration with generalized linear models*   203
FRANS WILLEKENS AND NAZLI BAYDAR

   9.1 Introduction   203
   9.2 Analysis of the time-series migration data for
       forecasting purposes   205
   9.3 Modelling the components of migration   220
   9.4 Forecasting migration   239
   9.5 Conclusions   241

10 *Demographic processes and household dynamics: a microsimulation approach*   245
MARTIN CLARKE

   10.1 Introduction   245
   10.2 Microsimulation: an outline of methodology and a
       review of practice   247
   10.3 The generation of an initial population using synthetic
       sampling   254
   10.4 A microsimulation model of household dynamics   263
   10.5 Results of numerical simulations   268
   10.6 Concluding comments: present problems and future
       priorities   272

11 *A demographic–economic model of a metropolis*   273
MOSS MADDEN AND PETER BATEY

   11.1 Introduction   273
   11.2 An input–output approach to demographic–economic
       modelling   276
   11.3 Methodological developments and empirical
       applications   278
   11.4 The household consumption framework as a
       forecasting device   286
   11.5 Conclusions   295

Part III *RECONSTRUCTION, ESTIMATION AND EVALUATION OF DEMOGRAPHIC PATTERNS*   299

12 *Demographic estimation: problems, methods and examples*   301
PHILIP REES AND ROBERT WOODS

   12.1 A definition of estimation   302
   12.2 The concepts used in defining the population stocks
       and flows   303

CONTENTS

12.3   The age–time frameworks adopted   305
12.4   The spatial frameworks adopted   312
12.5   The temporal and accounting frameworks adopted   319
12.6   Example 1: external migration flows from a set of
       United Kingdom zones, 1976–81   323
12.7   Example 2: India's spatial demography   329
12.8   Lessons   341

13   *Regional population analysis in developing countries:
     the creation of a database for Thailand*   344
     WIM DOEVE

13.1   Introduction   344
13.2   Problems of creating a database   346
13.3   The establishment of a benchmark integrated database
       for Thailand   357
13.4   Discussion   365

14   *Assessing the United Nations urbanization projections
     for the Asian Pacific*   367
     JACQUES LEDENT AND ANDREI ROGERS

14.1   Introduction   367
14.2   Projected population growth and urbanization in the
       Asian Pacific   367
14.3   The components of growth   371
14.4   Urbanization dynamics   376
14.5   Urbanization and development   380
14.6   Conclusion   388

Bibliography   390

Index   410

List of tables

		page
2.1	Contributory elements of contrasting demographic regimes	13
3.1	Estimated life expectation at birth and gross reproduction rate for England and Wales, France and Sweden, 1800–1980	24
3.2	The effects of population redistribution on the level of life expectation at birth, England and Wales, 1811–1911	37
3.3	Involvement stages in the mortality and fertility transitions	38
4.1	Variations in the general fertility rate, Trinidad and Tobago, 1946–80	50
4.2	Standardized urban and rural mortality rates for selected European countries	53
4.3	Hypothesized relationships with the general fertility rate, Trinidad and Tobago, 1960	55
4.4	Correlations between variables, Trinidad and Tobago, 1960	56
4.5	Stepwise regression results for general fertility rate, Trinidad and Tobago, 1960	57
4.6	Children ever born, desired family size and use of contraception among women ever in a marital union aged over 45, in Trinidad and Tobago, 1977	57
4.7	Variations in fertility measures, counties and metropolitan counties of England and Wales, 1981	59
4.8	Hypothesized relationships with fertility measures, England and Wales, 1981	62
4.9	Correlations between variables, England and Wales, 1981	62
4.10	Stepwise regression results for crude birth rate, England and Wales, 1981	63
4.11	Stepwise regression results for marital fertility, England and Wales, 1981	64
5.1	World Fertility Survey and vital registration data on Colombia's recent fertility trends	73

5.2 Cohort-period fertility measures (rates and trend
     indices) by level of education, Philippines survey, 1978   78
5.3 Partial correlation coefficients, controlling for linear
     trend, for regional groupings and regional averages   90
6.1 Description of the variables entering different
     multiregional population analyses   100
6.2 Sources of the variables entering different multiregional
     population analyses   100
6.3 American females, 1968, projected to 1998 using
     birthplace independent and birthplace dependent
     projections   114
6.4 Changes in population number and households, Great
     Britain, 1961–81   117
6.5 Components of the increase in numbers of households
     between 1951 and 1981, Great Britain   118
6.6 Projected headship rates, England and Wales   120
7.1 Comparisons of Rogers's different aggregations and
     decompositions with the full 9×9 multiregional model
     at 2008   131
7.2 A transition accounts table for cohort a 134
7.3 A movement accounts table for cohort a in one time
     interval   136
7.4 An extract from a movement accounts table for a
     20-zone UK system, 1976–81, for cohort 20–24 to
     25–29   138
7.5 Components of change for a region, Central Clydeside,
     1976–81   139
7.6 An extract from a movement rates table for a 20-zone
     UK system, 1976–81, for cohort 20–24 to 25–29   140
7.7 The research design   149
7.8 The age-group classifications of the raw data at zonal
     level   151
7.9 The cohort classifications used in the demographic
     information system   152
7.10 The projected populations of the UK zones in 2006   155
7.11 The projected population distribution by zone for the
     UK, 2006   156
7.12 The projected age distribution of the UK population,
     2006   157
7.13 Comparisons of the projection models   157
8.1 Model migration schedule estimates of age-group flows
     from Tyne and Wear to Northern Ireland, 1966–71   166
8.2 Three largest absolute net migration balances; study
     zones, 1966–71   172

8.3 Age-specific net migration balances; study zones, 1966–71   173

8.4 Age-specific interzonal and intra-zonal migration totals and proportions, 1966–71   177

8.5 Inmigration and outmigration proportions; study zones, 1966–71 and 1976–81   179

8.6 Zones arranged in hierarchical order according to number of net inflows, 1966–71 and 1976–81   180

8.7 Five-year age-group proportions of annual interzonal moves, 1976 to 1982   189

8.8 Outmove proportions from Greater London to other zones, 1975–6 to 1981–2   192

9.1 Number of municipalities by urbanization category, 1961 and 1971   208

9.2 The origin–destination-specific migration flows by the type of municipalities in the Netherlands, selected years   209

9.3 Distance measures for the migration generation vectors   213

9.4 Distance measures for the migration distribution matrices   221

9.5 Average percentage share of information divergence for each category of municipalities where migrations originate   221

9.6 Parameters of the illustrative simple models   224

9.7 Observed and fitted probabilities for the illustrative simple models   226

9.8 Summary indices for the models of the generation component   232

9.9 Summary indices for the models of the distribution component   234

10.1 Some differences between population and household forecasting   246

10.2 A list of individuals and their attributes: a microlevel specification   249

10.3 Attributes and their classifications as used in the microsimulation model   257

10.4 The probability of sex, marital status and age categories for heads of household, Yorkshire and Humberside, 1971   259

10.5 Population age and sex structure, Yorkshire and Humberside, 1975: model and observed distributions   261

10.6 Household structure, Yorkshire and Humberside, 1975: model and observed distributions   262

10.7 Household size, Yorkshire and Humberside, 1975: model and observed distributions   262

10.8	Age distribution of population, Yorkshire and Humberside, 1981 and 1986	270
10.9	Household size, Yorkshire and Humberside, 1974–5, 1980 and 1986	271
10.10	Household type, Yorkshire and Humberside, 1974–5 and 1986	271
11.1	Quadrant Δ: economic production multipliers	284
11.2	Quadrant Π: employment multipliers	284
11.3	Quadrant Λ: demographic–economic multipliers	285
11.4	Quadrant Γ: multisector multipliers	286
11.5	Merseyside demographic–economic forecasts	293
11.6	Population aged 15 + in different marital states	294
12.1	The two approaches to spatial population analysis	304
12.2	External migration: information for 1976	325
12.3	Emigration flows for 1976	327
12.4	Survival and fertility rates for projecting Indian populations	332
12.5	Life expectancy trends for India	333
12.6	Life expectancy estimates for selected Indian states, 1961–71	334
12.7	Total fertility rates in India, past and future	336
12.8	Regional differentials in crude birth rates	337
12.9	Estimates of crude birth and death rates for Indian states, 1961–71 and 1971–81	338
12.10	Socio-economic variables for Indian states, 1961	340
13.1	Integrated benchmark database derived from selected information in the 1970 Population and Housing Census of Thailand	360
13.2	Life expectation by region of residence at age x and future possible residence, Thailand, 1970	362
13.3	Multiregional population projections for Thailand, 1970–2005	363
13.4	Regional population structures for Thailand, 1970, compared with the stable age structures	364
14.1	Population estimates and projections and average annual rates of growth: Asian Pacific, urban and rural, 1950–2000	368
14.2	Estimated and projected percentages of population in urban areas: Asian Pacific, 1950–2000	370
14.3	The tempo of urbanization: Asian Pacific, 1950–2000	371
14.4	Estimates of rural net migration rates: Asian Pacific, 1950–2000	373
14.5	Percentage of urban growth due to natural increase: Asian Pacific, 1950–2000	373

14.6 Alternative population projections and average annual
      rates of growth: Asian Pacific, urban and rural,
      1975–2000   374

14.7 Alternative projections of the percentages of population
      in urban areas: Asian Pacific, 1975–2000   377

14.8 Alternative tempos of urbanization: Asian Pacific,
      1975–2000   377

14.9 Alternative rural net migration rates: Asian Pacific,
      1975–2000   378

14.10 Alternative percentages of urban growth due to natural
      increase: Asian Pacific, 1975–2000   378

14.11 Summary of alternative projections to the year 2000:
      Asian Pacific, 1950–2000   379

14.12 Urbanization and per capita GNP: selected Asian
      Pacific countries, 1975   384

14.13 Annual per capita GNP growth rates: historical and
      projected   386

14.14 Changes in per capita GNP over two quarter-centuries:
      historical and projected   387

List of contributors

Peter Batey
Senior Lecturer, Department of Civic Design, Town and Regional Planning and Transport Studies, University of Liverpool, Liverpool L69 3BX

Nazli Baydar
Postdoctoral Fellow, Stanford University, California 94305, USA

Martin Clarke
Lecturer, School of Geography, University of Leeds, Leeds LS2 9JT

John Coward
Lecturer in Geography, School of Biological and Environmental Studies, University of Ulster, Coleraine, Northern Ireland BT52 1SA

Wim Doeve
Lecturer, Department of Econometrics, University of Manchester, Manchester M13 9PL

Tim Dyson
Lecturer in Population Studies, London School of Economics, London WC2A 2AE

Jacques Ledent
Research Fellow, Institut National de la Recherche Scientifique, INRS-Urbanisation, 345 Durocher, Montreal H2X 2L6, Canada

Moss Madden
Senior Lecturer, Department of Civic Design, Town and Regional Planning and Transport Studies, University of Liverpool, Liverpool L69 3BX

Mike Murphy
Lecturer in Population Studies, London School of Economics, London WC2A 2AE

Philip Rees
Reader, School of Geography, University of Leeds, Leeds LS2 9JT

Andrei Rogers
Professor and Director, Population Program, Institute of Behavioral Sciences, University of Colorado, Boulder, Colorado 80309, USA

John Stillwell
Lecturer, School of Geography, University of Leeds, Leeds LS2 9JT

Frans Willekens
Deputy Director, Netherlands Interuniversity Demographic Institute, Lange Houtstraat 19,2511 CV, The Hague, The Netherlands

Robert Woods
Senior Lecturer, Department of Geography, University of Sheffield, Sheffield S10 2TN

1

Spatial demography: themes, issues and progress

ROBERT WOODS and PHILIP REES

The word 'demography' is commonly used in two senses: as a synonym for 'population studies' and to refer to the statistical analysis of vital events. The latter usage implies a particular subject area and methodology; the former is far broader and clearly contains the latter, but it gives no indication of how the subject is to be approached (see Bourgeois-Pichat 1973). 'Spatial demography' refers to the conscious use of a spatial perspective in demography. It differs from population geography mainly in terms of its equal emphasis on mortality, fertility and migration as the components of population change and distribution (see Fig. 2.1): its use of the statistical demographer's methods; and its multidisciplinary approach (Woods 1984a). The term 'spatial demography' is used here in its broader sense to refer to the spatial analysis of past, present and future population systems and structures. 'Spatial demography' is both a member of the demography family and a close relative of population geography.

Within spatial demography there have emerged three distinct yet related strands. The analysis of spatial and temporal patterns in demography has a long history and represents a particularly influential line of enquiry. It dates from the statistical revolution which began in Europe and America in the 19th century and resulted from the combination of regular population censuses with vital registration data organized and manipulated within a framework of administrative units by a bureaucracy of professional statisticians (Cullen 1975, Cassedy 1984). Dr William Farr's work at the office of the Registrar General in London provides numerous examples of attempts not only to describe spatial patterns, particularly in respect of mortality, but also to infer cause from pattern (Eyler 1979). In the 1930s influential American and English demographers, like Lotka and Glass, also approached demographic issues via a spatial perspective (Lotka 1936, Glass 1938). Since World War II the pattern analysis strand of spatial demography has been strengthened by regular use. Davis's (1951) work on India, Taeuber's (1958) on Japan and that of Brass et al. (1968) on sub-Saharan Africa all subscribe

1

to the view that regional variations in population characteristics are interesting and provide clues to underlying social, economic and cultural influences.

Part I of this volume outlines the various forms and uses of this pattern-oriented aspect of spatial demography. It also discusses its problems and limitations as well as illustrating some of the most important issues for new research that are being tackled in the 1980s.

The second important strand in spatial demography deals with modelling and forecasting in a multiregional framework. It has its origins in Stone's work on national accounting systems (Stone 1971), that of Rogers (1968, 1975) on multiregional cohort survival and life table models, that of Land and Rogers (1982) on multistate mathematical demography in general and that of Rees and Wilson (1977) on multiregional demographic accounting. Part II of this volume traces recent developments as well as illustrating the practical applications for planning of this aspect of spatial demography. The connection of spatial demography with accounting concepts is an important one. Careful attention to demographic book-keeping is essential if the derived population models are to have a sound empirical base. The demographic book-keeping takes place within two frameworks: the first is that of age–time, with which demographers are thoroughly familiar but which cannot be neglected in spatial population modelling; the second is that of space or the specification of the interactions of the internal system being modelled and its external environment. Immigration and emigration flows must be treated along with migration flows internal to a country and must be incorporated in any projection models.

However essential, demographic accounting is still only a small start in understanding population change. The next step is to investigate the patterns over time and space of the components that make up the accounts, and to specify the very many elements of population change in a multiregional system in terms of more parsimonious sets of equations of spatial interaction, of time–space series or of age schedule form. Having proceeded through an endogeneous analysis, it is then necessary to connect the structural characteristics or the detailed variables themselves to events that influence the natural and migrational flows of the population. These are connections explored in part in Part I of the book, but they need to be specified tightly and reliably for incorporation in spatial population forecasting models. Part II touches on these aspects, but there is clearly much to be done in connecting macro-models of the way the economy and society are changing to the detailed spatial level of, say, interregional migration flows for two sexes and detailed age groups.

In the first chapter of Part II (Ch. 6) the field of spatial population modelling is reviewed. Our understanding of demographic accounting is extended in new directions in Chapter 7. In Chapter 8 spatial patterns of migration using spatial interaction models as descriptive devices are examined, and the question of whether they are practicable over time using these and simpler models is posed. The authors of the next chapter, Chapter 9, bring together a time-series of migration flows and, after decomposing them into level, generation and distribution components, use the techniques of log-linear modelling to investigate the time-series. Whereas most models of spatial populations involve person-aggregates, the simulation model of Chapter 10 works at the individual level and is able thus to connect individual units in a population with household units. Finally, in Chapter 11 connections between population processes and economics within an input–output framework for an urban system are built.

The third strand, which is developed in Part III, is concerned with the estimation of regional demographic patterns from faulty or inadequate data. It is therefore particularly appropriate for statistically underdeveloped countries, in both contemporary and historical contexts. Advances in this area are clearly related to the development of model life table systems and the application of stable population theory (United Nations 1955a, 1967). At first estimation techniques were applied to age-structure data for countries as single regions, but the realization that mortality structures varied with disease patterns, and even cultures, led to the construction of model life tables specific to world regions. Coale and Demeny (1966) provided the necessary framework and impetus both to develop new techniques and to attempt additional applications. The development of new techniques is illustrated by Brass's (1975) work on a more flexible estimation procedure using logit models, and there are numerous examples of attempts at additional applications from Latin America (Carvalho 1974), Africa (Adegbola 1977, Kpedekpo 1982) and Asia (Woods 1982a, pp. 72–85, Dyson & Crook 1984). The new family of model life tables and stable populations also takes particular account of mortality variations among the populations of developing countries (United Nations 1982a). Many of these themes, together with discussion of the most recent developments in demographic estimation, are considered in Chapter 12.

When combined these three strands form a strong, flexible and most useful thread. Spatial demography is not an end itself, merely a means of focusing on particular aspects of population studies in ways that have proved enlightening and in which there is considerable potential for new advances in theory, methodology and practical applications. The chapters illustrate the strands and the book itself symbolizes our hopes for the thread.

3

PART I

Spatial variations in demographic structures

2
Spatial and temporal patterns

ROBERT WOODS

One of the most important objectives of spatial demography outlined in Chapter 1 is the use of a spatial perspective to identify and describe demographic patterns which might otherwise go unremarked. There is, in addition, considerable potential for statistical explanation since demographic attributes will be associated with the other economic, social, political etc. attributes of populations which have been delimited in spatial units. Change over time can also be incorporated in this framework so that cross-sectional static and dynamic aspects are captured by the study of spatial time series. To oversimplify, analysis may be performed in the static or dynamic modes: it may merely serve to identify new patterns for their own sake or it may use those patterns as a device to unmask the underlying causal structures of demographic relationships.

In order to realize these particular objectives it is necessary to tackle three related questions. First, to what forms of demographic relationships can the spatial perspective be most usefully applied? Secondly, must any particular assumptions be made before analysis can be effected? Thirdly, what are the problems and limitations of this form of approach?

2.1 Demographic relationships

It may not be appropriate to apply spatial analysis to all elements of the demographic system; some levels of aggregation will be more susceptible than others. Figure 2.1 provides a means of exploring these issues. It is not a systems diagram, but merely a way of ordering some of those items which should occur in any complete model of the demographic system. At the most general level there is concern with the size of a population, how it changes over time and has a particular spatial distribution, as well as with the influence size has on economy and society. Even if this level of abstraction is the one ultimately sought, it is usual for research to proceed via the three components of mortality, fertility and migration, although the

7

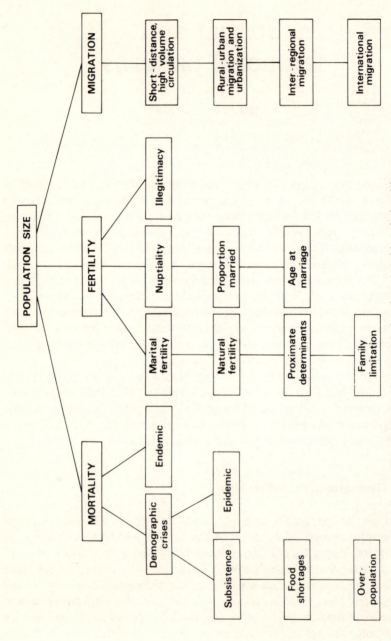

Figure 2.1 A framework for demographic relationships.

influence of migration is occasionally assumed away. It is here that spatial demography will prove most useful for it provides a means of exploring the variety of complex patterns that mortality, fertility and migration display. In Figure 2.1 ways in which these three demographic factors may in turn be tackled are suggested. For example, fertility rates are influenced by the level of marital fertility, nuptiality and illegitimacy, and migration can be classified by the scale at which the move takes place and the sorts of boundaries crossed. Thus, as one moves downwards and outwards in Figure 2.1, each box contains a dependent variable which is in turn affected by the variables in the boxes below. All the variables in Figure 2.1 are likely to exhibit some spatial manifestation and, although the analysis of pattern and its subsequent interpretation is the legitimate focus for spatial demography, some variables will display a recognizable pattern far more readily than others and certain levels will be more amenable to this approach.

Figure 2.1 only deals with demographic variables or those linked by definition to the concepts of mortality, fertility and migration, but the spatial demographic approach must seek to encompass elements from other socio-economic systems in order to examine cause and to trace impact. This is often possible within a spatial framework, but it tends to re-emphasize one particular scale of analysis and the use of empirically verifiable middle-range theory. These represent limitations to the approach which are just as important as data dependence and lack of sophistication in pattern recognition. Part I of this volume serves to illustrate these possibilities and limitations, and this chapter in particular outlines some of the objectives, methods and problems.

2.2   Methods

A distinction must first be made between pattern description, where methods of analysis are often very simple, and attempts to construct causal models, where more formal devices drawn from inferential statistics are readily available. The former has obvious value as a first step, but it is particularly important in cases where little is known about the demographic structures. The Princeton European Fertility Study, for example, has mapped regional variations in overall fertility, marital fertility, nuptiality and illegitimacy in 19th-century Europe and by so doing has confirmed earlier speculations regarding the existence of a peculiar west European marriage pattern in the early modern period and much of the 19th century (Coale 1969, van de Walle & Knodel 1980, Coale & Watkins 1986). In a large area of north-west Europe the mean age at first marriage was relatively high and celibacy was not uncommon. Overall fertility was thus depressed even though family limitation was not practised. This apparently unique demographic regime had a particular regional expression which the simple methods of spatial demography have helped to establish. Similarly, research on international variations has shown the existence of continental regions which have reached similar positions in the transition from high to low fertility and mortality. Sub-Saharan Africa, the Middle East and North Africa and much of Latin America display particular patterns. In the African case crude birth rates have remained high (50 per thousand) although death rates have fallen to 20 per thousand, leading to annual growth rates of 2.5, 3.0 or, in the case of Kenya, up to 4.0%. For Latin America, in Mexico for example the growth rate is 3.0%, but the birth rate is 30 per thousand and the death rate 10 per thousand (United Nations 1980a, 1982b, Woods 1986).

These illustrations stress the point that mapping or simple classification of demographic characteristics serves to highlight significant images and clues for further research. Description of a spatial or temporal pattern can of course go further by charting the changing level of variance over time, by searching for autocorrelation among variables or residuals, and by attempting to regionalize characteristics into discrete multi-unit entities. On the first point, it has often been remarked that a population's passage through the demographic transition will lead to an increase in the variation among regional or local levels of mortality, fertility and migration, but once the transition is complete variation, and thus the variance, will decline as mortality and fertility are universally low (Section 4.2). The point is usually well made, but the implicit assumption that pre-transition variation will be low, that mortality and fertility will be universally high and migration low, begs rather too many questions. We now know that short-distance high-volume circulatory migration was particularly important in early modern Western societies and that, as remarked above, overall fertility varied considerably because the pattern of nuptiality also varied, and even natural fertility (marital fertility in the absence of family limitation) was not constant (see Fig. 2.1).

The search for autocorrelation among variables and residuals has not been particularly thorough in demographic research, yet there is some potential here for pattern identification and exploratory analysis. Temporal and spatial autocorrelation indices have both been defined and used to some effect in simulation analyses of the development of spatiotemporal patterns, especially where it has proved useful to compare observed and simulated series or distributions (Cliff & Ord 1973, Bennett 1979).

There has been little attempt to group population characteristics into multifactor regions, although there would seem to be certain advantages here in the quest for distinctive demographic regimes. Figure 2.2 helps to make the point by plotting the crude birth and death rates (in parts per thousand) of countries classified into major world regions. Although the observations do not coincide there is some clustering. The most striking examples are Europe with the USSR: sub-Saharan Africa; and Australia, New Zealand, Canada and the USA. However, even the Middle East with

10

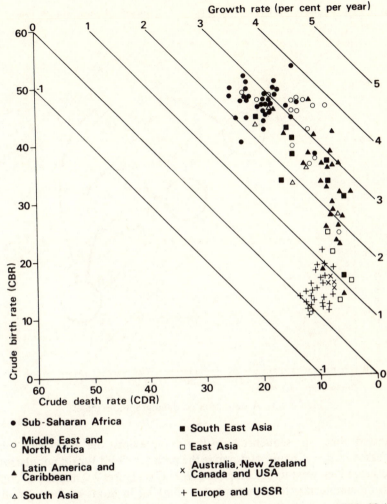

Figure 2.2 International variations in crude birth and death rates, 1975–80 (CBR and CDR in parts per thousand).
(*Source:* United Nations 1981c).

North Africa and East Asia show some degree of conformity. Figure 2.3 takes the definition of demographic regimes further in three ways. First, it traces the possible bounds of certain transitory positions where growth is rapid (*B*), where it is less rapid but still considerable (*b*), and the bounds of stable regimes where growth is low or zero (*A*, *a*, *c*). The areas of the circles suggest the likely degree of variation among populations. Secondly, two temporal sequences are illustrated (*A* → *B* → *C* and *a* → *b* → *c*) where the destinations are similar but the origins differ in terms of the levels of mortality and fertility, not the rate of growth. Thirdly, it may further be

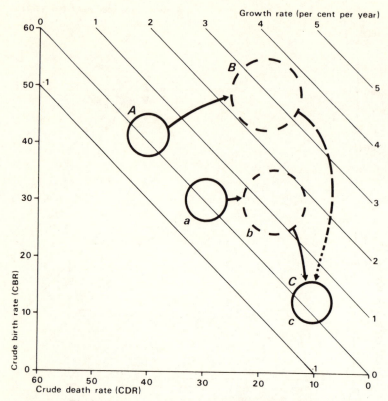

Figure 2.3 A definition of demographic regimes.

suggested that the sequence $a \to b \to c$ represents the European path whereas $A \to B \to C$ could summarize the path for Third World populations if the second leg were to be completed ($B \to C$). Figures 2.2 and 2.3 in combination summarize the arguments for thinking in terms of demographic regimes, their spatial manifestation and their movement over time along particular routes from several old to a single new stable position. In Chapter 5 several issues are taken up relating to the commonly observed increase in fertility associated with $A \to B \to C$ in Asia, Africa and Latin America. We may also speculate on the reasons for differences between A and a. Table 2.1 suggests some possibilities. In regime A mortality is higher, marriage takes place earlier, but marital fertility is lower, as are mobility and migration. But a takes an opposite form: mortality and nuptiality are lower since marriage is later and marital fertility and migration are higher. In c, mortality and marital fertility are not only lower but low by the standards of A and a, although marriage is earlier and the volume and range of migration is higher and high. Regime a has been well documented by European and North American historical demographers (see, for example,

Table 2.1 Contributory elements of contrasting demographic regimes.

	Higher	Later	Lower	Earlier
mortality	A		a, (c)	
marriage		a		A, (c)
marital fertility	a		A, (c)	
(migration)	a, (c)		A	

Note
See Figure 2.3 for a key to A, a and c. Migration and c are in parentheses because the former is not strictly a regime element and c has a significantly different form from A or a, mortality and fertility being low in c.

Vinovskis 1979, Wrigley & Schofield 1981); however, the form of A remains sketchy. But Cook (1981) provides an example of the demographic impact of Spanish colonialism in Inca Peru; Page and Lesthaeghe (1981) and Bongaarts *et al.* (1984) show how early marriage and lower marital fertility were combined in sub-Saharan Africa; and Barclay *et al.* (1976) and Coale (1984) give a sketch of the traditional rural Chinese regime. Hajnal (1982, 1983) has also compared the culturally embedded social rules for family and household formation in A and a. The ability of pre-modern, pre-transition populations to influence indirectly the balance of demographic constraints with which they lived, and thereby to defer the Malthusian positive check, must not be underestimated.

However, the identification and description of patterns can only be a first step. Demography has come of age in recent years with the discussion of important theoretical and explanatory issues alongside the traditional concern for empirical knowledge. Several of these issues can be linked with the development of micro-economic theory, the population and development debate or the emergence of historical sociology. But there has been a tendency for the positivist methodology to be dominant and for one particular framework to be employed in the verification of hypotheses. This framework has often involved ecological correlation together with causal or structural equation models. It is this particular aspect of the attempt to explain the form of population structures that has been concerned explicitly with spatial demography. For example, although E. G. Ravenstein listed the 'laws of migration' in the 1880s, his generalizations were based entirely on casual observation (Grigg 1977). When Olsson (1965) addressed similar problems in the 1960s he had recourse to multiple regression analysis which provided means of establishing both the signs and the strengths of functional relationships between a whole series of independent variables (e.g. size of origin and destination, employment levels etc.) and the length of migration streams. Hypotheses were derived from more general interaction theories and rigorously tested on data for Swedish administrative areas. The results of Olsson's analysis, although they have not gone unchallenged, provide clear instances of the advances possible through spatial demography. Since Olsson's work in the mid-1960s, a voluminous literature has developed on the use of multivariate ecological analysis in migration research (see, for example, Greenwood 1981). Much of this has been concerned with empirically testing the human capital hypothesis (Sjaastad 1962) in ways that take account of the peculiarities of regional systems and the distinctive nature of migration streams specific to stages in the life cycle or levels of economic development. Thus migration between two areas i and j becomes, for example, a function of the potential returns to migrants in making the $i \rightarrow j$ move, the costs of the move, the educational level of the movers, and other characteristics of origins and destinations − political violence in i perhaps (see Woods 1982a, pp. 142–53).

In the study of fertility the Princeton project provides numerous examples of the use of multivariate ecological analysis where the fertility and nuptiality characteristics of a spatially defined population are inter-related with other social, economic, cultural, environmental, demographic and political variables. In Lesthaeghe's (1977) study of the Belgian fertility transition, marital fertility (measured by I_g), illegitimate fertility (I_h) and nuptiality (proportion ever married aged 20–24) are taken in turn as dependent variables. Five independent variables are included in the models in order to capture, respectively, industrialization–urbanization, language homogeneity, literacy, infant mortality, and secularization. Of these variables Lesthaeghe found industrialization–urbanization and secular-ization to be the most important since, when Wallonia and Flanders were treated separately, they accounted in combination for from two-thirds to three-quarters of the regional variation in marital fertility (I_g). The other independent variables made relatively little contribution. In a related study of the Netherlands (1850–90) by Boonstra and van der Woude (1984) the dependent variable was the birth rate as it varied between a sample of 375 municipalities. Once again clear distinctions were made between static cross-sectional and dynamic analyses and between cultural regions (defined in terms of religious observance and specifically adherence to Roman Catholicism) and geographical regions (related to agricultural systems developed on clay or sandy soil). In their static analysis Boonstra and van der Woude (1984) found that the birth rate was related to, in descending order of importance, the death rate (especially infant mortality they claim); the surplus of immigrants in a municipality (and thus economic attraction); the agricultural system in operation; religious adherence and, to a lesser extent, literacy. Population density was of no particular significance. The dynamic analysis revealed the importance of changes in the first three of these six independent variables, but religious adherence, literacy and population density did not make significant contributions to explaining changes in the level of the birth rate.

These examples serve to illustrate some of the elements of a methodology that has become all but standard practice for the exploration of causal associations among demographic and non-demographic variables. Let us examine this methodology in a little more detail so that its sequential nature, its strengths and weaknesses can be made explicit.

The method employed by Olsson, Greenwood, Lesthaeghe, Boonstra and van der Woude comprises four distinct stages. The first is depicted in Figure 2.4. The dashed boxes encompass entire systems with circles for dependent variables and rectangles for independent variables. In Figure 2.4 the entire demographic system is viewed as the outcome of, or as having been caused by, the system on the left which summarizes under five subheadings those categories from which important independent variables might be drawn. Each of these categories is likely to be important in its own right, but the strength and sign of the contribution each makes can only be evaluated once it has been operationalized in measurable form. The second stage involves the precise definition of variables together with the elaboration of hypothetical associations. Figure 2.5 is developed from Figure 2.4 and shows how the focusing procedure might operate. The full range of demographic theory is now engaged. Migration is related to the compared characteristics of origin and potential destination as well as to the characteristics of potential migrants. Mortality is affected by environmental

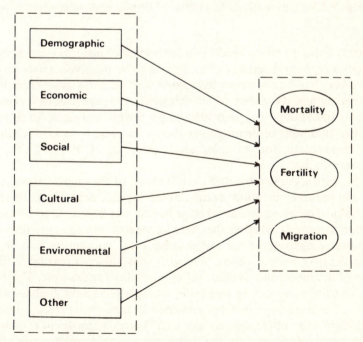

Figure 2.4 The multivariate analysis of demographic relationships: the three components.

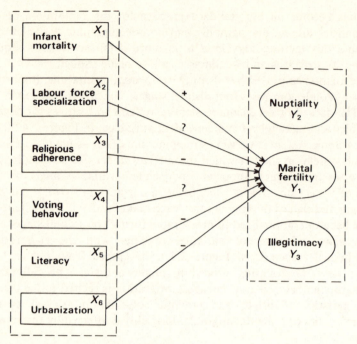

Figure 2.5 The multivariate analysis of demographic relationships: fertility.

quality, living standards and the effectiveness of medical science. Fertility, specifically marital fertility (Fig. 2.5), may be positively related to infant mortality, but it is inversely associated with religious adherence, the level of literacy and the extent of urbanization, although labour force specialization and voting behaviour have as yet unspecified signs. In this context the two traditions of demographic theory focus on economic relations and the implications for attitudes and behaviour of what is often called 'modernization'.

The third stage involves the quantification of the model shown in Figure 2.5 and thus the operationalization of the variable definitions, the choice of the units of observation and whether these are to be treated in a static cross-sectional form or whether they involve relative change over time. It also requires recognition of the fact that both the independent and dependent variables may be interrelated. Nuptiality may influence marital fertility; the level of urbanization will affect infant mortality for example. The demands of this third stage can be met using multiple regression analysis when the units of observation are areas and the variables are correctly scaled. The coefficient of multiple determination (R^2) gives a numerical expression for the amount of variance in the dependent variable explained by the combined effects of the independent variables; the regression coefficients (β)

provide a means of assessing the contribution of each independent variable on its own; and the correlation coefficients (r) give the association between individual pairs of independent or dependent variables. Variables can be respecified in terms of r or dropped from the model because of low β values and, if R^2 appears unsatisfactory, new variables can be included after the regression residuals have been examined.

The fourth stage is partially illustrated in Figure 2.6, which shows the imaginary results from the operationalized model in Figure 2.5, but does so with the aid of conventions developed in path analysis (see Blalock 1961, 1969, Duncan, 1975, and, for an application of structural equation models in migration, Cadwallader 1985). The independent variables ($X_1 \ldots X_6$) all have significant βs and thus each one is linked by an arrow to Y_1. Several of the independent variables have significant correlations with other variables (X_2 is influenced by X_1, X_5 and X_6; X_5 influences X_1 but is influenced by X_2 and X_6; X_3 and X_4 are interrelated etc.). All the variables influence Y_1 both directly and indirectly (X_6 via X_1, X_4 and X_5). The dependent variable is also influenced by Y_2 and Y_3. A full representation of the model in Figure 2.6 would specifiy the β coefficients on the $X \rightarrow Y$ links and either r on the $X \rightarrow X$ links or, in its most elaborate form, βs derived by allowing each of the independent variables in turn to become the dependent variable (each $X_1 \ldots X_6$ and Y_1 would then be affected by an

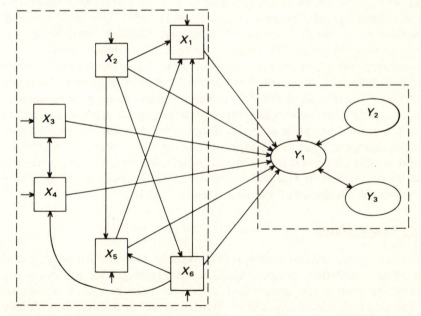

Figure 2.6 The multivariate analysis of demographic relationships: marital fertility.

as yet unspecified bundle of variables which account for the remaining unexplained variance, i.e. $\sqrt{(1 - R^2)}$.

How is Figure 2.6, and models like it, to be interpreted? Variations, or changes, in marital fertility are associated with a bundle of independent variables to the extent that $R^2 \times 100\%$ of the variation is explained statistically. Each of the independent variables in turn makes certain direct and indirect contributions, as do the unspecified variables and those, such as nuptiality and illegitimacy, that may be thought of as 'temporary' independent variables when marital fertility is the sole focus for attention. Variables in the bundle may be ordered according to their relative contribution, the signs checked against hypotheses, the form of the intervariable associations specified and the residuals examined, Ultimately interpretations similar to those drawn from the work of Olsson, Greenwood, Lesthaeghe, Boonstra, and van der Woude, outlined above, emerge to frame our understanding of what influences variations and changes in demographic patterns.

The techniques of simulation, projection and forecasting represent in their own right powerful means of exploring demographic structures since they tend to oversimplify the perceived 'rules' that underlie contemporary relationships in order to produce or reproduce future or past patterns. There are obvious differences between the intent of simulation and projection and thus of their objectives. The simulations of long-term population growth often made by econometricians (Lee 1977), and those of microscale redistribution made by geographers (Woods 1981), rely on the formal statement of simple operational rules derived from hypothesis. The objective is to produce expected patterns of variation which, when compared with observed patterns, provide means of evaluating the rules upon which those expected distributions have been generated. There are certain important philosophical problems – those concerning equifinality for example – that bedevil this form of exercise; yet the experimental nature of the method has great potential since it should be capable of providing a clear image of what would happen *if the rules were changed*. Projections and forecasts are based on the same principle, but here of course there can be no comparison of expected and observed. (The modelling side of spatial demography is discussed and illustrated in Part II.)

2.3 Limitations

Let us now return to the problems to be encountered in the use of ecological analysis, simulation, projection and modelling in general as devices for revealing spatial and temporal demographic patterns and as means of exploring their underlying causes. Apart from the issues that have already been raised in passing, there are two main types of problem: those that are data dependent and those that are inherent in the methods themselves.

We need not pursue the former in any detail here, save to recall that both historical demographers and demographers of most contemporary underdeveloped countries depend entirely for their images of past or present on estimations based on ecclesiastical records, rudimentary censuses and special sample surveys. Even the demography of the statistically advanced West has certain major lacunae often resulting from the lack of interest of governments in population monitoring, especially the collection of detailed migration and mobility records. Chapters 8 and 9 reflect the varied nature of this problem. It is obvious that the difficulties encountered in pattern identification will hinder the construction of causal models. Where it is difficult to reconstruct demographic structures it will also prove difficult to discern the other social, economic and cultural characteristics of the populations to which the demographic variations may be related.

The methods themselves may prove problematic for three main reasons. First, the perils of the ecological fallacy restrict the value of conclusions drawn with the aid of area-based causal models. For example, even though there is a strong positive association between the distribution of coalminers and marital fertility it does not mean that coalminers' wives have large families; it means rather that large families are common in areas where coalmining is an important occupation (see Section 3.5). It is likely, however, that there will prove to be some link if the positive association is very strong, and it is certain that there will be no link if the correlation coefficient shows a non-significant association. In these circumstances causal modelling within spatial demography should provide means to test theoretical statements of the middle range, but it could also act as a way of screening out the least fruitful aspects of explanatory frameworks and of focusing attention on more meaningful relationships which can be analysed using other, complementary methods. Research on fertility and migration behaviour has sought to meet this need by isolating the attitudes and actions of individuals whose decision making is affected by irrationality and ignorance, and whose ability to implement decisions may be severely constrained (on fertility, see Woods & Smith 1983, Bulatao & Lee 1983, and, on migration, Lieber 1978, Desbarats 1983).

Secondly, regardless of the ecological fallacy, the assumptions necessary for regression analysis impose a burden which not only limits the process of empirical validation but also constrains the scope and form of theory as initially constructed. Only measurable variables may be used. They should be in a normalizable form and clearly distinguishable into dependent and independent sets; the latter set should not contain highly related variables. In this regard, the intangible and the unobservable are given only secondary consideration since their influence on 'pattern' may either not be measured at all or may only be measured through surrogates. The relationships between husbands and wives within marriage clearly provide the fundamental context for working out fertility intentions and practices, yet sexual relationships can play no direct part in the formal presentation of causal models designed to explore spatial demographic patterns. Losses of this kind are by no means critical, but they do illustrate the limited and temporary sense in which the words 'exploration' and 'cause' are used. Spatial demography merely provides a single viewing point along the way to understanding.

Thirdly, the pattern of the consequences of aggregation – by area, social class or time, for example – will become more visible as detail is lost, but the effectiveness of interpretation may be impaired in consequence. This issue is certainly not peculiar to spatial demography, yet the scale problem can be particularly irksome, especially when the scale of analysis is dictated by the availability of data. Preston's (1976) work on international mortality patterns provides an interesting example, since in order to incorporate cause of death characteristics unequal countries had to be used as units for observation. The resulting correlation analyses did, however, yield extremely interesting evidence regarding the limited association between mortality decline and income per head in the underdeveloped world.

Not only do these various methodological problems serve to emphasize the need for caution in approaching population issues via spatial demography, they also help us to begin to appreciate that web of interrelationships which limits our understanding of human society.

The various problems inherent in the analysis of spatial and temporal patterns in demography are examined in Chapters 3, 4 and 5. The demographic transition in the West ($a \rightarrow b \rightarrow c$ in Fig. 2.3) is considered in Chapter 3, and contemporary variations in fertility in a developed economy and a developing one (i.e. c and $B \rightarrow C$) are considered in Chapter 4. In both these chapters spatial perspective is used to reveal pattern, but also an explanation of variation and change over time is sought through ecological analysis. The authors of Chapter 5 take a consciously temporal view and explore the $A \rightarrow B$ sequence at the international level. Each of the three chapters illustrates in its own way the potential and the pitfalls of spatial demography.

3

The spatial dynamics of the demographic transition in the West

ROBERT WOODS

3.1 Introduction

The West European demographic regime of 1930 was substantially different from that of 1800. Life expectation at birth was up to 20 years higher, and fertility was directly and effectively controlled within marriage. Both of these changes – the significant extension of life chances and the practice of family limitation – were particularly important events in the process of modernization, yet neither is well understood. In combination they are referred to as the 'demographic transition' or the 'vital revolution' – phrases that have their origins in the descriptive and conceptual writings of Thompson (1929), Landry (1934) and Notestein (1945). 'Demographic transition' is now used in two senses: first, as a model of how demographic change occurred over time; and, secondly, as a theory to explain why other social, economic and technological changes were in some combination contributory causes. Although this distinction between model and theory, modelling and theorizing, is an important one, it suggests that the model is all but complete and that an explanation is not beyond the realms of possibility. The 'demographic transition model' has been represented in a variety of related forms (Woods 1979, p. 6, Grigg 1982); the theory too, although based on Notestein (1945), becomes more diffuse by the decade (Woods 1982a, pp. 159–73). The 'demographic transition theory' can be reduced to two elements which operate on two levels. The levels are: first, that of the 'structural context', the dominant economic, social, cultural and technological organization of human society; and, secondly, that of 'individual behaviour' and decision making. The two elements are the static or slow moving and the dynamic or rapidly changing; the former conditions the general form of the structural context and the unchanging aspects of man's social existence whereas the latter affects certain parts of the overall structure in ways that can alter its influence on the attitudes and behaviour

21

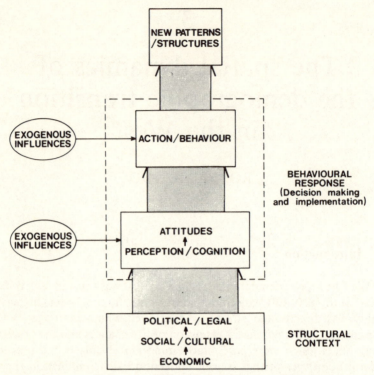

Figure 3.1 Framework for a general theory of demographic relationships.

of individuals. Figure 3.1 sketches a framework for the analysis of these levels of association. It has a foundation in materialism, but material conditions are not considered to determine behaviour: rather they condition the responses of individuals who act within the constraints of their economic, political and cultural positions in ways that are always rational but rarely calculated to maximize benefits. Demographic behaviour – the attempt to postpone death, to avoid conception, to migrate – is also covered by this framework in ways that will be discussed more fully in the final section of this chapter.

It is the objective of this chapter to examine in greater detail some of the points raised above. More specifically, three arguments will be elaborated. First, our existing models of the form and processes of historical demographic transitions are by no means complete. We do not fully understand the ways in which such fundamental demographic changes occurred in so relatively short a time. Secondly, in pursuing the first argument it is important to explore the spatial dynamics of the transition in order to reveal new patterns and regularities. Thirdly, although the general form of the theory necessary to explain the demographic transition can be outlined, as above, the specific sets of factors relevant to particular circumstances, together with their relative contributions, are persistently difficult to isolate. One way of tackling this problem would be to accept that demographic transitions are the cumulative products of bundles of influences. The presence of certain influences is necessary for revolutionary demographic change to occur; some influences are more important than others and some are unique to specific contexts. The particular composition of the bundles varies among transitions, but many of the influences may prove to be common. It is these common influences that we must seek to isolate, although it may be necessary to reconstruct a number of bundles before the general can be separated from the specific, and the significant from the marginal.

Although this chapter is largely concerned with the European experience it is necessary to begin by outlining the course of the transition in the West, that is the advanced industrial countries.

3.2 The transition described

The demographic transition model is usually depicted by showing changes in the crude birth and death rates over time with the two time-series divided into three or four stages. Yet such crude rates are not ideal for the measurement of mortality and fertility; their only advantages appear to be ease of calculation and the fact that the difference between them shows the rate of natural population change. However, in many European countries series of more sophisticated demographic measures exist which have either been calculated directly or are based on reasonably reliable estimates. Mortality can be measured by life expectation at birth (e_0) and fertility by the gross reproduction rate (GRR, the average number of female children a woman is likely to have on passing through the reproduction age groups 15–49). In their work on English population history Wrigley and Schofield (1981) have combined these two measures in order to judge the relative contributions of mortality and fertility to population growth rates. Figure 3.2 has been constructed on the same principle from the data in Table 3.1. It shows the demographic transition in Sweden, England and Wales, and France from 1800 to 1980 by plotting GRR against e_0. The isolines link points with the same population growth rates (r, the intrinsic rate of natural increase in per cent per year – compare with Fig. 2.3). They were constructed using Coale and Demeny's (1966) West family of model life tables for females and by assuming that the mean age at maternity was 27. From the isolines one can identify both the combination of GRR and e_0 necessary to produce a given growth rate and the extent to which population would grow under certain mortality and fertility conditions. Two boxes have been drawn in to represent the range of the pre-industrial demographic regime (solid) and the contemporary post-transition regime (dashed). The former circumscribes the mortality and fertility variations that occurred in England from 1551 to

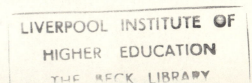

Table 3.1 Estimated life expectation at birth (e_0) and gross reproduction rate (GRR) for England and Wales, France and Sweden, 1800–1980.

	England and Wales		France		Sweden	
	e_0	GRR	e_0	GRR	e_0	GRR
1800	37	2.50	36	2.01	39	2.10
1810	38	2.68	37	1.94	36	2.17
1820	39	2.79	38	1.92	39	2.40
1830	40	2.39	38	1.86	39	2.22
1840	40	2.24	39	1.80	42	2.24
1850	41	2.26	39	1.70	44	2.23
1860	41	2.28	39	1.71	44	2.21
1870	42	2.36	41	1.67	45	2.20
1880	44	2.25	41	1.61	48	2.15
1890	46	1.97	42	1.45	51	2.10
1900	48	1.70	47	1.39	53	1.95
1910	53	1.40	51	1.37	55	1.84
1920	58	1.17	55	1.18	57	1.29
1930	60	0.90	57	1.09	63	0.95
1940	63	0.90	61	1.00	67	1.18
1950	69	1.04	66	1.43	71	1.11
1960	71	1.34	70	1.33	74	1.05
1970	72	1.16	72	1.20	75	0.94
1980	74	0.94	74	0.90	76	0.81

Sources:
Estimates based on the following: England and Wales, Glass (1938, p. 168), Wrigley and Schofield (1981, p. 230) and Registrar General's *Annual Reports*; France, Bourgeois–Pichat (1965); Sweden, Hofsten and Lundström (1976).

1801 as estimated by Wrigley and Schofield (1981, p. 230); however, it is possible that in certain areas, and even nationally for limited periods during demographic crises, e_0 was less than 30 (see Russell 1948, Gottfried 1978, Razi 1980). Apart from this temporary exception, the demographic experience of most of pre-industrial western Europe is unlikely to have strayed beyond the bounds of the solid box in Figure 3.2. The pre-industrial demographic system was not completely stable, however, either in terms of mortality or fluctuations in fertility (Flinn 1981). In certain respects the contemporary post-transition demographic regime (dashed box) is more difficult to define (c in Fig. 2.3): e_0 is approaching an upper maximum and although it will continue to increase its rate of change will decline; and fluctuations in fertility are likely to persist, but they may do so with an ever decreasing amplitude (Ermisch 1983).

Movement between the boxes represents the demographic transition, that is the secular decline in both mortality and fertility. As Figure 3.2 shows the paths taken by national populations were similar but by no means the same

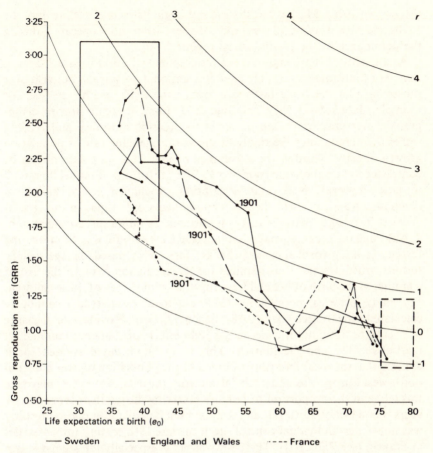

Figure 3.2 The demographic transition in England and Wales, Sweden and France, 1800–1980 (the years 1800, 1810, 1820, ..., 1980 are represented by dots). (*Sources*: see footnote to Table 3.1.)

either in terms of the rates of growth experienced or the timing of change. In Sweden the decline in mortality was in advance of that in England and Wales or in France, but fertility remained relatively static longer than in these other two countries; population growth rates were therefore higher, especially in the 1890s and 1900s. In France, at the other extreme, e_0 and GRR changed in step and in certain decades during the 19th century the French population was stationary. In England and Wales the rapid acceleration in population growth that began in the second half of the 18th century was probably linked with the relaxation of the Malthusian preventive check and the resultant rise in nuptiality and overall fertility (Wrigley & Schofield 1981). Decreases in the mortality rate were slow at first, but, as in France and Sweden, they had started to quicken by the 1870s

(McKeown 1976). Marital fertility did not begin its secular decline until the 1870s and then it did so in ways quite distinct from those operating during the dominance of the pre-industrial regime.

As a means of representing the demographic transition Figure 3.2 has a number of advantages not only over conventional portrayals, but also over those that plot the crude birth rate against the crude death rate (see, for example, Jabukowski 1977 and Fig. 2.2). First, it treats precise demographic measures which are designed to describe mortality and fertility rather than crude rates. Secondly, it shows the changing rate of population growth directly. Thirdly, the experience of individual populations can be contrasted within the same framework. What this form of model does tend to lack, however, is a clear description of change in the individual components and, in turn, their sub-components over time. In the case of changes in fertility patterns this is a particularly important consideration.

Although the gross reproduction rate (GRR) is a useful way of measuring fertility it has two distinct drawbacks. First, it is based on age-specific fertility schedules and thus requires for its calculation data on the age of a mother at the birth of her children, together with the sex of those children. For many historical populations GRR has to be estimated; it cannot be calculated directly (see Glass 1938). Secondly, GRR provides one measure of overall fertility, but it conceals the joint effects of changes in nuptiality, marital fertility and illegitimacy. This is an important drawback for it appears that the overall fertility of much of the population of pre-industrial north-west Europe was under 'social control'; the mean age at first marriage was late and the proportion of females marrying during their reproductive years was substantially less than the maximum possible. But marital fertility was not under 'individual control' until the late 19th century (much earlier in France) (see Table 3.1). These drawbacks − especially the second − can be avoided using A. J. Coale's fertility indices which are indirectly standardized on the age-specific marital fertility of those Hutterite women who married in the 1920s (Woods 1979, pp. 18−21). Coale defines four indices which are related in the following way:

$$I_f = I_m I_g + I_h (1 - I_m) \qquad (3.1)$$

where I_f is the index of overall fertility; I_m, the proportion married; I_g, marital fertility, and I_h, illegitimate or non-marital fertility. If illegitimate fertility is negligible, as was the case in much of western Europe (Shorter *et al.* 1971), then Equation 3.1 can be reduced to

$$I_f = I_m I_g \qquad (3.2)$$

Figure 3.3 utilizes the relationship given in Equation 3.2 to trace the combined influence of marital fertility and nuptiality on overall fertility.

26

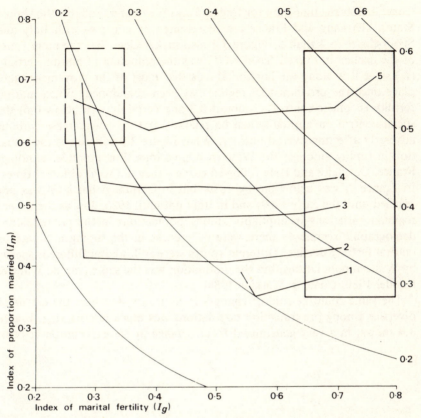

Figure 3.3 Generalized time paths for populations passing through the fertility transition.

The lines numbered 1 to 5 depict generalized time paths for populations passing through the fertility transition from the pre-industrial regime (solid box) to the post-transition (dashed box). In the pre-industrial regime marital fertility was high ($I_g > 0.6$) and 'natural', although it may have varied within narrow bounds (Leridon & Menken 1979, Hinde & Woods 1984), and nuptiality, influenced by the mean age at first marriage and the proportion of females marrying under 50, varied quite markedly over time and particularly between regions. By this means pre-industrial populations could display strikingly different levels of overall fertility (I_f).

In Figure 3.3, curves 1 and 5 chart the two extremes; in the former I_m is particularly low, marriage is delayed and celibacy is common but in the latter marriage takes place early and is almost universal. Post-famine Ireland provides an example for 1 and European Russia for 5. Curve 2 approximates the pattern of northern Europe, Sweden for instance, where I_m was relatively lower than in most of the remainder of north-west Europe.

Curve 3 plots the time path for England and Wales and probably the United States. Germany and France are represented by curve 4, with Italy and Spain closer to 4 than 5. Figure 3.3 also makes clear that the main cause of the decline in overall fertility (I_f) was the reduction in marital fertility (I_g) since it is along the horizontal axis that most of the movement takes place once the pre-industrial regime has been abandoned. When marital fertility is 'under control' (I_g about 0.3 and certainly well below 0.6) the social control on nuptiality can be relaxed, and I_m can increase without adversely affecting overall fertility. What Figure 3.3 conceals is the variation in timing amongst the Western populations. For example, although France, Germany and Italy followed curve 4 they did so at different times. In France I_g was below 0.6 by 1830, but in Germany that level was not reached until the early 1900s and in Italy not until 1920. Just as there were regional variations in nuptiality among populations in the pre-industrial demographic regime so there were differences in the timing and rate of marital fertility decline. Different routes were followed at different speeds by Western populations, but the destination was the same (van de Walle & Knodel 1980, Coale & Watkins 1986).

The same could be said of changes in mortality, but here the extent of diversity among pre-transition populations was much less striking. Figure 3.4 shows, in a very generalized form, change in life expectation at birth

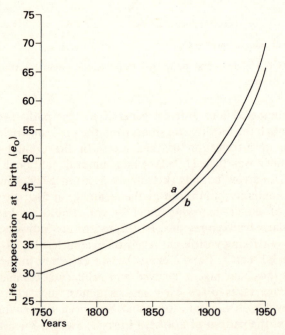

Figure 3.4   Change in life expectation at birth (e_0), 1750–1950.

(e_0) during the 200 years since the middle of the 18th century. Curve *a* summarizes the course of change in England and Wales, northern Europe and North America and *b* traces movement in France and southern Europe in general. Although mortality may have begun to decline before the middle of the 19th century the rate of change only accelerated after 1850 and by the middle of the 20th century its pace had slackened once again.

3.3 Spatial variations

It is apparent from Figures 3.2 and 3.3 that the course of the demographic transition varied in Western countries; it is also the case that regional and local variations were accentuated during the transition and have only recently diminished. The most obvious example of this phenomenon is to be found by considering changes in overall fertility (I_f) and its components. A. J. Coale first defined his fertility indices and then outlined the broad regional variations (Coale 1967, 1969). The results of this and subsequent research have shown the wide diversity of fertility patterns in late 19th-century Europe. Some of the variations can be related to national boundaries, but there are also broader cultural differences between eastern and western Europe – northern and southern Belgium, for example – as well as urban and rural contrasts. Figure 3.5 provides one simple illustration of the heterogeneity that is likely to be experienced during the fertility transition in a single country. It shows *départemental* variations in the decline of marital fertility (I_g) in France between 1831 and 1901 (van de Walle 1974, 1978, 1979, 1980). Even in 1831 I_g was less than 0.6 in France as a whole and it is likely, therefore, that fertility was being controlled within marriage, but in the periphery of the country and in the remoter corners, like the Massif Central, natural fertility persisted up until the end of the century and even beyond. Comparable regional variations are to be found in Germany (Knodel 1974) and Italy (Livi Bacci 1977).

In England and Wales where marital fertility began to decline among certain sub-populations from the 1870s and is apparent nationally from the early 1890s (Fig. 3.6) – far later than in France, but relatively early by general European standards – regional variations are to be seen. The 630 registration districts which were used for the recording of vital statistics between 1837 and 1910 provide a framework for the analysis of spatial variation in mortality, fertility and population redistribution at a relatively fine scale (Woods & Smith 1983, Teitelbaum 1984). Their use has advantages over and above comparable administrative units such as counties, *départements* or provinces. Figure 3.7 shows I_g for 1891 by registration districts, and London is treated separately in Figure 3.8. The year 1891 is a convenient datum point for I_g in England and Wales as a whole probably went below 0.6 for the first time in the early 1890s. Figure 3.7 suggests that

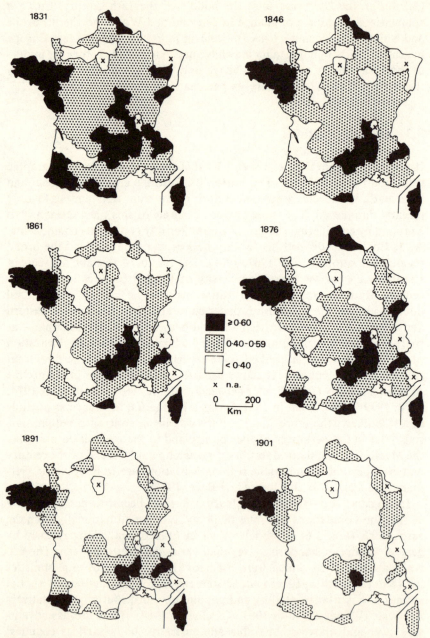

Figure 3.5 Variations in marital fertility (I_g) between rural French *départements*, 1831–1901.
(*Source:* derived from van de Walle 1974.)

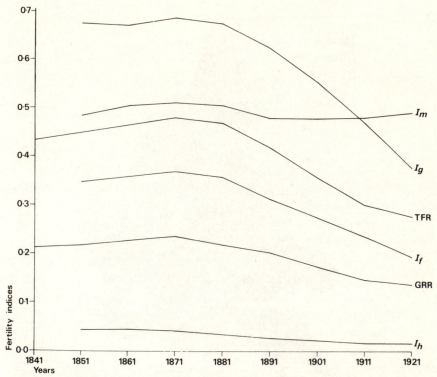

Figure 3.6 The fertility transition in England and Wales, 1841–1921. (Scale × 10 for GRR and TFR.)
(*Source:* the gross reproduction rate (GRR) and the total fertility rate (TFR) are from Glass 1938, p. 168.)

there were two main kinds of districts in which marital fertility declined early: those in the rural south and east (mainly east of a line from the Humber to the Severn) and those comprising the textile districts of Lancashire and the West Riding of Yorkshire. The late decline districts were more widely scattered, but those with the very highest marital fertility tended to be concentrated in the coalfield areas of the North East, South Yorkshire, South Lancashire, Staffordshire and South Wales. In London in 1891 the differences in I_g between the East End and the West End were sharp. Marital fertility was clearly under direct control in the latter, but not in the former. Even in 1861, as Figure 3.8 shows, I_g was below 0.6 in several West End districts (Woods 1984b).

These examples drawn from France and England and Wales serve to illustrate an important general point and to suggest an additional implication. Regional and local variations in the speed and timing of the fertility transition, as well as in pre-transition levels, were inherent characteristics of the breakdown in the natural fertility system and the move to a new demographic regime. One possible implication to be drawn from these

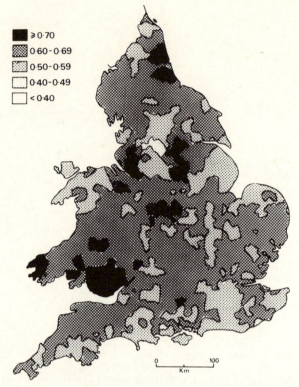

Figure 3.7 Variations in marital fertility (I_g) between registration districts, England and Wales, 1891.

variations is that they may provide a means of identifying the associated economic, social and cultural correlates of demographic change and thereby a procedure for identifying the bundles of influences responsible for such change. Although this is certainly an entirely justifiable route to follow there are, as we shall see, many pitfalls along the way (see also Section 2.2).

These points can be illustrated just as effectively by considering spatial variations in the pattern of mortality decline. Figure 3.9 shows life expectation at birth (e_0) for females for the rural *départements* of France in the 1800s, 1850s and 1890s (van de Walle 1973, Preston and van de Walle 1978). Although estimates for the 1800s are liable to considerable distortion, Figure 3.9 none the less reveals regional disparities in the course of mortality decline. In the 1890s, particularly when e_0 for females was about 47, there were still regions in the extreme west, east and south with e_0s in the 30s or low 40s, although even in these areas e_0 had increased since the 1850s. Just as in the case of marital fertility (Fig. 3.5), there were regional leads and lags in the process of mortality reduction. In England and Wales local variations were more apparent or, rather, their existence is more easily

32

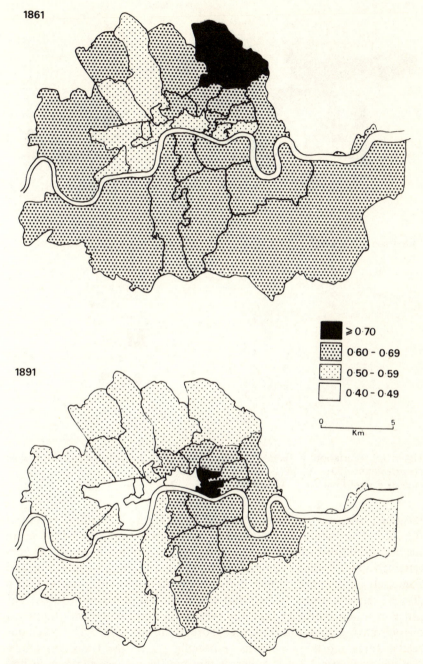

Figure 3.8 Variations in màrital fertility (I_g) between registration districts, London, 1861 and 1891.

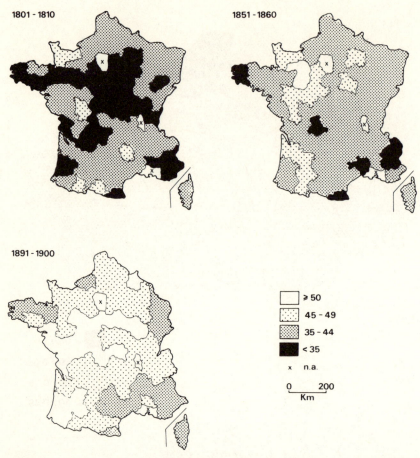

Figure 3.9 Variations in female life expectation at birth (e_0) between rural French *départements*, 1801–10, 1851–60 and 1891–1900.
(*Source:* derived from van de Walle 1973.)

identified using the registration district data. Figure 3.10 shows female e_0 for 1861. The picture is dominated by particularly high mortality levels in the industrial towns of the North of England, where e_0 was in the 30s, and relatively lower levels in many of the rural districts. In much of Devon and Somerset, for example, female e_0 was in excess of 50. There was at least a 20-year range between the best and worst districts in the early 1860s. The range in infant mortality (q_0) was even more accentuated with the worst districts having q_0s as much as twice those of the best (Fig. 3.11). When one relates these mortality patterns, especially e_0, to the transition model outlined in Figure 3.2 it is apparent that mortality levels common in pre-industrial Europe were still prevalent in certain French regions even at the end of the 19th century, although in the new urban and industrial districts

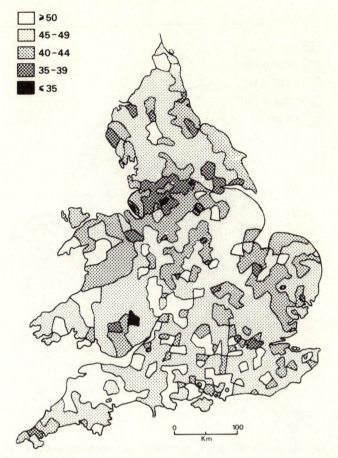

Figure 3.10 Variations in female life expectation at birth (e_0) between registration districts, England and Wales, 1861.

of England and Wales mortality probably increased during the early phase of the industrial revolution making it equivalent to that found in England in the late 17th century. The large-scale redistribution of population from the rural to the urban districts probably increased the importance of this localized deterioration in life chances (Woods & Woodward 1984).

This possibility is considered in Table 3.2. Panel (a) corresponds with Table 3.1 (except for the use of census years) while panel (b) gives the probability distribution of persons in England and Wales in 1811, 1861 and 1911 living in certain urban or rural environments. Panel (c) shows estimates of e_0 for those same urban and rural settlement categories. Multiplication of the appropriate columns in (b) and (c) gives the weighted averages for England and Wales in (a). The 1811 column in (c) is largely speculative, but the 1861 and 1911 columns are founded on recent and

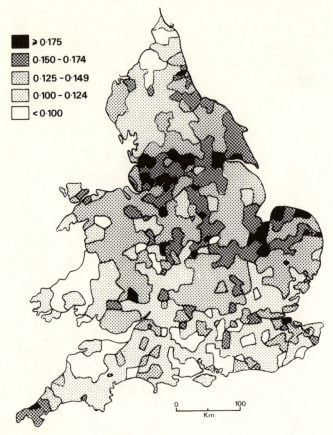

Figure 3.11 Variations in infant mortality (q_0) between registration districts, England and Wales, 1861.

contemporary estimates respectively. Table 3.2 implies that the redistribution of population in early 19th-century England from low-mortality rural areas to high-mortality towns and cities could have had a substantial impact by slowing the national rate of mortality decline (Woods 1985).

3.4 Transition theory

Many theories have been put forward to account for the demographic transition; each stresses its own bundle of influences from which it draws one or a small number of significant causal variables. None of the theories is entirely convincing, most are not formally stated and many lie beyond empirical verification. Four broad categories of theory will be distinguished here; but these categories are not entirely mutually exclusive.

Table 3.2 The effects of population redistribution on the level of life expectation at birth (e_0) for England and Wales, 1811–1911.

	1811	1861	1911
(a) e_0 in England and Wales (sexes combined)[a]			
	38	41	53
(b) Proportions of England and Wales population in rural, small town, large town and London categories[b]			
rural	0.7421	0.5104	0.2989
small town	0.1209	0.2018	0.2627
large town	0.0250	0.1480	0.3130
London	0.1120	0.1398	0.1254
(c) Estimated e_0s for categories[c]			
rural	41	45	55
small town	32	40	53
large town	30	35	51
London	30	37	52

Notes
[a] e_0s are based on Wrigley and Schofield (1981) for England with English Life Tables 1 to 8. ELT 8 is for 1910–12. It assumes that Wales and England are similar pre-1841.
[b] Based on Law (1967) with the addition of London. Small towns have populations in excess of 10 000 but under 100 000; large towns are 100 000 plus, excluding London; and 'rural' is the residual population.
[c] The figures for estimated e_0 for 1861 are based on approximations from Woods (1982b). For 1911 the e_0s are equivalent to those given for rural districts, urban districts, county boroughs and London for 1911–12 which accompany ELT 8. Multiplication of the 1861 and 1911 columns in (b) and (c) gives a close approximation of the e_0s in (a). The e_0s for 1811 in (c) represent one possible solution (see Woods 1985).

Notestein's (1945) transition theory is relatively clear. Mortality decline occurs first; it begins and is perpetuated as a consequence of the agricultural, industrial and sanitary revolutions. Fertility starts to decline after a certain time lag, during which there is rapid population growth. Changes are brought about by the adoption of fertility control behaviour among members of the new urban and industrial society in which individualism and materialism have become so important. The advantage of this first category is that it deals with both mortality and fertility, but it probably over-emphasizes the rôle of socio-economic change – what Notestein calls 'modernization' – by suggesting that industrialization and urbanization are the essential causal mechanisms. The other three categories of transition theories relate mainly to fertility. Although mortality and fertility may themselves be interrelated and affected by common social and economic influences, there are certain crucial differences in the ways such changes are likely to occur.

Table 3.3 illustrates some of these differences by outlining the progress

Table 3.3 Involvement stages in the mortality and fertility transitions.

Involvement stages

A, no action	B, social action	C, individual action
	1, intentional	1, intentional
	2, side-effect	

Mortality change sequence
A → (A + B1) → (B1 + C1)

Fertility change sequence
A → B2 → C1

---

of social and individual involvement. In both cases we begin from a 'no action' stage (A) in which mortality and fertility are out of direct control. This is not to say that they are both static: natural fertility may vary as may the epidemiological and environmental conditions that influence disease patterns. In the mortality change sequence, A is replaced by a combination of A and B1 as elementary public health measures are introduced by the state, hospitals are founded and medical science applied. Deliberate social action is taken with the explicit aim of improving life chances (B1), but mortality may still be beyond effective control. The third aspect of the mortality sequence involves the supplementary role of individual action which in this context implies the development of personal social services. The fertility change sequence is rather more straightforward with 'no action' replaced by social control through restrictions on nuptiality in the European regime and ultimately the direct limitation of fertility by married couples. In this sequence social control is merely a side-effect of the prevailing social and economic system (B2 rather than B1).

The second category of transition theory relates particularly to the move from B2 to C1 (even from A to C1) which it sees in terms of a small number of preconditions for change coming together and triggering off a secular decline in fertility. Coale (1973) provides one example of such a theory in which the pre-conditions are as follows: the technical means to limit fertility must be available; rational decision making must be practised in respect to family size and limitation; and 'perceived social and economic circumstances must make reduced fertility seem an advantage to individual couples' (Coale 1973, p. 65). Once all of these three conditions have been met then C1 should ensure both the demise of natural fertility and the decline of overall fertility.

The third and fourth categories place special emphasis on the role of particular preconditions. The economists' interpretations dwell on such concepts as the costs of and returns from children; the costs of family limitation; the balance between the factors influencing supply and demand; 'intergenerational wealth flows'; and 'relative status income compression'

38

(Leibenstein 1974, 1975, Caldwell 1982a). In essence this third category of transition theory deals with the 'perceived social and economic circumstances'; high-parity children will be avoided once their economic or social values have been reduced in comparison with the financial burden they represent. Low-parity children will still possess a social value for their own sake.

The fourth category sees the fertility transition in terms of innovation diffusion theory. Either new techniques of family limitation are developed and diffused within the temporal, spatial and social contexts or the idea of fertility control itself (C1) spreads through a population and is gradually adopted by larger and larger numbers of couples until it becomes the new social norm.

In short, transition theory has been thought of in terms of a general concept of total demographic change; a shortlist of preconditions; a single key determinant, often economic but occasionally cultural; and as a sequential movement in time and space. How appropriate are these notions for our understanding of the historical experience of the demographic transition in the West?

We have already outlined some of the distinguishing characteristics of the secular decline in mortality and fertility that began in most Western countries during the 19th century; now we must turn to their explanation.

3.5 Can the transition be explained?

Reference to the general framework in Figure 3.1 and to Table 3.3 suggests that we must concern ourselves with three structural elements (economic relations, social norms, cultural values) and with behaviour (motivation, action), whether the consequences are intended or not. We are also concerned with dynamic and static elements, and with the temporal and spatial dimensions. To give an example, cultural factors probably had a profound influence on the European fertility transition, but they did so as static structural elements which conditioned responses to rising living standards, new attitudes to children, the rôles of women and so forth. Such factors acted as background variables: they accelerated or retarded responses to the more dynamic structural elements (see van de Walle & Knodel 1980). Our brief review of the four categories of transition theory suggests that we should look for these dynamic elements in the following areas. First, economic growth, improving living standards and changes in relative income distributions may themselves have been directly influential in the mortality and fertility transitions – as prime movers even – but they were also associated indirectly with changes in the structure of employment and with the sectoral and spatial characteristics of the workforce. For example, women became increasingly more involved in non-domestic employment both before and during marriage; the rise of the lower middle class was spectacular, as was that of cities and suburbs. The age, sex, skill and place of employment of the workforce were all transformed. Secondly, society's values and attitudes were shifted, partly in response to economic changes. Attitudes to children and women changed only slowly as did the moral climate and religious observance. Public social welfare became a cause for concern and remedial action. Thirdly, some of the economic and social changes were themselves dependent upon technological advances, but some of these advances also affected the ability to extend life chances and to defer conception. Fourthly, we must be aware of the interrelationship between the demographic variables themselves. The decline of infant and child mortality will affect completed family size, unless fertility is reduced to compensate, and high fertility may itself be associated with low infant survival (Preston 1978).

Various attempts have been made to identify one or a number of these influences, although efforts to measure the effects of single variables or to provide an overall interpretation have posed problems. Here we shall provide an additional example drawn from the experience of 19th-century England and Wales. This example serves to cast some light on the entire historical process of the demographic transition, together with the particularity of the British experience; it also helps to reveal the issues associated with 'demographic explanation' and the insights that the spatial perspective can give. (General problems were discussed in Section 2.3).

It has already been shown (Fig. 3.2) how the transition in England and Wales compared with that in France and Sweden, and how marital fertility (Figs 3.7 & 3.8) and mortality (Figs 3.10 & 3.11) varied spatially. We can be reasonably certain that cultural differences were relatively unimportant within Victorian England – compared with Belgium, Germany, Switzerland and even Italy – but there were striking economic and social divisions. These divisions mediated the various influences of the dynamic structural elements – rising living standards, changing social attitudes, the growing involvement of the state – in ways that were analogous to the broader cultural divisions that were to be found in Europe as a whole. In order to approach these issues let us take marital fertility (I_g) in England and Wales as our dependent variable and consider the variables that were likely to have influenced its cross-sectional variation (see also Teitelbaum 1984, Coale & Watkins 1986).

In general, we would probably expect economic factors, especially those relating to occupation and the structure of the workforce, to have been particularly important when taken in conjunction with certain broader influences coupled with social class, social attitudes to children and the family, and the purely demographic influence of mortality and perhaps nuptiality. Most of these factors are beyond direct measurement: their influence can only be inferred from their position in the temporal sequence.

However, it is possible to construct some direct measures and others that have the status of surrogates. With these caveats in mind we can proceed to develop a causal model of the variations in marital fertility.

Equation 3.3 begins what is bound to be a process of iterative approximation. It gives marital fertility (I_g) as a function of four employment and two demographic variables:

$$I_g = f(C, F_s, -S, -T, -C_s, I_m) \tag{3.3}$$

They are: the percentage of adult males (20 and over) engaged in coalmining (C); the ratio of male and female farm servants to land proprietors, farmers and graziers (F_s); the percentage of adult women employed as domestic servants (S); the percentage of adult women in employment (excluding domestic servants) who were engaged in the manufacture of textiles (T); the probability of a child surviving from age 1 to age 10 (child survival, C_s); and the index of proportion married (I_m). We would expect I_g to be inversely related to both the domestic servants (S) and the textile workers (T) variables since the latter epitomizes the early involvement of females in the manufacturing workforce and thus the relative advantages to the family economy of postponing pregnancies and the avoidance of large families, and the former not only reflects female wage employment in the domestic economy but also serves as a surrogate measure of living standards. Marital fertility was probably higher where coalmining was important (C) since the local economies of such areas were buoyant in this period, male incomes could have been higher earlier compared with those in most other employment sectors, and the opportunities for non-domestic female employment were limited (Haines 1979). In the rural economy there appears to have been an important distinction between the arable areas in the south and east where landless agricultural labourers were employed on relatively large farms and the pastoral or mixed farming areas of the north and west where the system of 'servants in husbandry' persisted on the small farms even in the late 19th century (Kussmaul 1981). Where agricultural labourers predominated (low F_s) marital fertility may have been more responsive to economic vicissitudes. One would normally expect low child mortality (high C_s) to obviate the need for high marital fertility unless ideal family sizes were themselves increasing. There are, however, a number of complex issues at stake here and it may be that marital fertility must first be 'under control' before it can be effectively adjusted to the replacement of lost children (Knodel 1982). The last variable, I_m, should not bear any clear association with marital fertility, although nuptiality and marital fertility may act as alternative means of influencing overall fertility (see Fig. 3.2). Although our six independent variables capture some essential aspects they fail to relate to attitudinal changes or variations above and beyond those that may be influenced by labour force conditions. This is the single most serious omission from the causal model.

41

Figure 3.12 presents the results of two multiple regression analyses with I_g as the dependent variable for 1861 and 1891. The analyses are based on data for 590 districts in England and Wales (the areas used in Figs 3.7, 3.10 & 3.11) with London taken as a single district). Paths are only shown if significant linkages (correlation coefficients) exist between variables or between independent variables and the dependent variable (βs) (see Lesthaeghe, 1977, p. 210; Boonstra & van der Woude, 1984; Section 2.2).

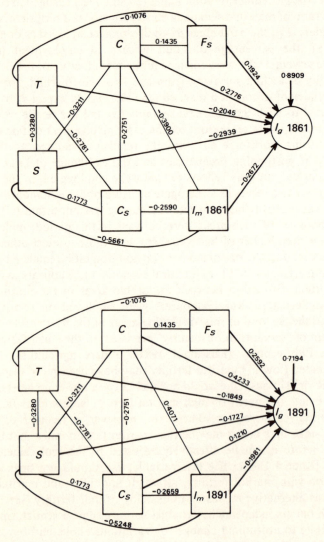

Figure 3.12 Path models of the variations in marital fertility (I_g) in registration districts, England and Wales, 1861 and 1891.

Four points should be noted. First, the coefficient of multiple determination (R^2) is low in both 1861 (20.64%) and 1891 (48.25%), but substantially better in the latter case. The model leaves much unexplained. Secondly, several of the independent variables are interrelated. This is inevitable given the nature of the socio-economic system under investigation, but is none the less worrying, especially in respect of the strong association between female servants (S) and nuptiality (I_m) even though r^2 is only 32.05 and 27.54% in 1861 and 1891 (see Woods & Hinde 1985). Thirdly, the signs of association are as expected in Equation 3.3, save that child survival (C_s) did not make a significant independent contribution to I_g 1861 although it did in 1891 when, contrary to expectation, it was positive. The contribution of I_m changed from a negative to a positive one between 1861 and 1891. Fourthly, a comparison of the causal models shown in Figure 3.12 reveals that the coalminers (C) and farm servants (F_s) variables increased in significance although the textile workers (T) and the domestic servants (S) variables became weaker.

The relative lack of success of these causal models in terms of R^2 can be accounted for in the following way. Although it is clear (even from Figure 3.7) that the districts in which marital fertility remained highest ($I_g \geqslant 0.7$) up to the 1890s were generally located on or close to the English and Welsh coalfields and that the districts in which it declined first ($I_g < 0.6$) – and in which it was already relatively low by the 1860s – were either associated with textile manufacture or had higher proportions of female domestic servants (which may also indicate their high social standing), the districts that fall outside these three categories and tend to have intermediate levels of I_g represent the great majority of districts in England and Wales. In these 'average' populations the correlates of marital fertility patterns are far more difficult to identify with the available independent variables and ecological analysis. It may be that other independent variables relating to social attitudes, such as religious observance or the extent of female literacy, would have proved valuable complements to the employment and demographic variables used in Figure 3.12. The timing of fertility decline – especially the control of marital fertility – is difficult to analyse using ecological correlations when a majority of the spatial units have very similar behaviour patterns. In this particular case an examination of national or regional time series may prove more fruitful (Fig. 3.6), although it would tend to obscure the extreme observations that the spatial perspective is capable of isolating.

The points raised by the above example also serve to illustrate some of the general problems in providing an empirically based explanation for the demographic transition in the West. Although our concept of the transition is fairly well developed – in terms of models and theories – our ability to formally test the theories is seriously limited by the availability of quantitative data, the multivariate nature of the influences involved and the multidimensional form of the several responses. Although we may be closer to a description of the bundle of influences involved in certain particular national demographic transitions, we are still not yet able to present a comprehensive statement on the causes of the demographic transition in the West.

4

The analysis of
regional fertility patterns

JOHN COWARD

4.1 Introduction

The explanation of spatial variations in fertility and mortality represents an important area for study not only in its own right but also in the contribution it may make to the broader fields of explaining and predicting regional population dynamics and the testing of hypotheses concerning the general determinants of fertility and mortality. In this chapter some general issues in the explanation of spatial demographic patterns are considered and, by way of example, variations in fertility with reference to Trinidad and Tobago, and England and Wales are investigated.

Depending on the availability of data, there are a variety of approaches one can take to the explanation of spatial patterns of fertility and mortality. With the majority of studies utilizing aggregate census and vital registration data, the most commonly used research design has been based on the ecological approach and, although this has received much criticism (Banks 1972), it remains a convenient method of identifying those factors that affect regional fertility and mortality and of exploring the general determinants of fertility and mortality differentials (Hermalin 1975, see Section 2.2). Utilizing individual data from surveys and registers widens the scope for explanation and reduces the likelihood of falling into the ecological fallacy. For example, the collection of individual data in connection with the British longitudinal mortality study (Fox & Goldblatt 1982) and the recently conducted World Fertility Surveys provide unique opportunities for more detailed analysis of spatial variations in fertility and mortality.

Thus many of the problems connected with the explanation of spatial demographic patterns, particularly those associated with the ecological approach, reflect limitations in the availability of data. Indeed, studies based on aggregate census and vital registration data can only offer a partial view in the explanation of spatial patterns because data are not available for certain potentially important variables and in many cases associations cannot be tested at the individual level. (Chapters 3 and 4 both illustrate this problem.) Thus, of the wide range of possible influencing factors affecting fertility – embracing demographic, biological, socio-economic, cultural and sociopsychological variables – the ecological approach based on census and vital registration data can normally only examine some of the more important demographic, socio-economic and cultural variables (see Fig. 4.1). It cannot of course directly examine childbearing norms or couples' decision-making processes, which ultimately govern fertility patterns. Indeed, the range and diversity of potentially important variables and possible levels of analysis ensures that it is virtually impossible for any single approach or research design to offer anything but a partial view on the general explanation of fertility. The value of the spatial approach lies in examining whether there are discernible area patterns of variation and the extent to which these can be related to variations in environmental and behavioural factors, and to processes such as spatial diffusion. In the case of the explanation of spatial fertility patterns there are two main underlying assumptions. First, there are certain regularities in individual behaviour which produce discernible spatially aggregated patterns of fertility. Secondly, although variations in factors such as social class, religious denomination or distance from a centre of innovation do not in themselves directly 'explain' fertility differences, the populations of particular areas, characterized by varying social class, religion or distance from a centre of innovation, have broadly similar norms and attitudes regarding family formation, the desired number of children and the use of family limitation which are expressed in fertility differentials. The second assumption generally has greater validity for small, socially homogeneous, spatially defined populations, although fertility differences between larger, more heterogeneous, populations generally reflect the presence of particular sub-populations with distinctive norms and with relatively high or relatively low levels of fertility.

Another feature concerning data availability relates to the manner in

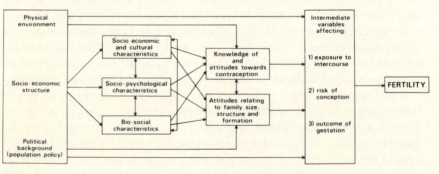

Figure 4.1 Summary of the major factors affecting fertility.
(*Sources:* Adapted from Beaver 1975, Balakrishnan *et al.* 1980, World Fertility Survey 1977.)

which theories of fertility are to be tested. Thus studies of fertility decline based on aggregate census data will inevitably concentrate on socio-economic structure and it is more difficult to give due consideration to other factors such as sociopsychological variables, fecundity or broader culturally ingrained variables such as degree of conservatism. The ecological approach is particularly suitable when applying mainstream demographic transition theory in a spatial framework by concentrating on various socio-economic aspects of modernization but is less suitable when, for example, adopting Caldwell's (1982a, 1982b) theory of fertility decline based on changing intergenerational wealth flows, since the pertinent explanatory variables can normally only be crudely inferred from available data sources. Finally, other problems concerning the explanation of spatial patterns can be briefly mentioned. For example, invariably there are problems connected with the spatial units of study in terms of the desired scale of analysis, the availability of data for such units and the varying geographical or population size of these units. Also there are statistical problems associated with the use of standard multivariate techniques in explaining spatial patterns, such as the presence of multicollinearity amongst the hypothesized explanatory variables and the assumptions of additive and linear models.

Before turning to the problems of multivariate explanation and the relationships outlined in Figure 4.1, it may prove valuable to sketch in more detail a relatively simple approach to the modelling of demographic change within a regional system through notions of divergence and convergence.

4.2 Divergence and convergence

Variations in the magnitude of regional differentials in fertility and mortality over time can be incorporated in a framework of divergence and convergence where, for any particular level of aggregation, the extent of regional differences would be expected to increase and then decline with the process of demographic transition (Spengler 1966). Thus, on the basis of demographic transition theory, it might be expected that regional differentials would be relatively small in the pre-transition phase with the population of most areas being subject to uncontrolled fertility and uniformly high mortality. The processes of modernization and socio-economic change which are thought to bring about reductions in fertility and mortality are initially limited in their spatial extent, and thus regional differentials increase or diverge and peak in the middle stage of transition, after which differences decline or converge with further modernization and regions that are demographic laggards catch up with leading regions. Eventually, fertility and mortality tend to level out at relatively low levels for the population of all areas, and it has been postulated that regional (and socio-economic) differentials in fertility and mortality could eventually

47

disappear, with all population groups sharing similar values and norms associated with mass society and having similar access to health facilities and services. Changing patterns of regional inequality over time and space constitute major themes in the development theories of, for example, Williamson (1965) and Myrdal (1957), and similar patterns of regional variation should be applicable to spatial patterns of fertility, mortality and migration (Zelinsky 1971; see also Woods 1979, p. 142).

However, this simple framework of divergence and convergence can be criticized and modified in a number of ways. For example, the post-transition phase is often characterized by oscillating, not uniform, fertility through time and, as suggested by Alonso (1980) and O'Connell (1981), such oscillations may be the product of diverse regional trends. Indeed O'Connell (1981) suggests that population groups at a relatively high level of socio-economic development, and generally with low fertility, display greater sensitivity to cyclical factors affecting fertility through changing patterns of family formation and family limitations; consequently, regional fertility levels will converge in cyclical upturns and diverge in downturns. Analysing inter-state variations in fertility in the USA from 1940 to 1975, he argued that 'a persistent cyclical pattern of converging and diverging rates can be expected to be the normal state of affairs'. In fact it has also been suggested that there could be regional swings in mortality, particularly infant mortality, as a result of changes in regional economic performance (Knox 1981), and this too could also lead to variations in the magnitude of regional differentials in mortality. These features of divergence and convergence can be amalgamated to extend the classic model of demographic transition by including a spatial perspective in terms of the magnitude of regional variations in fertility and mortality (see Fig. 4.2). Athough this model suffers from the same problems of oversimplification as that of demographic transition theory, it nevertheless provides a general framework for analysing changing regional variations in fertility and mortality. However, particular patterns concerning the degree of regional variation will be influenced by the level of aggregation and the measures of fertility and mortality utilized, although the general principles seem relevant to all levels of aggregation.

Many of the features of divergence and convergence need more detailed examination. For example, the distinctive features of demographic transition of many contemporary developing countries could also be associated with distinctive features of changing regional fertility and mortality. Thus rapid decline in mortality might occur for the population of all areas of a country within a relatively short space of time, hence reducing the length and intensity of an initial phase of divergence. Similarly, decline in fertility could also display particular patterns of divergence and convergence.

The applicability of the divergence and convergence framework to a developing country can be seen in relation to the recent decline in fertility

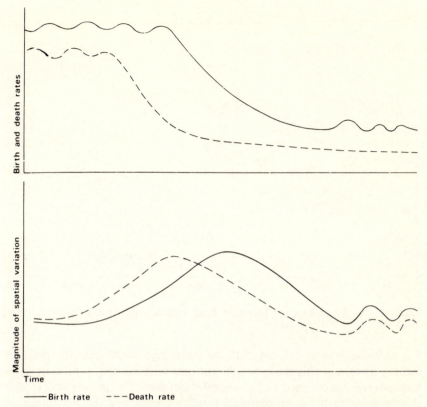

Figure 4.2   A model of divergence and convergence for spatial variations in fertility and mortality during the demographic transition.

in the Caribbean islands of Trinidad and Tobago. The crude birth rate (CBR) had generally fluctuated between 35 and 40 parts per thousand prior to 1960, but it declined dramatically during the 1960s (along with age-standardized measures) to 25 in 1970 and has remained at a broadly comparable level since then (Fig. 4.3). When examining changes in the general fertility rate (GFR, the number of live births per thousand women aged 15–44) at the ward level (mean population size (N) is 25 000), the degree of regional variation (measured by the coefficient of variation) was quite large in both 1946 and 1960 – prior to the onset of fertility decline (Table 4.1).[1] Furthermore, the magnitude of these spatial variations altered very little during the course of fertility decline; and the broad spatial patterns of variation, reflecting on the one hand relatively low fertility in and around the main urban areas of Port of Spain and San Fernando and on the other hand relatively high fertility in the less developed eastern half of Trinidad, were also quite similar during this period (Fig. 4.4). The factors contributing to these spatial patterns will be examined in Section

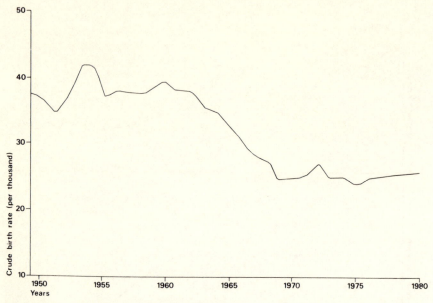

Figure 4.3   Variations in the crude birth rate (CBR), Trinidad and Tobago, 1949–80.

4.3; meanwhile it is evident that the changing spatial characteristics of fertility as seen at this scale do not conform with the model of divergence and convergence outlined earlier since distinct spatial variations were clearly evident prior to the main phase of fertility decline and the magnitude of such variations remained largely unchanged during the main phase of decline. However, the case of Trinidad and Tobago is by no means unique in displaying considerable spatial variations in fertility prior to decline. Similar characteristics have been observed, even at fairly coarse levels of aggregation, for Brazil in 1930–40 (Carvalho 1974), Pakistan in 1951 (Fuller & Khan 1978) and, at a finer scale, for Barbados in 1960 (Jones 1977a). Indeed these examples can be added to those of present-day developed countries which also displayed considerable spatial variations

Table 4.1   Variations in the general fertility rate (GFR), Trinidad and Tobago, 1946–80.

Year	General fertility rate	
	Mean	Coefficient of variation(%)
1946	172	19.7
1960	206	17.1
1970	145	20.5
1980	130	18.8

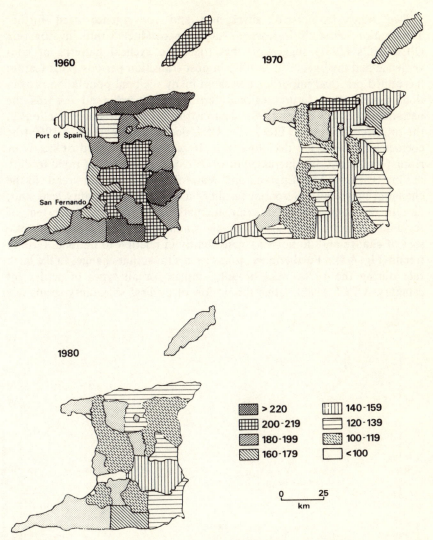

Figure 4.4   Spatial variations in the general fertility rate (GFR), Trinidad and Tobago, 1960, 1970 and 1980 (the national GFR was 178 in 1960, 127 in 1970 and 122 in 1980).

prior to fertility decline, as seen for Japan in 1920 and 1935 (Tsubouchi 1970) and many countries of Europe (Coale 1969) during the 19th century (see Chapter 3). Thus the presence of considerable spatial variations in fertility prior to the phase of main decline, attributable to variations in biological, demographic and behavioural variables, indicates that the initial assumptions concerning pre-transition lack of divergence need to be modified substantially.

Two other features of divergence and convergence need further examination. First, little research has been conducted into investigating O'Connell's (1981) suggestion that there are cyclical patterns of convergence and divergence in fertility in post-transition periods. This feature has added practical importance because many regional population projections assume that future regional fertility levels will tend towards the national mean. O'Connell (1981) demonstrates that inter-state variations in the total fertility rate (TFR) in the USA declined from 1940 to 1960 (the coefficient of variation declining from 16 to 9%) in a period of steady or rising fertility but then increased to 1977 (18%) in a period of rapid fertility decline. However, for England and Wales there are no clear trends in the changing magnitude of spatial fertility variation at the county level and, despite the considerable national fluctuations in fertility, the extent of regional variations in the crude and age-standardized birth rates show little sign of change and do not vary consistently in relation to national fertility trends (Fig. 4.5).[2] Furthermore, it has been shown that changes in the birth rate during the 1970s were broadly similar for all types of settlement category (OPCS 1982). Thus the notion of cyclical variability seems less

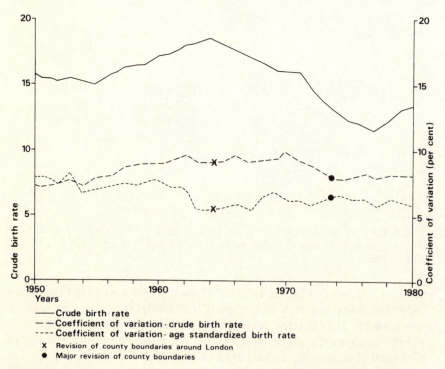

Figure 4.5   The magnitude of spatial variations in fertility by county, England and Wales, 1950–80.

relevant for England and Wales than the USA, and the distinctive features of the latter are perhaps a reflection of the considerable swings in regional economic performance where the recent prosperity of many of the southern states has helped maintain relatively high fertility despite the overall national decline. Further case studies are needed in order to clarify this issue of cyclical variability in spatial patterns in post-transition societies.

A second issue concerns whether regional differentials will, in the absence of regional cyclical variability, tend to disappear completely in post-transition societies. Once again the effects of level of aggregation and method of measurement are relevant here, although in the case of recent fertility patterns in developed countries it has been demonstrated that spatial variations in economic development, cultural attributes and demographic structure can give rise to quite marked spatial variations in age-standardized fertility rates even at fairly coarse levels of aggregation, as demonstrated for Scotland (Jones 1975, Wilson 1978), Northern Ireland (Compton 1978), the Republic of Ireland (Coward 1978, 1980, 1982a, 1982b), Italy (Rallu 1983) and Poland, Yugoslavia, the USSR and Hungary (Andorka 1978). Furthermore, broad regional variations in mortality in many contemporary developed countries show little sign of disappearing, as demonstrated for Britain by Chilver (1978), Knox (1981) and OPCS (1981a). In fact in a review of demographic trends up to the early 1970s it has been noted that regional mortality variations are still prominent in many developed countries (United Nations 1973), although more recent information on urban and rural differentials indicates that many of these differentials are quite large, particularly among males (Table 4.2).

The model of divergence and convergence as outlined here appears to provide a useful general framework for the analysis of changing spatial patterns, but it needs to be modified and clarified in terms of the extent of spatial variation in pre-transition societies, the presence of regional cyclical swings in post-transition societies and the likelihood of the eventual

Table 4.2 Standardized urban and rural mortality rates for selected European countries.[3] (Rates standardized on the age structure of England and Wales, 1981.)

Population and year	Males		Females	
	Urban areas	Rural areas	Urban areas	Rural areas
Netherlands, 1979	13.8	12.0	7.8	7.4
United Kingdom, 1973	17.3	15.3	10.3	10.0
Norway, 1979	14.2	12.5	8.2	7.8
Denmark, 1969	16.0	12.6	10.0	9.6
Finland, 1979	16.5	16.9	8.9	9.1

Source: United Nations (1980b).

elimination of regional variations in fertility and mortality. In relation to the latter point, it would seem that, although spatial differentials might be expected to display a decreasing degree of magnitude in post-transition societies, the elimination of such differentials is as unlikely as the attainment of complete regional uniformity of socio-economic and demographic structure, the provision of services, cultural norms and environmental characteristics.

Having considered the possibility of divergence and convergence in regional population structures during the demographic transition, we may now return to our ultimate goal: the explanation of demographic change. As before, two contrasting examples will be examined: first, Trinidad and Tobago, which as we have already seen in Figures 4.3 and 4.4 has experienced a substantial decline in fertility since the 1960s and, secondly, England and Wales, where there have been cyclical fluctuations in fertility since the 1940s.

4.3   The fertility transition in Trinidad and Tobago

The magnitude of and spatial variations in fertility decline in Trinidad and Tobago were marked from the 1960s onwards. Thus the dominant spatial pattern of the general fertility rate was characterized by relatively low levels in and around the major urban areas of Port of Spain and San Fernando with higher rates in the eastern half of Trinidad and the island of Tobago. In this case ecological analysis can shed some light on the major factors influencing the pattern of spatial variation. Such variation could be the product of at least seven major groups of influencing factors. First, differences in fecundity could affect the spatial patterns. Unfortunately there are no data available to investigate this relationship, but it is unlikely that this variable could account for the considerable differences in fertility observed on a relatively small island, although it can be noted that malaria had not been fully eradicated by 1960 (Fonaroff 1968). Secondly, the general fertility rate could be influenced by varying age structure within the female population aged 15–44, reflecting higher fertility levels at younger ages. Thirdly, fertility differentials could reflect the response to varying levels of mortality, particularly infant mortality. Fourthly, variations in coital frequency and the status of marital unions could affect the general fertility rate. Again, this factor is difficult to measure in a society with a high proportion of extramarital births and distinctive patterns of informal union formation. In the 1960 census a category of 'no union status' was identified, referring to persons who had never been married or in a common-law union and were not in a visiting union at the time of the census. This group had the lowest (though not zero) fertility of all union categories. Fifthly, variation in the cultural attributes of the population could affect fertility. In the case of Trinidad and Tobago the most distinctive cultural cleavage has been that of ethnic origin, differentiating between the population of Indian descent, whose fertility has generally been higher than that of the population of African descent (Harewood 1975, 1978). Sixthly, the spatial variations in fertility could reflect variations in modernization and socio-economic change that had taken place prior to 1960, with lower fertility being associated with the urban population employed in non-manual occupations and with relatively high levels of educational attainment.[4] Finally, the particular spatial patterns could reflect variations in the availability of contraceptive methods and the diffusion of information concerning family planning (Fuller 1974, Blaikie 1975). In this case it would be expected that availability and information would be greatest in the two largest urban areas of Port of Spain and San Fernando. In fact prior to 1970 the main family planning services were concentrated in and around these two major centres of population.[5]

The various hypothesized explanatory variables are summarized in Table 4.3, along with their zero-order correlations with the general fertility

Table 4.3 Hypothesized relationships with the general fertility rate (GFR), Trinidad and Tobago, 1960.

Independent variables	Mean	Standard deviation	Hypothesized direction	Zero-order correlation with GFR(Y)
Age structure				
X_1 females aged 15–29 as % of females aged 15–44	59.6	2.9	+	−0.01
Infant mortality				
X_2 infant mortality rate	44.3	6.9	+	0.27
Union status				
X_3 % females 15–44 with no union status	24.2	5.2	−	−0.59
Cultural characteristics				
X_4 % population of Indian descent	36.9	24.2	+	0.04
Socio-economic characteristics				
X_5 % males working in white-collar occupations	15.0	8.1	−	−0.84
X_6 % females > 15 with secondary education	7.5	6.5	−	−0.83
Family planning availability and information				
X_7 straight-line distance to nearest major urban area	26.5	16.9	+	0.62

Table 4.4 Correlations between variables, Trinidad and Tobago, 1960. (Variables are defined in Table 4.3.)

Variables	Y	X_1	X_2	X_3	X_4	X_5	X_6	X_7
Y	1.00	−0.01	0.27	−0.59	0.04	−0.84	−0.83	0.62
X_1		1.00	0.20	0.13	0.66	−0.10	0.71	−0.03
X_2			1.00	0.09	0.04	−0.16	−0.19	0.22
X_3				1.00	−0.34	0.74	0.71	−0.09
X_4					1.00	−0.26	−0.34	−0.29
X_5						1.00	0.97	−0.55
X_6							1.00	−0.48
X_7								1.00

rate (GFR). The signs of the relationship generally accord with their hypothesized direction, with the exception of age structure, and most of the variables are strongly related to the general fertility rate, with the exceptions of age structure and cultural characteristics (Table 4.3).[6] Those variables measuring socio-economic structure display the strongest associations with fertility, and the correlations between the explanatory variables do not show a particularly high degree of multicollinearity, although the two measures of socio-economic structure are very highly interrelated, along with their relationships with union status (Table 4.4). On this basis it appears that, although variations in fertility in 1960 were influenced by a variety of factors, the major source of variation was that of the differing socio-economic characteristics of regional populations. A stepwise regression model indicates that the varying magnitude of occupational differences accounts for the major part (70%) of the variations in fertility, and as this particular factor is quite highly related to some of the other major explanatory factors, no further variables make a substantial contribution to the variations in fertility (Table 4.5).[7] Thus the variations in socio-economic structure that had evolved in Trinidad and Tobago up to 1960 were also associated with distinctive patterns of fertility, perhaps indicating that changes in the direction of intergeneration wealth flows had already started to appear in those populations characterized by, among other things, urban living, the presence of relatively large numbers of white-collar workers in the labour force and increasing levels of educational attainment. Interestingly, the spatial variations observed in 1960 could well reflect long-standing differences; for example, data on cohort fertility, measuring the average number of children ever born among women aged 45–64 in 1960, also displayed a considerable degree of variation with a broadly similar pattern to that of the general fertility rate. Again these cohort patterns are most closely related to indices of socio-economic structure.[8] Similarly, the spatial patterns observed in 1970 and 1980 are broadly similar to that of

Table 4.5 Stepwise regression results for general fertility rate (GFR), Trinidad and Tobago, 1960. (The regression equation is $Y = 260 - 3.6X_5$.)

	Included variables			Excluded variables	
Step	Variable	R	$R^2(\%)$	Variables	Partial correlation with GFR
1	X_5	0.84	70	X_1	-0.15
				X_2	0.26
				X_3	0.06
				X_4	-0.33
				X_6	-0.14
				X_7	0.34

1960 and a separate stepwise regression analysis of the 1970 data indicated that the factors of female educational attainment and ethnic grouping accounted for 77% of the variation in the general fertility rate. In this sense the case study of Trinidad and Tobago differs from that of neighbouring Barbados, where Jones (1977a, 1977b) has shown that the relative effects of modernization variables tended to decline in importance from 1960 to 1970 although the importance of family planning inputs increased. In Trinidad and Tobago the increasing importance of family planning services is not marked at the ward scale. However, the relative importance of family planning among women older than 45 in 1977 can be seen from recent data from the World Fertility Survey (1981) which indicate that broad spatial differences – in this case between aggregate urban and rural areas – reflect the greater success of the urban population in matching actual family size with desired family size through differing levels of contraceptive use and that there was, seemingly, little difference between urban and rural areas in desired family (Table 4.6; see also Cleland & Hobcraft 1985).

The Trinidad and Tobago case study raises a number of interesting points which tend to support the value of ecological correlation as a means of

Table 4.6 Children ever born, desired family size and use of contraception among women ever in a marital union aged over 45, Trinidad and Tobago, 1977.

Women aged over 45 (ever in a union)	Urban areas	Rural areas
children ever born (mean)	5.6	6.5
desired family size (mean)	4.6	4.8
percentage of women who ever used any contraceptive method	64	48

Source: World Fertility Survey (1981).

exploring the changing regional demography of an area undergoing transition, but the limitations of this approach are probably best illustrated in studies of fertility variation in contemporary developed societies.

4.4 Contemporary fertility variations in England and Wales

The extent of spatial variations in fertility in England and Wales are unlikely to be particularly marked, except at a local scale where it may prove difficult to assess certain key themes in the explanation of fertility, such as the interaction of couples' earning power, education and social class. However, although the ecological approach can add little to the development of a truly general theory of fertility in such situations, it can nevertheless provide a convenient way of assessing the rôle of certain major compositional factors in contributing to spatial fertility patterns. Thus, in a discussion of recent fertility trends and differentials in the United Kingdom, Overton (1982) suggests that:

Areal differences in fertility will reflect the social and economic characteristics of the local population. They will themselves be a function of the different social class and religious characteristics of areas or their industrial structure (including whether or not there are employment opportunities for women, and of what kind), of the nature and accessibility of the dwelling stock and also of certain cultural traditions associated with different areas, which are more difficult to quantify . . . We now expect to see higher fertility in certain conurbations with sizeable immigrant populations as well as in ex-urban growth areas which attract young couples ready to settle down to family life.

Similar patterns of association have been suggested by Compton (1982) and Rees (1979a).

The relative importance of some of these variables can be assessed in relation to variations in fertility in England and Wales in 1981 at the county and metropolitan county scale. Here, in the absence of detailed information on longitudinal or age-specific fertility, recent variations are assessed in terms of the crude birth rate and Coale's (1967) indices of fertility. At this level of aggregation the magnitude of variation is quite small for overall fertility (I_f), marital fertility (I_g) and proportion married (I_m) and is, as expected, somewhat greater for the birth rate (Table 4.7). Interestingly, the greatest degree of relative variation is observed for non-marital fertility (I_h), indicating that the changing characteristics of this aspect of fertility, which are similar to the changes that occurred in the 1960s (Illsley & Gill 1968), reflect patterns that vary markedly at the subregional level (Figs 4.6 & 4.7). The present analysis will concentrate on variations in the birth rate (CBR) and marital fertility (I_g). The spatial distribution of the former reflects the

Table 4.7 Variations in fertility measures, counties and metropolitan counties of England and Wales, 1981.

Fertility measures	Mean	Standard deviation	Coefficient of variation (%)
crude birth rate	12.6	1.03	8.2
overall fertility (I_f)	0.150	0.0076	5.1
marital fertility (I_g)	0.207	0.0099	4.8
proportion married (I_m)	0.645	0.0302	4.7
illegitimate fertility (I_h)	0.047	0.0120	25.5

relatively low rates for the populations of many of the south coast and southwestern counties with higher rates in inner London, Berkshire, Bedfordshire and Cleveland; and the spatial distribution of the latter reflects the relatively higher rates in London, Berkshire, Bedfordshire, South Glamorgan and Merseyside, in contrast to somewhat lower rates occurring in a broad zone of counties extending from the counties of the West Midlands region through to the east coast counties of North Yorkshire, Humberside, Lincolnshire and Norfolk.

The major demographic, socio-economic and cultural explanatory variables are summarized in Table 4.8. It is hypothesized that fertility will be negatively related to social status, as measured by housing tenure and unemployment, and the participation of young married women in the labour force, and that it will be positively related to average wage levels and the proportion of households headed by immigrants from the New Commonwealth and Pakistan.[9] One further factor which could be important in influencing fertility is that populations characterized by relatively large proportions of young married couples are likely to have relatively high fertility rates, not only through the effects of age and marital structure but also because of a selective process as a consequence of which such couples may have migrated to those areas from major metropolitan areas with the specific intention of family building (Lawton 1973, Overton 1982, Eversley 1982). Thus Eversley (1982) argues:

> There are increasing numbers of two-adult, two-earner households in the metropolitan areas. If such a couple decide to have children, and especially if they are thinking in terms of two or more children, there is greater pressure on them to relocate in another area: they can only afford family housing on the income of one wage earner if they move to a town where house prices are relatively low when compared to the earnings potential of the principal wage earner.

This particular factor is difficult to measure with county data, but an approximate indicator based on proportions married is Coale's index (I_m),

Figure 4.6   Spatial variations in the crude birth rate (CBR), England and Wales, 1981 (CBR for England and Wales was 12.8 per thousand).

which is heavily weighted by the proportions married at ages 20–29. Thus it is anticipated that areas with relatively high proportions married in the peak childbearing ages will be linked with selective migration and positively associated with fertility.

For variations in the birth rate (CBR, Y_1) the signs of the zero-order correlations with the hypothesized explanatory variables are all in the

60

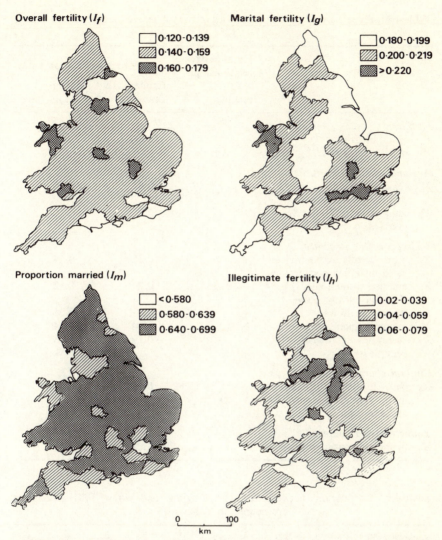

Figure 4.7 Spatial variations in I_f, I_g, I_m, I_h, England and Wales, 1981 (for England and Wales, I_f was 0.16; I_g, 0.21; I_m, 0.62; I_h, 0.052).

expected direction, with the exception of married women's participation in the labour force, but, as might be expected, variations in age structure are most highly associated with variations in the birth rate. Zero-order correlations between the explanatory variations are displayed in Table 4.9, and a stepwise regression model emphasizes the importance of age and marital structure in influencing birth rates – in this case accounting for 80% of the variation (Table 4.10). However, four other variables embracing socio-economic structure and cultural characteristics of the population

Table 4.8 Hypothesized relationships with fertility measures, England and Wales, 1981.

	Hypothesized relationship with fertility	Zero-order correlation with:	
		Crude birth rate	Marital fertility rate
Fertility			
Y_1 crude birth rate			
Y_2 marital fertility (I_g)			
Age and marital structure			
X_1 females aged 15–34 as % of total population	+	0.85	
X_2 females aged 20–24: % married	+	0.25	
Socio-economic structure			
X_3 economically active males: % in unskilled occupations	+	0.25	0.24
X_4 married women aged 15–34: % economically active	–	0.24	0.12
X_5 average male wages (£)	+	0.43	0.51
X_6 unemployment rate	+	0.20	0.14
X_7 % households owner occupied ·	–	–0.19	0.03
Cultural characteristics			
X_8 % of household heads born in the New Commonwealth and Pakistan	+	0.46	0.42
Young married couples			
X_9 proportion married (I_m)	+	0.09	–0.53

Table 4.9 Correlations between variables, England and Wales, 1981. (Variables are defined in Table 4.8.)

Variables	Y_1	Y_2	X_1	X_2	X_3	X_4	X_5	X_6	X_7	X_8	X_9
Y_1	1.00	0.56	0.85	0.25	0.25	0.24	0.43	0.20	–0.19	0.46	0.09
Y_2		1.00	0.56	0.41	0.24	0.12	0.51	0.14	0.03	0.42	–0.53
X_1			1.00	–0.02	0.11	0.40	0.64	–0.01	–0.33	0.55	–0.11
X_2				1.00	0.15	–0.20	–0.50	0.22	–0.02	–0.34	0.88
X_3					1.00	–0.10	–0.08	0.78	–0.47	–0.35	–0.19
X_4						1.00	0.26	–0.24	–0.06	0.52	–0.21
X_5							1.00	–0.27	–0.19	0.50	–0.45
X_6								1.00	–0.37	–0.39	–0.08
X_7									1.00	0.11	0.19
X_8										1.00	–0.32
X_9											1.00

Table 4.10 Stepwise regression results for crude birth rate (CBR), England and Wales, 1981. (The regression equation is $Y_1 = -10.7 + 0.9X_1 + 0.08X_2 + 0.11X_6 + 0.03X_7 + 0.66X_8 + 0.01X_5$.)

	Included variables			Excluded variables after final step	
Step	Variables	R	$R^2(\%)$	Variables	Partial correlation with CBR
1	X_1	0.85	74	X_3	0.22
2	X_2	0.90	80	X_4	-0.09
3	X_6	0.91	83	X_9	0.05
4	X_7	0.93	86		
5	X_8	0.94	89		
6	X_5	0.95	90		

contribute to the variations, with fertility being positively associated with levels of unemployment, owner occupation, immigrant populations and male wages. In this case the six variables account for 90% of the variation in the birth rate.[10] These results suggest that differing aspects of socio-economic structure have varying effects on fertility since areas with relatively high levels of unemployment are associated with relatively high birth rates and areas with relatively high average wages – generally with low levels of unemployment – are also associated with relatively high fertility. The final positive (and not negative) relationship between levels of owner occupation and fertility is difficult to interpret because it has been demonstrated recently that, although the relationships between housing and fertility are multifaceted, owner-occupiers have lower fertility than local authority dwellers even when social class is controlled for (Murphy & Sullivan 1983). The positive association observed in the regression equation could reflect the selective migration effects of those couples planning to have children moving away from the main metropolitan areas which are, generally speaking, associated with relatively low levels of owner occupation. This particular problem of interpretation is perhaps illustrative of the general problem of establishing patterns of association from this type of analysis. A separate analysis indicated that the four socio-economic and cultural variables contributing to variations in the birth rate account for 45% of the variations in overall fertility (I_f).

For variations in marital fertility (I_g) the signs of three of the zero-order correlations do not accord with the directions hypothesized, involving those variables measuring the participation of married women in the labour force, owner occupation and the incidence of young married couples. However, a stepwise regression model indicates that three of the variables – male wage levels (X_5), unemployment (X_6) and immigrant households (X_8) – account

Table 4.11 Stepwise regression results for marital fertility (I_g), England and Wales, 1981. (The regression equation is $Y_2 = 123.4 + 1.3X_5 + 0.44X_6 + 10.5X_8$.)

	Included variables			Excluded variables after final step	
Step	Variables	R	$R^2(\%)$	Variables	Partial correlation with I_g
1	X_5	0.52	27	X_3	0.17
2	X_6	0.59	35	X_4	-0.09
3	X_8	0.68	46	X_7	0.28

for almost one half of the variation in fertility, and all are positively related to fertility in the regression equation (Table 4.11).[11] Again, the interpretation of the unemployment variable is not clear cut: it could be a general measure of social status or, at the risk of falling into the ecological fallacy, indicate that unemployment itself is often associated with relatively high fertility. Indeed, several studies, such as Askham's (1976) of Aberdeen, have indicated that unemployment is one aspect of deprivation which is, in turn, associated with high fertility. However, more research is needed in a variety of spatial settings in order to verify the existence of such a relationship. If the overall relationship proves not to be spurious, then the implications of rising unemployment for fertility, particularly in areas of high unemployment, may be considerable (see Ermisch 1983).

The spatial patterns of proportions married and non-marital fertility will not be discussed in detail here, but it can be noted that economic factors (male wages) are most highly correlated with the former although variations in the latter, generally reflecting the highest rates in the metropolitan counties, inner London, Berkshire, South Glamorgan, Nottinghamshire and Humberside, are most strongly correlated with certain socio-economic variables, particularly the proportion of the labour force in unskilled occupations and male unemployment.[12] However, to assess spatial variations in illegitimate fertility accurately further information is needed, such as data concerning variations in the proportion of illegitimate births jointly registered (by both the mother and the father) and details concerning spatial variations in the other options open to couples – namely abortion and marriages producing a birth within eight months.

4.5 Conclusion

In this chapter several themes have been investigated concerning the analysis of fertility and, to a lesser extent, mortality. These themes have involved the magnitude of spatial variations, a model of demographic divergence and convergence, the identification of regional patterns and their evolution over time and the explanation of spatial patterns. An attempt has been made to demonstrate that the spatial perspective can offer additional insights into the description, analysis and explanation of variations in fertility and mortality, although in each case there remains considerable potential for further research either by using more traditional sources, such as published census and vital registration data, or by utilizing more recently exploited sources, such as small-area statistics or individual data derived from population registers or social surveys. The spatial demographic approach will continue to provide a useful contribution to the study of fertility and mortality, providing it can successfully exploit the ever widening range of data sources available for detailed analysis.

Notes

1 It is possible that the extent of regional differences, as measured by the coefficient of variation, could be reduced considerably if an average of three years' births around each census date were used instead of births for a single year. However, this does not appear to be the case: in 1946 the coefficient of variation based on births for 1945–7 is 21.7%, compared with 19.7% based on 1946 alone. Similar checks have not been carried out on the data for 1960, 1970 and 1980 because birth data were derived from a census question asking women if they had a birth in the year prior to the census. This seems to be an accurate reflection of the number of births, although the data for Port of Spain in 1970 are likely to be subject to error because of the civil disturbances in the capital around the time of the census enumeration.

2 In order to ensure broad comparability in relation to changing county boundaries over the period 1950–80 certain areas have been combined for the whole time series. These are (1) Cambridgeshire, Ely, Huntingdonshire and Peterborough; (2) Rutland and three sub-areas of Lincolnshire; (3) two sub-areas of Suffolk; (4) Hereford and Worcestershire; and (5) Westmorland and Cumberland. In order to ensure broad comparability in terms of population size the following areas were combined prior to 1974: (1) Anglesey, Caernarvon, Cardigan, Merioneth and Montgomery; (2) Brecknock, Carmarthen, and Pembroke; and (3) Denbigh and Flint. Hampshire (Southampton) and Isle of Wight have been combined for the whole series. However, consistency cannot be maintained for the boundary changes around London in 1964–5 and the major revision of counties in 1974, although such changes do not appear to have particularly distorting effects on the overall pattern of variations through time.

65

3   Urban areas are defined as follows. Netherlands: urban municipalities with populations over 2000 plus non-rural semi-urban areas; United Kingdom: county boroughs, municipal boroughs and urban districts; Norway: localities of more than 200 inhabitants; Denmark: localities of over 2000 inhabitants; Finland: urban communes.

4   Several writers, such as Cochrane-Hill (1979) and Thomas (1980), have suggested that in many cases the factor of education can be difficult to interpret because it does not always vary consistently with fertility. For Trinidad and Tobago in overall terms, however, census data for 1960 and 1970 indicate that there is a consistent negative relationship between female level of educational attainment and children ever born, even when age is controlled for.

5   There is no precise method of measuring variations in the use and provision of family planning facilities at the ward level because such data are only available for larger population aggregates. However, these data indicate relatively high levels of use among the populations residing in and around Port of Spain and San Fernando.

6   The variables all approximate to a normal distribution and, as each independent variable is more or less related in a linear manner to the general fertility rate, no transformations were necessary.

7   An analysis of the residuals indicated that there was no clear pattern over space. The regression equation overpredicted fertility in some areas around the main urban centres – suggesting that family planning services could have led to lower than expected fertility on the basis of socio-economic development alone – but fertility was also over-predicted for many other wards away from the main urban centres.

8   Thus the coefficient of variation among children ever born to women aged 45–64 in 1960 was 14.9%, compared with 17.1% for the general fertility rate in 1960. The association between the two spatial patterns was quite high, $r = 0.45$. Variables measuring female education, ethnic composition, distance from the main urban areas and infant mortality are the main contributors to the spatial pattern, accounting for 62% of the variation.

9   The variables all approximate to a normal distribution, although X_8 (immigrant heads of household) has been logarithmically transformed to maintain greater linearity with the dependent variables. In order to maintain broad comparability of population size of the spatial units, the following areas were combined for the statistical analysis: (1) Hampshire and the Isle of Wight; (2) Powys and Dyfed; and (3) Gwynedd and Clwyd.

10   There was no clear spatial pattern in the residuals and relatively large and relatively small residuals – as well as positive and negative residuals – were scattered throughout England and Wales.

11   Variable X_9, measuring the relative incidence of young married

females, was omitted from the regression analysis. Again the spatial pattern of the residuals showed no clearly discernible features.

12 The zero-order correlations between extramarital fertility and these two variables are 0.60 and 0.56 respectively. A separate analysis indicates that extramarital fertility is also quite highly related to variations in female unemployment (the percentage of single women aged over 16 seeking work) where $r = 0.48$.

5

Rising fertility
in developing countries

TIM DYSON and MIKE MURPHY

5.1   Introduction

Rapid population growth has understandably meant that fertility research in developing countries has concentrated on the issue of fertility decline and, particularly with improvements in data, it has become clear that decline is now widespread (Kirk 1979). In contrast, the issue of rising fertility has received much less attention – even though the notion that a fertility increase may precede a subsequent fall is certainly not new. Nag (1980) has recently stated that 'Evidence of increase in fertility measures in the wake of modernization is not very common in the demographic literature.' In this chapter it will be argued that increases in national fertility levels among developing countries have in fact been far more common than has generally been supposed. Much of the data that support the case for recent fertility decline also support an earlier fertility rise. As a result we may have to reinterpret some aspects of recent demographic history.

5.2   The evidence

Our review of the evidence that fertility rises have been widespread follows the evolution of our research. First, we examine the indications from registration data from India, Egypt and China – half the world's population at present. Secondly, we summarize – and reinterpret – relevant data from the World Fertility Survey (WFS) programme (Cleland & Hobcraft 1985). Thirdly, we examine registration data for selected remaining developing countries grouped by world region; we also refer to relevant country case studies. Fourthly, we analyse some interesting similarities in birth rate trends between a sample of developing and developed countries over the long run. Finally, we discuss some of the implications of our research.

5.2.1 India

There can be little doubt that India has recently experienced some fertility decline. Various studies suggest a fall in the birth rate of between 9 and 16% over 1972–8, and there was almost certainly a modicum of fertility decline prior to 1972 (Jain & Adlakha 1982, Dyson & Somawat 1983). These studies are based on several fairly reliable data sources that have become available since the late 1960s.

At the national level vital registration is certainly very deficient and cannot provide us with any indication of fertility trends, but in certain states – notably Maharashtra, Gujarat, Tamil Nadu (previously called Madras), Punjab and Haryana – birth registration coverage is well above average at 70% or more (India 1980). Annual crude birth rates in parts per thousand (CBRs) for these states have been published for many years and, unlike those for the other states, from a relatively continuous and consistent series over time. For those years in which comparison is possible the fertility trends implied by vital registration in these five states are broadly comparable to those implied by the dual survey Sample Registration Scheme (SRS) – a modern demographic surveillance system which is thought to be fairly reliable. Thus the weighted average registration CBR for these five states declined by 17% over 1972–8 compared with a figure of 15% implied by the SRS (Dyson & Somawat 1983).

Perhaps the most interesting feature of the annual birth rates in these states with better registration lies in their pattern of variation over time. In the smaller more socio-economically advanced states of Punjab and Haryana registered crude birth rates declined from the late 1950s onwards, but the three larger states appear to exhibit a more complex yet broadly similar trend. In each of these the registered crude birth rate fell during the early 1950s, reaching a minimum around 1955–8. It then rose in each to peak around 1962–5, and thereafter a fairly sustained fall set in. This pattern of variation is essentially that shown in Figure 5.1a for the erstwhile Bombay State (contemporary Gujarat and Maharashtra combined). (The figure is based on Bombay in order to minimize discontinuities that result from its subdivision in 1957.)

Faced with such an annual CBR series, it is interesting to note the difficulty of designating any specific time as marking the onset of fertility decline (a topic covered in greater detail below). Similarly Figure 5.1a underlines the fact that an approximately constant average birth rate over two decades can conceivably hide a significant change – in this case a 17% birth rate rise in a period of only six years in Bombay State.

5.2.2 Egypt

Since the early 1960s Egypt has also definitely experienced a significant degree of fertility decline. Various estimates put this at a little under 20%

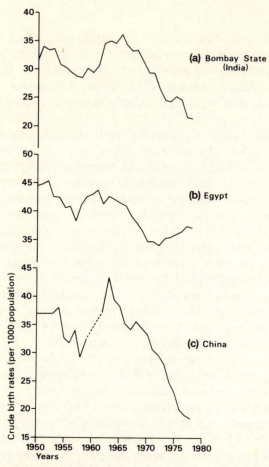

Figure 5.1 Annual vital registration crude birth rates (CBRs) for Bombay State (Gujarat and Maharashtra combined since 1957), Egypt and China.

(Omran 1973, Panel on Egypt 1982). Figure 5.1b depicts the path of the country's vital registration CBR. Again, a short period of increase is indicated around the early 1960s prior to the subsequent decline. Although there is little doubt that birth registration coverage declined during 1956 – and declined even more in 1957, perhaps as a result of the Suez crisis – it is less certain that the CBR decline in the early 1950s also reflects a deterioration in coverage. At least some analysts consider that, 1956–7 apart, the pattern of CBR variation shown in Figure 5.1b reflects the real trend in the birth rate over that decade (El-Badry 1965, Omran 1973). All scholars seem to agree that levels of fertility around 1960 were significantly higher than in the late 1940s (e.g. Panel on Egypt 1982).

70

5.2.3   China

Several demographers have compiled time-series of birth rates for China based on the writings of Chinese population specialists and reports of the State Statistical Bureau (Coale 1981a, Aird 1982, Chen & Kols 1982). These series are all similar because each is largely derived from official national household registration statistics. Figure 5.1c summarizes arguably the most up to date of such series, that made by Yuan Tien (1983). The figure illustrates what most observers now agree: that the Chinese birth rate has declined very substantially in recent years.

As Aird (1982) has written, few demographers would dispute the general trends indicated by the official data in Figure 5.1c. However, there is some uncertainty in connection to the food crisis period around 1960. According to Yuan Tien (1983), the household registration system did not provide data for a birth rate estimate for 1960, and he considers that the official CBR of 19.1 for 1961 is almost certainly much too low – although the true figure in that year was nevertheless probably lower than average due to the events of the previous years.

Again, for our purposes, the key feature of Figure 5.1c is the indicated birth rate rise prior to the fall. This rise exists even if we entirely exclude the problematic period 1960–4. Thus the birth rates in each of the years 1955–9 are lower than those for the years 1965–9 inclusive. Averaging CBRs for these two quinquennia implies that the birth rate was 11% higher in 1965–9 than in 1955–9.

Recently, partial reconstitution of CBR trends has become possible for three major Chinese provinces – Anhui, Jiangxi and Hunan (Yuan Tien, 1983). Each of these reconstituted series is broadly consistent with this general pattern of birth rate variation over time.

The suggestion of a common trend exhibited by Indian, Egyptian and Chinese data in Figure 5.1 is interesting and is an issue to which we return later. However, here we continue to concentrate specifically on rising fertility and turn to the evidence from the World Fertility Survey.

5.2.4   World Fertility Survey: Colombia

Of those countries in the WFS programme Colombia is particularly important because it was a study based on the 1976 National Fertility Survey which served as an 'illustrative analysis' for evaluating fertility trends using WFS data (Hobcraft 1980). We will therefore consider the case of Colombia in some detail.

The illustrative analysis utilized two types of WFS material. First, household survey data were subjected to own-children analysis, a form of reverse survival. Secondly, fertility trends were estimated from detailed maternity histories. The own-children analysis was restricted to children under 15. Therefore, given that the survey was undertaken in 1976, the resulting fertility estimates cover only years after 1960–1. However, the maternity history data on trends can cover the period 20–24 years prior to the survey and, possibly, a little beyond. The maternity history trend data can be thought of as age-truncated period total fertility rates (TFRs). (The rates are truncated because women beyond a given age – usually 50 – were generally excluded from the WFS individual questionnaire containing the maternity history. It is perhaps worth noting that the maternity history data constitute the main way of obtaining indications of fertility trends from the WFS.)

Table 5.1 compares these two types of WFS fertility trend data with annual CBRs from Colombia's vital registration. It is organized around the same quinquennia as the available maternity history estimates. For these quinquennia simple averages of the registration CBRs and own-children TFRs are also given in order to facilitate comparison. The truncated TFRs represent cumulative fertility to age 30. These rates are used here because they maximize the number of women on which WFS fertility estimates for the period 20–24 years prior to the survey (i.e. for the early 1950s) can be based.

Both WFS time-series indicate a substantial fertility decline between 1966–70 and 1971–5. Also, over 1961–5 to 1966–70 the vital registration CBR, truncated TFR, and own-child TFR indicate falls of 11, 7 and 12% respectively. However, we are again particularly interested in the period preceding this decline. In this context Figure 5.2a compares the fertility trends indicated by vital registration and maternity histories, indexed on their respective arithmetic means for the period 1951–70 as a whole. Interestingly, both sources suggest a 7% increase in fertility between the early and late 1950s. Figure 5.2b stretches this comparison to the limits of the available data in order to encompass the quinquennia 1946–50 and 1971–5. It is based on WFS maternity history TFRs truncated at age 25 and on an estimate of the vital registration crude birth rate for the quinquennium 1971–5 derived by linear interpolation between our average figure for 1966–9 and the published figure for 1976. In view of the various data limitations involved (see below) the overall degree of agreement between the two sources is really remarkably close. Figure 5.2b suggests that Colombia's fertility rise extends back at least to the late 1940s. The alternative explanation requires an unlikely combination of specific and very different patterns of errors in these two independent sources.

WFS analyses have consistently rejected the implication from maternity histories that Colombia's fertility did in fact rise during the late 1940s and early 1950s (Hobcraft 1980, Goldman & Hobcraft 1982). However, such analyses seem to have completely neglected vital registration data on birth rate trends. Certainly, in our view, the results depicted in Figure 5.2 make it difficult to agree that the country's fertility was probably approximately constant before the mid-1960s (Goldman & Hobcraft 1982).

Table 5.1 World Fertility Survey (WFS) and vital registration data on Colombia's recent fertility trends.

Year/ quinquennia	Vital registration crude birth rate[a]	WFS: cumulative fertility to age 30, within five-year periods[b]	WFS: own-children total fertility rate estimates[c]	
1951	36.1		na	
1952	36.4		na	
1953	38.1	37.32	2.908	na	
1954	37.2		na	
1955	38.8		na	
1956	39.6		na	
1957	40.1		na	
1958	40.4	39.92	3.116	na	
1959	40.7		na	
1960	38.8		6.75	
1961	39.4		7.24	
1962	39.6		7.36	
1963	39.3	38.74	3.027	7.72	7.08
1964	38.5		6.05	
1965	36.9		7.03	
1966	35.9		6.10	
1967	35.3		6.67	
1968	32.0	34.45	2.801	6.19	6.22
1969	34.6		6.18	
1970	na		5.94	
1971	na		5.11	
1972	na		4.83	
1973	na	2.173	4.01	4.46
1974	na		4.22	
1975	na		4.13	
1976 (survey)	30.0			

Sources

[a] United Nations (1966) and (1977); the figure for 1976 is from United Nations (1980b). Of course these CBRs are underestimates; here we are only concerned with trends.

[b] This figure is cumulative fertility to exact age 30 within five-year periods centred upon the years for which figures are given. These data are therefore the truncated period total fertility rates referred to in the text. For simplicity we have assumed both here and subsequently that the WFS survey was undertaken at the beginning of the year (here 1976). Data in this column are taken from Hobcraft (1980).

[c] Hobcraft (1980). Strictly, estimates pertain to part of year specified and part of subsequent year.

Note: na = not available.

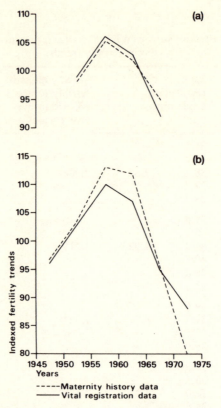

Figure 5.2 Comparison of vital registration and WFS maternity history data on Colombian fertility trends.

5.2.5 World Fertility Survey: other countries

The Colombian example prompted a wider investigation. Comparable WFS maternity history data have been published for 18 other developing countries (see Goldman & Hobcraft 1982). In five − Pakistan, Nepal, Bangladesh, Indonesia and the Republic of Korea − vital registration or similar data on fertility are unavailable, and for the Dominican Republic and the Philippines it proved very difficult to construct an unambiguous and consistent set of vital registration crude birth rates over time. However, for the remaining eleven countries it was possible to construct a reasonably satisfactory time-series of annual vital registration CBRs. This was done almost entirely by using data from the periodic editions of the United Nations *Demographic yearbook* specializing in fertility (United Nations 1955b, 1966, 1976, 1980b) supplemented occasionally by data from other statistical publications (e.g. United Nations 1977, Sri Lanka 1979, Thailand 1980).

It is perhaps worth noting that the use here of CBRs, rather than more refined indices of fertility, was largely dictated by considerations of regular annual availability. In a few instances CBRs for the same year(s) from different editions of the *Demographic yearbook* differed slightly; where these differences could not be unambiguously resolved averages were used instead, but in no case does the use of this procedure substantially alter the conclusions we draw below. As in the Colombian example, simple average CBRs were obtained for the same quinquennia as the available maternity history estimates. Again these figures were indexed to facilitate comparison of trends. Generally we have only extended the comparison back to the early 1950s. This was done so that the truncated World Fertility Survey TFRs could be based on women at a time in the past when they were under 30. However, for four countries it proved necessary to consider the late 1940s, and in these instances the truncated TFRs pertain to the experience of women aged under 25. Clearly, for any past time period, rates based on women aged under 30 stem from larger numbers of respondents and are thus less subject to sampling errors than rates based on respondents at the time when they were under 25. We would expect this lower age group to be more sensitive to timing changes and in general for smaller age groups to be more prone to age-structure distortions when comparing age and non-age standardized measures.

The resulting comparisons between WFS and registration data are summarized in Figure 5.3. Several preliminary points must be made. First, although we have tried to construct the indices so that they relate to the 'same' national populations, in fact it is likely that there are many discrepancies between the two. The reasons range from probable territorial divergences and changes in national and registration jurisdictions over time (perhaps most acute in the comparison for Malaysia) to the fact that the WFS figures are based solely on the experience of surviving respondents rather than on all the population alive at a given time. Secondly, the two indices relate to somewhat different fertility measures. For example, CBRs are affected by the age structure of the population, whereas the WFS measures are not. However, Bogue and Palmore (1964) found a correlation of 0.982 between the crude birth rate and the total fertility rate (TFR) for a sample of 50 countries in the period 1955–60. On the other hand, unlike the truncated maternity history data, past registration birth rates are based on births occurring to women of all ages. A final general point to bear in mind is that both vital registration and maternity histories have many other limitations as instruments for gauging fertility trends.

In view of such considerations the degree of correspondence between the two indices in Figure 5.3 is undoubtedly much greater than many demographers would expect. The correspondence is the more noteworthy because in several cases adjustments might plausibly be made to the registration data that would further enhance the level of agreement.[1] For

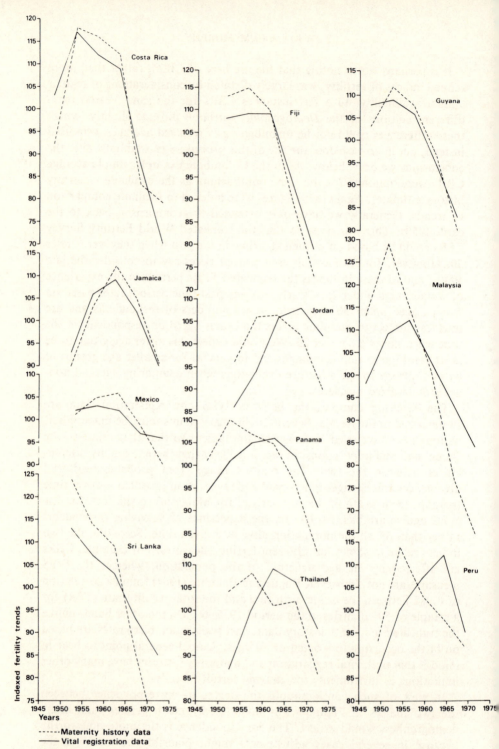

Figure 5.3 Comparison of vital registration and WFS maternity history data by country.

Costa Rica, Guyana, Jamaica and Fiji the correspondence is almost as close as it is for Colombia. It is also fairly good for Mexico, Sri Lanka and Panama – all countries generally thought to have comparatively good vital registration. For Jordan, Malaysia and Peru the comparison is less than satisfactory – although overall movements in the two indices for these countries certainly appear to be related, the peaks are found to differ substantially. Perhaps the comparison is poorest for Thailand, where, if anything, the variation of the WFS index is the most irregular.

In every country in Figure 5.3 both vital registration and WFS indices show some measure of fertility decline between the late 1960s and early 1970s. A more interesting feature is that in virtually every case the maternity history measure exhibits the sharper degree of recent decline (this is also evidenced for Colombia in Fig. 5.2b). One consideration here may be delays in registering births, a possibility especially for Jordan, Peru and Thailand, and for Mexico, where the delay is estimated as almost two years (Figueroa 1980). More important, it seems certain that during the 1970s developing country CBR trends were being influenced by increasing proportions of women in the prime reproductive years, a phenomenon which is largely a result of recent fertility decline.

Perhaps the most interesting feature of Figure 5.3 is the indication of increasing fertility, particularly during the 1950s. This is supported by both indices in 10 of the 11 countries. The country where neither index shows a fertility rise, Sri Lanka, is also that with arguably the earliest and most pronounced fertility decline. In fact there is good reason to think that Sri Lanka did experience a period of fertility increase during the 1940s (Langford 1981, ESCAP 1976). Registration data quite clearly suggest that this was the case, but unfortunately WFS material does not provide any basis for considering trends that far back.

As in the case of Colombia, WFS analyses of such maternity history trend data usually conclude that the indicated 1950s fertility rise is probably fictitious. Instead the explanation put forward is that older women have failed to report some of their early births (i.e. those most distant in time), and have also systematically displaced (i.e. misdated) those early births towards the survey date (thus injecting into the data a spurious past fertility rise). The almost routine use of this rationale in successive WFS analyses stands in sharp contrast to its early exploration by Potter (1977). He stressed, among other things, that any displacement biases may be partially self-cancelling and that there was no guarantee that net biases would always vary in the same direction between populations. Unfortunately, however, although this 'omission plus displacement' hypothesis may have some relevance – particularly in one or two countries where WFS data are of especially poor quality, e.g. Nepal (see Goldman *et al.* 1979) – its common usage runs into at least two major difficulties. First, the surprising fact is that in most WFS analyses all the suggested probes and checks have usually failed to establish the presence of a significant number of birth omissions. It is interesting to note that Potter has also recently written to this effect (Ordorica & Potter 1981). Secondly, when truncated period TFRs from maternity histories have been tabulated by educational level of women, the seeming proportional rise in 1950s fertility has, if anything, usually been found to be average, or even above average, for better educated women. Yet we would expect precisely these women to be superior in matters of both dating and recall; additionally, such women have usually had lower than average fertility. This somewhat anomalous feature is reflected in the data – for example, for Colombia, the Dominican Republic, Guyana and Peru (Hobcraft 1980, Guzman 1980, Balkaran 1982, Cespedes 1982). Table 5.2 illustrates the point with indexed data from the Philippines (Reyes 1981). Although, as expected, the recent fertility fall is greater among more educated women – those of high school education or more – so too is the 1950s fertility rise. In these circumstances perhaps a more plausible alternative explanation to the omission plus displacement hypothesis is that better educated women are subjected earlier – and possibly to a greater extent – to any fertility-enhancing effects of modernization.

To conclude this section, although response errors may partly account for the seeming past rise in fertility shown by WFS data, the possibility that these rises are largely real certainly deserves much greater weight than analysts have accorded it hitherto. This is especially so given the overall degree of correspondence between the vital registration and maternity history data shown in the figures presented above.

Table 5.2 Cohort-period fertility measures (rates and trend indices) by level of education, Philippines survey, 1978.

Level of education	Years before the survey				
	20–24	15–19	10–14	5–9	0–4
Primary or less					
rate	317	341	328	309	309
index	99	106	102	96	96
Intermediate					
rate	309	331	326	338	283
index	97	104	103	106	89
High school or more					
rate	235	283	232	238	191
index	100	120	98	101	81

Source: derived from Reyes (1981).

5.2.6 Other evidence

The evidence assembled so far surely supports the case that fertility rises have been common in the fairly recent past among developing countries. What additional indications of rising fertility exist? We now briefly address this question with reference to time-series of vital registration CBRs published by the United Nations. We also refer to some studies of relevant countries.

Data on trends are scarcest for Africa, but there are fairly strong indications that rises may have occurred in parts of the continent. In North Africa registration birth rates for Algeria suggest a CBR fluctuating slightly above 40 during the early 1950s. This rate then declined very substantially to approximately 32 during 1957 and 1958, followed by a sharp rise, peaking at around 47 in 1965. Thereafter a minor decline seems to have set in (Algeria 1981). A UN study (United Nations 1977) has also concluded that Algeria may well have experienced an upward fertility swing in the years around 1960. It is interesting to note the unusually low birth rates in 1956 and 1957 in a North African country not directly involved in the Suez crisis, although of course Algeria did experience substantial internal problems around this time. Indeed, overall, the progression of the Algerian registration CBR since 1950 is broadly reminiscent of that of Egypt in Figure 5.1b. For Tunisia both raw and adjusted CBRs imply that birth rates rose from the mid-1950s, peaking in the early 1960s, before moving into significant decline (Marcoux 1971, Vallin 1971).

South of the Sahara there is little doubt that fertility increases have occurred in some populations affected by venereal disease. Perhaps the best evidence is that provided by continuous registration data for Zaire. There the birth rate is estimated to have risen from around 42 in 1940–5 to approximately 48 in the early 1970s (Romaniuk 1980). For Kenya WFS maternity history data strongly support a past rise in fertility, although there is debate as to its timing, and changes in the incidence of venereal disease may be only part of its cause (Henin *et al*. 1982). In much of sub-Saharan Africa there is reason to think that changes in traditional breastfeeding and abstinence patterns may have led to increases in fertility (Lesthaeghe *et al*. 1981). Lastly, in Africa registration crude birth rates for Mauritius exhibited a rise of about 50% during the 1940s followed by a very rapid decline. There is every reason to believe that this rise was not wholly an artefact of better registration (Xenos 1976).

There is much better evidence of a pre-decline increase in fertility for Latin America (especially middle mainland America) and the Caribbean. More than half of the WFS countries examined above are from this region; and indeed the general coincidence between registration and maternity history data that we have demonstrated must considerably weaken objections that recorded rises in birth rates in this area were simply due to improving coverage of registration. In addition to the WFS data there are fairly persuasive country-level analyses supporting past fertility increases for many nations in this region – for example Costa Rica, Cuba, El Salvador, Guyana, Honduras, Jamaica, Nicaragua, Panama, Surinam, Trinidad and Tobago and Venezuela (see the following, and references cited therein: United Nations 1977, Mauldin 1978, Hollerbach 1980, Nag 1980).

In order to examine Latin American experience in somewhat greater detail we constructed vital registration crude birth rate time-series for years from around 1930. In so doing we employed the same general data sources (League of Nations 1935, United Nations 1949, 1955b, 1966, 1976) and the principles used above when dealing with WFS data. Unfortunately those countries for which a fairly unambiguous time-series could be constructed were usually countries we had already considered in connection with WFS data (although all countries thus 'rejected' nevertheless showed some sign of a past registration birth rate rise). Nevertheless, an examination of the results is instructive, and a fairly representative selection is shown in Figure 5.4.

Perhaps the most interesting feature of Figure 5.4 is the suggestion of a similar regional birth rate trend. This involved a substantial and sustained rise from the mid-1930s. By 1960 a strong downward trend had usually set in. It is worth emphasizing that this common trend seems to be reflected in data for other countries in the Caribbean region. However, we must recognize that there are important exceptions to any common trend. For example, as Figure 5.4 also shows, Puerto Rico's birth rate rise, if any, was much shorter and did not embrace the 1950–60 decade. This said, Puerto Rico's general demographic situation – particularly as regards its relationship with the United States – clearly makes it a special case (see Mosher 1980). One other country that follows the common trend, but in a much attenuated form, is Mexico. Its CBR time-series since 1930 tends to confirm the impression of a much more gentle birth rate rise and fall, as previously conveyed in Figure 5.3.

Turning to consider Asia, there are really very few additional developing countries for which it is possible to construct anything like a satisfactory fertility time-series over either the medium or long run. All that can be said is that data for Cyprus, Singapore and two countries considered previously, Thailand and Sri Lanka, indicate credible past birth rate rises. Recent country studies – usually of more socio-economically and demographically advanced nations – have generally concluded that fertility increases in the 1950s and before preceded declines during the 1960s and 1970s. This is true, for example, for the Republic of Korea (Coale *et al.* 1980), Taiwan (Sun & Soong 1979), Singapore (Chang 1979) and Indonesia (Cho *et al.* 1980). There are even suggestions of significant fertility increases among some West Asian populations – for example, among Palestinians (Hill 1983), in Turkey (Shorter & Macura 1982), and in the Central Asian Republics of the USSR (Coale *et al.* 1979).

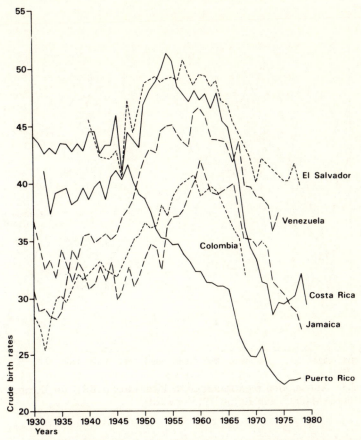

Figure 5.4 Annual vital registration crude birth rates (CBRs) for selected countries in the Caribbean region.

Given Asia's tremendous diversity and, still more, the aforementioned paucity of time-series data, it would clearly be asking too much to expect to find any strong resemblance of past birth rate trends between most of the countries of the continent. But India, with its comparatively good data, certainly merits a second glance. We therefore undertook a wider review of registration crude birth rate trends over the long run for our better registration states of Bombay and Tamil Nadu. The results are summarized in Figure 5.5. The general similarity of CBR trends seems to have existed at least since 1915.[2] An initial reaction might be to attribute this correspondence to a similar variation in registration completeness in these two Indian states, but this explanation loses much of its force when we are faced with the surprising fact that both Indian time-series also bear a resemblance to the progression of registration CBRs in Egypt since 1915

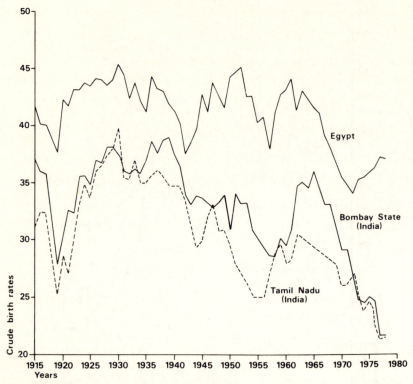

Figure 5.5 Annual vital registration crude birth rates (CBRs) for Bombay State, Tamil Nadu (Madras) and Egypt, 1915 onwards.

(see Fig. 5.5). Given this, together with the previous suggestion of a common trend in Latin American and Caribbean CBR time-series, we now proceed to focus a little more rigorously upon such possible similarities.

5.3 Describing common fertility trends: analytic approaches

Previous sections have strongly suggested that where validation with alternative sources has been possible, the CBR series have been found to provide adequate indices of fertility movements. Where independent validation is not possible, the rather similar patterns exhibited by series from different countries suggest that they are generally reflecting real movements rather than artefacts due to data errors. We therefore feel justified in using CBR series to measure patterns of fertility change in the countries discussed earlier. The analysis will now be broadened to include a number of other developing countries in order to provide a more geographically balanced coverage – implicitly assuming that the CBR series are of comparable quality to those considered earlier; it will also include a number of developed countries from Europe and the USA using data from the sources mentioned earlier, together with those of Mitchell (1981, 1982), in order to compare and contrast long-term CBR movements in the world's main geographical regions.

To summarize the common features of these series we shall employ two complementary techniques. The first is reference cycle analysis, the methodology of defining turning points; the second is partial correlation analysis. These approaches and their results will be described in the next two sections.

5.3.1 *Defining turning points in crude birth rate series*

All the CBR series shown earlier have turning points. Although the most obvious way to pick out such points is by eye, this would involve an inevitably subjective element, especially with erratic series such as those examined here, or ones with poorly defined peaks and troughs where some analysts will tend to ignore 'weak' cycles. The problem is exacerbated since any common cycles are not necessarily absolute peaks or troughs but may show themselves as periods of lesser or greater than average deviations from a non-constant long-term trend. To overcome these problems we have decided to use methods of the type developed for the determination of peaks and troughs of economic time-series by the use of cyclical indicators at the National Bureau of Economic Research (Burns & Mitchell 1946) and later by researchers such as Moore and Shiskin (1967) and O'Dea (1975).

The period of interest here is that before the mid-1960s, since after that time virtually all countries examined were experiencing declining fertility levels and the main focus of attention here is on fertility trends in the pre-decline period. We have therefore cut off the analysis at 1967. The starting date was taken as 1932. The reason is that a number of the Latin American and Caribbean series only became available in suitable form from that date. We have therefore excluded from this analysis two countries whose CBR series were shown earlier, China and El Salvador, because they had substantial gaps in availability of data in this period. The adjustments made to the data set are described in note 2 at the end of this chapter with the addition that missing values for Taiwan in 1944–6 were replaced by the mean value of the adjacent years' estimates.

To identify peaks and troughs we started by smoothing the series by means of a five-point moving average with equal weights in order to remove short-term variation. Such variation is not of interest in the present context and, for example, the smoothing will tend to remove spurious variation such as displacement of births from one year to another; in spectral analysis terms, it removes power at high frequencies but leaves low-frequency power effectively unaltered.

A potential peak (P) is defined as a value which is greater than, or equal to, its immediate neighbours; for potential troughs (T) the reverse definition applies. These values were subsequently deleted from consideration if they fulfilled the following criteria sequentially. First, contiguous sets of peaks and troughs were deleted; in any case the differences were always small. If three turning points were adjacent, e.g. PTP, the less significant, i.e. smaller P value and T value, were deleted; and analogously for a TPT triad. Secondly, the same procedure was adopted for a pair of turning points separated by one other value, as in the first criterion. Thirdly, an adjacent peak and trough which fulfilled the appropriate conditions but whose difference was less than 0.5 per thousand, were deleted (this involved the rejection of only two pairs in the results presented below).

This algorithm was applied not only to the original smoothed series but also to a smoothed detrended series. The detrending procedure chosen was to subtract a linear trend from each of the 1932–67 series. This trend was chosen as being monotonic over the period; thus its elimination would not remove peaks and troughs (it is also compatible with the partial correlation analysis below). Another reason for the choice of a regression-based detrending method rather than the symmetric linear filter approach of, for example, O'Dea (1975), was that we did not wish to lose observations at the ends of the series. In spectral analysis terms, the regression may be considered as a common asymmetric linear filter applied to each series for a given year, but one whose weights differ for each year. An additional reason for the exclusion of post-1967 observations is that the recent decline would tend to generate spurious turning points earlier in the series, since the fact that such observations would be below the long-term trend would imply that earlier observations would be found to be above the long-term trend because the regression residuals must, by definition, sum to zero.

Although the results of this approach are arbitrary since different approaches are likely to produce slightly different results in some cases, the method is objective, replicable and, we believe, would be regarded as reasonable by most analysts. The results of this exercise are shown in Figure 5.6 which gives the reference chronology for 23 series covering Latin America (which hereafter will be taken to include the Caribbean series), Afro-Asia and Europe (which also includes the USA) for both the original and the detrended series.

Although caution must be exercised in attempting detailed analysis of a particular country's patterns because of potential data errors (with the exception of some of the European series), we can nevertheless see general patterns in these results. Turning to the Latin American set shown in Figure 5.6a, there is a high degree of homogeneity in behaviour, with fertility rising until the latter part of the 1950s, followed by a subsequent uniform decline. Three countries stand out as departing from this overall pattern. Puerto Rico is a well-documented special case and it will not be discussed further here. Of more interest are the rather different patterns of the former British colonial islands of Jamaica, and Trinidad and Tobago. Jamaica's pattern is out of synchronization with the other series for most of the period before 1960, and in general its fertility movements appear to occur rather later than the general pattern. Trinidad and Tobago, on the other hand, appears to have experienced its turning points rather before the majority of neighbouring states. Although it is tempting to try to explain these movements as partly spurious, because of the high rates of emigration from these islands to the USA and Great Britain we believe that the delayed behaviour of Jamaican fertility patterns compared with other countries considered here is also supported by the data in Figure 5.3. If migration effects are important, they appear to work through factors such as exposure to risk rather than directly through age- and sex-structure effects.

By their nature chronologies based on detrended series, such as those presented in Figure 5.6b, are likely to be more complex, but we would stress that an average level of fertility, say 5% above the long-term trend, has similar implications for differential population growth as an average level, say 5% above a long-term constant trend. This data set shows a less marked rise in the prewar fertility patterns, and a tendency for the wartime period to be associated with relatively falling fertility in Colombia and Venezuela. However, the postwar patterns are very similar to the earlier analysis with virtually all countries showing rising fertility around 1950, reaching a peak during the 1950s followed by a general decline.

The Afro-Asian patterns are less clear-cut. In the prewar period, the behaviour is rather mixed with some series showing rises and some declines. During the war itself there was a tendency for fertility to rise, although the postwar pattern diverges considerably with only the 'continental' series of Egypt, Tamil Nadu and Bombay State exhibiting a short-term rise in fertility around 1960. The other four 'island' societies show a rather different pattern with a rise in fertility in the postwar period which had reversed by the early 1950s into a sharp decline. (Japan did show a rather weak pattern of fertility increase in the 1960s which is rather reminiscent of the European pattern discussed below.) The detrended series (Figure 5.6b) show a broadly similar pattern with the common behaviour of the continental series becoming even more apparent. The profile of increased fertility is pronounced with all societies showing rises in the late 1940s and all declining in the early 1950s. Although the behaviour of the island and continental societies in later periods appears to be rather different, a more detailed analysis shows that Sri Lankan fertility did not decline uniformly over this period. The percentage declines in the five-year CBR averages centred around 1950 to 1955, 1955 to 1960 and 1960 to 1965 were 6.3, 2.0

(a) Original Series

Rising fertility ——— Falling fertility - - - - -

X-axis: 1935 1940 1945 1950 1955 1960 1965

Country	Values (as plotted along timeline)
Colombia	39·9
Venezuela	45·3
Guyana	32·3 — 43·4
Trinidad and Tobago	39·1 — 36·7 — 39·2
Jamaica	40·2
Mexico	45·6
Costa Rica	31·2 — 49·8
Puerto Rico	41·3
Bombay State (India)	38·3 — 29·1 — 33·4
Tamil Nadu (India)	24·6 — 29·7
Egypt	39·6 — 43·8 — 40·5 — 42·9
Sri Lanka	39·5
Mauritius	47·4
Taiwan	39·1 — 46·3
Japan	26·9 — 30·9 — 17·4
Norway	21·0
Sweden	19·8 — 14·0 — 15·6
USA	25·2
England and Wales	14·6 — 18·2 — 15·3 — 18·1
France	14·1 — 20·9
Bulgaria	22·0 — 24·8 — 15·5
Portugal	24·5 — 25·6 — 23·8 — 24·4
Spain	20·1 — 24·1 — 20·2 — 21·5

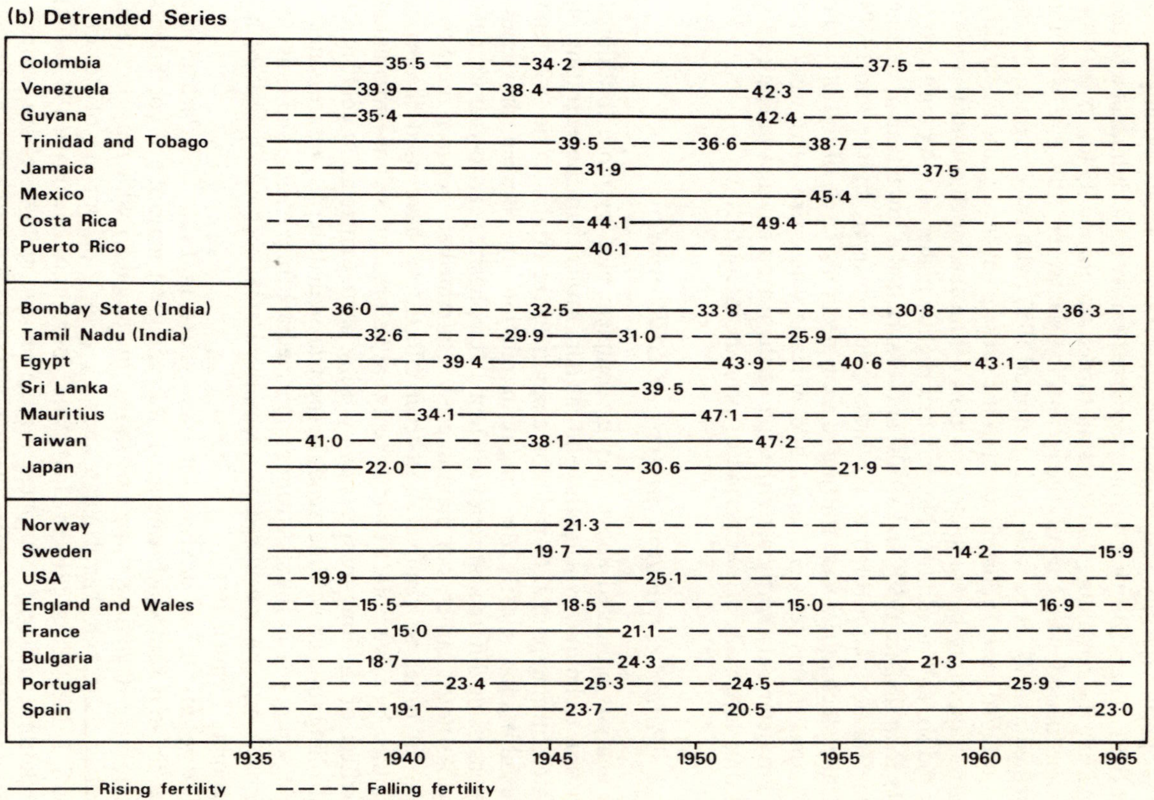

(b) Detrended Series

Figure 5.6 Reference chronologies for 23 crude birth rate series.

Legend: ——— Rising fertility - - - - Falling fertility

Years axis: 1935 1940 1945 1950 1955 1960 1965

Colombia: 35·5 — 34·2 — 37·5
Venezuela: 39·9 — 38·4 — 42·3
Guyana: 35·4 — 42·4
Trinidad and Tobago: 39·5 — 36·6 — 38·7
Jamaica: 31·9 — 37·5
Mexico: 45·4 — 49·4
Costa Rica: 44·1
Puerto Rico: 40·1

Bombay State (India): 36·0 — 32·5 — 33·8 — 30·8 — 36·3
Tamil Nadu (India): 32·6 — 29·9 — 31·0 — 25·9
Egypt: 39·4 — 43·9 — 40·6 — 43·1
Sri Lanka: 39·5 — 47·1
Mauritius: 34·1 — 38·1 — 47·2
Taiwan: 41·0
Japan: 22·0 — 30·6 — 21·9

Norway: 21·3
Sweden: 19·7 — 14·2 — 15·9
USA: 19·9 — 25·1 — 15·0
England and Wales: 15·5 — 18·5 — 16·9
France: 15·0 — 21·1
Bulgaria: 18·7 — 24·3 — 21·3
Portugal: 23·4 — 25·3 — 24·5 — 25·9
Spain: 19·1 — 23·7 — 20·5 — 23·0

and 9.1 respectively. This indicates that the late 1950s was a period of below average decline compared with surrounding periods. However, the Taiwanese and Mauritian series do not show such a hiatus.

'European' fertility experience reflects rather more homogeneous behaviour. The recovery in fertility occurred earlier in Scandinavia and the USA, but the remaining countries all turned up around 1940, so that the wartime period was one of rising fertility. However, this rise was not sustained and all series were falling around 1950 (with the exception of the USA original series). Participation in the subsequent resurgence of fertility does not appear to be complete, but most of the developed countries shown here did so, and in addition Norway had slightly higher fertility in the early 1960s than the late 1950s and 1960s, and France had a lower rate of decline in the former period than in the latter one. However, by the mid-1960s virtually all countries were starting to show declining levels of fertility. The exceptions in this set were Japan and Bulgaria where rises were weak and were to peter out shortly after the end of the period covered in Figure 5.6 and thus move out of our period of primary interest.

5.3.2 Partial correlation analysis of CBR trends

The analysis presented above may be complemented by more traditional statistical techniques which utilize all the data rather than concentrating on isolated turning points. Correlation analysis of the original series will tend to exhibit most clearly the long-term relationship between the series, whereas using differenced series will tend to emphasize year-to-year changes only. As noted earlier, our main interest is intermediate between these two cases. In order to remove short-term effects, we have used the series smoothed by a five-point moving average as before, and we have attenuated the effect of the long-term trends by using partial correlation coefficients controlling for a linear time trend. In spectral analytic terms, we are concentrating on power in the spectrum at intermediate frequencies, and thus this approach may be considered as a simplified cross-spectral analysis of intermediate frequencies.

The results of this analysis are summarized in Table 5.3. Perhaps the most obvious fact which emerges is that the great majority of coefficients are positive (including those not shown in the table) with only Jamaica, Bombay State and Tamil Nadu showing a high proportion of negative values. If these three cases are laid aside, four out of five of the 190 partial correlation coefficients computed for the remaining 20 series are positive, indicating rather similar overall movements in both developed and developing countries. (In passing, it should be noted that it is inappropriate to apply standard tests of significance to these coefficients because the observations for a given series are, of course, highly correlated; but they do show common trends in these series.)

In other ways too the results in Table 5.3 tend to reinforce the conclusions drawn from the reference cycle analysis. For example, it can be seen from Table 5.3a, that the pattern in Jamaica is out of line with the patterns in other Latin American countries; moreover, it is the only member of this set to exhibit a negative correlation with either the Afro-Asian or European average series. It is interesting to note that among the European series the highest overall correlations by far of the Latin American countries are found to be with the United States (see Table 5.3c), suggesting that the American continent as a whole exhibits a similar behaviour pattern. By contrast, correlations with the Iberian countries are especially poor, in spite of the linguistic and migrant ties between these two areas.

The dichotomy between the 'island' and 'continental' societies mentioned earlier also emerges in Table 5.3b, with the Indian states showing a similar pattern, as do the set of Taiwan, Mauritius and Sri Lanka. Egypt shows some similarity with both these groups. Indeed, of all the countries considered, only Egypt outside the Indian subcontinent would seem to have patterns in common with Bombay State, since the great majority of other countries have strongly negative partial correlations with the Indian subcontinent states, especially those in Latin America. Thus, although all countries considered have shown a tendency for fertility to rise before the recent fall, the form and timing of that rise was rather different in different parts of the world, and to some extent in different types of areas. Fertility movements appear to have been more pronounced in relatively small and isolated developing countries, particularly islands, than in large societies such as Mexico and Egypt. Among the Afro-Asian group, Japan stands out as having a distinctly more 'European' pattern, reflected by its particularly high correlation with the European average and low one with the Latin American average.

In contrast to the Afro-Asian set, European trends are rather similar, with the exception of the Iberian countries, which tend to have rather different patterns from the others, as indeed they do from all the other countries considered. Looking at the individual members, the high association between Latin America and the USA has already been noted; but for the Afro-Asian set the closest link appears to be between the French and Bulgarian experience which may be characterized as highly disrupted by World War II. These are also societies where there was little sign of the baby boom in the late 1950s experienced in much of the rest of Europe. This pattern was typical – although not necessarily for the same reasons – of the dominant Afro-Asian pattern; but we are inclined to view this association as coincidental rather than related.

Table 5.3 Partial correlation coefficients, controlling for linear trend, for regional groupings and regional averages.

(a) Latin American data set.

	Colombia	Venezuela	Guyana	Trinidad and Tobago	Jamaica	Mexico	Costa Rica	Puerto Rico
Colombia	—							
Venezuela	0.87	—						
Guyana	0.71	0.84	—					
Trinidad and Tobago	0.52	0.61	0.63	—				
Jamaica	0.19	-0.22	-0.28	-0.51	—			
Mexico	0.45	0.63	0.59	0.83	-0.68	—		
Costa Rica	0.82	0.84	0.78	0.42	0.13	0.37	—	
Puerto Rico	0.07	0.32	0.41	0.80	-0.87	0.78	-0.05	—
Latin American average	0.84	0.92	0.91	0.82	-0.29	0.75	0.80	0.51
Afro-Asian average	0.03	0.39	0.60	0.26	-0.63	0.30	0.19	0.51
European and USA average	-0.01	0.17	0.50	0.69	-0.66	0.52	-0.03	0.85

(b) Afro-Asian data set.

	Bombay State	Tamil Nadu	Egypt	Sri Lanka	Mauritius	Taiwan	Japan
Bombay State	—						
Tamil Nadu	0.66	—					
Egypt	0.31	0.08	—				
Sri Lanka	-0.58	-0.63	0.17	—			
Mauritius	-0.44	-0.70	0.42	0.91	—		
Taiwan	-0.40	-0.77	0.34	0.45	0.62	—	

	Norway	Sweden	USA	England and Wales	France	Bulgaria	Portugal	Spain
Japan	0.01		0.01	0.37	0.63	0.62	-0.15	—
Latin American average	-0.74		-0.87	0.03	0.81	0.78	0.78	0.13
Afro-Asian average	0.10		-0.29	0.70	0.66	0.83	0.39	0.78
European and USA average	-0.48		-0.35	0.21	0.79	0.75	0.03	0.82

(c) European/USA data set.

	Norway	Sweden	USA	England and Wales	France	Bulgaria	Portugal	Spain
Norway	—							
Sweden	0.90	—						
USA	0.72	0.37	—					
England and Wales	0.58	0.72	0.01	—				
France	0.71	0.41	0.76	0.39	—			
Bulgaria	0.55	0.30	0.59	0.41	0.94	—		
Portugal	-0.35	-0.42	-0.24	0.22	0.21	0.43	—	
Spain	0.09	0.07	-0.06	0.57	0.41	0.64	0.79	—
Latin American average	0.50	0.13	0.95	-0.28	0.56	0.38	-0.30	-0.26
Afro-Asian average	0.46	0.26	0.51	0.18	0.81	0.72	0.07	0.13
European and USA average	0.86	0.69	0.69	0.66	0.91	0.87	0.14	0.51

Notes

Partial correlation coefficients are based on five-year moving average of 1932–67 data.

Regional averages are the average values of the individual countries within each region shown above (with the addition of El Salvador in the Latin American set in the period 1940–67).

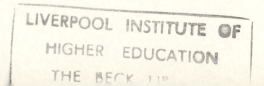

5.4 Summary and discussion

In our view an examination of available data confirms the proposition that increases in developing country fertility levels prior to the recent sharp declines have been widespread. The similarities in birth rate trends found between countries cast doubt on the suggestion – made particularly *vis-à-vis* Latin America and the Caribbean – that improved registration was mainly responsible for increases in reported crude birth rates during the 1950s. But if CBRs generally increased in that decade, then age-standardized fertility rates probably rose even more. The reason is simply that widespread mortality decline prior to 1960 led directly to reductions in the proportion of the population in the childbearing years. In fact this latter generalization seems to be valid for virtually every developing country in the world with available census age and sex data enclosing the 1950–60 decade (see United Nations 1956, 1964).

Given that past fertility increases have been common, a number of subsidiary points should be made. To begin with, the data we have examined suggest that in some instances past fertility increases may well have been of broadly the same order of magnitude (or only slightly less) than any subsequent decline. Consider, for example, the case of Colombia in Figure 5.2b or Jamaica in Figure 5.3. Moreover, as Figure 5.4 implies, in many developing countries – particularly those that are more advanced – we may have to consider years prior to 1950 in order to fully appreciate the scope of any past fertility rise.

A second related point concerns the acceleration of developing country population growth rates during the postwar period. The conventional view (formed to a considerable extent in the years immediately after the 1960 round of censuses when enumerated populations substantially exceeded those projected), was – and remains – that these high rates of population growth were 'caused by rapid declines in mortality combined with *high fertility that remained almost unchanged*' (our italics, Coale 1982, p. xiii). We consider that, even as a characterization of experience in developing countries outside of Latin America and the Caribbean, this statement may understate the contribution of rising fertility to rapid population growth during the 1950s.

Our conclusion that CBR trends in different countries are sometimes similar should remind us that factors such as major wars, economic upheavals, advances in preventive medicine, and influenza pandemics can exert a global influence and clearly even a stronger common influence at the world regional level. Such factors also affect age structures in similar ways and thus help bring similarity to subsequent crude birth rate trends. Yet another influence that may be relevant here is changes in ideas among the community of policy makers (Caldwell 1976), not least in respect of the desirability of programmes for population control. Clearly, however, the effects of any such 'global' influences will be mediated by 'local' circumstances – hence the suggestion of 'regional' rather than global birth rate trends and the existence of exceptions within regions. We suspect that exactly what constitutes 'regional' in this context may have more to do with cultural and economic considerations than with simple matters of geography or proximity. For example, Egypt, Bombay State and Tamil Nadu are all predominantly agricultural 'peasant', 'national' populations (of Egyptians, Marathis and Tamils respectively); each contains a major capitalist urban centre (Cairo, Bombay and Madras) which for much of this century acted as an important linkage in Britain's imperial design. Thus it may not be quite so surprising that Egyptian birth rate trends resemble those in parts of India, rather than those in some other areas of Africa such as Zaire (Romaniuk 1980). Similarly, small island societies (or ones relatively isolated from their immediate neighbours) such as Sri Lanka, Mauritius and Taiwan appear to exhibit rather similar and particularly strong movements – in part perhaps because the diffusion of attitudes and the implementation of health and family planning programmes are easier in such societies.

Finally, three methodological issues arise. First, vital registration data for developing countries certainly merit greater attention than they often receive. Simply because such data are deficient it should not necessarily mean that they are ignored. Occam's razor suggests that the existence of similar trends is in itself evidence that in some countries the rate of change of the degree of omission of births has probably remained roughly constant over time. Hence implied trends may be informative – though by no means necessarily exact – even though the level of birth registration is seriously deficient. As indicated earlier, some WFS analyses have almost certainly neglected registration data to an unwarranted degree. We have seen that this has probably led to an undervaluation of the quality of WFS maternity history data, so far as measuring past fertility trends is concerned.

Secondly, the fact that demographers have come to rely heavily on 'indirect' techniques of fertility estimation has probably been a major reason why the scope of past fertility increases in developing countries has generally remained obscure. Fertility estimates derived from such indirect techniques typically relate to a period which is often undated and of several years in length. Thus, so far as gauging trends is concerned, indirect techniques may sometimes be rather blunt instruments lacking the potential sensitivity afforded by annual vital registration. For example there is no real inconsistency between the general pattern of fertility variation suggested by Figure 5.1a and the conclusion from several intercensal analyses that Indian fertility changed only slightly between the 1951–61 and 1961–71 decades.

Our final point is also essentially a qualification regarding indirect techniques. Several of these estimation methods are based upon the assumption that fertility has remained approximately constant in the population over the recent past. Yet the evidence we have presented here indicates that often this assumption may be invalid. There may thus be a need, either in the application of indirect techniques or in the interpretation of their results, to give somewhat greater weight to possible past fertility change.

Notes

1 The sole *ad hoc* adjustment we made was to exclude in the CBR averaging for Jordan the CBRs for 1967, 1968 and 1969 of 65.9, 62.6 and 53.9, which are right out of line (probably in some way related to the 1967 war).
2 Simple linear adjustments to the data for Tamil Nadu for the years 1954–6 and 1963–7 have been made in order to correct for obvious inconsistencies in the raw data base of the CBRs for those years. In addition, in Figure 5.4 the following values were linearly interpolated because of missing data: Colombia, 1970–5; Guyana, 1972–5; and Puerto Rico, 1974 (but these are outside the main time period considered here).

PART II

Modelling and forecasting

6

Developments
in the modelling of
spatial populations

PHILIP REES

6.1 What are the Part II chapters about?

The chapters in Part II address aspects of a common problem. Given that
the characteristics of the population vary in interesting ways across space
and that their time paths of development may be very different, as the
chapters in Part I have demonstrated, how do we represent the processes
of demographic change in formal models which will make predictions about
the future path of development possible? Implicit in this activity is the
notion that the ability to make accurate predictions will be useful to society
and to the people who plan its future.

What do the authors of the chapters in Part II mean by models?
Generally, they agree that models are simplified but formal representations
– usually in mathematical notation – of processes occurring in the real
world. The mathematics used is fairly simple: it involves subscripted
variables arranged in difference equations with excursions on occasion into
their matrix equivalents (Chs 7 and 11) or algorithmic representation
(Ch. 10). The main purpose in using mathematics is to identify and label entities in a population system precisely and to translate hypotheses about
their behaviour into more precise form. It is Stillwell (Ch. 8) and Willekens
and Baydar (Ch. 9) who follow this model most closely; Rees (Ch. 7),
Clarke (Ch. 10) and Madden and Batey (Ch. 11) are concerned more with
the definition and description of modelling frameworks within which the
behaviour of the population systems of interest can be studied.

Although there are commonalities – in method – in all the chapters in
Part II, there are also contrasts, particularly in the kinds of systems studied
and the degree to which the population is the focus of interest.

The first three chapters in Part II (Chs 7, 8 & 9) are concerned with
systems of many interacting regions. Rees (Ch. 7) and Stillwell (Ch. 8) use

a common system of 20 zones that exhaustively partition the United Kingdom. Willekens and Baydar (Ch. 9) employ a grouping of municipalities in the Netherlands into six classes which have spatial significance although not spatial contiguity.

By contrast both Clarke (Ch. 10) and Madden and Batey (Ch. 11) focus on a single region, although careful consideration is given to external flows across the region boundary in both cases. To supply migrants to and take migrants from Merseyside, for which their full model is developed, Madden and Batey use four regions in their multiregional cohort survival model.

The five chapters can be divided into three sets in terms of the components or entities studied. Stillwell (Ch. 8) and Willekens and Baydar (Ch. 9) examine migration in a variety of guises. Willekens and Baydar focus on the temporal trends in migration activity and thereby address a sorely neglected dimension of population movement, since most studies examine migration patterns for a single period or perhaps two, as Stillwell does – although the patterns of the two periods cannot be compared directly because of differences in the migration measures he adopts. Stillwell adds age to the spatial classification of migration and is able to look at the propensity of migrants in different age groups to overcome the friction of distance.

In Chapter 7 Rees considers all the components of population change – births and deaths, internal and external migrations – and classifies them by age. The focus is on the conversion of the classical components of the growth model into a consistent multiregional form.

For Clarke (Ch. 10) and for Madden and Batey (Ch. 11) the population and its associated demographic processes are but a small part of a much larger system of urban demographic–economic models. In these two chapters the focus shifts from individuals and the events influencing them to households, the units that are the basis of much socio-economic decision making. There have been attempts to build demographic models of household change using transition matrix methods (Harsman & Marksjo 1977), but these methods depend on a sophisticated database not available in most countries. The transition of a household from, say, having two members to having one could result from the demographic process of death, the social process of divorce or the mixed sociodemographic process of members leaving home and migrating to form a new household. The simpler demographic and social processes are measured: the household transitions are not. Clarke adopts the alternative and elegant strategy of microsimulation and list processing. In the microsimulation model demographic events happen to individuals, but any consequences for the household can be logged in a matched list of households.

In both the chapter by Clarke and that by Madden and Batey the marriage process is included in the authors' models. Clarke uses a marriage market in which pairs of individuals are matched probabilistically according to their characteristics, and Madden and Batey use a more traditional transition model in which the states are the marital categories 'never married', 'married', 'widowed' and 'divorced'. Not all moves between marital states are possible: people only leave the 'never married' state; but they both enter and leave the other states. Although it is possible for an individual to move from a widowed or divorced state to the other only in two steps, via the married state, transitions over a fixed time interval between widowed and divorced states are possible. This example illustrates the general problem faced in spatial populations modelling, the problem of handling population stocks, the events that occur to them, and the transitions of the population between states in a consistent fashion.

Having reviewed what the chapters in Part II are concerned with, let us now look at the developments in spatial population modelling since the late 1970s. What has been learnt about the theory and practice of multistate population analysis[1] will be assessed in the next five sections of this chapter. In Section 6.2 a clear distinction is drawn between the different kinds of data that can be used. Section 6.3 looks at the consequences of these differences for the measurement of components of change. The computation and interpretation of demographic rates (Section 6.4), their use (Section 6.5) and their modelling (Section 6.6) are then reviewed. The need for household analysis and the methods for achieving it − neglected topics in spatial population modelling − are discussed in Section 6.7. Finally, in the penultimate section of the chapter an attempt is made to place the modelling of spatial populations in a much wider context.

6.2 Movement, transition and last residence data

The 1970s saw the development of methods of multistate population analysis and their application to the description of the dynamics of multiregional population systems. However, there was some confusion in this application because, very often, the method did not match the data employed. This led Ledent and Rees (1980), for example, to characterize many of the multiregional life tables constructed and population projections carried out in the Migration and Settlement Study (Rogers & Willekens 1986) of the International Institute for Applied Systems Analysis (IIASA) as 'hybrid' in character because they used 'transition' data in a 'movement' model.

Let us try here to resolve the confusion by setting out systematically what is now known and accepted by most practitioners. Although readers may say at the conclusion of this account that it was all so obvious, I think it does need spelling out explicitly.

In Table 6.1 are set out the variables entering the components of the

Table 6.1 Description of the variables entering different multiregional population analyses.

Component of population change	Moves between states	Concept Transitions from initial states	Transitions from last states
birth	births to mothers resident in a region	persons starting life in a region (sometimes classified by mother's initial location)	persons born during period classified by current or last residence
death	deaths to residents of a region at time of death	deaths to persons initially resident in a region	deaths to persons classified by last residence
migration	migrations between one region and another	persons classified by initial region and final region	persons classified by last region and final region
population at risk	average population in a period	initial population in a period	initial population in a period

Table 6.2 Sources of the variables entering different multiregional population analyses.

Component of population change	Events or moves between states	Concept Transitions from initial states	Transitions from last states
birth	vital statistics registration	vital statistics registration or retrospective census	retrospective census
death	vital statistics registration	vital statistics registration data transformed	vital statistics registration data transformed
migration	address register	retrospective census tables based on: Q. 'Where were you living n years ago?'	retrospective census tables based on: Q. 'Where did you last live within the past n years?'

growth equation in the multiregional case, which involves migration between geographical areas. Three concepts are distinguishable.

(1) Moves are events in which only the immediately anterior state and immediately posterior state are known, not the states of the mover at the beginning or end of the time interval.
(2) Transitions are classifications of the populations by initial and final states in a time interval; the intermediate states through which a person may have passed are unknown. There are two kinds of transition: (a) transitions in which the initial and final states are known; (b) transitions in which the final states and the immediately previous states in a time interval are known.

Table 6.2 shows the relationship between the component variables of different conceptual type and the common data sources from which they are derived.

6.3   How are the components of change formulated?

6.3.1   Components of change for movement and transition data

For a multiregional system it is possible to write down for each of these concepts (a) a set of components of change equations in flow terms, and (b) a set of components of change equations in rate terms suitable for projection or stationary and stable population analysis.

Before this is done two points should be noted. The first is that the conceptual differences arise only because in practice discrete time intervals, discrete age groups and discrete regions have to be used if useful results are to be obtained. They all reduce to the same continuous formulation. The second point is that because the equations involve discrete variables measured in different ways no one set produces 'the truth' about the system being studied. Thus, for example, the distribution of life expectancy across many regions is not perfectly measured by any particular set of equations. The movement method probably exaggerates the out-of-birth-region life expectancy, whereas transition methods tend to underestimate these quantities.

Thus we can write the movement concept version of the components of change equation as

$$P^i(t+1) = P^i(t) + B^i - D^i + \sum_j M^{ji} - \sum_j M^{ij} \qquad (6.1)$$

where $P^i(t+1)$ = the population at the end of the time interval in region i;
$\quad\quad\ \ P^i(t)$ = the population at the start of the time interval in region i;
$\quad\quad\ \ B^i$ = births occurring to mothers usually resident in region i;
$\quad\quad\ \ D^i$ = deaths occurring to persons usually resident in region i;
$\quad\quad\ \ M^{ij}$ = moves from region i to region j.

It does not matter whether moves within a region are set to zero or included as they cancel out in the equation. Note, however, that this equation applies only if migration movements to and from all regions j have been included.

Normally we would wish to disaggregate the population and the component events by age and perhaps by other characteristics (sex, ethnic group, marital condition, labour force status). For the present purpose we shall introduce age disaggregation only and assume that age a refers to a 'period-cohort' (age–time plan II in Fig. 12.2), and is a label for the age group at the start of the time interval. The second subscript, a dot, indicates summation over age at the time of the event, which could be age a or age $a + 1$. For ages greater than the first the components of change equation reads

$$P^i_{a+1}(t+1) = P^i_a(t) \quad - D^i_{a\cdot} - \sum_j M^{ij}_{a\cdot} + \sum_j M^{ji}_{a\cdot}. \qquad (6.2)$$

and that for the first age group is

$$P^i_1(t+1) = B^i_\cdot - D^i_{0\cdot} - \sum_j M^{ij}_{0\cdot} + \sum_j M^{ji}_{0\cdot}. \qquad (6.3)$$

where subscripts have been added to indicate age, except in the case of births where the statistics are aggregated rather than broken down by age of mother.

The equivalent components-of-change equations for data gathered under the transition from initial state concept are

$$K^{e\cdot si}_{\cdot\,a+1} = K^{ei\cdot\cdot}_{a\cdot} - K^{eid\cdot}_{a\cdot} - \sum_j K^{eisj}_{aa+1} + \sum_j K^{ejsi}_{aa+1} \qquad (6.4)$$

$$K^{b\cdot si}_{01} = K^{bi\cdot\cdot}_{0\cdot} - K^{bid\cdot}_{0\cdot} - \sum_j K^{bisj}_{01} + \sum_j K^{bjsi}_{01} \qquad (6.5)$$

where K refers to a count of persons transferring between initial and final states in a period. The first two superscripts refer to life state and location at the start of the time interval; the second two superscripts refer to life state and location at the end of the time interval. The two subscripts refer to initial age group in the time interval and final age group respectively. The dot symbol indicates summation over the subscript or superscript replaced. Thus

K^{eisj}_{aa+1} = persons in existence in region i in age group a at the start of the time interval who were in age group $a + 1$ and surviving in region j at the end of the time interval;

and

K^{eidj}_{aa+1} = persons in existence in region i in age group a at the start of the time interval who died in region j at age $a + 1$ before the end of the period.

The summary variables in Equation 6.4 are made up of the following two types of transitions:

$K_a^{ei\cdot\cdot}$ = persons in existence in region i in age group a at the start of the time interval (summed over all possible final life states, locations and ages);

and

$K_a^{eid\cdot}$ = persons in existence in region i in age group a at the start of the time interval but who died during it (summed over all possible locations and ages).

The third term on the right-hand side of Equation 6.4 involves surviving outmigrants from region i and the fourth term involves surviving inmigrants to region i.

The terms in Equation 6.5 parallel those in Equation 6.4, except that the superscript b (for birth) replaces e (for existence), and the initial age is labelled 0 (zero). On the left-hand side are

$K_{\cdot a+1}^{e\cdot si}$ = persons aged $a + 1$ who are surviving in region i at the end of the time interval (and who were in existence at the start);

$K_{\cdot 1}^{b;si}$ = persons in the first age group who are surviving in region i at the end of the time interval (and who were born during it).

What are the equivalences between the movement concept equations and those of the transition concept, and what are the differences?

The stock terms are directly equivalent:

$$P_a^i(t) = K_a^{ei\cdot\cdot} \tag{6.6}$$

$$P_{a+1}^i(t + 1) = K_{\cdot a+1}^{e\cdot si} \tag{6.7}$$

$$B_\cdot^i = K_0^{bi\cdot\cdot} \tag{6.8}$$

$$P_1^i(t + 1) = K_{\cdot 1}^{b;si} \tag{6.9}$$

However, the flow terms are different: the M terms refer to moves; and the K terms involve migration of persons. Generally, the count of moves will exceed the count of migrants by a fair margin. The terms that refer to death involve the same mortality statistics, but they appear in a rather different guise in each equation. The movement concept term can be defined in terms of person transitions as

$$D_{a\cdot}^i = \sum_j K_{a\cdot}^{ejdi} = K_{a\cdot}^{eidi} + \sum_{j \neq i} K_{a\cdot}^{ejdi} \tag{6.10}$$

That is, deaths in a region are the sum of all persons who die there summed over all their initial locations. The transition term is defined differently as

$$K_{a\cdot}^{eid\cdot} = \sum_j K_{a\cdot}^{eidj} = K_{a\cdot}^{eidi} + \sum_{j \neq i} K_{a\cdot}^{eidj} \tag{6.11}$$

That is, the deaths of persons in existence in a particular region at the start of a time interval are treated as the sum of all persons born there who die either there or in another location. The deaths variable on the left-hand side of Equation 6.10 is the one normally reported in the registration statistics. The deaths variable on the left-hand side of Equation 6.11 must be found by first estimating its constituent terms (the two terms on the right-hand side of Eqn. 6.11), using a transition accounts based model.

This model estimates non-survivor flows thus:

$$K_{a\cdot}^{eidi} = K_{a\cdot}^{e\cdot di} - \sum_{j \neq i} K_{a\cdot}^{ejdi} \tag{6.12}$$

$$K_{a\cdot}^{eidj} = \frac{\frac{1}{2} d_{a\cdot}^{j}}{1 - \frac{1}{4} d_{a\cdot}^{j}} K_{aa+1}^{eisj} \qquad \text{for } i \neq j \tag{6.13}$$

where $d_{a\cdot}^{j}$ is the death rate in region j for persons aged a at the start of the time interval. It is computed using the deaths statistics usually available:

$$d_{a\cdot}^{j} = \frac{K_{a\cdot}^{e\cdot dj}}{\hat{K}_{a\cdot}^{e\cdot dj}} \tag{6.14}$$

where the $\hat{K}$ term refers to the population at risk of dying in region j. It is estimated as either the average population

$$\hat{K}_{a\cdot}^{e\cdot dj} = \tfrac{1}{2}(K_{a\cdot}^{ej\cdot\cdot} + K_{\cdot a+1}^{\cdot sj}) \tag{6.15}$$

or the multiregional weighted population

$$\hat{K}_{a\cdot}^{e\cdot dj} = K_{aa+1}^{ejsj} + \tfrac{1}{2} \sum_{j \neq i} K_{aa+1}^{ejsi} + \tfrac{1}{2} K_{a\cdot}^{ejdj} + \tfrac{1}{4} \sum_{j \neq i} K_{a\cdot}^{ejdi}$$

$$+ \tfrac{1}{2} \sum_{j \neq i} K_{aa+1}^{eisj} + \tfrac{1}{4} \sum_{j \neq i} K_{a\cdot}^{eidj} \tag{6.16}$$

Since the right-hand sides of both population-at-risk equations contain the non-survivor flows being estimated, the system of equations must be solved iteratively (for details see Rees & Wilson 1977, Rees 1981a).

6.3.2 Where does last residence data fit in?

In Table 6.1 a second variety of transition concept was identified, that generated by the following census question applied to a time interval: 'Where were you last living?' This question has been favoured by more nations than use the fixed interval question which generates the transitions discussed above (for further details see United Nations 1978, Willekens 1984). It is thus important to define the components-of-change equation in this context, although much current practice is to use Equations 6.2 and 6.3. To construct the conceptually correct equation we need to extend our notation for the transitions experienced by persons in a period to

$K_{a \cdot a + 1}^{eilksi}$ = persons in existence in region i aged a at the start of time interval who were in region j aged $a + 1$ at the end of the time interval, but reported their last residence in the interval to be region k.

Note that here if the 'last residence' is the same as that at the end of the time interval, then the initial location must also be that same region. That is,

$$K_{a \cdot a + 1}^{eiljsi} = 0 \qquad (6.17)$$

Last residence need not be involved in the person terms that end in death. The components-of-growth equations can be written as

$$K_{\cdot a + 1}^{e \cdot si} = K_a^{ei \cdot \cdot} - K_a^{eid \cdot} - \sum_j \sum_k K_{a \cdot a + 1}^{eilksi} + \sum_j \sum_k K_{a \cdot a + 1}^{ejlksi} \qquad (6.18)$$

and

$$K_{\cdot 1}^{b \cdot si} = K_0^{bi \cdot \cdot} - K_0^{bid \cdot} - \sum_j \sum_k K_0^{bilksj} + \sum_j \sum_k K_{0 \cdot 1}^{bjlksi} \qquad (6.19)$$

These equations are slightly more disaggregated versions of the normal transition equations. Equations for estimating the additional disaggregation need to be added to the model based on transition accounts.

$$K_{a \cdot a + 1}^{eilksj} = K_{a \cdot a + 1}^{e \cdot lksj} P(i/k) \qquad (6.20)$$

where

$P(i/k)$ = probability that a person giving region k as their last region of residence will have originated at the start of the time interval in region i estimated as

$$= \frac{K_{a \cdot a + 1}^{e \cdot lisk}}{K_{a \cdot a + 1}^{e \cdot l \cdot sk}} \qquad (6.21)$$

Thus, when we only have data of the last-residence kind to measure migration (or transfers between states in general), we should estimate the full start-of-period − last residence − end-of-period transitions and then aggregate over the last-residence states. If this is satisfactorily accomplished, all the methods for using transition data involving fixed-interval data are available to us (for further details see Rees 1985).

6.4 The measurement of rates

6.4.1 Rates measured using movement data

So far we have specified only historical accounting equations. These need to be converted into model equations for application in stationary, stable or realistic projections. The model equations are derived by substituting flows in the components-of-change equation. Equation 6.2 then becomes

$$P^i_{a+1}(t+1) = P^i_a(t) - d^i_{a\cdot}.\hat{P}^i_{a\cdot} - \sum_j m^{ij}_{a\cdot}.\hat{P}^i_{a\cdot} + \sum_j m^{ji}_{a\cdot}.\hat{P}^j_{a\cdot}. \tag{6.22}$$

where $\hat{P}$ is the population at risk of a demographic event and m is the migration rate. How should this population be defined? In a particular region any risk, say that of dying, is proportional to the time a person has spent in the region. So ideally we should define the population at risk as

$$\hat{P}^i_{a\cdot} = \frac{\displaystyle\sum_{y=1}^{N} t^i_a(y)}{T} \tag{6.23}$$

where $t^i_a(y)$ is the time spent in region i by individual y aged a at the start, N is the number of individuals spending time in region i, and T is the time interval. In practice, such a statistic can rarely be measured. In Equation 6.16 the population at risk was computed by guessing the fractions of time spent in region j by bundles of individuals collected together in the transition flow terms.

With movement data no such sets of persons can be estimated. Instead the population at risk is assumed to be the sum of the person years lived by the average population divided by the interval. This boils down to taking an average of the initial and final populations:

$$\hat{P}^i_{a\cdot} = \text{average of} [\, P^i_a(t), \, P^i_{a+1}(t+1)] \tag{6.24}$$

The form the average takes depends on the assumption about the functional form of the population path from the start to the end of the time interval. The simplest assumption is the linear one: that change between time t and $t+1$ can be represented as a straight line. The population at risk is then the arithmetic average of start and finish populations:

$$\hat{P}^i_{a\cdot} = \tfrac{1}{2}[P^i_a(t) + P^i_{a+1}(t+1)] \tag{6.25}$$

Other alternatives are exponential and cubic averages. For most purposes the linear assumption is sufficiently robust.

Substituting the right-hand side of Equation 6.25 for the population at risk in Equation 6.22 we obtain

$$P^i_{a+1}(t+1) = P^i_a(t) - d^i_{a\cdot}.\tfrac{1}{2}[P^i_a(t) + P^i_{a+1}(t+1)]$$

$$- \sum_j m^{ij}_{a\cdot}\tfrac{1}{2}[P^i_a(t) + P^i_{a+1}(t+1)]$$

$$+ \sum_j m^{ji}_{a\cdot}\tfrac{1}{2}[P^j_a(t) + P^j_{a+1}(t+1)] \tag{6.26}$$

Neglecting for the moment the two migration terms, we can rearrange

Equation 6.26 by gathering all end-of-period population terms onto the left-hand side:

$$P_{a+1}^i(t+1) + \tfrac{1}{2}d_a^i \cdot P_{a+1}^i(t+1) = P_a^i(t) - \tfrac{1}{2}d_a^i \cdot P_a^i(t) \tag{6.27}$$

which gives

$$P_{a+1}^i(t+1) = \frac{1 - \tfrac{1}{2}d_a^i \cdot}{1 + \tfrac{1}{2}d_a^i \cdot} P_a^i(t) \tag{6.28}$$

This last equation shows how, in the absence of migration, the initial population is transformed into the final one. When survivorship rates are defined as

$$s_{aa+1}^i = \frac{1 - \tfrac{1}{2}d_a^i \cdot}{1 + \tfrac{1}{2}d_a^i \cdot} \tag{6.29}$$

most demographers have, in the past, interpreted these rates as transition probabilities which tell us what the probability is of persons in the region i population surviving to age $a + 1$ at the end of the time interval.

For a while in the 1970s researchers had difficulty in deriving an equation equivalent to Equation 6.29 for multiregional systems in which migration played a vital role. The problem was solved by Rogers and Ledent in 1976, and the solution was incorporated in the Willekens and Rogers (1978) computer program. The key was to rearrange the rates in matrix form thus:

$$\mathbf{M}_{a\cdot} = \begin{bmatrix} d_a^1 \cdot + \sum_j m_a^{1j} \cdot & -m_a^{21} \cdot & \cdots & -m_a^{n1} \cdot \\ -m_a^{12} \cdot & d_a^2 \cdot + \sum_j m_a^{2j} \cdot & \cdots & -m_a^{n2} \cdot \\ \vdots & \vdots & & \vdots \\ -m_a^{1n} \cdot & -m_a^{2n} \cdot & \cdots & d_a^n \cdot + \sum_j m_a^{nj} \cdot \end{bmatrix} \tag{6.30}$$

The populations are arranged as vectors:

$$\mathbf{p}_a(t) = \begin{bmatrix} P_a^1(t) \\ P_a^2(t) \\ \vdots \\ P_a^n(t) \end{bmatrix} \qquad \mathbf{p}_{a+1}(t+1) = \begin{bmatrix} P_{a+1}^1(t+1) \\ P_{a+1}^2(t+1) \\ \vdots \\ P_{a+1}^n(t+1) \end{bmatrix} \tag{6.31}$$

Then, assuming that the populations at risk are linear averages of start and finish populations, the model equation linking them is

$$\mathbf{p}_{a+1}(t+1) = [\mathbf{I} + \tfrac{1}{2}\mathbf{M}_{a\cdot}]^{-1}[\mathbf{I} - \tfrac{1}{2}\mathbf{M}_{a\cdot}]\mathbf{p}_a(t) \tag{6.32}$$

and we can define the survivorship rates as

$$S_{aa+1} = [I + \tfrac{1}{2}M_{a\cdot}]^{-1}[I - \tfrac{1}{2}M_{a\cdot}] \qquad (6.33)$$

and the model equation is

$$p_{a+1}(t+1) = S_{aa+1}p_a(t) \qquad (6.34)$$

Exemplification of these equations is given in Chapter 7.

The derivation above is not quite that of Rogers and Ledent (1976). These authors were concerned with the estimation of survival rates for use in multiregional stationary (life-table) and stable (constant-rate projection) models. Let us label these survival rates as

p_{xx+n}^{ij} = the rate at which a person attaining birthday x in region i will survive to attain birthday $x+n$ in region j, where n is the age interval.

The relationship between the age-group a notation and the exact age x notation is shown in Figure 12.2.

Let

$$P_{xx+n} = [I + \tfrac{1}{2}M_{xx+n}]^{-1}[I - \tfrac{1}{2}M_{xx+n}] \qquad (6.35)$$

in the same way as the S survivorship rates were derived. The M matrix in Equation 6.35 is arranged in the same structure as in Equation 6.33, except that for events counted in age–time plan III (Fig. 12.2). Since events in many countries are not counted in this fashion Rogers and Ledent (1976) derived an approximate version of Equation 6.32:

$$P_{xx+n} = [I + \tfrac{1}{2}M \cdot a]^{-1}[I - \tfrac{1}{2}M \cdot a] \qquad (6.36)$$

where events in the M matrix are counted at the age at which they occur using age–time plan I (Fig. 12.2). If events are counted using this age–time plan, then the survivorship rate equivalent of Equation 6.36 is

$$S_{aa+1} = [I + \tfrac{1}{2}M \cdot a]^{-1}[I - \tfrac{1}{2}M \cdot a+1] \qquad (6.37)$$

Which particular equation is chosen to estimate the S and the P rates depends on which age–time plan is used to collect the data on flow components and whether any age–time plan transformations are attempted (see Chapter 12 for a much fuller discussion).

6.4.2 Rates measured using transition data

Rates are normally measured using transition data in a rather different fashion from movement data. Rates that assess the likelihood of given outcomes over a time interval (i.e. transitions) are computed by dividing the transition flow term by the initial population in the state.

Survivorship rates are measured directly as

$$s_{aa+1}^{ij} = \frac{K_{aa+1}^{eisj}}{K_a^{ei\cdot\cdot}} \tag{6.38}$$

$$s_{01}^{ij} = \frac{K_{a1}^{bisj}}{K_a^{bi\cdot\cdot}} \tag{6.39}$$

where

s_{aa+1}^{ij} = the rate at which persons existing in region i in age group a at the start of the period survive in region j in age group $a + 1$ at the end of the time interval;

and

s_{01}^{ij} = the rate at which persons born in region i survive in region j at the end of the time interval.

Rates of non-survivorship are similarly measured by dividing the flow term by the initial population.

The matrix version of these equations involves defining matrices of the population flow terms (see Table 7.2) and premultiplying by a diagonal matrix of the reciprocals of the regional populations (that is, the inverse of the diagonalized vector of regional populations):

$$\mathbf{K}_{aa+1} = \begin{bmatrix} K_{aa+1}^{e1s1} & K_{aa+1}^{e1s2} & \cdots & K_{aa+1}^{e1sn} \\ K_{aa+1}^{e2s1} & K_{aa+1}^{e2s2} & \cdots & K_{aa+1}^{e2sn} \\ \vdots & \vdots & & \vdots \\ K_{aa+1}^{ens1} & K_{aa+1}^{ens2} & \cdots & K_{aa+1}^{ensn} \end{bmatrix} \tag{6.40}$$

$$\tilde{\mathbf{K}}_a^{-1} = \begin{bmatrix} \dfrac{1}{K_a^{e1\cdot\cdot}} & 0 & \cdots & 0 \\[2ex] 0 & \dfrac{1}{K_a^{e2\cdot\cdot}} & \cdots & 0 \\[1ex] \vdots & \vdots & & \vdots \\[1ex] 0 & 0 & \cdots & \dfrac{1}{K_a^{en\cdot\cdot}} \end{bmatrix} \tag{6.41}$$

$$\mathbf{S}_{aa+1}' = \tilde{\mathbf{K}}_a^{-1}\mathbf{K}_{aa+1} \tag{6.42}$$

with similar equations for the first cohort (born during the time interval).

How are the P rates used with age–time plan III estimated from transition data? If migration data were collected using this age–time plan, then the equation would simply be

$$\mathbf{P}_{xx+n}' = \tilde{\mathbf{K}}_x^{-1}\mathbf{K}_{xx+n} \tag{6.43}$$

(as in Rees & Wilson, 1977 Part 4). However, since no such data are collected, Ledent and Rees (1980, 1986) suggest various forms of interpolation between survivorship rates computed using age–time plan II data (census migration). The simplest method is linear interpolation:

$$\mathbf{P}_{x+n} = \tfrac{1}{2}(S_{a_x} + S_{a_{x+n}}) \tag{6.44}$$

though cubic spline interpolation is more accurate (see Ledent & Rees 1980, 1986).

6.4.3 Are the survivorship and survival rates probabilities?

For rates to be regarded as probabilities they must satisfy at least the following properties:

(1) All outcomes of the process must be known.
(2) The sum of the probabilities of all outcomes must be 1.
(3) No individual probability can exceed 1.
(4) No individual probability can fall below 0.
(5) The denominator in a probability definition must be the sum of all possible outcomes.
(6) The numerator in a probability definition must be a subset of the denominator.

Let us consider the properties of the rates so far defined:

(a) observed rates based on movement data;
(b) survivorship rates and survival rates based on movement data;
(c) survivorship rates and survival rates based on transition data.

Observed occurrence–exposure rates based on movement data fail to be probabilities on all counts except 1 and 4. The numerators consist of counts of events; the denominators are counts of persons at risk. If the population makes an average of more than one move in a time interval, the mobility rate can exceed unity. If this is the case, when such rates are used to define survivorship rates (age–time plan II) or survival rates (age–time plan III) then the diagonal terms can be less than zero.

So why have demographers persisted in regarding survival or survivorship rates as probabilities when such logic suggests they are not. The reason is that if you can reduce the system studied to a single region closed to outside influences then the following equality holds:

$$\frac{\text{the number of persons dying in}}{\text{the initial population}} = \frac{\text{the observed number of}}{\text{mortality events}} \tag{6.45}$$

Then the survivorship rate satisfies all the properties described above, but only because of the equivalence of transitions and events. However, remove the assumption of closed regions and Equation 6.45 no longer holds and movement-based survivorship rates are no longer probabilities. Survivorship rates based on transition data satisfy all the conditions for defining probabilities as long as they are derived from full sets of population accounts or through adherence to the accounting relationships built into such accounts.

6.5 The use of rates in population models

Do these conclusions really matter in practice? The answer is probably not, for two reasons. The first, shallower, reason is that in most real situations survival or survivorship rates based on occurrence–exposure rates derived from movement data and those based on transition data are going to be rather similar. The second reason, which is more profound, is that the applications in which the rates are used depend for their validity on the components-of-change equations used, not on whether or not the rates are probabilities. As long as data type and method used match comparable results should be obtained.

Having estimated S and P rates, we can put them to work in their respective age–time plan frameworks (II or III) to carry out population projections with a real population, life-table analysis with a stationary population, or stable population analysis with constant rates. For the first and third analyses it is also necessary to measure fertility rates and add equations for generating births to the model. These issues are not discussed in detail here because the fertility process is not central to an understanding of developments in multistate or multiregional population analysis, although it is crucial in any practical application.

To project the population using S rates we apply Equation 6.34 successively:

$$\mathbf{p}_{a+1}(t+1) = \mathbf{S}_{aa+1}\mathbf{p}_a(t) \tag{6.46}$$

$$\mathbf{p}_{a+2}(t+2) = \mathbf{S}_{a+1a+2}\mathbf{p}_{a+1}(t) \tag{6.47}$$

and so on. However, this well known set of equations can also be used for stationary population analysis. Assuming a fixed birth cohort, the stationary populations in successive age groups are generated thus:

$$\mathbf{k}_1 = \mathbf{S}_{01}\mathbf{l}_0$$
$$\mathbf{k}_2 = \mathbf{S}_{12}\mathbf{k}_1$$
$$\vdots$$
$$\mathbf{k}_{a+1} = \mathbf{S}_{aa+1}\mathbf{k}_a$$
$$\vdots$$
$$\mathbf{k}_z = \mathbf{S}_{z-1z}\mathbf{k}_{z-1} + \mathbf{S}_{zz}\mathbf{k}_z \tag{6.48}$$

111

where l_0 = a column vector of the regional radices or the regional hypothetical cohorts;

k_a = a column vector of regional stationary populations in age group a.

Since the stationary population can be interpreted also as an estimate of life years lived by the population if it is multiplied by the age interval, we can derive life expectancies in terms of the survivorship rates (following Ledent & Rees 1980, 1986). However, in order to do this we must classify life years by region of birth. The initial cohort vector becomes a diagonal matrix of initial regional radices:

$$\tilde{L}_0 = \begin{bmatrix} l_0^1 & 0 & \ldots & 0 \\ 0 & l_0^2 & \ldots & 0 \\ \vdots & \vdots & & \vdots \\ 0 & 0 & \ldots & l_0^n \end{bmatrix} \tag{6.49}$$

with each initial regional cohort set to unity (probability formulation) or to, say, 100 000 (hypothetical cohort formulation). When we introduce place-of-birth disaggregation and the length of the age interval, the stationary population vectors become life-years-spent matrices:

$$L_1 = S_{01} n \tilde{L}_0$$
$$L_2 = S_{12} L_1$$
$$\vdots$$
$$L_a = S_{a-1a} L_{a-1}$$
$$\vdots$$
$$L_z = S_{z-1z} L_{z-1} + S_{zz} L_z \tag{6.50}$$

where

$$L_a' = \begin{bmatrix} {}^1L_a^1 & {}^1L_a^2 & \ldots & {}^1L_a^n \\ {}^2L_a^1 & {}^2L_a^2 & \ldots & {}^2L_a^n \\ \vdots & \vdots & & \vdots \\ {}^nL_a^1 & {}^nL_a^2 & \ldots & {}^nL_a^n \end{bmatrix} \tag{6.51}$$

Equation set 6.50 can be expressed as

$$L_a = \prod_{b=0}^{a-1} S_{bb+1} n L_0 \tag{6.52}$$

and if these are cumulated to yield total life years lived beyond age c,

$$T_c = \sum_{a=c}^{z} L_a = \sum_{a=c}^{z} \prod_{b=0}^{a-1} S_{bb+1} n L_0 \tag{6.53}$$

Life expectancies at birth are derived as

$$e_0 = T_0 \tilde{L}_0^{-1}$$

$$= \sum_{a=1}^{z} \prod_{b=0}^{a-1} S_{bb+1} n l_0 \tilde{L}_0^{-1}$$

$$= \sum_{a=1}^{z} \prod_{b=0}^{a-1} S_{bb+1} n \qquad (6.54)$$

This is called the 'direct' method of life expectancy calculation by Ledent (1978a) and Ledent and Rees (1980, 1986) because life expectancies are a function solely of the observed survival rates and age interval.

To compute life expectancies beyond given ages we need to estimate survival probabilities for given ages, and these can be linearly interpolated between successive stationary populations for which the region of birth classification has been retained (as in Philipov & Rogers 1982):

$$l_{x+n} = \tfrac{1}{2}(k_{a_x} + k_{a_{x+n}}) \qquad (6.55)$$

so that

$$e_x = \sum_{a=x}^{z} \prod_{b=0}^{a-1} S_{bb+1} n l_0 L_x^{-1} \qquad (6.56)$$

where a_x is the age group starting at age x.

An important point to make about the discussion above is that the life-table model in its entirety has been derived using age–time plan II and observed survivorship rates. Normally, the life-table model is derived initially using age–time plan III survival rates and the survivorship rates are estimated later. With movement-type data on migration it is possible to take either route (see Chapter 12 for further discussion); with transition-type data on migration it makes sense to take the age–time plan II route (as recommended in Ledent & Rees 1980, 1986).

There is, however, one crucial distinction between the different uses to which survivorship or survival rates are put. Researchers may be interested in projecting population stocks or life years lived classified by current region, or by current region and region of previous residence (such as region of birth). In the first case, it probably does not matter that in reality the Markovian assumption of most multistate population models – that current transitions depend on current state, not any prior states – is violated. In the second case, as Ledent (1981) and Philipov and Rogers (1982) have demonstrated, very different results are produced if one assumes that migration in a current period or age interval is independent of place of birth than if one assumes it is dependent on place of birth. In the projection model one can assume that the independence model (in age–time plan II) is

$$K_{aa+1}^{eisj} = s_{aa+1}^{ij} K_{aa+1}^{ei\cdot\cdot} \qquad (6.57)$$

and that the life-table model (in age–time plan III) is

$$l_{xx+n}^{ij} = p_{xx+n}^{ij} l_x^i \tag{6.58}$$

rather than

$$K_{aa+1}^{eisj} = \sum_k {}^k s_{aa+1}^{ij} \, {}^k K_a^{ej\cdot\cdot} \tag{6.59}$$

or

$$l_{xx+n}^{ij} = \sum_k {}^k p_{xx+n}^{ij} \, {}^k l_{xx+n}^{ij} \tag{6.60}$$

where the k superscript indicates a state prior to age a or age x, such as birthplace.

Table 6.3 illustrates the differences that can result from projections disaggregated by place of birth (Philipov & Rogers 1982). Birthplace-dependent and birthplace-independent projections produce virtually identical projections of the national population in 1998. The birthplace-dependent projections produce higher percentages of the population remaining in their native region because of the higher than average return migration rates: 2.6% higher in the South, 3.5% higher in the non-South. However, the regional distributions aggregated over birthplace are much closer – only 0.7% different. These results are thus comforting for the user of conventional population projections, where a birthplace disaggregation is not usually required; but they are uncomfortable for anyone wishing to use multiregional life tables. Using an equation like 6.58 rather than 6.60 undoubtedly leads to an overestimate of lifetime migration out of the birth region.

These considerations explain the differences observed between life tables based on migration data with a one-year time interval and those with a five-

Table 6.3 American females, 1968, projected to 1998 using birthplace independent and birthplace dependent projections.

Projection type	% resident in South			% resident in non-South			Total population projected (millions)
	Born South	Born non-South	Total	Born non-South	Born South	Total	
birthplace independent projection	25.2	7.8	33.0	58.9	8.1	67.0	138.6
birthplace dependent projection	27.8	4.5	32.3	62.4	5.3	67.7	138.6

Source: Philipov and Rogers (1982, Table 6, p. 465).

year time interval: the latter estimate a much higher proportion of lives spent in the birthplace region than the former.

6.6 Should observed rates or models of rates be used?

One criticism has been consistently levelled at multiregional and multistate population modelling: it is that there are far too many rates involved and that it is therefore difficult to know how such rates change over time or are influenced by changes in population behaviour. A solution that has been proposed is to represent sets of rates in the multistate model by submodels with fewer parameters.

Rogers and Castro (1981, 1982) have summarized their extensive work on the modelling of migration schedules by age, whch has been widely applied (see, for example, Martin Voorhees Associates & John Bates Services 1981). Rogers (1982, Rogers & Planck 1984) combined migration schedule models with similar models for mortality and fertility to develop 'parameterized' projection models which give results (Rogers & Planck 1984, Table 3, p. 32) very close to the observed schedules. Then Rogers and Planck related the model parameters for migration, fertility, first marriage and divorce schedules from a large number of countries to the gross transition rates for each process in sets of regression equations. This enabled them to carry out a two region and four marital state illustrative projection for Sweden by stipulating changes in a small number of gross transition rates.

One aspect of this issue not addressed by Rogers and Planck is whether the spatial patterns of migration flows can be similarly treated. Both Stillwell (Ch. 8) and Willekens and Baydar (Ch. 9) explore different methods of representing migration flows between regions or settlement classes by a smaller number of parameters. In Chapter 8 Stillwell compares the results of a simple observed-rates model with those of a set of spatial interaction models. Although the models fit well to observed data, they performed significantly less well than methods based closely on observed rates.

Willekens and Baydar (Ch. 9) find in their analysis a very smooth, almost constant trend in the distribution component of migration among settlement types in the Netherlands. The key to forecasting migration in both the United Kingdom and the Netherlands is to predict the level of migration activity accurately. The fluctuations revealed over the past two decades are considerable – probably due to the level of economic activity – and are therefore difficult to forecast.

Numerous other approaches have been applied to the problem of handling migration flows in systems of a great many regions. These are reviewed in detail by Rees (1981a, 1983), so only a brief word is included here. Reduction of a system of n by n flows to one of n sets of 2 by 2 flows for the region and the rest of the country gives relatively accurate results (Rogers 1976). Masser (1976) outlines a hierarchical accounting system that could be adapted for use with multiregional population models. The Greater London Council uses a model originally developed by Gilje and Campbell (1973) that incorporates chains of probabilities in a hierarchical fashion, but the model structure is specific to the system studied. The Department of the Environment now employs, along with the Office of Population Censuses and Surveys, a model (Martin Voorhees Associates & John Bates Services 1981) that decouples the outmigration process from the destination selection process, as does Frey (1983) in his city—suburb model. Probably the most useful way to regard these models is to look on them as models that seek to estimate the rates that enter a standard multiregional population model.

Some final points should be mentioned before concluding this discussion of how to model spatial population systems. We have assumed that the systems being used are properly specified; otherwise the components of growth equations fail to hold, and so does most of the subsequent methodology. This concern with proper system definition and model closure is addressed in detail in Chapter 7. Alexander (1983) has looked at what happens to the population system when a population model involving constant migrant numbers (rather than rates) is used. This might be the appropriate way to represent immigration quotas in forecasts, for example. Under certain conditions, such as positive natural increase within the system and negative net external migration at the right level, or such as net reproduction rates of less than unity within the system and net positive external migration, the population of regions within the system may become stationary. Espenshade *et al.* (1982) explore what happens to stable population theory in such circumstances and the implications with respect to immigration policy. Models involving a degree of control of population systems have also been specified, but these have found uses in the manpower planning activities of firms and other organizations rather than in larger systems with many more decision takers, looser constraints and more freedom of individual movement.

6.7 The individual and the household

6.7.1 Why the household deserves more attention

All the works reviewed so far in this chapter have adopted the individual as the principal actor in the system. He or she is subject to rates or probabilities of dying, migrating, marrying, having children and so on. Yet many of the decisions involved in these processes are taken by families or households. And it is the household unit and its characteristics which is of crucial interest to planners of housing or retail facilities, for example.

Table 6.4 Changes in population numbers and households, Great Britain 1961–81.

Year/ Period	Population (millions)	Change (%)	Households (millions)	Change (%)	Population per household	Headship rate (%)
1961	51.380		16.189		3.17	31.51
					(3.09)	(32.36)
61–6		3.48		4.62		
1966	53.167		16.937		3.14	31.86
					(2.99)	(33.44)
66–71		2.26		8.15		
1971	54.369		18.317		2.97	33.69
					(2.89)	(34.60)
71–6		0.54		⎫		
1976	54.664		—	⎬ 6.41	(2.76)	(36.23)
76–81		0.27		⎭		
1981	54.814		19.492		2.81	35.59
					(2.71)	(36.90)
81–3		– 0.02				
1983	54.804		—		—	

Sources
Population – OPCS (1984, Table 2, p. 37): mid-year estimates.
Households – Central Statistical Office (1984, Table 2.3, p. 24): census figures.
Notes
Great Britain = England and Wales, and Scotland.
  The unbracketed figures for population per household are the ratio of population to private households. The bracketed figures (from Central Statistical Office 1984) are the ratio of population in private households to households.
  The headship rates are the number of households as a percentage of the population (total is unbracketed; private household population is bracketed).

The number of households has tended to increase faster than the population in recent decades in developed countries. Increases in living standards have been translated into better housing and increased income has provided families and primary individuals with the means of living in independent households at each stage of their life cycle. For Britain these trends are illustrated in Table 6.4. Since 1961 the pace of population growth has progressively slackened and in the early 1980s it reached zero. However, the growth in numbers of households has remained positive: it was 13.1% in the 1961–71 period and 6.4% in the 1971–81 period. The consequence has been a fall of 12% in the average household size and an increase in the percentage of the population who are heads of households from 32 to 37%.

Table 6.5 reveals that in the 1951–61 and 1961–71 periods some 42% of the growth in the number of households was due to population growth *per se*. This had shrunk to 13% in the 1971–81 period. Changes in the age–sex structure of the population (towards groups more likely to form independent households such as widowed females in the older age groups) contributed 15% to the changes in the 1951–61 period, but nothing in the

117

Table 6.5 Components of the increase in numbers of households between 1951 and 1981, Great Britain.

Period	Total increase in households		Increase due to the population growth		Increase due to change in population structure		Increase due to change in headship rates	
	No.	%	No.	%	No.	%	No.	%
1951–61	1.523	100	0.644	42.3	0.231	15.2	0.648	43.5
1961–71	1.869	100	0.790	42.3	−0.007	−0.3	1.072	57.4
1971–81	1.175	100	0.150	12.8	1.025	87.2		

Source: Plessis-Fraissard (1979, Table 10.10, p. 454) and the author's calculations.
Note: The figures in the No. columns are in millions.

1961–71 period. The largest contribution is likely to have come from the increasing propensity of individuals to head separate households in both 1961–71 and 1971–81.

These trends, no doubt familiar to most population researchers, have not been given the attention they deserve in spatial population modelling. Exceptionally, Plessis-Fraissard (1979) has provided a fascinating picture of the way in which household characteristics vary across British regions and

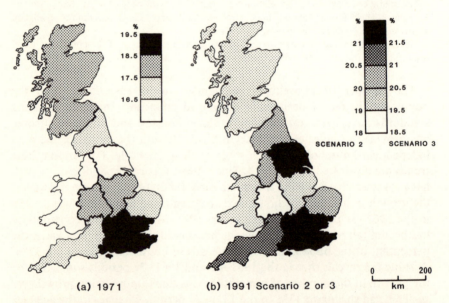

(a) 1971   (b) 1991 Scenario 2 or 3

Figure 6.1 Regional distribution of the percentage of one-person households among all households in Great Britain, 1971 and 1991.
Source: Plessis-Fraissard, 1979, Fig. 12.4, p. 624. (See Table 6.6 for a description of the scenarios.)

118

how they are likely to change in the near future. Figure 6.1 shows how the proportion of households made up of one individual varies from region to region, and how this proportion is likely to change by 1991. The extent to which one-person households are formed is crucial in household forecasting, and this will depend in part on conditions in the housing market, that is, on the availability of suitable housing units.

In Chapter 10 Clarke considers the connections between individuals, demographic processes and households at the microlevel in a simulation model and links the evolution of households to events in the housing and job markets in the urban region in the wider work from which Chapter 10 has been extracted. The transition of an individual between one state and another can easily be translated into a change in the characteristics and number of households by applying a few simple rules. The household is viewed as a group of individuals whose various individual decisions and histories determine its evolution over time. To put the work of Clarke and his collaborators into context, it will be useful here to review some of the alternative approaches to the problem of modelling the ways in which households change over time.

We can distinguish four types of method: (1) the headship rate method, (2) the household transition matrix method, (3) the household composition method and (4) the microsimulation method. The first three are briefly reviewed here. The fourth is outlined by Clarke in Chapter 10.

6.7.2   Headship rate method

The headship rate method has long been used in forecasting the numbers of households. Here we draw on the review and analysis of Plessis-Fraissard (1979), who carried out a set of household projections for the regions of Great Britain.

A headship rate is the ratio of the number of heads of household with given attributes to the number of people in general with those attributes. However, it may be extended to encompass the disaggregation of heads by type of household headed, in terms of size or relationship of members. For example, households might be divided into one-person households, married-couple households (with or without children), lone-parent households and non-family households with two or more members.

In the forecasting of households' headship rates are measured for groups distinguished by age, sex and marital status. This tripartite division is need-ed because all three factors produce important variations in headship rates. In the past only age has been consistently used in multiregional population projections. Thus Rees (Ch. 7) uses age but not sex to disaggregate his 20 regional populations; and this is also the case in the multiregional projections of the Migration and Settlement Study (Rogers & Willekens 1986). Multistate methods have been used for marital condition projection only

Table 6.6 Projected headship rates, England and Wales.

Sex	Age group	Married				Single				Widowed/divorced			
		1951	1971	1991 S2	1991 S3	1951	1971	1991 S2	1991 S3	1951	1971	1991 S2	1991 S3
men	15–39	0.801	0.974	0.982	0.985	0.037	0.088	0.114	0.127	0.037	0.088	0.114	0.127
	40–59	0.962.	0.987	0.990	0.992	0.269	0.368	0.417	0.442	0.678	0.779	0.831	0.857
	60 +	0.966	0.983	0.984	0.990	0.389	0.520	0.585	0.618	0.637	0.726	0.770	0.793
women	15–39	—	0.028	0.028	0.028	0.037	0.088	0.114	0.127	0.037	0.088	0.114	0.127
	40–59	—	0.026	0.026	0.026	0.290	0.399	0.452	0.479	0.778	0.883	0.930	0.950
	60 +	—	0.032	0.032	0.032	0.468	0.600	0.666	0.699	0.681	0.786	0.840	0.867

Source: Plessis-Fraissard (1979, Table 11.1, p. 516).

Notes

S2 = scenario 2: low growth of headship rates.

1971–81 change is at 2/3rds of 1951–71 rate;

1981–91 change is at 1/3rd of 1951–71 rate.

S3 = scenario 3: medium growth of headship rates.

1971–81 change is at the same rate as 1951–71;

1981–91 change is at 1/2 of 1951–71 rate of change.

For the 15–39 age group the rate for widowed/divorced is a combined one for both sexes and for non-married persons.

(Willekens *et al.* 1982). Madden and Batey (Ch. 11) use a marital state population model for their projected Merseyside population and so combine regional, age–sex and marital condition classifications. However, the marital state model was used for the study area population alone. It is only with the model of Rogers and Planck (1984) for a population distinguished by two regions, two sexes and four marital states in Sweden that all transitions are explicitly included.

Thus the more usual sequence in projecting the numbers of households has been to apply forecast marital condition proportions to projected regional populations, disaggregated by age and sex, to obtain projected populations by age, sex and marital status to which projected headship rates can be applied (Plessis-Fraissard 1979, Ch. 10). There are a number of consistency checks that need to be applied to the marital condition proportions such as 'Do they sum to unity?' and 'Are the resulting numbers of married men and women roughly the same?' They will never be exactly the same in any one region because of the combined effects of marital separation and migration. In forecasting how headship rates will evolve it is necessary to adapt the rates of change observed over the recent past as ceilings are reached in the proportion of a group who are heads, and to adjust the headship rates so that the projections produce reasonable estimates of mean household size and of the number of one-person households (Plessis-Fraissard 1979, Ch. 11). Table 6.6 summarizes the way in which headship rates are expected to shift in England and Wales if the trends noted earlier in Tables 6.4 and 6.5 slow drastically (scenario 2) or moderately (scenario 3). There is still considerable room for growth in the number of households as the headship rates change and as people spend more time in their lives in the single state before marriage or in the divorced or widowed states after marriage, even if the population itself remains stationary – a probable state of affairs according to the Chapter 7 forecasts, although the official projections anticipate slight growth in the UK population.

6.7.3 Transition matrix method

It is possible to approach the problem of forecasting household numbers by estimating the transitions between sets of household types and by using the transition rates so measured in a matrix projection model (Harsman & Marksjo 1977). Attempts to estimate such matrices from demographic or social data already collected have not proved very satisfactory. Several authors have spelled out why this is so (for example, Plessis-Fraissard 1979, Table 10.14, p. 485). A transition from one household type to another may occur as a result of many different demographic events, or as a result of an event not normally recorded, such as marital separation or merely a change in the catering arrangements within a multifamily household, creating two separate single-family households.

6.7.4   Household composition matrix method

Akkerman (1980, 1983) has developed a method for the simultaneous projection of population and households which is essentially a generalization and extension of the headship rate method. Adopting a slightly different notation from that of Akkerman, the household composition matrix can be defined as consisting of elements a_{ij} representing the average number of persons in age group i in households with head in age group j. Thus

$$A = \begin{bmatrix} a_{11} & a_{12} & \dots & a_{1n} \\ a_{21} & a_{22} & \dots & a_{2n} \\ \cdot & \cdot & & \cdot \\ \cdot & \cdot & & \cdot \\ \cdot & \cdot & & \cdot \\ a_{n1} & a_{n2} & \dots & a_{nn} \end{bmatrix} \tag{6.61}$$

If $p(t)$ is a vector of population by age at time t and $h(t)$ is a vector of households by age of head at time t, it then follows that

$$p(t) = Ah(t) \tag{6.62}$$

and

$$h(t) = A^{-1}p(t) \tag{6.63}$$

By way of comparison the headship rate model formulated as a matrix model would involve the pre-multiplication of a vector of population disaggregated by age, sex and marital status category, $p(t)$, by a row vector of similarly disaggregated headship rates, r:

$$h(t) = rp(t) \tag{6.64}$$

where $h(t)$ is the scalar number of households.

Akkerman introduces fertility into the model by treating the first five-year age group separately from the others:

$$a = (a_{12}a_{13}\dots a_{1n}) \tag{6.65}$$

$$P_1 = ah(t) \tag{6.66}$$

Although Akkerman claims that his method makes possible the simultaneous projection of population and households, in essence it is a generalization of the headship rate method which yields more useful data on households that relate ages of heads and other members and generate mean sizes at the expense of neglecting marital status. The method also requires cross-tabulations of household data beyond those currently provided in most censuses, unless those censuses provide public use samples such as the one Akkerman uses in his application of the method to the Toronto metropolitan area.

6.8 The modelling of spatial populations within wider systems

Models of spatial population can be divided into three broad classes: (1) extrapolative, in which the demographic component rates and/or flows are statistically or judgementally trended into the future; (2) economic–demographic, in which the demographic component rates and/or flows are modelled as functions of other socio-economic influences; and (3) comprehensive models of an urban or regional system in which the interactions between the population and other model sectors are represented.

The projections reported in Chapter 7 are the simplest form of the first class: namely, they assume constancy of future rates and flows, although it would be very simple to introduce time variable inputs to the movements accounts model described. The investigations of Stillwell (Ch. 8) and of Willekens and Baydar (Ch. 9) into migration also fall into the first class, although in each careful attention is paid to decomposing the forecasts into time-variable and time-invariant constituents, and to assessing the goodness of fit of the forecasts. Clarke (Ch. 10) describes the demographic submodel that is elsewhere embedded in a comprehensive model of a regional system. Madden and Batey (Ch. 11) give an account of an integrated model based on a greatly extended Leontief input–output model of the population and economy of an urban region, and Batey (1985) provides a general review of this type of model.

The second class of model is thus unrepresented in Part II of this volume, although much of what is said in Part I is relevant to constructing such models. Isserman (1985) has recently reviewed this second class of model with respect to fertility and internal migration. Despite a large volume of social science research on the determinants of fertility and migration, Isserman expresses disappointment with achievements to date. He says (p. 41):

> This empirical work, however, is usually an analysis either (1) of a single place over time, or (2) of a cross-section of places at a single time. To be useful in multiregional forecasting, on the other hand, the theory must either (1) explain changes in every region in the model, not just in a single place, or (2) generate cross-section parameters that are constant or predictable. Such tests are far more demanding than those to which most social science theories have been subjected.

Why is it that we have not achieved the improved multiregional population modelling capability that Isserman seeks? Three broad reasons can, I think, be advanced.

First, it has not been easy to convert conventional demographic and economic methods – such as the cohort survival model, the life-table formulation or accounting procedures – into multiregional or multistate models. Debates about the right equations to use in measuring survival probabilities, about how multiregional systems should be closed and about the robustness of the Markovian assumption have now, it is hoped, been resolved, although a comprehensive set of computer programs (a population package for the social sciences?) incorporating our current understanding remains to be developed.

Secondly, research into the explanation of spatial and temporal trends in the components of demographic change does, at the very minimum, require the existence of good time-series of the dependent variables. Good time-series of migration statistics – essential if the population of many regions are to be studied simultaneously – have been lacking in many countries. The national household survey, carried out each year, may effectively monitor most social characteristics, but it simply does not provide adequate spatial detail and tends to be subject to much bias when measuring migration. National registers can provide excellent monitoring devices (see Chapter 8 on the British system and Chapter 9 on the Dutch system), but often lack cross-classificatory reference variables. The national census provides many of these cross-classificatory variables but suffers from being periodic rather than continuous, from often asking less than ideal questions on migration, and from failing to compute some crucial missing variables (infant migration in the British census is one). An emerging solution is the development of longitudinal data sets which combine the comprehensive profiles of the periodic censuses with the continuous monitoring of key demographic events, recorded in registration systems, although these data sets are not yet as easily available as either census or register information.

Thirdly, as Isserman (1985) points out, if we were to develop a good set of explanatory models for fertility and migration, we would need an equally good set of future predictions of the explanatory variables that enter these models.

6.9   Conclusion

This chapter has attempted to put the other contributions of Part II into context through a review of recent developments in spatial population modelling. Attention has been most focused on an attempt to synthesize the achievements of what history may call the 'Rogers school'. In the latter part of the chapter a broader perspective is developed which reveals the lacunae not covered by that school of work. The chapters that follow contain examples of the developments and issues raised here.

Note

1   In the account of multiregional population analysis given here the detailed acknowledgment of individual insights is very difficult, and the

authors may not necessarily agree with my interpretations. However, I think a collective acknowledgment is in order. I have benefited greatly from reading the papers of Andrei Rogers, Frans Willekens, Jacques Ledent, Kao-Lee Liaw, Richard Stone, Ken Land, Luis Castro and Dimiter Philipov and talking with each of them at length. Fortunately for us all, the ideas of multistate population analysis were freely exchanged in a fruitful period of collaboration centred on Andrei Rogers's leadership at the International Institute for Applied Systems Analysis over the 1975–83 period. Since all of the researchers mentioned above have contributed to the development of spatial population modelling, and because the contributions in this volume of the first three listed do not reflect their contribution fully, a longer review is justified here.

7

Choices in the construction of regional population projections

PHILIP REES

7.1 Introduction

7.1.1 Overview

Projecting the population of geographical areas into the future is an exercise now routinely carried out at both national and local levels. The projected numbers of people have a profound effect on the demand for public services, as Craig (1983) has recently demonstrated so elegantly using national population projections.

Of course, population projections are always subject to error and must be continually revised to take account of the most up-to-date information on trends in the components of change that 'drive' the projections. But the forecaster needs also to be aware of the likely sources of variation – besides real world events – that will affect the projections made. Some of these sources of variation are well known; others are not. It is intended in this chapter to explore the likely effects of two sources that involve 'model' and 'system' design, both of which have been neglected to date. These two sources are the accounting framework employed in the population projection, and the way in which the system of regions being studied is closed. A set of empirical experiments using a United Kingdom (UK) twenty-zone system are used to tease out the significance of these sources of variation. All sources of variation in population projections are reviewed in Section 7.2.

Section 7.3 contains a description of the alternative accounting frameworks that underpin population projections, and that based on movement data is examined in detail. The variety of ways accounts can be built, using the component information in different ways, are specified in Section 7.4. The different ways in which the system may be closed are specified in Section 7.5. A brief description of the demographic information

126

system consisting of raw data files, estimation procedures and processed data files that had to be constructed is given in Section 7.6. Section 7.7 contains an outline of the research design governing the projection experiments, the results of which are reviewed and evaluated in Section 7.8.

In the remainder of this introduction some essential preliminary points are made concerning the age–time plan involved in population projection, and the crucial distinctions between the different migration measures are set out.

7.1.2 The age–time plan of population projection

Any regional population projection model must work with the population disaggregated into regular age groups, because most services have client groups concentrated in a particular age span. This means that the most natural model to use will involve 'cohort survival'. It is essential in projec-

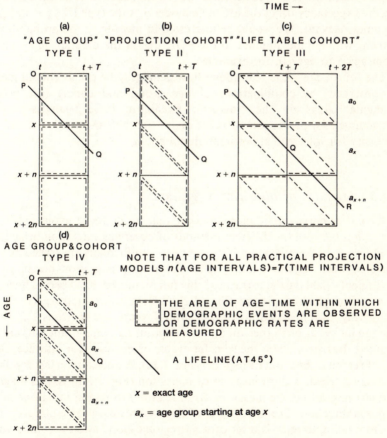

Figure 7.1 Alternative age–time observation plans.

tion to focus on cohorts, as this is the way in which a projection model works. Unfortunately, data for most components of change in the UK are tabulated only by age at the time of the event.

To understand the importance of the age–time plan used it is essential to think 'diagrammatically'. Four age–time plans in a series of Lexis diagrams are set out in Figure 7.1. The Lexis diagram labelled 'type I' shows the way in which demographic events in the UK are usually recorded: by age group at time of the event (the pecked square areas on the diagram). The type II Lexis diagram shows the way in which demographic events should be counted for entry into projection models, that is in the pecked parallelogram areas. This is because persons in a cohort move from being in one age group at the start of a time interval to being in the next at the end. Thus the person with lifeline PQ starts aged 0–4 at time t and moves to be aged 5–9 at time $t + 5$. The third type of Lexis diagram involves cohorts observed over two consecutive periods between two exact ages. The pecked parallelogram areas enclose the relevant events. It is when measuring life expectancy using the life table model that the type III age–time plan becomes relevant. We would be interested in measuring the probability of persons with similar lifelines to the PQR line in the diagram of surviving from age 5 to age 10, for example.

The fourth age–time plan shows how demographic events should ideally be observed: by combinations of age group and cohort (the pecked triangular areas on the diagram). Events in these triangles can be reassembled for projection purposes or for life table purposes, without the necessity for intermediate estimation equations.

7.1.3 Methods of observing migration

A second essential preliminary concept that needs to be explained is the distinction between the different methods of observing migration behaviour. In Figure 7.2a the migration histories of five individuals are traced as they move between regions i and j (Fig. 7.2a). Our migration measurement instruments yield partial extracts of this full picture. A fixed period question in a census yields a picture (Fig. 7.2b) of transitions retrospectively by comparing current location with location T years ago (persons 1,2) or, if you are lucky, at birth (person 5). One migrant and one infant migrant are counted. Registers count the transfer events or moves – for instance, three out of region i, three out of region j (Fig. 7.2c). A question on last residence in a census yields a third measure of migration (Fig. 7.2d). In this diagram two last migrations are measured from region j to region i and one in the opposite direction. The importance of these three migration concepts is that corresponding to each is a set of multiregional population accounts and a multiregional projection model.

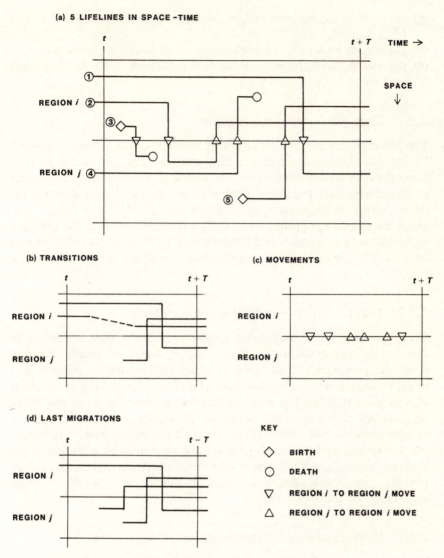

(a) 5 LIFELINES IN SPACE –TIME

t   *t* + *T*   TIME →

SPACE
↓

REGION *i*

REGION *j*

(b) TRANSITIONS

t   *t* + *T*

REGION *i*

REGION *j*

(c) MOVEMENTS

t   *t* + *T*

REGION *i*

REGION *j*

(d) LAST MIGRATIONS

t   *t* − *T*

REGION *i*

REGION *j*

KEY

◇   BIRTH

○   DEATH

▽   REGION *i* TO REGION *j* MOVE

△   REGION *j* TO REGION *i* MOVE

Figure 7.2 The different kinds of migration measure.

7.2 Sources of variation in population projection

We can identify the following sources of variation:

(a) the assumptions about the way in which the component demographic rates or flows input to the projection are likely to change in the future;

(b) the influence of events outside the demographic system which disturb its momentum and alter the direction of change;

129

(c) the level of aggregation and/or decomposition of the regional system being studied;

(d) the way in which the regional system under study is closed; and

(e) the way in which the data for the base period are assembled and made consistent.

7.2.1 Changes in input assumptions

The first influence is obviously of crucial importance and is well recognized. Projections based on alternative fertility levels are regularly carried out (e.g. Central Policy Review Staff 1976). Occasionally the effect of curing cancer or of reducing cardiovascular death rates are explored, and although the overall effect on population size is small (Craig 1983) such changes can affect the elderly age groups a lot. Only a few researchers in the UK have explored the consequences of different mobility levels (Stone 1970) because only recently has a good time-series become available (Ogilvy 1979, see also Ch. 8).

7.2.2 Events outside the demographic system

Events outside the demographic system are clearly very important in influencing component rates. Social norms, ideas of family life and economic prospects are all likely to affect fertility levels, perhaps in a phased intergenerational fashion (Easterlin 1980). The slowing of economic growth since 1974 has had a profound effect on mobility levels and hence on projected populations. Major changes in interregional and international competitiveness will also affect future migration flows. However, interesting and vital though these issues are, they must be left aside in this chapter, although, with the demographic information system established for the experiments described later, it should be possible to begin exploration of some of them.

7.2.3 Aggregation and decomposition

The third source of variation, aggregation and decomposition, has been explored in a seminal paper by Rogers (1976). Rogers has long argued that regional population projections should be carried out using a multiregional model that incorporates gross migration rates amongst regions, rather than by using a model based on net migration flows or rates (for the full arguments see Rogers 1985). This strong and valid case has still to win many converts in national demographic offices, although other branches have recognized the need for a multiregional projection model (Martin Voorhees Associates & John Bates Services 1981).

Rogers (1976) explores the differences between the projected results of a full 9 by 9 multiregional model for the USA and a series of eight alternative models, ranging from a components of growth model (no age disaggregation) through to a model in which the system is decomposed into two sets. Within each set the regions interact but between the sets the flows

Table 7.1 Comparisons of Rogers's different aggregations and decompositions with the full 9×9 multiregional model at 2008.

No.	Model Title	Difference in US total population (1000 s) (1)	Absolute values of differences (1000 s) (2)	Absolute percentage differences (3)	Index of dissimilarity (4)
1	4-region model	− 397	1 854	1.91	0.22
2	components of growth	57 253	57 253	112.07	1.59
3	bi-regional aggregation	− 6 675	7 699	16.01	0.74
4	single region, net migration	− 28 920	54 700	108.74	6.83
5	decomposition A with net migration	− 19 590	37 060	77.32	4.76
6	decomposition B with net migration	− 13 373	25 665	53.37	3.28
7	single region with components of growth	2 689	13 637	28.55	1.58
8	decomposition B with bi-regional aggregation	− 1 308	5 432	10.94	0.62
	Meaning of statistic	US under- or over- prediction	Total deviations	Equal weights for each region	Relative distribution statistic

Source: computed from the projected population tables in Rogers (1976).

Definitions of comparison statistics:

$P(i, m)$ = population of region i in 2008 projected by model m.

$P(\cdot, m)$ = population of US in 2008 projected by model m.

$m = 9 \times 9$ multiregional model.

(1) Difference in US total population = $P(\cdot, 9) - P(\cdot, m)$. Negative values indicate overprediction, positive values underprediction.

(2) Absolute value of differences = sum for all regions of absolute values of $P(i, 9) - P(i, m)$.

(3) Absolute percentage difference = sum for all regions of absolute values of 100 times $[P(i, 9) - P(i, m)]/P(i, 9)$.

(4) Index of dissimilarity = sum for all regions of absolute values of $[P(i, 9)/P(\cdot, 9)] - [P(i, m)/P(\cdot, m)]$, multiplied by 100 and divided by 2.

and the rates are pooled. The performance statistics for each model compared with the full multiregional model are set out in Table 7.1. The 'best buy' among the alternatives is the third model, involving biregional aggregation, because of the simplicity of its data requirements: just in- and outmigration to the rest of the country by age for each region. The eighth model, decomposition B with biregional aggregation, performs better but demands a full interregional migration matrix for implementation. In such a situation it would be simpler to use a full multiregional model since the data requirements are the same.

7.2.4 The importance of external migration and the issue of system closure

However, in the Rogers's school of projection attention has been concentrated on intra-national multiregional systems, assumed closed to outside influences. The theoretical influence of external migration on national populations has recently been explored by Alexander (1983). She shows that projection trajectories in a 'this country and rest of the world' system need not necessarily exhibit the stable (that is, constant rate) growth or decline of internal regional systems: stationarity can be achieved when natural gain within the country is balanced by net emigration loss or when natural loss is balanced by net immigration gain.

Empirically, for many countries, international migration flows are an important component of population change. It has been estimated (Rees & Willekens 1981, Table 8) that immigration flows from outside the country make up about 32% of total inmigration flows into both Dutch and British regions, and 46% of such flows into Canadian provinces. Note that in the United Kingdom, whereas the overall balance of external migration was very small in relation to other population changes, for individual regions the external balance is a significant contributor to population change. Greater London, for example, is a substantial net importer of external migrants.

A commonly voiced objection to the full and explicit incorporation of external migration flows in multiregional population projection models is that data on such flows are unavailable (particularly on emigration) or unreliable. However, in countries in which migration data derive from population registers, immigration and emigration are carefully monitored. In countries dependent on periodic censuses for migration data, immigration data are as available and reliable as internal migration data. Emigration can often be estimated from survey data or as a residual flow if population stocks at the start and end of the base period are known. There is thus no longer any excuse for neglecting the issue of system closure, that is, how external migration flows should be incorporated in the projection model.

However, there are a variety of different ways in which external migration flows should be handled in regional projection models, which raise the same concerns that were addressed by Rogers (1976) with respect to internal migration. Should gross or net migration terms be used, and should these be handled using flows or rates in the model? For a number of reasons, the answers to these questions are a little different from those involving internal migration terms, as will be explained later.

7.2.5   Base period accounts

The fifth source of variation identified above, namely the way in which the data for the projection base period are assembled, concerns the interface between the available demographic data and the projection model. I have long argued that such an interface should take the form of a set of demographic accounts, appropriately tailored to the nature of the data and population system being studied. The rôle of migration data is crucial here. Three kinds of migration are employable in multiregional projections:

(1) migrants or transitions;
(2) migrations or moves;
(3) last residence migrants or last residence migrations.

For each type there exists a different accounting framework. If you have census-based migrant data to hand you must construct *transition* accounts; however, if your data are moves based on counts of changes of address reported to a registration system, you must construct *movement* accounts. If your data consist of migration measured in a census or survey by place of last residence, as in many Third World countries, you must build *last residence* accounts, although the theory and models for accounts of this type have yet to be fully worked out (for more details see Rees 1984a). The empirical applications reported in this chapter use movement accounts.

There are a number of choices to be made in constructing sets of population accounts, depending principally on what kind of population stocks data are available and whether independent estimates of emigration are to hand.

In the next section the accounting framework to be used with moves data is outlined and compared with the accounts hitherto developed for transitions data.

7.3   Accounting frameworks for population projection

7.3.1   Transition accounts

Transition accounts are only described briefly as they are precursors to, and contrast with, the movement accounts used later in the empirical applications.

133

Table 7.2 A transition accounts table for cohort a.

Initial state in period	Final state in period									
	Survival at time $t+T$					Death in period t to $t+T$				Totals
	Internal regions				Outside world	Internal regions				Outside world	
	1	2	...	N	O	1	2	...	N	O	
internal regions 1	K_a^{e1s1}	K_a^{e1s2}	...	K_a^{e1sN}	K_a^{e1sO}	K_a^{e1d1}	K_a^{e1d2}	...	K_a^{e1dN}	K_a^{e1dO}	$K_a^{e1\cdots}$
2	K_a^{e2s1}	K_a^{e2s2}	...	K_a^{e2sN}	K_a^{e2sO}	K_a^{e2d1}	K_a^{e2d2}	...	K_a^{e2dN}	K_a^{e2dO}	$K_a^{e2\cdots}$
...	...	...		...	...	...	...		...	...	...
N	K_a^{eNs1}	K_a^{eNs2}	...	K_a^{eNsN}	K_a^{eNsO}	K_a^{eNd1}	K_a^{eNd2}	...	K_a^{eNdN}	K_a^{eNdO}	$K_a^{eN\cdots}$
outside world O	K_a^{Os1}	K_a^{Os2}	...	K_a^{OsN}	0	K_a^{Od1}	K_a^{Od2}	...	K_a^{OdN}	0	$K_a^{O\cdots}$
totals	$K_a^{e\cdot s1}$	$K_a^{e\cdot s2}$	...	$K_a^{e\cdot sN}$	$K_a^{e\cdot sO}$	$K_a^{e\cdot d1}$	$K_a^{e\cdot d2}$	...	$K_a^{e\cdot dN}$	$K_a^{e\cdot dO}$	$K_a^{e\cdots}$

Notes

1 Infant accounts have the same structure: a b superscript is substituted for e and the value of a is set to $-n$.

2 The a subscript means 'aged a to $a+n$ at time t, aged $a+n$ to $a+2n$ at time $t+T$' for survivor variables; the subscript means aged a to $a+n$ at time t, dying before attainment of ages $a+n$ to $a+2n$ at time $t+T$ for non-survivor variables.

Definitions of variables:

t time at start of period

T length of period

$t+T$ time at end of period

K count of transitions or persons making a transition

K_a^{eisj} persons in cohort a in existence in region i who survive in region j at time $t+T$

K_a^{eidj} persons in cohort a in existence in region i who die in region j before time $t+T$

$K_a^{ei\cdots}$ population aged a to $a+n$ of region i at time t

$K_a^{e\cdot dj}$ total deaths in cohort a in region j in time interval

$K_a^{e\cdot sj}$ population aged $a+n$ to $a+2n$ of region j at time $t+T$

$K_a^{eO\cdots}$ total existing immigrants to all internal regions in cohort a in time interval

$K_a^{e\cdot sO}$ total surviving emigrants in cohort a from all internal regions in time interval

$K_a^{e\cdot dO}$ total non-surviving emigrants in cohort a from all internal regions in time interval

Where O is substituted for i this means the variable refers to external transitions from the outside world, O.

The theory (Rees & Wilson 1977) and practice (Rees 1981a) of multiregional demographic accounting has to date been developed using census migration data which are counts of transitions between regions over a fixed time interval, as in Figure 7.2b. The accounts variables are positioned and defined in Table 7.2. Note that because a type II (projection cohort) age–time observation plan (as in Fig. 7.1b) has been adopted the accounts table is quite simple in structure. In order to fill in accounts tables for all cohorts the researcher enters known items in the table and selects an appropriate set of equations for estimating missing elements, principally the existence–death transitions (for operational details see Rees 1981a). The models used for estimation may easily be used for projection, or the rates needed for a multiregional cohort survival model can be estimated from the accounts as

$$h_a^{eisj} = \frac{K_a^{eisj}}{K_a^{ei \cdot \cdot}} \tag{7.1}$$

where K_a^{eisj} is the number of persons in the age cohort a in existence in region i at the start of the period who survive in region j at the end of the period (i.e. migrants from region i to region j), $K_a^{ei \cdot \cdot}$ is the population of age cohort a in existence in region i at the start of the period, and h_a^{eisj} is the corresponding transition rate for region i to region j migrants.

7.3.2 Movement accounts

Although rates generated from multiregional transition accounts match exactly the rates needed in multiregional projection models, they have two disadvantages from a practical point of view. The first is that, in countries where census migration tables of the transition type are available, they are produced intermittently at lengthy intervals. The second is that in many countries movement data are gathered via registers and no migration question is used in the national census.

The movement accounts table that uses counts of moves between regions over a fixed time interval (as in Fig. 7.2c) in a type II (projection cohort) age–time observation plan (Fig. 7.1b) is set out in Table 7.3. The structure of the table is remarkably simple. Interregional mortality transitions which occupied an N region by N region matrix in the Table 7.2 transition accounts become a column vector of regional deaths; the two column vectors of surviving and non-surviving emigrants become one vector of regional emigrations; the two row vectors of surviving and non-surviving immigrants become one row vector of regional immigrations; the N by N matrix of interregional surviving migrants and surviving regional stayers becomes an N by N matrix with interregional migrations in the off-diagonal elements and accounting balances in the principal diagonal. The initial and final population vectors in the movement accounts are exactly equivalent

135

Table 7.3 A movement accounts table for cohort a in one time interval.

					State after move		
		Destinations Internal regions			Outside world		
State before move	1	2	...	N	O	Death	Totals
Origins internal regions 1	R_a^1	M_a^{12}	...	M_a^{1N}	M_a^{1O}	D_a^1	$P_a^{1\cdot}$
2	M_a^{21}	R_a^2	...	M_a^{2N}	M_a^{2O}	D_a^2	$P_a^{2\cdot}$
.	.	.		.	.	.	.
.	.	.		.	.	.	.
N	M_a^{N1}	M_a^{N2}	...	R_a^N	M_a^{NO}	D_a^N	$P_a^{N\cdot}$
outside world	M_a^{O1}	M_a^{O2}	...	M_a^{ON}	0	0	$M_a^{O\cdot}$
totals	$P_a^{\cdot i}$	$P_a^{\cdot 2}$	...	$P_a^{\cdot N}$	$M_a^{\cdot O}$	$D_a^{\cdot}$	$T_a^{\cdot\cdot}$

Notes

1 The infant accounts for $a = 0$ follow the same structure except that variables $B^1 \ldots B^N$ replace $P_0^{1\cdot} \ldots P_0^{N\cdot}$.

2 The a subscript refers to a 'projection cohort' occupying the age–time space a, t; $a + n, t$; $a + n, t + T$; $a + 2n, t + T$ in Figure 7.1 (type II observation plan).

Definitions of variables:

Population

$P_a^{i\cdot}$ population in region i aged a to $a + n$ at start of time interval

$P_a^{\cdot j}$ population in region j aged $a + n$ to $a + 2n$ at end of time interval

Deaths

D_a^i deaths in region i to persons in cohort a during time interval

$D_a^{\cdot}$ total deaths in all internal regions

Emigrations

M_a^{iO} emigrations from region i by persons in cohort a to the outside world, O, during the time interval

$M_a^{\cdot O}$ total emigrations from all internal regions

Internal migrations

M_a^{ij} migrations from region i to region j by persons in cohort a during the time interval

Residual term

R_a^i residual accounts balancing term for region i

Immigrations

M_a^{Oj} immigrations from the outside world, O, to region j by persons in cohort a during the time interval

$M_a^{O\cdot}$ total immigrations to all internal regions

$T_a^{\cdot\cdot}$ total of all inflows and inputs to the internal system or total of all outflows and outputs from the internal system to the initial and final population stocks in the transition accounts. The column vector of regional deaths in the movement accounts is also equivalent to the row vector of total regional deaths in the transition accounts.

An extract from a movement accounts table for a 20-zone UK system is given in Table 7.4. Consider the row of the table for the Central Clydeside conurbation (the City of Glasgow and adjacent districts). The region starts with a mid-year 1976 population aged 20–24 of 124 800. This population is subjected to the attrition of some 487 deaths, 8278 emigrations, 391 outmigrations to Wales, 885 to the North-West Remainder and so on, including 16 200 outmigrations to Scotland Remainder and 304 to Northern Ireland over the period 1976–81. The balance element in Central Clydeside is 83 820. Note that this is not the number of persons who do not move over the period, nor the number of stayers: it is the number of interregional stayers less the number of interregional outmigrations surplus to the number of transitions for the region in question! To the balancing element are added 261 inmigrations from Northern Ireland, 9115 from Scotland Remainder ... 490 from the North-West Remainder and 278 from Wales, together with immigrations from overseas of 2552, leaving some 103 237 persons aged 25–29 living at mid-1981 in Central Clydeside.

The figures can be reassembled in simpler form, region by region, to show the components of change in gross and net terms. Table 7.5 shows the components of change for Central Clydeside. Internal outmigrations totalled 32 215 and the counterstream was only 16 865. The net external migration balance was -5726 and the net internal balance $-15\,350$; total net outmigration was 21 076. Central Clydeside was not a popular region for those in their twenties in the later 1970s and early 1980s.

From the transition accounts table, matrices of interregional survivorships rates can be computed by dividing elements in the existence–survival half of the table by their population at risk, the initial populations of the origin region, as in Equation 7.1. These rates can be entered directly into a multiregional cohort survival model projection.

For movement accounts, the population at risk is the average population in the period, which can most conveniently be estimated as half of the initial and final populations. The rates can thus be computed, using lower-case letters for rates, as

$$m_a^{ij} = \frac{M_a^{ij}}{\frac{1}{2}(P_a^{i\cdot} + P_a^{\cdot i})}$$

$$m_a^{iO} = \frac{M^{iO}}{\frac{1}{2}(P_a^{i\cdot} + P_a^{\cdot i})}$$

(7.2)

These are transmission rates because the origin region population at risk is

137

Table 7.4 An extract from a movement accounts table for a 20-zone UK system, 1976–81, for cohort 20–24 to 25–29.

State before move	State after move								
	Destination in UK						Emigrations	Deaths	Totals
	NI	CC	SR	...	NWR	W			
Northern Ireland (NI)	103 466	261	631	...	493	288	2 363	591	115 400
Central Clydeside (CC)	304	83 820	16 200	...	885	391	8 278	487	124 800
Scotland Remainder (SR)	714	9 115	196 429	...	1 636	926	10 643	994	250 300
...	...	...	...	...	...	...	...	...	...
North West Remainder (NWR)	377	490	1 282	...	101 801	2 782	5 482	552	149 000
Wales (W)	215	278	945	...	2 464	142 560	6 782	615	186 500
immigrations	1 289	2 552	6 795	...	5 678	3 848	0	0	167 811
totals	112 139	103 237	247 354	...	153 872	182 940	189 011	13 037	4 039 011

Table 7.5 Components of change for a region, Central Clydeside, 1976–81.

Gross component	Gross flows	Net flows	Net component
initial population	124 800	124 800	initial population
deaths	− 487	− 487	deaths
emigrations	− 8 278	− 5 726	net external immigrations
total internal outmigrations	− 32 215	− 15 350	net internal inmigrations
residuals	= 83 820	(− 21 076	net migrations)
total internal inmigrations	+ 16 865		
immigrations	+ 2 552		
final population	= 103 237	= 103 237	final population

used. Death rates are, as conventionally:

$$d_a^i = \frac{D_a^i}{\frac{1}{2}(P_a^{i\cdot} + P_a^{\cdot i})} \tag{7.3}$$

but for immigrations we must use the population at risk of the destination regions, since the population of the origin region (the outside world) does not appear in the accounts. Thus the immigration rates are admission rates:

$$m_a^{Oi} = \frac{M_a^{Oi}}{\frac{1}{2}(P_a^{i\cdot} + P_a^{\cdot i})} \tag{7.4}$$

Table 7.6 shows the rates equivalent to the flows previously displayed in Table 7.4.

7.3.3 A projection model based on movement accounts

How should these movement rates be employed in a multiregional population projection model? It turns out that all that is needed is the rearrangement of the rate equations into the equivalent flow equations:

$$M_a^{ij} = m_a^{ij}\tfrac{1}{2}(P_a^{i\cdot} + P_a^{\cdot i})$$
$$M_a^{iO} = m_a^{iO}\tfrac{1}{2}(P_a^{i\cdot} + P_a^{\cdot i}) \tag{7.5}$$
$$D_a^i = d_a^i\tfrac{1}{2}(P_a^{i\cdot} + P_a^{\cdot i})$$
$$M_a^{Oi} = m_a^{Oi}\tfrac{1}{2}(P_a^{i\cdot} + P_a^{\cdot i})$$

These items we enter in the accounts table to estimate the residual balancing terms are

$$R_a^i = P_a^{i\cdot} - D_a^i - M_a^{iO} - \sum_{j \neq i} M_a^{ij} \tag{7.6}$$

Table 7.6 An extract from a movement rates table for a 20-zone UK system, 1976–81, for cohort 20–24 to 25–29.

State before move	State after move						Emigrations	Deaths	Populations at risk
	Destination in UK								
	NI	CC	SR	...	NWR	W			
Northern Ireland (NI)	—	0.002 29	0.005 55	...	0.004 33	0.002 53	0.020 77	0.005 19	113 769.5
Central Clydeside (CC)	0.002 67	—	0.142 08	...	0.007 76	0.003 43	0.072 60	0.004 27	114 018.5
Scotland Remainder (SR)	0.002 87	0.036 63	—	...	0.006 57	0.003 72	0.042 77	0.003 99	248 827
...	...	...	...	...	...	...	...	...	...
North West Remainder (NWR)	0.002 49	0.003 24	0.008 47	...	—	0.018 37	0.036 20	0.003 45	151 436
Wales (W)	0.001 16	0.001 50	0.005 12	...	0.013 34	—	0.036 72	0.003 33	184 720
immigrations	0.011 33	0.022 38	0.027 31	...	0.037 49	0.020 83	—	—	0.04354
totals	−0.028 66	−0.189 12	−0.011 84	...	0.032 17	−0.019 27	0.049 04	0.003 38	3 854 081.5

Notes
1 Rates in the NI to W rows are transmission rates, flows divided by origin population at risk.
2 Rates in the immigrations row are admission rates, flows divided by destination population at risk.
3 Rates in the totals row are population change divided by population at risk, except for the emigrations and deaths columns which contain UK rates.
  The total UK change rate = −0.008 88.

and the final populations are

$$P_a^{\cdot i} = R_a^i + \sum_{j \neq i} M_a^{ji} + M_a^{Oi} \qquad (7.7)$$

'But', you object, 'you can't use the Equation 7.5 set because you don't know the final populations until you get to Equation 7.7.' Well, simply enter them as zero the first time Equation set 7.5 is computed, work out an initial estimate of the final populations and then return with this estimate to Equation 7.5. Repeat this sequence of calculations until your population at risk estimates no longer change very much, and you will then have projected the population forward one time interval. These iterative calculations can be speeded up by using the initial populations as populations at risk on the first iteration through the equations.

The infant cohort (persons born during the time interval) should be computed after all the 'existing' cohorts have been projected. Births will simply be projected as

$$B_a^i = b_{a\frac{1}{2}}^i (P_a^{i\cdot} + P_a^{\cdot i}) \qquad (7.8)$$

where B_a^i are births in region i to mothers in projection cohort a for all fertile cohorts, say $a = 10{-}14$ to $15{-}19$ through $40{-}44$ to $45{-}49$, and then summed:

$$B^i_{\cdot} = \sum_a B_a^i \qquad (7.9)$$

These are then equivalent to the row total in the infant cohort accounts, that is

$$P_0^{i\cdot} = B^i_{\cdot} \qquad (7.10)$$

and the projection model above is used again.

This structure of equations is very flexible in that we can easily alter our estimates for any components. For example, we could assume immigrations to be fixed by legal quota:

$$M_a^{Oi} = M_a^{Oi} \text{ (fixed)} \qquad (7.11)$$

7.3.4 A multiregional cohort survival model

Is iteration through the projection model equations strictly necessary? In certain circumstances, when rates are assumed constant over the whole of the projection period, it may be convenient to substitute an analytical solution to the projection equations for the iterative. All we have to do is to substitute Equations 7.7 and 7.6 back into Equation set 7.5 to yield rate equations of the kind:

$$m_a^{ij} = \frac{M_a^{ij}}{\frac{1}{2}\left(P_a^{i\cdot} + P_a^{\cdot i} - D_a^i - M_a^{iO} - \sum_{j=i} M_a^{ij} + \sum_{j=i} M_a^{ji} + M_a^{Oi}\right)} \qquad (7.12)$$

The problem with this equation is that the migration terms appear on the right-hand side of the equation as well as on the left-hand side – and in two guises, in the outmigration and inmigration sums – and that the equation for one interregional migration flow is dependent on the others. We need to rearrange terms so that we have equations of the form:

$$\text{final population} = \text{rates} \times \text{initial population} \tag{7.13}$$

It is easiest to do this with a matrix formulation. The task is to define $\mathbf{S}_a$ such that

$$\mathbf{p}_a(t+T) = \mathbf{S}_a \mathbf{p}_a(t) \tag{7.14}$$

where $\mathbf{p}_a(t+T)$ is a vector of final populations of regions in cohort a at time $t+T$, $\mathbf{p}_a(t)$ is a vector of initial populations in cohort a, $\mathbf{S}_a$ is the rates matrix that transforms the initial population vector into the final one.

The matrix of $\mathbf{S}$ rates can be defined in a way similar to that of the matrix of $\mathbf{P}$ rates (survival probabilities) in life-table analysis (Rogers & Ledent 1976, Willekens & Rogers 1978).

Let $\mathbf{M}_a$ be a matrix of migration and mortality rates arranged in the following way, keeping to the definition of a as a 'projection cohort':

$$\mathbf{M}_a = \begin{bmatrix} \left(d_a^1 + \sum_{j=i} m_a^{1j} + m_a^{1O} - m_a^{O1} \right) & -m_a^{21} & \cdots & -m_a^{N1} \\ -m_a^{12} & \left(d_a^2 + \sum_{j=i} m_a^{2j} + m_a^{2O} - m_a^{O2} \right) & \cdots & -m_a^{N2} \\ \vdots & & \ddots & \vdots \\ -m_a^{1N} & -m_a^{2N} & \cdots & \left(d_a^N + \sum_{j=i} m_a^{Nj} + m_a^{NO} - m_a^{ON} \right) \end{bmatrix} \tag{7.15}$$

Then

$$\mathbf{S}_a = [\mathbf{I}_a + \tfrac{1}{2}\mathbf{M}_a]^{-1}[\mathbf{I}_a - \tfrac{1}{2}\mathbf{M}_a] \tag{7.16}$$

Equation 7.15 extends the previous formulation by adding emigration rates to the diagonal term in the $\mathbf{M}$ matrix and subtracting immigration rates.

If we substitute Equation 7.16 into the right-hand side of Equation 7.14, we now have a one-equation projection model based on movement accounts:

$$\mathbf{p}_a(t+T) = [\mathbf{I} + \tfrac{1}{2}\mathbf{M}_a]^{-1}[\mathbf{I} - \tfrac{1}{2}\mathbf{M}_a]\mathbf{p}_a(t) \tag{7.17}$$

This is convenient for the analytical exploration of the consequences of the current pattern of multiregional population change (stable growth analysis), but it involves commitment to only one of the methods for handling external migration. Since this is one of the key issues addressed in this chapter the more flexible projection model is used. The non-iterative form of the projection model based on movement accounts has been adapted as the basis of a multiregional forecasting model for the provinces of the Netherlands (Willekens & Drewe 1984).

It should be stressed that the matrix of survivorship rates defined in Equation 7.16 is not a matrix of transition probabilities. These rates do not yield the probability that a person living in one region at the start of a period will be in another at the end. They are merely those rates, based on observed mortality and mobility, that transform the initial into the final population distribution across regions.

7.4 Accounts based models: the ways in which the data are assembled

There are a variety of ways of putting together the components of multiregional change to form population accounts, the basis of projections. The various methods are set out in Figure 7.3. The top diagram in Figure 7.3 names the components of movement accounts that have already appeared in algebraic and numerical form. To construct accounts tables it is essential to know the regional distribution of mortality, fertility and immigration and the interregional distribution of internal migration. Thus, in all four alternative ways of assembling accounts (Fig. 7.3a to d) these components are numbered and shaded. It is necessary, in addition, to be able to estimate at least two of the following components: initial regional populations, final regional populations and emigration flows from the regions. Combinations of these components lead to four types of model for constructing population accounts.

7.4.1 The forecast model

Here initial populations and emigrations are used as inputs and final populations are generated from the accounts as the totals for the columns. Figure 7.3b shows the forecast model graphically.

7.4.2 The backcast model

For periods ending with a decennial census, rather than using the initial populations it may be preferable to use the final populations reliably estimated from a recent census, along with emigration flows. This is the backcast model exhibited in Figure 7.3c. From this model the initial populations are estimated by adding across the rows of the accounts table.

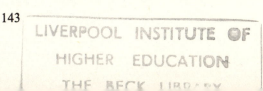

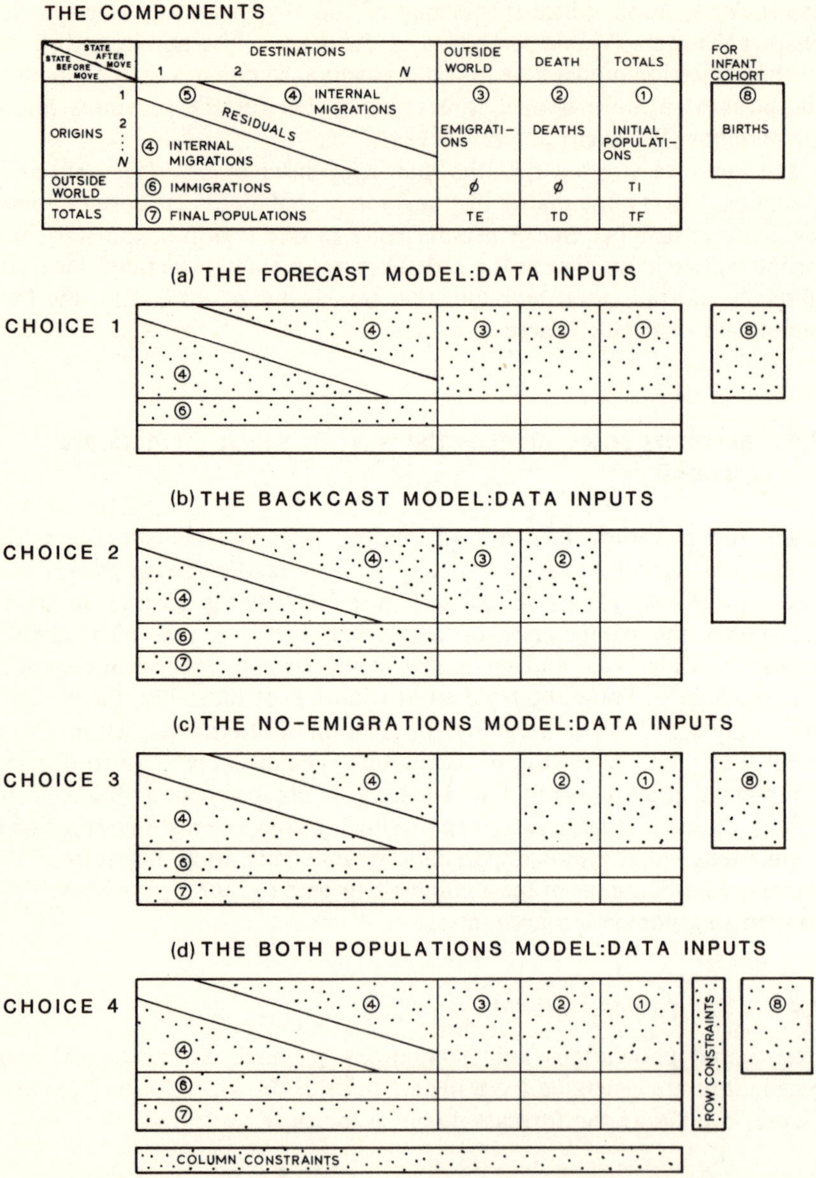

THE COMPONENTS

STATE BEFORE MOVE \ STATE AFTER MOVE	DESTINATIONS			OUTSIDE WORLD	DEATH	TOTALS	FOR INFANT COHORT
	1	2	N				
ORIGINS 1 2 ⋮ N	⑤ RESIDUALS	④ INTERNAL MIGRATIONS		③ EMIGRATI-ONS	② DEATHS	① INITIAL POPULATI-ONS	⑧ BIRTHS
	④ INTERNAL MIGRATIONS						
OUTSIDE WORLD	⑥ IMMIGRATIONS			∅	∅	TI	
TOTALS	⑦ FINAL POPULATIONS			TE	TD	TF	

(a) THE FORECAST MODEL:DATA INPUTS

CHOICE 1

(b) THE BACKCAST MODEL:DATA INPUTS

CHOICE 2

(c) THE NO-EMIGRATIONS MODEL:DATA INPUTS

CHOICE 3

(d) THE BOTH POPULATIONS MODEL:DATA INPUTS

CHOICE 4

ROW CONSTRAINTS

COLUMN CONSTRAINTS

Figure 7.3 The different ways of assembling movement accounts.

7.4.3 The no-emigration model

In certain situations emigration may not be available or may be very unreliable. Then emigration flows can be estimated as residuals if both initial and final populations are input, as in Figure 7.3d. However, with this model there is the problem that all data errors pile up in the emigration terms, and in some instances negative estimates may result. The no-emigration model is most appropriately used with transition data that link two successive censuses, as is the situation in Canada and in France. When movement data can be used reasonable estimates of external moves can be made, and this model will not be used. The model is not employed in the projection experiments described later in this chapter.

7.4.4   The model based on both populations and on the use of constraints

All eight components of the movement accounts can be introduced into the tables. However, in this case there will be inconsistency either between the final populations computed from the columns of the table and those input as data when the estimates are based on a forecast model, or between the initial populations computed from the rows of the table and those input as data when the estimates are based on a backcast model.

The solution is to adjust the estimates of a forecast or backcast model to independent sets of row and column constraints containing the initial and final population vectors, emigration total, deaths total and immigration total, modified to ensure equality of the sum of row and column totals. If $A(i, j)$ are defined to be the estimates of accounts elements in row i and column j in each cohort table, and $R(i)$ and $C(j)$ are the independent row and column constraints, then constrained re-estimates of the accounts elements are obtained by iteration through the following sets of equations:

$$A(i, j) = A(i, j) \frac{R(i)}{\sum_j A(i, j)} \qquad (7.18)$$

$$A(i, j) = A(i, j) \frac{C(j)}{\sum_i A(i, j)} \qquad (7.19)$$

until all elements differ by less than half a person from one iteration, $p - 1$, to the next, p:

$$|A^p(i, j) - A^{p-1}(i, j)| < 0.5 \qquad (7.20)$$

Note that adjustment to constraints is only possible if

$$\sum_i R^i = \sum_j C^j \qquad (7.21)$$

and some of the constraints must be adjusted if this is not true.

The empirical experiments described later are designed to measure the degree to which the base period accounts and projected populations for a

20-zone UK system differ according to the way in which the data are assembled.

7.5 The ways in which the population system is closed

The second set of choices to be explored empirically relates to the ways in which a system of regions is closed. Here we assume the system consists of a number of regions of interest together with the rest of the country.

7.5.1 External migration ignored

The first choice is to ignore external migration. This assumes the country is a closed system. But the system will still be influenced by external flows if surviving stayer (transition accounts) or residual (movement accounts) terms are computed as one minus the sum of regional internal outmigration rates and minus the regional death rates. In these cases the surviving stayer flows or residual elements will be overestimated by the sizes of the emigration flows; this error will be partly compensated for by the absence of any immigration terms.

Figure 7.4 sets out the closure choices in diagrammatic fashion. Figure 7.4a shows how this first choice is implemented in the movement accounts model and programme (Rees 1984b). All emigrations and immigrations are entered as zero flows.

7.5.2 Net migration flows or rates

The second choice is to incorporate net external migration as net flows or rates. One of these alternatives has been the usual choice applied in national population projections; those of the United States or the United Kingdom use vectors of net immigration flows. Academic forecasters prefer to use net immigration (admission) rates. The multiregional cohort survival model based on movement rates incorporated net external migration rates (Eqn 7.15). Figure 7.4b shows that these are introduced into the movement accounts model as net immigration flows or rates – which may be positive or negative – and emigrations are input as zeroes.

This second choice improves on the first but has similar disadvantages to those of conventional net migration models as identified by Rogers (1976). A net migration is not a move and so cannot be traced in the projection.

7.5.3 Gross migration flows or rates

The third choice is to introduce external migrants as gross flows or rates (Fig. 7.4c). This does not produce very different results from the corresponding net flow or rate model if the corresponding gross and net flows

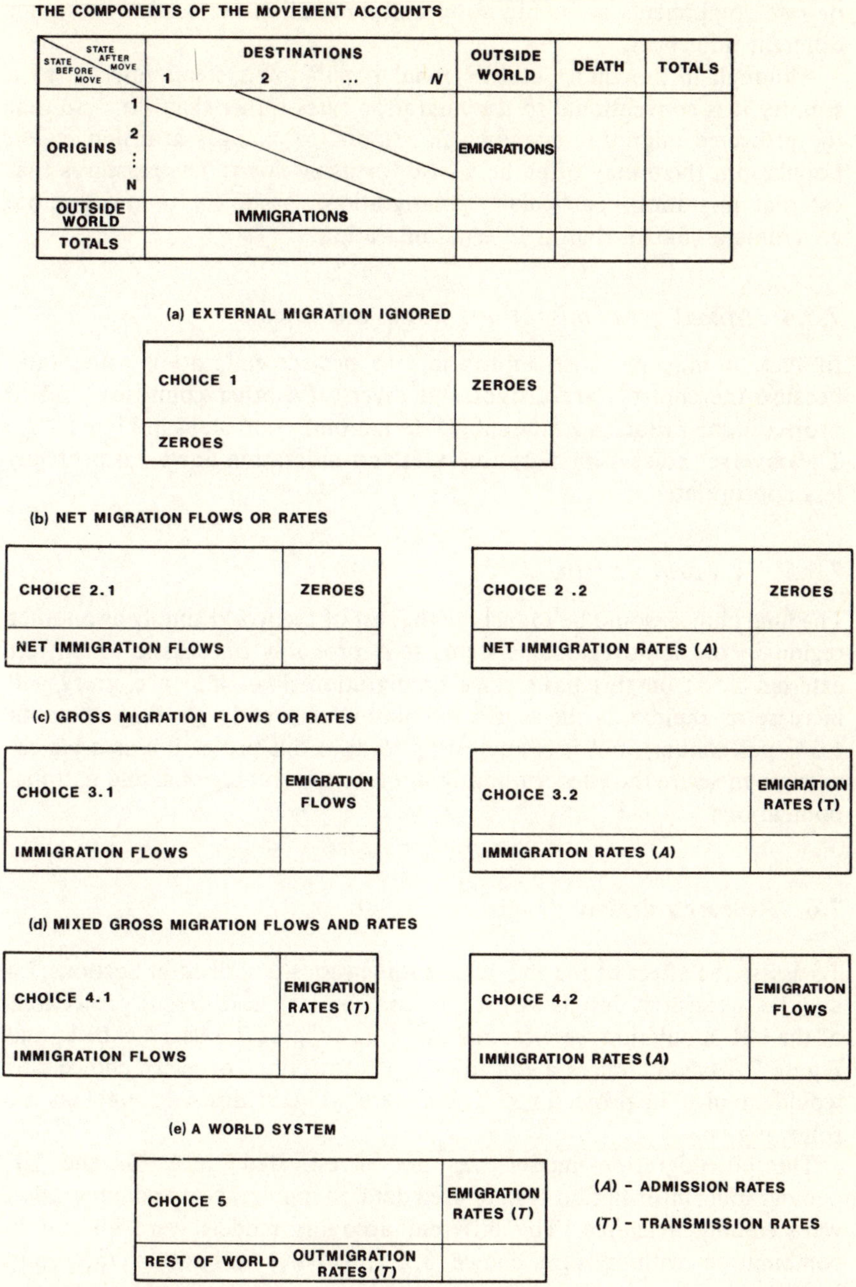

THE COMPONENTS OF THE MOVEMENT ACCOUNTS

STATE BEFORE MOVE \ STATE AFTER MOVE	DESTINATIONS				OUTSIDE WORLD	DEATH	TOTALS
	1	2	...	N			
ORIGINS 1 2 : N					EMIGRATIONS		
OUTSIDE WORLD	IMMIGRATIONS						
TOTALS							

(a) EXTERNAL MIGRATION IGNORED

CHOICE 1	ZEROES
ZEROES	

(b) NET MIGRATION FLOWS OR RATES

CHOICE 2.1	ZEROES
NET IMMIGRATION FLOWS	

CHOICE 2 .2	ZEROES
NET IMMIGRATION RATES (A)	

(c) GROSS MIGRATION FLOWS OR RATES

CHOICE 3.1	EMIGRATION FLOWS
IMMIGRATION FLOWS	

CHOICE 3.2	EMIGRATION RATES (T)
IMMIGRATION RATES (A)	

(d) MIXED GROSS MIGRATION FLOWS AND RATES

CHOICE 4.1	EMIGRATION RATES (T)
IMMIGRATION FLOWS	

CHOICE 4.2	EMIGRATION FLOWS
IMMIGRATION RATES (A)	

(e) A WORLD SYSTEM

CHOICE 5	EMIGRATION RATES (T)
REST OF WORLD OUTMIGRATION RATES (T)	

(A) – ADMISSION RATES

(T) – TRANSMISSION RATES

Figure 7.4 The different ways of closing the system using movement accounts.

are used; but it is easier in the gross version to change the separate flows or rate components as immigration and emigration are subject to rather different influences.

Although in modelling multiregional population systems internal to a country it is conventional to use migration rates rather than flows so that the projected migration streams can respond to changes in origin region population, there may often be a case for using flows. The reason is that external migration, particularly immigration, is subject to much more government control than is internal migration.

7.5.4 Mixed gross migrations flows and rates

In fact, it may be most appropriate to project emigration using rates because the controls are distant and diverse (in other countries) and to project immigration as a flow subject to national control, as in Figure 7.4c. The obverse choice – immigration rates and emigration flows – is probably less appropriate.

7.5.5 A world system

The final choice would be to include the rest of the world simply as another region in the multiregional system. It is probably unrealistic to project external flows on this basis since immigration flows into a country will increase as rapidly as the world population (currently growing at about 1.5% per annum), but it is interesting to have this projection as a bench-mark to measure the effect of immigration control on regional and national populations.

7.6 Research design

To assess the effect of the two choice dimensions described in Sections 7.4 and 7.5 a research design was set up and some eight different projections of the UK population were carried out. Since Figure 7.3 lists 4 choices and Figure 7.4 has 8 choices a full matrix of projections of every choice pair would involve 32 projections. These were whittled down to eight in the following way.

The no-emigration model was not investigated since for the UK demographic information system used data on immigration and emigration were equally available. The different accounts models were all run in combination with closure choice 3.2, involving emigration rates and immigration flows.

From the system closure alternatives, choice 1, involving no external migration, choice 2.2, involving net immigration rates, choice 3.1, involving

Table 7.7 The research design.

| Ways of closing the system | Ways of assembling movement accounts | | |
	Choice 1: Forecast model	Choice 2: Backcast model	Choice 4: Constrained model
Choice 1 external migration ignored	projection model 4		
Choice 2.2 net migration rates	projection model 5		
Choice 3.1 gross migration flows	projection model 6		
Choice 3.2 gross migration rates	projection model 1	projection model 2	projection model 3
Choice 4.1 emigration rates, immigration flows	projection model 7		
Choice 5 a world system	projection model 8		

gross migration flows, choice 3.2 involving gross migration rates and immigration flows and choice 5, involving a world system were selected, all in combination with the forecast model option. The result is eight projections, shown in Table 7.7, which cover both choice dimensions. However, this research design assumes that there are no interaction effects in the table between the dimensions. This hypothesis should be tested in further analyses.

7.7 A demographic information system for 20 UK zones

To gauge the effect of data assembly and system closure choices, it was necessary to put together the components of a set of movement accounts for a real world system. This turned out to be a very extensive task, of which only the barest bones are sketched here.

7.7.1 Zones

The zone system consists of 20 units for which demographic data were published with some degree of age disaggregation. The zones used completely cover the United Kingdom, and Figure 8.1 shows their boundaries. Eight zones are metropolitan counties or their administrative or statistical equivalents; seven zones consist of the whole or part of the rest of a standard region, that is, the region minus the metropolitan zone; and five zones are standard regions in which a metropolitan core is not distinguished. Another study (Rees & Stillwell 1984) showed that the main contrasts in population change in this 20-zone system were between metropolitan and non-metropolitan zones rather than between northern and southern zones. This spatial disaggregation is thus a considerable improvement over previously used standard region systems, although it is still not as fine as the functional urban region system developed by the Centre for Urban and Regional Development Studies at the University of Newcastle.

7.7.2 Time periods

The time period chosen was the interval mid-year 1976 to mid-year 1981. A five-year period was needed to match the anticipated level of reliable age disaggregation (five-year age intervals). But, most importantly, movement data for the UK have only recently become available from mid-1975. The end-point of the period, mid-year 1981, comes just after the 1981 Census, and the 1981 population estimates thus provide a sound basis on which to project the population.

7.7.3 Age classifications

The age classifications used in the various component data sets proved to be many and varied. Table 7.8 sets out the various age disaggregations in terms of best, worst or standard cases.

The age classification of a component was rarely consistent across all zones and all years. Three different 'national' agencies provide demographic data for England and Wales, Scotland and Northern Ireland respectively. The best data were generally for Scotland and the worst for Northern Ireland. The age classifications also varied from year to year: the best breakdowns were for 1977 to 1980 inclusive. They tended to be worse in 1981 because of the time-lag in publication or because of a reduction in the number and detail of tables as a result of cutbacks in government statistical services.

The best situation was for births: type I data for all zones and for all years for nine age groups were available. The worst situation was for emigrations and immigrations where the only age disaggregation was for the UK as a whole and was for only five broad age groups.

The Table 7.8 age-classified data (type I) had to be converted into cohort-classified data (type II) for the 19 cohorts listed in Table 7.9.

Table 7.8 The age-group (type I) classifications of the raw data at zonal level.

Populations		Deaths		Emigrations and immigrations	Births	Internal migrations
Best case	Worst case	Best case	Worst case	National case	Standard case	Standard case
0, 1–4		0, 1–4	0, 1–4			
0–4	0–4	0–4	0–4	0–14		0–4
5–9	5–14	5–9	5–14			5–9
10–14		10–14			< 15	10–14
15–19	15–24	15–19	15–24	15–29	15–19	15–19
20–24		20–24			20–24	20–24
25–29	25–34	25–29	25–34		25–29	25–29
30–34		30–34		30–34	30–34	30–34
35–39	35–44	35–39	35–44		35–39	35–39
40–44		40–44			40–44	40–44
45–49	45–54	45–49	45–54	45–59/64	45–49	45–49
50–54		50–54			50 +	50–54
55–59	55–64	55–59	55–64			55–59
60–64		60–64		60 + /65 +		60–64
65–69	65–74	65–69	65–74			65–69
70–74		70–74				70–74
75–79	75 +	75–79	75–84			75 +
80–84		80–84				
85–89		85–89	85 +			
90 +		90 +				

7.7.4 The demographic information system

The process by which this and other estimations were achieved is laid out in Figure 7.5. The process involved 5 sets of about 80 information files (file sets I to V) and 4 sets of about 20 programs (program sets A to D).

Magnetic tapes (files I–M) with the National Health Service Central Register data on transfers between Family Practitioner Areas were supplied by the Office of Population Censuses and Surveys. These data were checked, aggregated and rearranged in a FORTRAN program (see Chapter 8) (program A-M) and files referring to the 20-zone UK system created for 1975–6 to 1981–2 (file set II-M). Another FORTRAN program (program B-M) was then used to solve the three-face problem (Willekens *et al.* 1981) for these data to produce files containing interzonal migrations classified by age from the aggregate interzonal matrix and age-disaggregated zonal inmigrations and outmigrations (file set III-M). These separate year files were then consolidated and the age–time plan converted into cohort form in a Waterloo BASIC program (program C-M).

The other components were processed in the same sequence of operations, although the details differed between components and years.

Table 7.9 The cohort (type II) classifications used in the demographic information system.

Cohort number	Initial populations	Deaths, emigrations, internal migrations, immigrations and births		Final populations	Cohort order in files
		From	To		
1		birth	0–4	0–4	19
2	0–4	0–4	5–9	5–9	1
3	5–9	5–9	10–14	10–14	2
4	10–14	10–14	15–19	15–19	3
5	15–19	15–19	20–24	20–24	4
6	20–24	20–24	25–29	25–29	5
7	25–29	25–29	30–34	30–34	6
8	30–34	30–34	35–39	35–39	7
9	35–39	35–39	40–44	40–44	8
10	40–44	40–44	45–49	45–49	9
11	45–49	45–49	50–54	50–54	10
12	50–54	50–54	55–59	55–59	11
13	55–59	55–59	60–64	60–64	12
14	60–64	60–64	65–69	65–69	13
15	65–69	65–69	70–74	70–74	14
16	70–74	70–74	75–79	75–79	15
17	75–79	75–79	80–84	80–84	16
18	80–84	80–84	85–89	85–89	17
19	85 +	85 +	90 +	90 +	18

Notes
1 Births data assembled for cohorts 4 to 10 inclusive, which refer to mother's cohort at time of maternity.
2 All cohorts are 'projection' cohorts (type II in Fig. 7.1).

Published data were extracted from OPCS publications (file set I), coded up and input via a VDU terminal to computer files (operation A) to form 'rawdata' files (file set II). These 'rawdata' files were input to a series of Waterloo BASIC programs (program set B) that estimated the full age disaggregation for age–time plan type I which were written to 'abmdata' files (file set III).

These 'abmdata' files for six separate calendar years were consolidated into data for the mid-year 1976 to mid-year 1981 period by a series of Waterloo BASIC programs (program set C), and at the same time the data were converted to projection cohort form to produce one data file for each component (file set IV). These files were input to a FORTRAN program (Rees 1984b) (program set D) to construct movement accounts tables, various tables of rates and tables of projected populations for the base period 1976–81 and for five periods of projection: 1981–6, 1986–91, 1991–6, 1996–2001 and 2001–6.

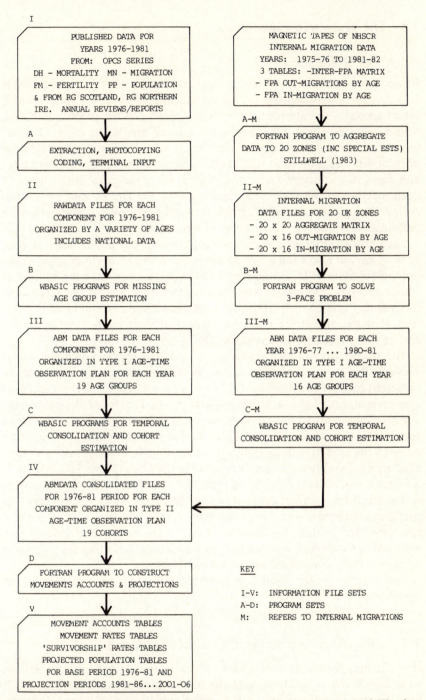

I

PUBLISHED DATA FOR
YEARS 1976-1981
FROM: OPCS SERIES
DH - MORTALITY   MN - MIGRATION
FM - FERTILITY   PP - POPULATION
& FROM RG SCOTLAND, RG NORTHERN
IRE.   ANNUAL REVIEWS/REPORTS

MAGNETIC TAPES OF NHSCR
INTERNAL MIGRATION DATA
YEARS: 1975-76 TO 1981-82
3 TABLES: -INTER-FPA MATRIX
- FPA OUT-MIGRATIONS BY AGE
- FPA IN-MIGRATION BY AGE

A

EXTRACTION, PHOTOCOPYING
CODING, TERMINAL INPUT

A-M

FORTRAN PROGRAM TO AGGREGATE
DATA TO 20 ZONES (INC SPECIAL ESTS)
STILLWELL (1983)

II

RAWDATA FILES FOR EACH
COMPONENT FOR 1976-1981
ORGANIZED BY A VARIETY OF AGES
INCLUDES NATIONAL DATA

II-M

INTERNAL MIGRATION
DATA FILES FOR 20 UK ZONES
- 20 x 20 AGGREGATE MATRIX
- 20 x 16 OUT-MIGRATION BY AGE
- 20 x 16 IN-MIGRATION BY AGE

B

WBASIC PROGRAMS FOR MISSING
AGE GROUP ESTIMATION

B-M

FORTRAN PROGRAM TO SOLVE
3-FACE PROBLEM

III

ABM DATA FILES FOR EACH
COMPONENT FOR 1976-1981
ORGANIZED IN TYPE I AGE-TIME
OBSERVATION PLAN FOR EACH YEAR
19 AGE GROUPS

III-M

ABM DATA FILES FOR EACH
YEAR 1976-77 ... 1980-81
ORGANIZED IN TYPE I AGE-TIME
OBSERVATION PLAN FOR EACH YEAR
16 AGE GROUPS

C

WBASIC PROGRAMS FOR TEMPORAL
CONSOLIDATION AND COHORT
ESTIMATION

C-M

WBASIC PROGRAM FOR TEMPORAL
CONSOLIDATION AND COHORT ESTIMATION

IV

ABMDATA CONSOLIDATED FILES
FOR 1976-81 PERIOD FOR EACH
COMPONENT ORGANIZED IN TYPE II
AGE-TIME OBSERVATION PLAN
19 COHORTS

D

FORTRAN PROGRAM TO CONSTRUCT
MOVEMENTS ACCOUNTS & PROJECTIONS

V

MOVEMENT ACCOUNTS TABLES
MOVEMENT RATES TABLES
'SURVIVORSHIP' RATES TABLES
PROJECTED POPULATION TABLES
FOR BASE PERIOD 1976-81 AND
PROJECTION PERIODS 1981-86... 2001-06

KEY

I-V: INFORMATION FILE SETS
A-D: PROGRAM SETS
M: REFERS TO INTERNAL MIGRATIONS

Figure 7.5 Steps in the assembly of demographic data for the United Kingdom movement accounts.

7.8   The projection experiments

7.8.1   General description

Projections were carried out using some eight models (as specified in Table 7.7). Accounts were constructed for the base period 1976–81, and from this set of accounts the appropriate rates and flows for the projection model were extracted. These were then applied in all models to the 1981 zonal populations, so that each projection began with the same, accurate base population. The projection then rolled forward using the appropriate rates and flows in a constant fashion, applying either the rates or the flows or both together to the projected populations at the end of each projection period. The projections were carried forward over five five-year periods, a sufficient time span for the present experiments.

Each model provides not only a projection of the populations of each zone by age but also a full set of accounts and components of growth. These are too voluminous to reproduce or discuss here but will be the subject of future analysis. The projections thus contain forecasts of the volume of internal and external migration, of births and deaths as well as of population. Here we concentrate attention on the final projected populations at the end of the projection time span in 2006.

The results for the eight models are collected together in four tables. Table 7.10 gives the 2006 populations, in millions, for each of the zones as projected by the eight models. Table 7.11 converts these zonal populations into percentages of the total UK population. In Table 7.12 the percentage age distribution over 19 age groups projected in 2006 by each model is given for the UK as a whole. Finally, Table 7.13 shows the results of comparing seven of the models with an eighth (model) using the same statistics as were used earlier to evaluate Rogers's results for the USA (Table 7.1). Model 7, a forecast model using emigration rates and immigration flows, was chosen as the norm for comparison as this was the model which, on the basis of previous arguments, would probably have been used for producing population forecasts. In this projection the data for the base period 1976–81 are accepted at face value, and the closure option best reflecting the influences of immigration control on external flows is used.

The results of the model projections will now be considered and evaluated.

7.8.2   What happens to the UK zonal populations?

If we accept, for the moment, that model 7 provides the best projection, what does it tell us will happen to the populations of our 20 UK zones? It first suggests that the overall UK population will decline by nearly three-quarters of a million from its 1981 value of 56.29 millions, although there

Table 7.10 The projected populations of the UK zones in 2006, in millions.

Zone	1981 population	1 f er, ir	2 b er, ir	3 c er, ir	4 f emi	5 f nmr	6 f ef, if	7 f er, if	8 f World
Northern Ireland	1.547	1.712	1.720	1.605	1.764	1.712	1.716	1.709	1.723
Central Clydeside	1.725	1.307	1.244	1.411	1.426	1.307	1.292	1.315	1.341
Scotland Remainder	3.425	3.433	3.551	3.400	3.541	3.433	3.435	3.430	3.503
Tyne and Wear	1.161	0.976	0.967	1.029	1.020	0.976	0.974	0.980	0.997
Northern Remainder	1.953	1.831	1.865	1.923	1.895	1.831	1.831	1.834	1.867
South Yorkshire	1.315	1.248	1.268	1.258	1.260	1.248	1.249	1.250	1.274
West Yorkshire	2.065	1.923	1.942	2.012	1.951	1.923	1.925	1.926	1.964
Yorkshire and Humberside Remainder	1.526	1.548	1.591	1.577	1.555	1.548	1.550	1.547	1.585
East Midlands	3.840	3.926	4.054	4.158	3.998	3.926	3.932	3.923	3.995
East Anglia	1.895	2.115	2.227	2.173	2.187	2.115	2.123	2.109	2.159
Outer South East	4.734	5.633	5.986	5.245	5.655	5.633	5.643	5.591	5.767
Outer Metropolitan Area	5.442	5.422	5.594	5.738	5.564	5.422	5.429	5.428	5.613
Greater London	6.851	6.055	5.942	6.161	5.971	6.055	6.075	6.120	6.510
South West	4.363	4.669	4.815	4.682	4.711	4.669	4.675	4.657	4.771
West Midlands County	2.674	2.293	2.262	2.309	2.300	2.293	2.294	2.304	2.354
West Midlands Remainder	2.507	2.738	2.891	2.692	2.672	2.738	2.737	2.731	2.807
Greater Manchester	2.624	2.341	2.335	2.349	2.379	2.341	2.341	2.347	2.394
Merseyside	1.525	1.269	1.242	1.274	1.298	1.269	1.268	1.276	1.302
North West Remainder	2.315	2.323	2.401	2.300	2.327	2.323	2.325	2.321	2.382
Wales	2.807	2.751	2.809	2.868	2.818	2.751	2.753	2.751	2.800
United Kingdom	56.289	55.515	56.705	56.165	56.294	55.515	55.569	55.548	57.106

Source: runs of the MOVE program with the data sets described above in the University of Leeds Amdahl mainframe computer. See Rees (1984b) for full details of the program.

Notes
1 Ways of assembling accounts: f, forecast model; b, backcast model; c, constrained model.
2 Ways of closing the system:

er, ir	emigration rates, immigration rates.
emi	external migration ignored.
nmr	net migration rates.
ef, if	emigration flows, immigration flows.
er, if	emigration rates, immigration flows.
world	world as one internal system.

Table 7.11 The projected population distribution by zone for the UK, 2006. (Percentages of the UK population.)

Zone	1981 %	Projection model							
		1 f er, ir	2 b er, ir	3 c er, ir	4 f emi	5 f nmr	6 f ef, if	7 f er, if	8 f World
Northern Ireland	2.75	3.08	3.03	2.86	3.13	3.08	3.09	3.08	3.02
Central Clydeside	3.06	2.35	2.19	2.51	2.53	2.35	2.33	2.37	2.35
Scotland Remainder	6.08	6.18	6.26	6.05	6.29	6.18	6.18	6.18	6.13
Tyne and Wear	2.06	1.76	1.71	1.83	1.81	1.76	1.75	1.76	1.75
Northern Remainder	3.47	3.30	3.29	3.42	3.37	3.30	3.30	3.30	3.27
South Yorkshire	2.34	2.25	2.24	2.24	2.24	2.25	2.25	2.25	2.23
West Yorkshire	3.67	3.46	3.42	3.58	3.47	3.46	3.46	3.47	3.44
Yorkshire and Humberside Remainder	2.71	2.79	2.81	2.81	2.76	2.79	2.79	2.78	2.78
East Midlands	6.82	7.07	7.15	7.40	7.10	7.07	7.08	7.06	7.00
East Anglia	3.37	3.81	3.93	3.87	3.89	3.81	3.82	3.80	3.78
Outer South East	8.41	10.15	10.56	9.34	10.05	10.15	10.16	10.06	10.10
Outer Metropolitan Area	9.67	9.77	9.86	10.22	9.88	9.77	9.77	9.77	9.83
Greater London	12.17	10.91	10.48	10.97	10.61	10.91	10.93	11.02	11.40
South West	7.75	8.41	8.49	8.34	8.37	8.41	8.41	8.38	8.35
West Midlands County	4.75	4.13	3.99	4.11	4.09	4.13	4.13	4.15	4.12
West Midlands Remainder	4.45	4.93	5.10	4.79	4.75	4.93	4.93	4.91	4.91
Greater Manchester	4.66	4.22	4.12	4.18	4.23	4.22	4.21	4.23	4.19
Merseyside	2.71	2.29	2.19	2.27	2.31	2.29	2.28	2.30	2.28
North West Remainder	4.10	4.19	4.23	4.09	4.13	4.19	4.18	4.18	4.17
Wales	4.99	4.95	4.95	5.11	5.01	4.96	4.95	4.95	4.90
United Kingdom	100.00	100.00	100.00	100.00	100.00	100.00	100.00	100.00	100.00

Source and Notes: see Table 7.10.

Table 7.12 The projected age distribution of the UK population, 2006. (Percentages of the UK population.)

		Projection model							
		1	2	3	4	5	6	7	8
	1981	f	b	c	f	f	f	f	f
Age	%	er, ir	er, ir	er, ir	emi	nmr	ef, if	er, if	World
0–4	6.13	5.86	6.04	5.58	5.80	5.86	5.86	5.93	5.99
5–9	6.54	6.24	6.39	5.92	6.18	6.24	6.24	6.27	6.31
10–14	7.90	6.74	6.90	6.40	6.67	6.74	6.73	6.72	6.73
15–19	8.31	6.86	7.03	6.57	6.79	6.86	6.86	6.87	6.84
20–24	7.45	6.59	6.76	6.28	6.48	6.59	6.58	6.65	6.66
25–29	6.76	6.12	5.99	5.92	6.05	6.12	6.12	6.26	6.32
30–34	7.33	6.45	6.30	6.31	6.46	6.45	6.43	6.58	6.76
35–39	6.40	7.68	7.50	7.65	7.76	7.68	7.69	7.61	7.77
40–44	5.70	7.98	7.81	8.01	8.11	7.98	8.01	7.82	7.93
45–49	5.52	7.03	6.91	7.21	7.19	7.03	7.05	6.95	6.94
50–54	5.71	6.26	6.17	6.47	6.38	6.26	6.26	6.24	6.17
55–59	5.89	6.59	6.50	6.90	6.64	6.59	6.60	6.52	6.41
60–64	5.29	5.42	5.39	5.69	5.42	5.42	5.42	5.40	5.30
65–69	4.99	4.38	4.33	4.58	4.35	4.38	4.37	4.38	4.29
70–74	4.28	3.62	3.52	3.78	3.59	3.62	3.61	3.62	3.54
75–79	3.03	2.89	2.77	3.07	2.87	2.89	2.89	2.89	2.83
80–84	1.72	2.01	1.97	2.11	1.99	2.01	2.01	2.01	1.96
85–89	0.75	0.96	1.08	1.02	0.95	0.96	0.96	0.96	0.94
90+	0.30	0.31	0.66	0.51	0.31	0.31	0.31	0.31	0.30
UK	100.00	100.00	100.00	100.00	100.00	100.00	100.00	100.00	100.00

Source and notes: see Table 7.10.

Table 7.13 Comparisons of the projection models with model 7.

Projection number	Model description	Difference in UK total population (1000 s) (1)	Absolute value of differences (1000 s) (2)	Absolute percentage differences (3)	Index of dissimilarity (4)
1	f; *er, ir*	− 33	194	6.01	0.18
2	b; *er, ir*	1157	1713	54.20	1.27
3	c; *er, ir*	617	1698	60.29	1.53
4	f; *emi*	746	1177	46.26	0.74
5	f; *nmr*	− 33	194	6.01	0.19
6	f; *ef, if*	21	214	7.39	0.21
8	f; world	1558	1559	47.80	0.48

Notes
1 The statistics are computed from the projected figures in Tables 7.10 and 7.11.
2 The statistics are defined in Table 7.1.
3 Model descriptions: see Table 7.10.

will be increases to 1991 and decreases thereafter. The 'demetropolitan-ization' of the UK continues with all eight metropolitan zones losing population over 1981–2006, particularly Central Clydeside (-24%), Merseyside (-16%) and the West Midlands Metropolitan County (-14%). Not all the other non-metropolitan zones gain population: the Northern Remainder, the Outer Metropolitan Area and Wales lose population. The nine other non-metropolitan zones continue to grow, particularly the Outer South East (18%), East Anglia (11%) and the South West (7%). All eight metropolitan zones lose shares of the national population together with the Northern Remainder. The non-metropolitan zones are gainers, particularly those already mentioned together with the East Midlands and the West Midlands Remainder.

7.8.3 The effect of closure choices recognizing external migration

From the tables, particularly Table 7.13, we can see that models 1, 5, 6 and 7 give very similar results. These are the models using the same accounting method (forecast model); they recognize external migration but employ slightly different techniques for handling the flows. Models 1 and 5 are virtually identical in their results – the differences are probably only due to slight computational differences. Whether you use net migration rates, gross migration rates, or gross migration flows does not appear, at least in the short run, to have a profound effect on the projection outcomes.

7.8.4 The effect of ignoring external migration

The effect of ignoring external migration is quite substantial. Model 4 differs from the norm, model 7, by three-quarters of a million in the total UK population and has a substantial sum of absolute differences over the zonal populations, and the sum of absolute percentage differences, which gives each region in the analysis an equal weight, is high.

7.8.5 The effect of using a world system

The result of opening up the UK to world influences is, as expected, substantial in that overall growth increases and an increase of just over 800 thousand is projected by 2006 in the national population, as a result of the increased levels of immigration generated by a fast-growing world population.

7.8.6 The effect of accounting model choice

When we depart from the simple forecast model view that all the accounts components can be accepted at face value in the forecast model and use instead a backcast or constrained model, substantial changes are effected in the population of the UK and particularly in its distribution among the zones. The indices of dissimilarity, which compare the zonal distributions of each model with the norm, are high for models 2 and 3 (Table 7.13). In the backcast model all the accounting errors are loaded on the initial populations; in the constrained model the emigration values are the ones adjusted to take the strain. Both adjustments in the view of what is currently happening in the base period result in level changes in zonal populations in 2006 of the same order as those resulting from adopting a world system model (see columns 1 and 2 of Table 7.13) and distributional changes that are larger (see columns 3 and 4).

A very careful examination of the base period accounts and likely error sources is thus indicated. It is clearly foolish to think that the future can be accurately predicted if the past has been erroneously measured.

7.9 Conclusions

It is probably too early in the investigation of this new UK multiregional system to recommend a replacement for the forecast accounting, emigration rates and immigration flows model (model 7). More of the research design matrix (Table 7.7) needs to be explored, and the base period population changes need to be investigated thoroughly. However, this chapter has served to demonstrate that the two sources of variation in population projection outcomes that have been investigated, namely, accounting model choice and closure model choice, can be neglected by the forecaster only at his or her peril.

8

The analysis and projection of interregional migration in the United Kingdom

JOHN STILLWELL

8.1 Introduction

An explanation of historical migration behaviour is rarely straightforward because of the wide variety of influences upon the decision to migrate and upon the decision to choose one particular destination rather than another. Nevertheless, analysis of historical data is a necessary prerequisite of projection because it enables more informed hypotheses to be suggested about the likelihood of migration in the future. In turn, improvements in the forecasting capability will mean improved strategic planning and ultimately a more satisfactory distribution of resources and public services.

In the United Kingdom the redistribution of the population through migration has become the most significant influence upon subnational population change and upon the differential growth of cities and regions. This chapter stems from a wider research project designed to investigate the processes of spatial population change in the UK since 1961 and to develop a multiregion population projection system which links migration models with accounts-based population models (Rees & Stillwell 1984).

Section 8.2 contains a description of the age-disaggregated data on migration which is available from the 1971 census 'new area' tabulations and from the Office of Population Censuses and Surveys' (OPCS) 10% sample of National Health Service patient reregistrations since 1975. The limitations of both types of migration data are discussed and methods of estimating complete matrices of flows for a system of metropolitan counties and non-metropolitan regions are outlined. Section 8.3 presents some of the characteristic features of migration for this system of zones, and particular attention is paid to the spatial pattern and age structure of five-year migration during 1966–71 and changes in the pattern between 1966–71 and

160

1976–81. The distance decay parameters of a doubly constrained spatial interaction model are used to illustrate spatial variations in the propensity to migrate over distance, and trends in the level and pattern of annual inter-zonal movement are examined.

In Section 8.4, alternative methods of migration projection are considered and four different approaches are chosen to generate forecasts of age-specific flows which can be compared against estimated 'observed' data using a goodness-of-fit statistic measuring the average deviation for each age group.

8.2 Study area zones, data sources and estimation methods

8.2.1 Metropolitan and non-metropolitan zones

Several alternative sets of areas have been used for the analysis of migration in the past, including standard economic planning regions at a relatively coarse level (Department of the Environment 1971) and local government districts at a finer scale (Martin Voorhees Associates & John Bates Services, 1981). Analysis at a finer scale usually means the sacrifice of age and sex detail. The selection of study zones is important because of the motivations which tend to stimulate migration over different distances. In some studies (Hyman & Gleave 1978) regionalization methods have been used in an attempt to distinguish longer distance employment-related migration from shorter distance migration influenced by the desire to change home without changing employment.

The standard regions are probably the most convenient set of administrative zones to work with because of the wealth of published data which exists at the regional level and because much has been learnt already about modelling at this level. However, the regional scale does obscure one of the most important spatial characteristics of the migration pattern over the last two intercensal decades; namely the migration of persons from densely populated urban cores to more sparsely populated rural areas (OPCS, Census Division 1981). Ideally, it would be appropriate to work with a set of local government areas, but this was considered beyond current capabilities in terms of purchase and release of unpublished data.

A system of zones has been selected which includes the metropolitan counties, their region remainders, the remaining regions without metropolitan counties in Great Britain, and Northern Ireland (Fig. 8.1).

One advantage of this set of twenty zones is that age-specific migration data are available from special tabulations from the 1971 census for the areas as constituted on 1 April 1974 for England and Wales and on 16 May 1975 for Scotland (OPCS 1978d). This enables comparison with sets of data for later periods. The analysis focuses on five-year migration and five-year age groups in order to avoid problems of sparse matrices which arise with data

161

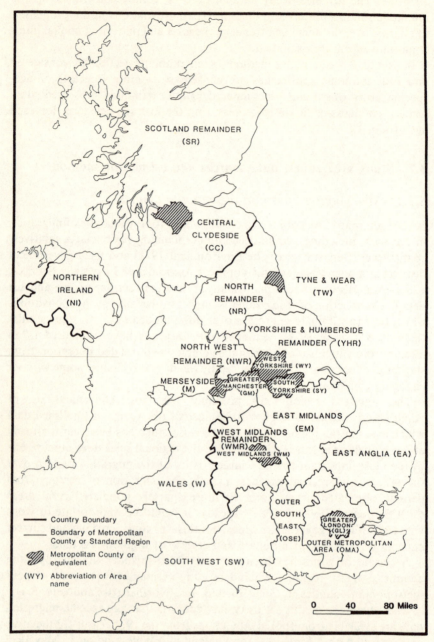

Figure 8.1 Metropolitan and non-metropolitan zones in the United Kingdom.

for single-year migration and one-year age groups. A further consideration is the need to limit the size of the computing task involved.

8.2.2   Census transition data: five-year migrant flows

Migration statistics derived from the results of national population censuses are frequently used for analysis in the UK in the absence of a population registration system. Prior to 1961, respondents were asked to identify their place of birth and place of usual residence. Consequently analysis was undertaken of 'lifetime' migration in the 19th century (Ravenstein 1876), and in the first half of the 20th century (Osborne 1956).

Since 1961, respondents to censuses have been asked to identify their place of usual residence either one year or five years beforehand. Five-year information is only available for the periods preceding the 1966 and 1971 censuses. The intermediate census taken in 1966 was organized on a 10% sample basis, whereas the migration data associated with the 1961 and 1971 censuses is based upon the selection, at random, of one household from each run of 10 private households and of one person from every 10 persons enumerated in non-private establishments.

Research studies based on published and unpublished census tabulations of five-year transition data at various spatial scales are numerous since censuses are more comprehensive and reliable sources of information than registers or surveys. Published flows between standard regions have been examined by Rees (1979a) and Stillwell (1978) and used in projection contexts by Joseph (1975), but other studies have considered migration between aggregated counties (Stillwell 1979) and flows associated with specific counties (Craig 1981). Flows within and between Metropolitan Economic Labour Areas on the other hand are described in Kennett (1980). More detailed, unpublished information has been extracted from the 1971 census 10% migration file (Edwards & Pender 1976) and used to prepare reports on intra-regional migration in Wales (Welsh Office 1979), and Yorkshire and Humberside (Department of the Environment, Yorkshire and Humberside Regional Office 1979). Data on flows between local authorities in the London Region, disaggregated by social class, have been extracted from the same source and used by Gordon (1982), for example, to separate migration streams according to motivation.

Despite the reliability of census information, the migration data are not without their limitations, and these are well known (Rees 1977). It is appropriate to think of census figures as numbers of migrants rather than migrations because they refer only to those persons who were in existence five years prior to the census and who migrated (at least once) during the period to a different place of usual residence and who survived the period. Various migrant subgroups are omitted from transition statistics. One such group consists of infant migrants or those aged less than 5 years on census

163

date, who were not in existence at the commencement of the five-year period. Persons who migrated and then died during the period are another group which is excluded. In addition, migrants who were resident at the same address at the start and end of the period but who might have lived elsewhere in between are not recorded. The incidence of return migration is difficult to measure, and it can be argued that return to the same address is less significant than return to an address in the same locality. In the latter case, the migration is recorded as a short-distance migration within the same area which has probably not involved the migrant in crossing an administrative boundary – perhaps concealing the fact that two or more longer distance, interregional or international moves may have been undertaken. Multiple migration is omitted from census figures because transition data represent a count of persons experiencing migration, rather than the number of times each person moves. Certain unknown flows can be estimated through the construction of population accounts (Rees & Wilson 1977), but several, such as surviving infant migrants, are required as inputs to the accounts-based model and must be determined independently. Infant migrants can be estimated as a function of migrants in the 5–9 age group and single-year flows as follows:

$$\left[\begin{array}{c} \text{Five-year} \\ \text{migrants aged} \\ \text{0–4 at census,} \\ 1971 \end{array} \right] = \left[\begin{array}{c} \text{Five-year} \\ \text{migrants aged} \\ \text{5–9 at census,} \\ 1971 \end{array} \right] \times 0.5 \times \left[\begin{array}{c} \text{9/8 one-year} \\ \text{migrants aged} \\ \text{aged 1–4} \\ \text{at census, 1971} \end{array} \bigg/ \begin{array}{c} \text{one-year} \\ \text{migrants aged} \\ \text{5–9 at census,} \\ 1971 \end{array} \right]$$

$$(8.1)$$

Migrants in age categories 75–79, 80–84, 85–89 and 90+ are estimated by deconsolidating flows in the last migrant age group (75+) using proportions based on 1971 population totals.

One set of internal migration flows unavailable from the census tables is the set of flows from zones in Great Britain to Northern Ireland of persons in each five-year age group. The first stage of estimation requires the total number of migrants to Northern Ireland from each zone. Northern Ireland Migration Tables (General Register Office, Northern Ireland 1975, Table 1B) yield figures of immigration from England, Wales and Scotland but with no subnational breakdown. If we assume that the distribution of out-migration flows to Northern Ireland from other zones is equivalent to the distribution of immigration flows to other zones from Northern Ireland, the total outflows from England and Scotland can be deconsolidated into zonal flows according to the inmigration proportions. It is surprising to find that over 20 thousand inmigrants are recorded with an area of origin which is 'not stated'. The 'not stated' inmigrants can either be ignored or distributed proportionately between the origin zones.

The second stage of estimation involves generating age-group flows from aggregate zonal flows. A simple method is to assume the same age

164

breakdown as that associated with all other internal migration flows. Estimated migrants ($\hat{M}$) from zone i to Northern Ireland (NI) in age group a at census date 1971 are determined using

$$\hat{M}_a^{iNi} = \hat{M}_.^{iNI} \sum_{\substack{j=1 \\ j \neq i}}^{19} M_a^{ij} \Bigg/ \sum_a \sum_{\substack{j=1 \\ j \neq i}}^{19} M_a^{ij} \qquad (8.2)$$

where $\hat{M}_.^{iNI}$ represents the non-disaggregated totals estimated previously, and $\cdot$ represents summation over the subscript replaced. An alternative method of deriving these flows is through calibrating model migration schedules (Rogers & Castro 1981) for outmigration from each zone to the rest of Great Britain. Model migration rates for each age group provide the basis for disaggregating the totals of outmigration to Northern Ireland from each zone. To exemplify this, the observed rates of outmigration from Tyne and Wear to all other zones in Great Britain have been standardized by the gross migraproduction rate, the sum of the age group rates; and a non-linear least squares algorithm has been used to estimate the parameters of a reduced model migration equation. The model schedule is plotted in Figure 8.2, and the model equation has the form:

$$m_a^{i\cdot} = b_1 e^{(-\alpha_1 a)} + b_2 e^{\{-\alpha_2(a-\mu_2)-e^{[-\lambda_2(a-\mu_2)]}\}} + c \qquad (8.3)$$

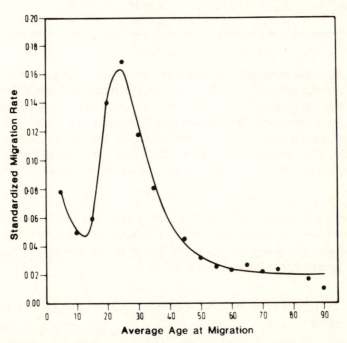

Figure 8.2 Model migration schedule for standardized outmigration rates for Tyne and Wear to other zones in Great Britain, 1966–71.

Table 8.1 Model migration schedule estimates of age-group flows from Tyne and Wear to Northern Ireland, 1966–71.

Age group at census date	Average age at migration	Standardized migration rate observed	Model migration rate prediction	Flow to Northern Ireland from Tyne and Wear Model estimates	
				Equation 8.4	Equation 8.2
5–9	5	0.0784	0.0780	14	19
10–14	10	0.0495	0.0512	9	11
15–19	15	0.0593	0.0568	10	13
20–24	20	0.1402	0.1435	26	33
25–29	25	0.1688	0.1626	30	30
30–34	30	0.1177	0.1226	22	19
35–39	35	0.0803	0.0830	15	13
40–44	40	0.0576	0.0566	10	10
45–49	45	0.0453	0.0409	7	9
50–54	50	0.0321	0.0317	6	6
55–59	55	0.0250	0.0265	5	5
60–64	60	0.0234	0.0235	4	4
65–69	65	0.0266	0.0218	4	4
70–74	70	0.0222	0.0208	4	3
75–79	75	0.0239	0.0203	4	2
80–84	80	0.0204	0.0199	4	1
85–89	85	0.0169	0.0198	4	1
90+	90	0.0110	0.0197	4	0

where $m_a^{i\cdot}$ is the predicted, standardized age-group outmigration rate from zone i for age group a. The first term on the right-hand side represents a single negative exponential curve of ages before entry into labour force; the second term represents a left skewed unimodal curve of the labour-force age range; and c is a constant which, with b_1 and b_2, determines the level of the schedule. The remaining parameters determine the shape of the schedule. Migrants from zone i to Northern Ireland are estimated as

$$\hat{M}_a^{iNI} = m_a^{i\cdot} \cdot \hat{M}^{iNI} \tag{8.4}$$

and Table 8.1 contains an example of the results obtained from using both methods to estimate flows from Tyne and Wear to Northern Ireland. The model-based method generates lower figures in the lower age groups and higher figures in the older age groups.

8.2.3 National Health Service reregistrations: annual movement data

The National Health Service maintains a Central Register (NHSCR) of changes of a patient's Family Practitioner Committee (FPC). Transfers occur when a patient registers with a new NHS doctor in an FPC other than that with which the patient was previously registered. The boundaries of FPC areas correspond with those of counties and metropolitan districts.

OPCS considers that this register data has a useful function as an indicator of internal migration in Great Britain in the absence of census information. The register has been in operation since 1971, recording details of aggregate flows, but since 1975 OPCS has taken a 10% sample of patient reregistrations and produced tabulations for local planning authorities, which include some age and sex disaggregation. Quarterly statistics were produced until 1980 when local authorities requested tables for 12-month periods, thereby removing seasonal fluctuations. The primary unit data which consist of a series of records containing information about origin FPC, destination FPC, date of birth and sex are aggregated to provide two computer summaries for each 12-month period. The first of these summaries contains the numbers of moves into and out of each FPC area disaggregated by sex and by age (the age groups are: all ages, 0–4, 5–9 ... 75 +, not stated). The second contains total numbers moving into each FPC from every other FPC in the UK (including the Isle of Man). Region and metropolitan county flows are also available, but the data in this table are not disaggregated by sex or age. The summary figures for recorded moves among the regions of England, Wales and Scotland are presented in OPCS monitors (OPCS MN series). Hitherto, NHSCR data have been used for national and regional analysis by Ogilvy (1979, 1980, 1982) and by Elias and Molho (1982) for labour-market modelling.

The NHSCR data have several limitations. There is no record of movers who fail to register. Some individuals may remain with the same doctor despite moving into another county or metropolitan district. Wide variation exists in the period between a person moving and the subsequent reregistration. The propensity of a mover to reregister immediately depends on several factors, and the OPCS estimates an average lag of about 3 months. When using the data it is important to recognize that, given this lag period, moves recorded between one September and the next are appropriate for mid-year to mid-year analysis. The figures are of course subject to sampling error and the quality of the registers tends to vary between urban and rural areas.

There are two major problems involved in aggregating the FPC area data to be consistent with the set of study zones defined in Figure 8.1. Only estimates of cross-border moves between Scotland and other zones in the rest of the UK are available from the register for England and Wales. Flows to and from Central Clydeside are not distinguished from flows to and from the Remainder of Scotland. The Scottish Central Register covers moves within Scotland and to and from England and Wales, and the data represent a 100% count rather than a sample. The other problem concerns the South East. Greater London is consistent for both zonal systems, but the counties in the Remainder of the South East do not aggregate into the Outer Metropolitan Area and the Outer South East and moves to and from these zones require estimation.

The procedure for obtaining complete sets of age-aggregated interzonal flows from the annual summaries is as follows: raw data for the FPC areas, metropolitan counties and regions comprising the set of study zones must be identified and a matrix consolidation program is used to generate the aggregated flows for each year. The Isle of Man is identified as a separate zone. Moves between Central Clydeside (and Scotland Remainder; Outer Metropolitan Area; Outer South East) and the 'other' zones in the UK are estimated by disaggregating the totals to and from Scotland (and the Remainder of the South East) according to the proportions indicated by the 1966–71 census flows. For example, moves from Central Clydeside (CC) to Tyne and Wear (TW) are estimated as follows:

$$\hat{M}^{CC\ TW}(\text{NHSCR, annual}) = M^{S\ TW}(\text{NHSCR, annual})\left[\frac{M^{CC\ TW}(\text{census, 1966–71})}{M^{S\ TW}(\text{census, 1966–71})}\right]$$

(8.5)

Moves between the two Scottish zones and the two zones in the Remainder of the South East (RSE) are estimated using a similar method; moves from Central Clydeside to the Outer Metropolitan Area (OMA) are estimated as

$$\hat{M}^{CC\ OMA}(\text{NHSCR, annual}) = M^{S\ RSE}(\text{NHSCR, annual})\left[\frac{M^{CC\ OMA}(\text{census, 1966–71})}{M^{S\ RSE}(\text{census, 1966–71})}\right]$$

(8.6)

The unknown moves remaining are those between Central Clydeside and Scotland Remainder (SR) and between Outer Metropolitan Area and Outer South East. The former are estimated on the basis of census proportions of total outmigration:

$$\hat{M}^{CC\ SR}(\text{NHSCR, annual}) = M^{S\cdot}(\text{NHSCR, annual})\left[\frac{M^{CC\ SR}(\text{census, 1966–71})}{M^{S\cdot}(\text{census, 1966–71})}\right]$$

(8.7)

One control total is available for moves between FPC areas in the Remainder of the South East. Flows between the Outer South East and the Outer Metropolitan Area are estimated by disaggregating the total according to 1966–71 outmigration proportions, and the remaining moves are assumed to be internal to the two zones and divided between them on the basis of these outmigration proportions. Corresponding off-diagonal elements of the five relevant annual matrices can be summed to provide a set of five-year data on aggregate moves during the period mid-year 1976 to mid-year 1981.

The procedure for obtaining sets of age-disaggregated interzonal flows from the annual summaries requires a similar initial identification of raw data to that used previously. Gross inmovement and outmovement totals are obtained for the sixteen age groups (0–4, 5–9 ... 70–74, 75+). The age-specific totals for Scotland require deconsolidation into totals for Central Clydeside and Scotland Remainder, and the Remainder of the South East totals are split between the Outer Metropolitan Area and the Outer South East. Deconsolidation of these totals is undertaken by applying the proportions obtained from the estimates of aggregate flows entering and leaving these zones. There remains the problem of estimating the age-specific interzonal flows, given the aggregate interzonal matrix and the age-specific outmove and inmove totals. This can be solved using an iterative balancing factor routine, but a more convenient formulation from a computational point of view is one in which the age-specific interzonal estimates (M_a^{ij}) are initially set to one and subsequently adjusted in three stages as follows:

$$\hat{M}_a^{ij} = \hat{M}_a^{ij} \frac{OD^{ij}}{\sum_a M_a^{ij}} \tag{8.8}$$

$$\hat{M}_a^{ij} = \hat{M}_a^{ij} \frac{D_a^j}{\sum_i M_a^{ij}} \tag{8.9}$$

and

$$\hat{M}_a^{ij} = \hat{M}_a^{ij} \frac{O_a^i}{\sum_j M_a^{ij}} \tag{8.10}$$

where the given information is

OD^{ij} aggregate moves by origin i and destination j;
D_a^j moves by destination j and age group a;
and O_a^i moves by origin i and age group a.

The final estimates from Equation 8.10 are reused in Equation 8.8, and the model reiterates until the absolute difference between each estimate on successive iterations is below a predefined tolerance level. In order to test alternative methods of projection in a later section, these age-disaggregated estimates are assumed to represent 'observed flows'.

8.3 Characteristics of internal migration in the UK

8.3.1 The spatial pattern and age structure of five-year migration, 1966–71

Analysis of migration behaviour is facilitated by the identification of three important dimensions: the overall level of mobility within the system, the spatial pattern of migration between zones in the system, and the age structure of migration.

During the five-year period prior to the census in 1971, nearly 4.1 million individuals (aged over 5 in 1971) were involved in migrating among the study area zones within the UK, and almost 13.8 millions moved *within* the same region. The interzonal total can be represented as a rate of 75 persons per thousand from the total usually resident population at the date of the 1966 census and 30% of this migration involved persons aged between 20 and 29 at the date of the 1971 census.

The spatial pattern of migration in aggregate net terms is characterized by gains to all the non-metropolitan zones in Great Britain and losses from all the metropolitan zones (Fig. 8.3), reflecting the process of decentralization from urban core areas to their surrounding hinterlands. Northern Ireland, for different reasons, has a negative net migration balance. Further evidence of the way in which decentralization dominates the migration distribution pattern is shown by the pairs of zones experiencing the most significant net gains or losses. The three largest net migration balances (in absolute terms) for each zone are presented in Table 8.2. The largest balance is the net loss of over a quarter of a million migrants from Greater London to the Outer Metropolitan Area during the period. All the metropolitan counties, apart from South Yorkshire, lose primarily to their region remainders and, correspondingly, the region remainders gain most migrants from their metropolitan cores. The North West Remainder gains more net migrants from Merseyside than from Greater Manchester, and Yorkshire and Humberside Remainder gains more from West Yorkshire than from South Yorkshire. A number of zones which are recipients of migrants from decentralizing metropolitan counties are also experiencing decentralization themselves. The Outer Metropolitan Area, which receives such a massive influx from Greater London, exports relatively large numbers to the Outer South East and the South West. Similarly the West Midlands Remainder gains from its metropolitan core yet loses to the South West and the Outer South East. Wales gains from Merseyside and Greater Manchester but loses to the South West.

Greater London and the Outer Metropolitan Area are key zones for migration activity within the system. The South West, East Anglia and the Outer South East each gain primarily from Greater London and secondarily from the Outer Metropolitan Area. The East Midlands likewise gains from Greater London although, like the Outer Metropolitan Area itself, loses to the South West. On the other hand there are zones in the North, including Scotland Remainder, Tyne and Wear and Central Clydeside, whose net outflows to Greater London and the Outer Metropolitan Area are of secondary or tertiary importance.

The spatial patterns of age-specific net migration conform to the aggregate pattern in all but a few cases. Metropolitan zones experience net

170

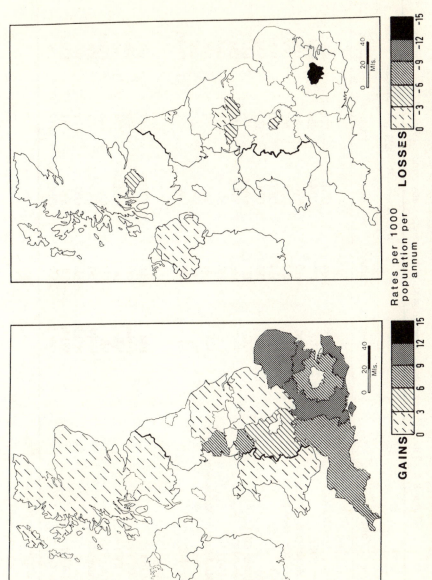

Figure 8.3 Annual aggregate net migration rates: gaining and losing zones, 1966–71.

Table 8.2 Three largest absolute net migration balances: study zones, 1966–71.

Zone	Interzonal net migration balance					
	Zone	Balance	Zone	Balance	Zone	Balance
Non-metropolitan zones						
Outer Metropolitan Area (OMA)	GL	2524	OSE	−624	SW	−260
Outer South East (OSE)	GL	1432	OMA	624	GM	49
West Midlands Remainder (WMR)	WM	619	SW	−68	OSE	−39
North West Remainder (NWR)	M	432	GM	267	WY	47
South West (SW)	GL	414	OMA	260	WM	131
East Anglia (EA)	GL	382	OMA	155	EM	40
Scotland Remainder (SR)	CC	257	OMA	−34	GL	−34
North Remainder (NR)	TW	146	YHR	−38	EM	−37
East Midlands (EM)	GL	136	SW	−86	GM	81
Yorkshire and Humberside Remainder (YHR)	WY	93	SY	57	NR	38
Wales (W)	M	67	SW	−67	GM	58
Northern Ireland (NI)	GL	−36	SW	−21	OMA	−19
Metropolitan zones						
South Yorkshire (SY)	EM	−68	YHR	−57	WY	−33
West Yorkshire (WY)	YHR	−93	NWR	−46	SW	−36
Tyne and Wear (TW)	NR	−146	OMA	−34	GL	−26
Central Clydeside (CC)	SR	−257	GL	−45	OMA	−37
Greater Manchester (GM)	NWR	−267	EM	−81	SW	−80
Merseyside (M)	NWR	−432	GM	−71	W	−67
West Midlands (WM)	WMR	−620	SW	−131	EM	−79
Greater London (GL)	OMA	−2524	OSE	−1432	SW	−414

Note: for a map of the zones see Figure 8.1

Table 8.3 Age-specific net migration balances: study zones, 1966–71.

| | | | | | | | Net migration balance (hundreds) Average age at migration, 1966–71 | | | | | | | | |
Zone	5	10	15	20	25	30	35	40	45	50	55	60	65	70	75+
Non-metropolitan zones															
OSE	161	130	134	213	252	160	121	125	117	119	164	240	270	109	70
OMA	196	94	55	209	475	261	150	74	84	64	32	−23	−15	29	65
SW	84	69	81	61	63	59	67	64	77	87	128	182	189	71	52
NWR	100	75	34	17	125	95	61	56	54	47	35	42	38	18	12
EA	74	51	39	67	82	65	42	44	32	35	44	63	66	22	15
WMR	50	28	30	72	169	58	39	26	23	18	14	19	14	6	10
EM	62	34	2	56	99	51	38	30	18	10	11	3	10	12	13
YHR	14	9	19	−35	−3	8	12	17	10	7	11	28	25	13	9
SR	29	24	−29	−75	2	22	18	8	3	17	20	28	30	13	5
W	4	83	−24	−80	−12	18	7	2	18	15	27	37	39	9	−1
NR	8	−2	−33	−56	22	15	9	6	8	0	5	5	3	5	0
NI	−9	−117	−18	−45	−23	−6	−4	−1	−1	2	2	5	5	2	2
Metropolitan zones															
WY	−6	−3	−21	−37	−23	−10	−12	−5	−11	−6	−9	−18	−22	−9	−5
SY	−31	−23	−22	−41	−43	−26	−25	−31	−13	−15	−5	−15	−10	−3	−5
TW	−32	−22	−31	−66	−65	−36	−24	−20	−21	−8	−8	−5	−8	−4	−10
GM	−42	−28	−29	−14	−16	−30	−30	−32	−42	−36	−44	−53	−52	−22	−16
CC	−54	−54	−40	−81	−68	−45	−30	−28	−22	−20	−22	−23	−24	−10	−13
M	−68	−51	−44	−133	−132	−65	−35	−34	−27	−23	−23	−24	−22	−11	−9
WM	−68	−49	−46	−108	−194	−79	−55	−48	−48	−48	−50	−62	−63	−24	−15
GL	−472	−280	−57	77	−711	−515	−346	−253	−259	−268	−332	−429	−476	−225	−180

Notes

1 The average age at migration is assumed to be the midpoint of the age transition. Thus 25 is the assumed average age of migrants who were aged 20–24 in 1966 (at census date) and 25–29 in 1971 (at census date).

2 For the key to zone abbreviations see Table 8.2.

losses in all age groups, apart from Greater London, which gains migrants in the 20–24 labour-force age group (Table 8.3). The non-metropolitan regions gain migrants in all age groups, apart from the Outer Metropolitan Area, which experiences net losses of migrants aged 60–69 (retirement), and the four most peripheral regions which lose migrants in certain lower age groups. In particular there are substantial net losses of 7.5, 8.0 and 5.6 thousand migrants aged 20–24 from Scotand Remainder, Wales and the North Remainder respectively. Our estimates for Northern Ireland suggest net losses in the age groups up to 45–49 and marginal net gains in the older groups.

Net migration is the difference between gross inward and outward migration, and the pattern of gross migration rates for 1966–71 (Fig. 8.4)

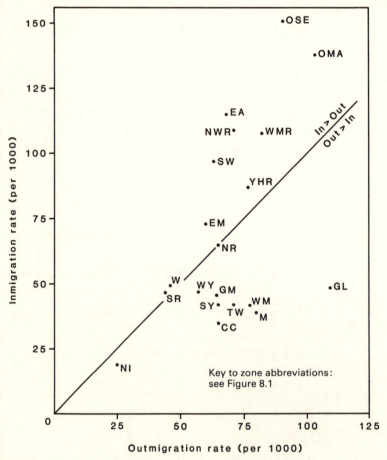

Figure 8.4 Gross rates of aggregate outmigration and inmigration: study zones, 1966–71.

indicates that, whereas metropolitan counties other than Greater London form a group of zones with a relatively small range of gross rate values, non-metropolitan zones have rates which vary more widely, with the Outer Metropolitan Area and the Outer South East experiencing inmigration rates of 151 and 138 per thousand. The rate of inmigration for Greater London conforms to that of the other metropolitan zones, but the outmigration rate for this zone is much higher.

The third important dimension of migration is its age structure. The general shape of the migration rate age schedule has been shown to have universal application (Rogers *et al.* 1978) with variations identified according to the type and level of migration, the latter being dependent upon the nature of the zonal system of interest or the average distance over which migration occurs between or within zones. The age schedule of inter-zonal migration for our system is illustrated in Figure 8.5, and the profiles

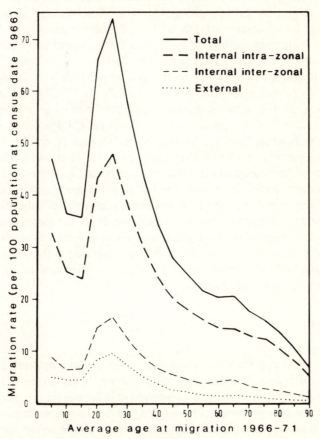

Figure 8.5 Age schedules for total, interzonal, intra-zonal and external migration rates, 1966–71.

for total, intra-zonal and external migration are included for comparison. The initial decline in the propensity to migrate in all schedules is followed by an increase until the so-called labour-force peak during age group 25–29 (average age 25) and subsequent decline thereafter, interrupted only by the retirement peak which occurs between the ages of 60 and 69. The rate of migration within zones is higher than the interzonal rate at all ages, but two features distinguish the shape of the two schedules. First, whereas intra-zonal migrants in their late teens have lower migration propensities than those in the preceding age group, interzonal migrants aged 15–19 have slightly higher propensities than those aged 10–14, as the labour-force component of interzonal migration begins to become apparent. Secondly, the retirement peak at age group 65–69 is more pronounced for interzonal migration than for intra-zonal migration where retirement causes only a temporary levelling out of the schedule.

The statistics presented in Table 8.4 provide further details of the extent to which migration by age group varies as a percentage of age-group population. In summary, 25.3% of the population aged over 5 moved within the same zone during 1966–71, and 7.5% moved between different zones within the UK. Broad age-group categorization shows that 18.6% of the total migration involved children aged 5–14 (16.4% of total population), 33.6% of migration involved young adults of 15–29 years (21.6% of population), 35.5% involved persons aged 30–59 (37.7% of population) and only 12.3% involved persons aged 60 and over (24.4% of total population). At the most popular age for migration (between 20 and 24 at the date of the 1966 census, 25 and 29 at the date of the 1971 census), nearly 65% of the population moved usual residence. The preceding discussion suggests that age structure should be taken into account when comparing migration rates between zones. It might be argued that high rates of migration occur because of higher proportions of young people in the population rather than a higher propensity for migration in the population as a whole. One method of comparison which allows for age structure is the calculation of gross migraproduction rates (gmr^i) defined as the sum of age-specific migration rates for each zone and calculated as

$$\text{gmr}^i = \sum_a \frac{\sum_j M_a^{ij}}{P_a^i} \tag{8.11}$$

where M_a^{ij} represents the flow of migrants in age group a between zone i and zone j, and P_a^i represents the population of zone i in age group a. However, age-structure differences are not an important influence on the spatial variation in migration propensity. The majority of non-metropolitan zones have relatively high interzonal gross migraproduction rates whereas the rates for metropolitan zones, with the exception of Greater London, are relatively low.

Table 8.4 Age-specific interzonal and intra-zonal migration totals and proportions, 1966–71.

End of period age group	Interzonal migration				Intra-zonal migration		
	Start of period population	Total flows	% of age group population	% of total migration	Total flows	% of age group population	% of total migration
5–9	4 706 437	425 451	9.0	10.4	1 550 226	32.9	11.3
10–14	4 214 364	280 633	6.7	6.9	1 066 069	25.3	7.7
15–19	3 841 613	258 376	6.7	6.3	922 876	24.0	6.7
20–24	4 278 018	624 817	14.6	15.3	1 850 601	43.3	13.4
25–29	3 619 076	603 553	16.7	14.8	1 739 030	48.1	12.6
30–34	3 280 478	401 962	12.3	9.8	1 245 765	38.0	9.1
35–39	3 225 990	289 096	9.0	7.1	965 782	29.9	7.0
40–44	3 394 772	229 465	6.8	5.6	812 024	23.9	5.9
45–49	3 646 693	194 933	5.3	4.8	727 989	20.0	5.3
50–54	3 405 740	156 370	4.6	3.8	606 947	17.8	4.4
55–59	3 573 392	142 383	4.0	3.5	564 978	15.8	4.1
60–64	3 488 943	146 093	4.2	3.6	510 742	14.6	3.7
65–69	3 095 606	144 668	4.7	3.5	443 909	14.3	3.2
70–74	2 469 119	82 679	3.3	2.0	318 178	12.9	2.3
75–79	1 828 844	52 082	2.8	1.3	224 950	12.3	1.6
80–84	1 265 550	31 426	2.5	0.8	133 240	10.5	1.0
85–89	722 811	14 127	2.0	0.3	58 816	8.1	0.4
90+	392 554	5 105	1.3	0.1	20 553	5.2	0.1
over 5	54 450 000	4 083 219	7.5	100.0	13 762 715	25.3	100.0

8.3.2   Changes in the pattern of five-year migration between 1966–71 and 1976–81

The 1981 census of population did not include a five-year migration question. In the absence of transition data for 1976–81, annual NHSCR moves data can be aggregated and used to examine whether there have been any significant changes in the spatial distribution patterns of migration in these two five-year periods. Direct comparisons of levels, flows and rates are not appropriate because of the conceptual differences in the two measures of migration discussed in Section 8.2. One feasible method of comparison is through examination of the migration to and from each zone as a proportion of total migration. Shifts in the inmigration and out-migration proportions between the two five-year periods (Table 8.5) indicate that whereas the overall pattern of movement in 1976–81 has remained similar to that in 1966–71 metropolitan zones have increased their proportional shares of inmigration and, except for West Yorkshire, have reduced their proportional shares of outmigration.

Many of the non-metropolitan zones, on the other hand, have reduced shares of inmigration and larger shares of outmigration. These shifts in proportions suggest a marginal deceleration in the process of decentralization. The most significant change is the reduction in Greater London's proportion of total outmigration by 5.2% and the corresponding increase of 2.1% in its proportion of total inmigration. As a result of this shift, the proportion of movements entering the Remainder of the South East region has declined by 3.2%, whereas the proportion moving out has increased by a similar amount. Four non-metropolitan zones (EA, EM, SR and W) have increased their share of inmigration but two (NI and SR) show a reduced proportion of total outmigration.

A second method of assessing changes in the migration distributions for the two periods is to examine the hierarchy (Table 8.6) which appears when zones are ordered according to the number of positive net inflows (Rees & Stillwell 1984). Non-metropolitan zones tend to appear higher up in the hierarchy than metropolitan zones, except for Greater London which gains from the 11 zones below it in the 1966–71 period, and loses to the 8 zones above it. The South West, East Anglia, Outer South East and East Midlands are the top four zones in the hierarchies for both periods whereas Northern Ireland, Central Clydeside, Tyne and Wear and Merseyside occupy the bottom four positions. Several of the intermediate zones in the hierarchy do not experience the same stability. The North West Remainder, ranked fifth in 1966–71 and receiving a net gain of movers from 15 other zones, drops to rank 12 in 1976–81, and gains from only 9 zones. On the other hand, the metropolitan county of South Yorkshire moves up the hierarchy by five places, losing migrants in net terms to only 9 zones in 1976–81 compared with 15 zones in the previous period. Wales, Greater

178

Table 8.5 Inmigration and outmigration proportions; study zones, 1966–71 and 1976–81.

Zones	Immigration proportions			Outmigration proportions		
	% 1966–71 Migrants (A)	% 1976–81 Moves (B)	% Change (B) – (A)	% 1966–71 Migrants (C)	% 1976–81 Moves (D)	% Change (D) – (C)
Non-metropolitan zones						
OMA	16.83	14.39	−2.44	12.54	14.56	2.02
OSE	14.47	13.74	−0.73	8.63	9.89	1.26
NWR	5.61	4.82	−0.79	3.63	4.44	0.81
SW	9.34	8.93	−0.41	6.07	6.92	0.85
WMR	5.80	5.45	−0.35	4.39	4.67	0.28
YHR	3.06	2.99	−0.07	2.71	2.72	0.01
NR	3.00	2.93	−0.07	3.01	3.01	0.00
NI	0.68	0.62	−0.06	0.93	0.89	−0.04
EA	4.41	4.48	0.07	2.60	3.28	0.68
EM	6.21	6.30	0.09	5.10	5.68	0.58
SR	3.98	4.28	0.30	3.69	3.65	−0.04
W	3.20	3.66	0.46	3.03	3.33	0.30
Metropolitan zones						
CC	1.53	1.64	0.11	2.83	2.78	−0.05
GM	3.08	3.21	0.13	4.27	4.11	−0.16
TW	1.26	1.51	0.25	2.14	1.88	−0.26
M	1.62	1.90	0.28	3.34	2.70	−0.64
WY	2.38	2.71	0.33	2.87	3.13	0.26
SY	1.34	1.67	0.33	2.10	1.76	−0.34
WM	2.82	3.27	0.45	5.17	4.87	−0.30
GL	9.39	11.51	2.12	20.97	15.77	−5.20

Note: for key to zone abbreviations see Table 8.2.

Table 8.6 Zones arranged in hierarchical order according to number of net inflows, 1966–71 and 1976–81.

Rank	Zone	1966–71 Number of inflows Exp	Obs	Number of outflows Exp	Obs	Zone	1976–81 Number of inflows Exp	Obs	Number of outflows Exp	Obs
1	SW	19	19	0	0	SW	19	19	0	0
2	EA	18	18	1	1	EA	18	18	1	1
3	OSE	17	16	2	3	OSE	17	16	2	3
4	EM	16	15	3	4	EM	16	15	3	4
5	NWR	15	15	4	4	W	15	14	4	5
6	OMA	14	14	5	5	GL	14	13	5	6
7	W	13	12	6	7	SR	13	12	6	7
8	WMR	12	12	7	7	OMA	12	12	7	7
9	GL	11	11	8	8	WMR	11	12	8	7
10	YHR	10	10	9	9	YHR	10	11	9	8
11	SR	9	8	10	11	SY	9	10	10	9
12	NR	8	8	11	11	NWR	8	9	11	10
13	GM	7	8	12	11	NR	7	7	12	12
14	WY	6	7	13	12	WY	6	7	13	12
15	WM	5	6	14	13	GM	5	5	14	14
16	SY	4	4	15	15	WM	4	4	15	15
17	M	3	4	16	15	TW	3	3	16	16
18	TW	2	2	17	17	M	2	2	17	17
19	CC	1	1	18	18	CC	1	1	18	18
20	NI	0	0	19	19	NI	0	0	19	19

Notes
1 Exp, Number of flows expected if hierarchical ordering is perfect.
2 Obs, Number of observed flows.
3 For key to zone abbreviations see Table 8.2.

London and Scotland Remainder move slightly up the hierarchy whereas the Outer Metropolitan Area and Greater Manchester move slightly downwards.

8.3.3 The propensity to migrate over distance

The observation that each zone interacts with every other zone but that more migration takes place between near zones than distant zones is the foundation upon which gravity models of migration are based. The negative relationship between migration interaction and distance is one of the 'laws of migration' (Ravenstein 1885) and the precise nature of the relationship has been investigated widely in the literature by Masser (1970) and Weeden (1973) in the UK for example, and by Somermeijer (1971) in the Netherlands. Traditional gravity models, calibrated using log linear

regression methods, have been rewritten by Wilson (1974) as spatial interaction models, derived by entropy-maximizing methods, which incorporate
additional knowledge in the form of constraints. A doubly constrained
spatial interaction model of migration takes the form:

$$M^{ij} = A^i B^j O^i D^j f(d^{ij}) \qquad (8.12)$$

where O^i is the total outmigration from zone i,
  D^j is the total inmigration to zone j, and
  $f(d^{ij})$ is a distance function.

The other terms on the right-hand side of the equation are balancing factors
defined as

$$A^i = \frac{1}{\sum_j B^j D^j f(d^{ij})} \qquad (8.13)$$

and

$$B^j = \frac{1}{\sum_i A^i O^i f(d^{ij})} \qquad (8.14)$$

which are used to ensure that the constraints

$$O^i = \sum_j M^{ij} \qquad (8.15)$$

and

$$D^j = \sum_i M^{ij} \qquad (8.16)$$

are satisfied. Distance is measured as road mileage between the zones and
historical tests suggest that the negative power decay function ($d^{ij-\beta}$) is
preferable to the negative exponential form. The optimum decay parameter,
β, is estimated using a Newton–Raphson iterative search routine and, in its
general form, it can be interpreted as a measure of the general propensity
to migrate over distance. Higher β values mean that the friction of distance
effect is greater, or that migrants show a greater rigidity towards moving
over distance. The same distance matrix was used to fit a number of doubly
constrained spatial interaction models to the transition data for 1966–71
and to the movement data for 1976–81. The aggregate flows model for
1966–71 has a generalized decay parameter value of 1.15 associated with an
observed mean migration distance for our zone system of 82.6 miles. In
comparison, the model for aggregate moves, 1976–81, has a β value of 1.08
and the mean movement distance is 86.6 miles.

Spatial variation in the propensity to move into and away from individual
zones in the system can be examined by calibrating origin- and destination-
specific parameters. Whereas the pattern of variation in mean outmigration

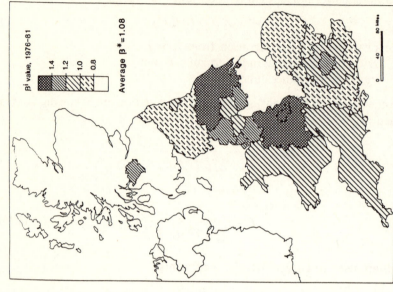

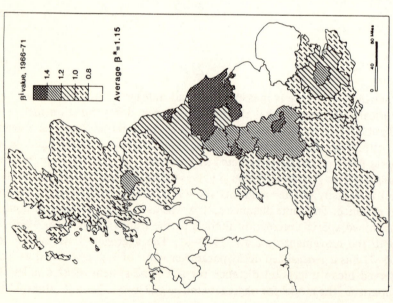

Figure 8.6 The spatial pattern of origin-specific distance decay parameters: 1966–71 and 1976–81.

or inmigration lengths reflects the relative location of each zone to all other zones, accessibility does not necessarily determine the propensity to migrate over distance. Origin-specific decay parameters for the two five-year periods are illustrated in Figure 8.6. For 1966–71 the West Midlands is the most accessible of all the zones and has the highest β^i value of 2.07 in contrast to Northern Ireland, the least accessible zone whose β^i is 0.14; however, there is no consistent relationship between β^i and mean migration distance since Greater London, Tyne and Wear, and Central Clydeside all have similar decay parameter values but very different mean outmigration distances of 68.7, 117.4 and 149.4 miles respectively. On the other hand, Merseyside and West Yorkshire, which have identical mean migration lengths, have dissimilar β^i values of 1.63 and 1.16. The spatial pattern which emerges from Figure 8.6 is one which shows that outmigrants from metropolitan zones tend to be more influenced by distance than migrants from non-metropolitan zones, although there are exceptions. West Yorkshire in 1966–71, and in 1976–81 together with Greater Manchester, has low β values compared with other metropolitan counties, whereas the Remainders of Yorkshire and Humberside and the West Midlands have relatively high decay parameters.

The variation in inmigration propensities is represented by the destination-specific parameters and Figure 8.7 illustrates that for

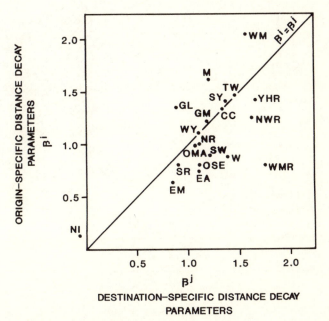

Figure 8.7 Origin and destination-specific decay parameters for aggregate inter-zonal flows, 1966–71.

183

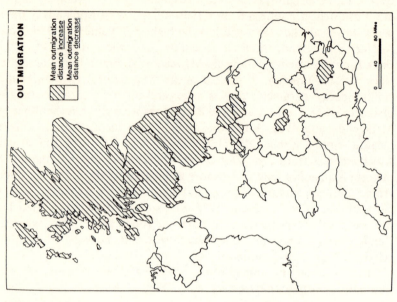

OUTMIGRATION

Mean outmigration
distance increase

Mean outmigration
distance decrease

0   40   80 Miles

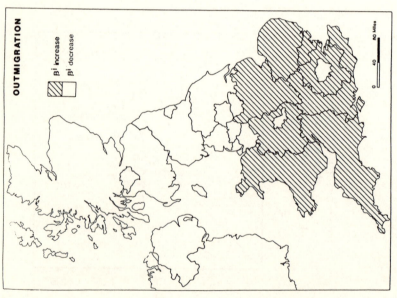

OUTMIGRATION

β^i increase

β^i decrease

0   40   80 Miles

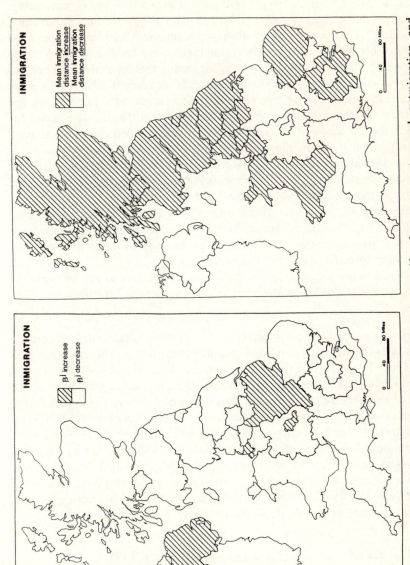

Figure 8.8 Changes in origin-specific and destination-specific decay parameters and outmigration and inmigration between 1966–71 and 1976–81.

metropolitan zones the friction of distance influences outmigration during 1966–71 more than it does inmigration, particularly in the cases of Greater London, Merseyside and West Midlands. Destination-specific parameters for non-metropolitan zones are higher than origin-specific parameters, indicating the greater effect of distance on migrants into these zones than on migrants out of them. The exception is Northern Ireland, whose β^i value is low and whose β^j value is positive, suggesting that migration increases as the zone of origin becomes further away! If we compare the zone-specific parameters and the mean migration distances for the two time periods, the patterns of change illustrated in Figure 8.8 are different. The zones for which the influence of distance on outmigration increases are the non-metropolitan zones in the south of the country. The origin-specific β^i parameter values decline for the metropolitan zones and for the Northern non-metropolitan regions. There are corresponding increases in the average distance migrated for these zones and decreases for the former set. Inmigration into only four of the zones (West Midlands, Merseyside, East Midlands and Northern Ireland) becomes more affected by distance from the first period to the second, and the average distance increases for migration into the majority of zones.

Migration flows disaggregated into five-year age groups can be modelled using a similar doubly constrained spatial interaction formulation:

$$M_a^{ij} = A_a^i B_a^j O_a^i D_a^j d^{ij - \beta_a^*}$$
(8.17)

in which a generalized age-specific decay parameter is calibrated. Figure 8.9 illustrates the variation in the age-specific parameters for the transition data for 1966–71 and for the estimated movement data for 1976–81. The results of modelling the transition data indicate that migrants aged 15–19 at the end of the period (average age at migration of 15) have the lowest of the β_a^* values and that propensities to migrate over distance generally decline up to retirement age with corresponding differences in the mean distances of migration. This pattern of age differentials is not so pronounced when the movement data is modelled. The age-group definition is different for this type of data, and the lack of variation is not unexpected since the distribution of flows for each age group being modelled has been estimated using the same aggregate flows matrix (Eqns 8.8 to 8.10).

8.3.4 Trends in annual movement data since 1976

The lack of time series data on migration within the UK has had a limiting effect on historical and forecasting analysis. Annual NHSCR data does provide a welcome source of information on movement in more recent years. The analysis of this section shows that although levels of mobility have declined since 1976 the patterns of gross and interzonal mobility have remained relatively stable.

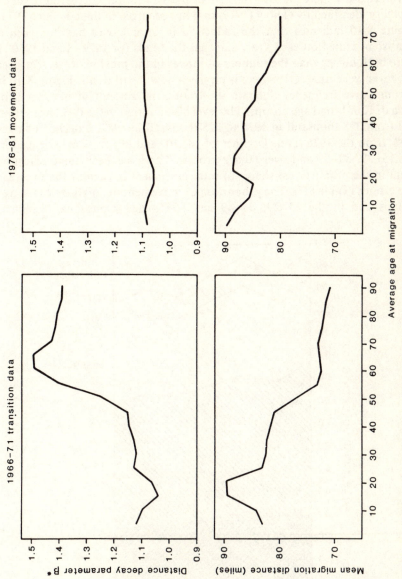

Figure 8.9 Age-specific distance decay parameters and mean migration distances: 1966–71 and 1976–81.

The number of transfers between metropolitan and non-metropolitan study zones in the 12 months ending mid-year 1982 totalled 1236 thousand compared with 1469 thousand moves in the 12 months ending mid-year 1976. This decline of nearly 16% is consistent with the decreasing level of mobility identified by Ogilvy (1979) that has occurred in the UK since 1973. Figure 8.10 indicates that the reduction in total moves has not been a consistent reduction each year, and that the totals for 1977–8 and 1980–1 were both higher than the number of moves in the previous year. Yet over the seven-year time series there is clearly a downward trend. Figure 8.10 is a cumulative frequency diagram illustrating the amount of movement in each of four broad age groups. The level of migration in the 0–14 age group fell from 328 thousand in 1976 to 235 thousand in 1982, a decline of over 28% from the 1976 level. Declines of 14, 10, and 8% were experienced in the 15–29, 30–59 and over 60 age groups. There has been some readjustment in the proportional shares of total movement in each of the five-year age groups (Table 8.7). The proportion of movement in the three lowest age groups and in the 25–29, 45–49 and 50–54 age groups has declined,

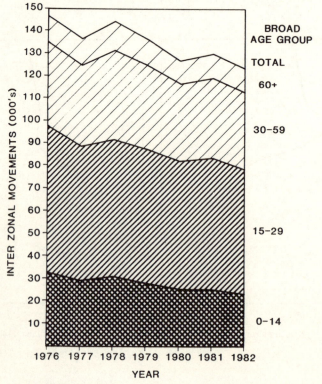

Figure 8.10 Cumulative age-group movement levels for single years ending mid-year 1976 to mid-year 1982.

Table 8.7 Five-year age-group proportions of annual interzonal moves, 1976–82.

Age group	% of total interzonal movement						
	1976	1977	1978	1979	1980	1981	1982
0–4	8.8	8.3	8.1	7.7	7.6	7.6	7.5
5–9	7.4	7.3	7.3	6.9	6.6	6.1	5.7
10–14	6.1	6.2	6.1	6.1	6.1	5.8	5.8
15–19	11.2	11.5	11.2	11.6	11.9	12.1	12.5
20–24	17.8	17.6	17.0	17.7	18.5	18.9	18.8
25–29	15.0	14.3	13.9	14.0	14.0	13.9	13.5
30–34	8.4	9.3	9.9	10.3	10.2	10.2	9.6
35–39	5.2	5.2	5.3	5.5	5.6	5.6	6.2
40–44	3.6	3.7	3.9	3.7	3.5	3.6	3.7
45–49	3.0	3.0	3.1	2.9	2.8	2.8	2.9
50–54	2.8	2.7	2.8	2.5	2.5	2.4	2.5
55–59	2.4	2.4	2.8	2.7	2.5	2.4	2.4
60–64	2.5	2.6	2.5	2.2	2.2	2.4	2.6
65–69	2.2	2.3	2.5	2.3	2.2	2.2	2.2
70–74	1.4	1.5	1.5	1.5	1.5	1.6	1.6
75+	2.1	2.2	2.3	2.2	2.3	2.4	2.6
Total moves (thousands)	1469	1366	1442	1362	1270	1303	1236

whereas the proportions in the remaining groups have either remained the same or have increased.

The decline in the level of mobility is a trend which appears to be consistent across virtually all the regions (Fig. 8.11), regardless of the differences in the levels of aggregate movement involved. But to what extent has the pattern of movement changed since 1976? The stability of the spatial structure of migration can be examined if we distinguish the generation component from the distribution component. The generation component can be represented by the proportion of total moves leaving each origin zone, given the total level of mobility, and Figure 8.12 presents the outmove probabilities in percentage terms for each of the 20 study zones. Although levels of outmigration have declined over time and are not directly comparable between zones of different size, outmove proportions are comparable and show a marked stability over time. The Outer Metropolitan Area and the Outer South East are the largest movement generating zones and have stable outmove probability schedules. Greater London is the zone for which there is most fluctuation in the outmove proportion, due largely to an increase from 11.4% in 1979–80 to 12.4% in 1980–1. The role of the South West as a generating zone is illustrated by the graph and this zone maintains a stable schedule of around 9%. These four zones account for almost half the total outmoves occurring in the system. A group of non-metropolitan zones, including the East Midlands, West Midlands

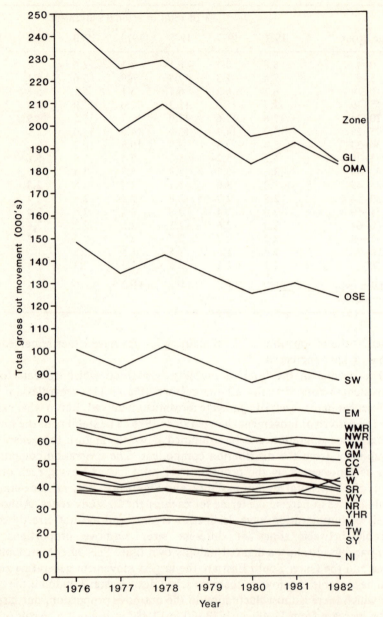

Figure 8.11 Levels of aggregate gross outmovement: study zones, 1975–6 to 1981–2.

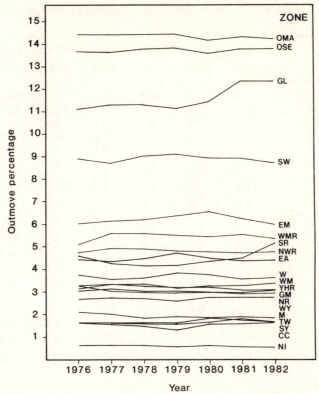

Figure 8.12 Outmove proportions: study zones, 1975–6 to 1981–2.

Remainder, Scotland Remainder, North West Remainder, and East Anglia, have proportions between 4 and 7% whereas the remaining zones have proportions below 4%. The metropolitan counties of Merseyside, Tyne and Wear, South Yorkshire and Central Clydeside each account for only between 1 and 2% of total outmoves and Northern Ireland accounts for less than 1%.

The second component of the spatial structure of migration is the distribution component which can be defined as the proportion of total moves from any one origin zone i which end up in destination zone j. The conclusion from a comparison of the distribution probabilities over the seven years is that the pattern of aggregate movement between zones has also remained stable. The proportions of total outmovement from Greater London to each of the other zones in each 12-month period are presented in Table 8.8 as an example of this stability for a zone which has a relatively unstable generation component. Outmovement from this zone is dominated by flows to the Outer Metropolitan Area, Outer South East and, to a lesser extent, to the South West, East Anglia, East Midlands, Wales and Scotland

Table 8.8 Outmove proportions from Greater London to other zones, 1975–6 to 1981–2.

Destination zone	% of total outmovement from Greater London						
	1976	1977	1978	1979	1980	1981	1982
OMA	39.8	39.8	40.3	40.0	39.1	39.9	40.5
OSE	21.1	21.0	21.3	21.2	20.7	21.1	21.4
SW	9.2	9.4	9.8	9.2	9.5	9.4	8.9
EA	6.2	6.2	6.1	6.6	6.4	5.8	5.8
EM	4.8	4.8	4.6	4.8	5.1	4.6	4.6
W	2.4	2.7	2.5	2.7	2.6	2.7	2.5
SR	2.4	2.0	2.0	1.9	2.2	2.2	2.1
WMR	1.8	1.9	1.8	1.7	1.8	1.7	1.8
WM	1.6	1.8	1.6	1.8	1.8	1.7	1.9
WY	1.4	1.3	1.2	1.2	1.3	1.5	1.4
GM	1.4	1.6	1.5	1.5	1.7	1.7	1.7
NWR	1.4	1.6	1.5	1.5	1.4	1.6	1.3
NR	1.2	1.1	1.1	1.1	1.2	1.2	1.1
YHR	1.2	1.1	1.2	1.0	1.1	1.3	1.1
CC	1.0	0.8	0.8	0.7	0.9	0.9	0.8
TW	0.9	0.8	0.6	0.8	0.9	0.7	0.9
M	0.9	0.9	0.7	0.8	0.9	0.9	0.8
SY	0.7	0.8	0.6	0.6	0.8	0.9	0.8
NI	0.6	0.5	0.7	0.7	0.7	0.4	0.6
Total out moves (thousands) from GL	244	226	229	215	195	198	184

Note: for key to zone abbreviations see Table 8.2.

Remainder. Flows to any other zone account for less than 2% of total outmovement from Greater London. The probabilities do not suggest that any significant changes are occurring in the pattern of movement, even though the level of outmovement has fallen by 24% from 244 thousand moves in 1975–6 to 184 thousand in 1981–2.

The analysis of aggregate movement data has demonstrated stability in the spatial structure of migration for the system of metropolitan and non-metropolitan zones. Consequently, techniques of short-term projection are preferred which are based upon the pattern of previous movement. Methods of modelling the historical effect are among those which are discussed in the next section.

8.4 A modelling system

8.4.1 Migration modelling and population projection

There exists in the literature a wide variety of migration models and, although a broad distinction can be drawn between spatial interaction models, intervening opportunities models, econometric models and probability models (Stillwell 1975) on the basis of structural form and calibration methodology, each has its own specific characteristics in terms of the definition and measurement of the migration variable, the zone system used and the effects which the model builds in. Regression techniques are frequently used for explanatory analysis in order to determine the effects of independent variables upon migration.

The development and use of migration models for projection and forecasting is less well advanced, and most studies have been undertaken in the context of population projection (Gilje & Campbell 1973, Joseph 1977, Martin Voorhees Associates & John Bates Services 1981). Given the importance of the migration component in population change, it becomes essential to develop a system which integrates the projection of both population and migration in such a way that it is possible to explore the consequences of using alternative migration models or of making particular choices about the way in which projections are constructed (see Chapter 7). The accounts-based model for age-disaggregated population projection described in Rees and Wilson (1977) has the advantage that interzonal flows rather than net flows can be incorporated explicitly. We must recognize that there is not necessarily a best method of projecting interzonal flows within a system; rather, there are likely to be a number of alternative methods which may be applicable, the choice of which will depend upon factors such as the availability of historical time-series, the characteristics of the flows and the purpose for which projections are constructed. It is therefore in our interest to develop a system which includes a range of models for migration projection so that different types of model can be selected under a variety of data situations and so that projections generated by different methods can be compared and evaluated.

If we assume no information about the projection period except the initial age-disaggregated population stocks, there are three questions to be asked which are particularly important since they dictate the type of models selected.

(1) Is interzonal migration to be projected directly or through stages involving projection of overall levels or gross flows?
(2) Is age-disaggregated interzonal migration to be projected directly or through stages involving age-group aggregation and deconsolidation procedures?
(3) Is there a requirement to incorporate non-demographic variables?

The first question provides the focus for the remainder of this chapter. Methods of projecting migration levels, zonal outmigration and inmigration totals and interzonal flows are outlined in the following section and age-disaggregated NHSCR movement data are then used to test a set of alternative models. The second question raises the issue of whether migration projections should be initially generated at an aggregate or broad age-group level and subsequently deconsolidated into smaller age groups. The decision to adopt this type of approach may become necessary if projections are required for one-year age-group flows; and methods involving model migration schedules can be employed in this situation. Further research is required to compare the results of projections involving aggregate modelling and age-group deconsolidation with those reported here. The incorporation of non-demographic data is feasible with several of the models outlined, but projections of variables influencing migration are frequently less reliable than projections of migration based on demographic information. Consequently migration projection has tended to be undertaken on the basis of rates analysis or trend extrapolation where time-series data are available.

8.4.2 Migration projection methods

There are theoretical arguments which suggest that migration occurring between a set of areal units can be partitioned into three components, each of which is likely to be influenced by a different set of factors. The first component is the general migration propensity, measured by the total number of interzonal moves that occur in the system. Secondly, there is the migration generation (or attraction) component whch is represented by the gross outflow (or inflow) from (or into) any given zone. The third component is the distribution component which refers to the flow of migrants from zone i to zone j. A variety of methods exist for projecting each of these components.

8.4.2.1 PROJECTING LEVELS OF MIGRATION

The projection of migration levels, like that of gross flows, depends upon the extent of the data time-series. If data for only one historical period are available, projections for age group a can be generated using a rate l_a defined as

$$l_a = \frac{\sum_i \sum_j M_a^{ij}(t, t + T)}{\sum_i P_a^i(t)} \tag{8.18}$$

where $\sum_i P_a^i$ refers to the total population in age group a at the beginning of the historical period $(t, t + T)$. This rate can then be applied to a projection period population. When data are available for two historical periods $(t, t + T)$ and $(t + T, t + 2T)$, projections can be generated according to the changes observed between the two periods. A migration propensity multiplier lm_a can be defined on the basis of change in flow totals:

$$lm_a = \frac{\sum_i \sum_j M_a^{ij}(t+T, t+2T)}{\sum_i \sum_j M_a^{ij}(t, t+T)} \qquad (8.19)$$

or change in rates:

$$lm_a = \frac{\sum_i \sum_j M_a^{ij}(t+T, t+2T)}{\sum_i P_a^i(t+T)} \left/ \frac{\sum_i \sum_j M_a^{ij}(t, t+T)}{\sum_i P_a^i(t)} \right. \qquad (8.20)$$

As the time-series is extended, more sophisticated methods of extrapolation can be used to generate trend-based projections. Ideally, projections should be sensitive to the likely effects on migration of fluctuations in the economy or changes in technology for example, but this requires formal measurement of the relationships involved.

8.4.2.2 PROJECTING OUTMIGRATION OR INMIGRATION TOTALS FOR ZONES

Similar methods to those described above can be used to prepare projections of gross zonal outmigration or inmigration or both. Historical outmigration rates, o_a^i, defined as

$$o_a^i = \frac{\sum_j M_a^{ij}(t, t+T)}{P_a^i(t)} \qquad (8.21)$$

can be applied to projection period populations either directly or after adjustment for changes in the general level of mobility using the multiplier defined in either Equation 8.19 or Equation 8.20. Gross inmigration projections should theoretically be produced using admission rates, where the at-risk population stocks are those persons in age group a in each zone at the end of the period. However, populations at the end of the projection period are often unavailable.

An alternative method of generating gross flow projections assumes that the overall level of migration has been projected independently. The empirical evidence presented in Section 8.3.4 indicated that the proportional distribution of outmigration remains stable over time, and consequently the overall total can be disaggregated on the basis of probabilities observed in the historical period. The outmigration probability po_a^i, is defined as

$$po_a^i = \frac{\sum_j M_a^{ij}(t, t+T)}{\sum_i \sum_j M_a^{ij}(t, t+T)} \qquad (8.22)$$

and, if an adequate time-series is available, projections of gross out-migration or inmigration probabilities can be based on trend. Further methods of gross inflow projection might involve the adjustment of historical inmigration rates using multipliers reflecting the changes in each zone's proportion of total employment, or the use of the relationship between inmigration rates and outmigration rates which have been shown to exist for mobility within certain zone systems (Cordey-Hayes & Gleave 1974).

8.4.2.3 PROJECTING INTERZONAL MIGRATION FLOWS

The distribution of migrants between origin and destination zones can also be achieved in several different ways, depending upon the amount of information that is provided exogenously and which can be used to constrain the flow projections. The simpler type of distribution model is one in which $\widetilde{M}_a^{ij}$, the projected migration flow between zone i and zone j of persons in age group a, is estimated by applying m_a^{ij}, the migration rate observed for a previous historical period, to $\widetilde{P}_a^i$, the age-group population at the commencement of the projection period. The model is

$$\widetilde{M}_a^{ij} = m_a^{ij}\widetilde{P}_a^i \qquad (8.23)$$

where the symbol $\sim$ indicates that the variable is associated with a projection period. The population stocks are generated as the final populations of the previous projection period by a suitable projection model and input to the migration model. This type of model is popular in forecasting (Joseph 1975) and the results obtained can be used as a standard for comparing projections constructed using other methods.

A second type of model is one in which projected totals of migration in each age group, L_a, are distributed on the basis of two probabilities derived from data for an historical period. This type of model has been used for historical analysis of Dutch data by Baydar (1983). A conditional probability projection model has the form

$$\widetilde{M}_a^{ij} = \widetilde{L}_a po_a^i pm_a^{ij} \qquad (8.24)$$

where po_a^i is the gross outmigration probability defined in Equation 8.22, and

$$pm_a^{ij} = \frac{M_a^{ij}(t, t+T)}{\sum\limits_j M_a^{ij}(t, t+T)} \qquad (8.25)$$

represents the probability of migration to zone j, given that the migrant originates from zone i. An alternative formulation can be expressed which distributes the total figure according to the probability of migration from zone i conditional on the probability of inmigration to zone j.

If gross outmigration and inmigration flows are projected independently, growth factor methods can be used to distribute these totals on the basis of the migration distribution associated with a historical period. A doubly constrained growth factor model for migrants in age group a has the form

$$\widetilde{M}_a^{ij} = \widetilde{A}_a^i \widetilde{B}_a^j \widetilde{g}_a^{ij} M_a^{ij} \qquad (8.26)$$

where the growth factor is

$$\widetilde{g}_a^{ij} = \frac{\widetilde{O}_a^i}{O_a^i} \frac{\widetilde{D}_a^j}{D_a^j} \qquad (8.27)$$

and where the balancing factor, $\widetilde{A}_a^i$ and $\widetilde{B}_a^j$, ensure that the row elements for each zone sum to the respective projected gross outflow total, and the column elements for each zone sum to the projected gross inflow total. The effect of historical dependence is implicit in this model which factors the observed matrix according to the product of the ratio between the projected and the historical row and column sums.

Spatial interaction models can also be used for the purpose of generating flow distributions from gross flow totals, although calibration is required prior to projection in order to estimate the best-fit parameters. In the doubly constrained model, the gross totals represent precise estimates of origin and destination zone 'attractiveness', and the impact of distance on migration is introduced through a negative power or a negative exponential distance function. Origin zone-specific decay parameters are used for projection if they improve model fits for the historical period. The projection model can be written as

$$\widetilde{M}_a^{ij} = \widetilde{A}_a^i \widetilde{B}_a^j \widetilde{O}_a^i \widetilde{D}_a^j d^{ij - \beta(i,a)} \qquad (8.28)$$

When projections of either gross outmigration or gross inmigration are unavailable, singly constrained models can be constructed in which the 'attractiveness' of either origins or destinations is represented by other types of data. The use of economic indicators to represent the destination 'attractiveness' term is one mechanism for linking migration projections with economic forecasts.

The methods which have been described in this section do not make up a comprehensive set of migration models. They represent a selection of models, the predictive capabilities of which we wish to compare in the next section.

8.4.3 A comparison of four approaches to movement projection

There are very few studies reporting the accuracy of alternative migration projections. The aim of this section is to explore the effectiveness of approaches described previously by using them to generate projections which can be compared against 'observed' flows. The NHSCR movement data are used for this purpose, and the year commencing mid-1979 has been chosen as the base period for producing forecasts of age-disaggregated interzonal moves during 1980–1 and 1981–2. Statistical indices are required to measure the degree of agreement between projected and 'observed' flow matrices. The results are reported in terms of the average deviation between the 'observed' and projected flows for each age group or

$$\frac{\sum_{ij}\left| M_a^{ij} - \tilde{M}_a^{ij} \right|}{\sum_{ij} M_a^{ij}}$$

This summary measure, usually expressed as a percentage, is rather crude but has the advantage of being relatively easy to interpret.

The projections are divided into four sets shown in Figures 8.13, 8.14, 8.15 and 8.16. The first set consists of those constructed using a simple rates model as specified in Equation 8.23. Figure 8.13 indicates the amount of variation in the average deviation between age-group projections for each of the two single-year periods. The average deviation varies from 7.8% (30–34 age group) to nearly 17% (65–69 age group) in the first period and there is a tendency for projection of movement to be more accurate for the younger age groups where the flows are larger. Projections for 1981–2 are less accurate than those for 1980–1 in the younger age groups but more accurate in certain of the older age groups.

The second set of projections are generated by a conditional probability model (Eqn 8.24) supplied with rate-based projections of age-group movement levels (Eqn 8.18). These projections tend to be only marginally

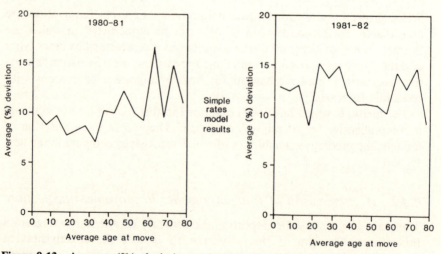

Figure 8.13 Average (%) deviations of 1979–80-based age-specific projections using a simple rates model.

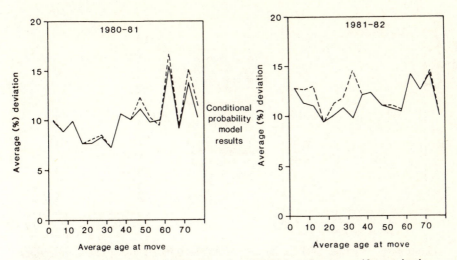

Figure 8.14 Average (%) deviations of 1979–80-based age-specific projections using a conditional probability model.

less accurate than those incorporating observed levels of movement, and the pattern of deviation across the age groups in both projection periods resembles the pattern observed from the first set of projections.

The third set of projections is prepared in two stages. Zonal outmigration and inmigration flows are forecast in the first stage and distributed among

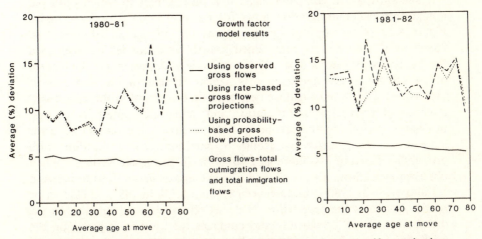

Figure 8.15 Average (%) deviations of 1979–80-based age-specific projections using a doubly constrained growth factor model.

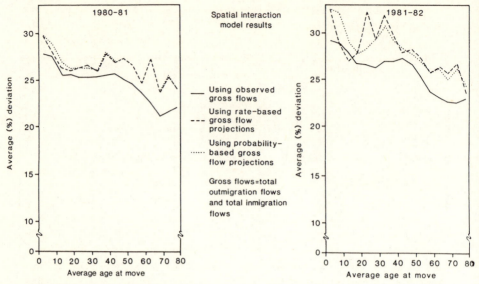

Figure 8.16 Average (%) deviations of 1979–80-based age-specific projections using a doubly constrained spatial interaction model.

zones in the second stage using a growth factor method (Eqn 8.26). One subset of projections in the first stage involves rate-based outmigration and inmigration flow projections (Eqn 8.21), whereas the other subset contains gross flow projections based on forecast movement levels (Eqn 8.18), which are disaggregated into zonal outflow and inflow totals using historical probabilities (Eqn 8.22).

These subsets are compared against a third subset in which observed inmigration and outmigration flows for the projection period are input. Figure 8.15 shows the average deviations for projections of interzonal moves in which a doubly constrained growth factor model has been used for distributing the gross flows. The magnitude of deviation and the pattern of variation between age groups is similar to that of the first sets of projections with little to choose between rate-based and probability-based methods of forecasting outmigration and inmigration totals in the first projection period. In the second projection period the margin of error increases in the younger age groups in particular, and projections with probability-based gross flows are superior in most age groups. When observed gross flows are distributed, the average deviation falls to between 5.1 and 4.1% in 1980–1 and between 6.2 and 5.1% in 1981–2. This set of results illustrates the proportion of deviation which is attributable to the distribution model specifically and confirms the need to improve on the methods of gross flow projection which have been used so far.

The fourth set of projections was also prepared in two stages. Zonal outmigration and inmigration flow projections described previously were distributed using a doubly constrained spatial interaction model with origin-specific decay parameters (Eqn 8.28). The results presented in Figure 8.16 indicate a decline in the goodness of fit as compared with other approaches. The average deviation fluctuates between 23 and 30% for both subsets involving projected gross flows for 1980–1, and most of the deviation is accounted for by the distribution model in both projection periods. There is a tendency for the model to generate better projections in the older age groups, where the influence of distance on migration is more pronounced.

8.5 Conclusions

The long-term aim of this research is to construct a system for producing projections of age-disaggregated migration that can be used in population forecasting. In the course of doing so, it is helpful to examine some of the characteristic features of internal migration in the UK. The empirical results presented in this chapter verify the potential of adopting the metropolitan and non-metropolitan regions as a set of study zones. The process of decentralization from large urban centres to their respective hinterlands is one of the most important characteristics of the pattern of UK internal migration in the past 20 years. In addition, there emerges a distinct hierarchy of areas, ordered on the basis of net inflows from other zones in the system. The aggregate pattern of metropolitan net losses and non-metropolitan net gains is consistent across most age groups, with certain exceptions, and although the general pattern of flows remained the same between 1966–71 and 1976–81 the evidence suggests a decline in each metropolitan area's share of total outmigration and an increase in each metropolitan area's share of total inmigration. A slowing down in the process of decentralization is most apparent for Greater London and, moreover, the annual movement data since 1975–6 indicate a decline in the level of mobility throughout the UK. Outmove and interzonal move proportions confirm that while the level of migration fluctuates the spatial pattern remains fairly stable. The main characteristic of change in the age structure of movement since 1975–6 is the downward trend in the proportion of infants and children aged 5–9 moving with their parents in the 25–29 age bracket.

The chapter has drawn attention to the limitations of both census-based transition data and register-based moves data and to the difficulties faced in preparing and comparing different types of data for a common zone system. The investigation of spatial and age-group differentials in the propensity to migrate over distance has shown that there is no necessary relationship between the location of one zone relative to others and the influence of distance upon outmigrants from that zone or migrants to that zone. There is a tendency for the friction of distance effect to be greater on outmigrants from metropolitan zones than on those from non-metropolitan zones, and on migrants in the latter half of the age range. The magnitude and spatial pattern of variation in zone-specific distance decay parameters calibrated for aggregate flows are similar between 1966–71 and 1976–81, but age differentials are not strictly comparable between the two periods.

The empirical analyses reported in Section 8.3 provide several clues about effective methods of constructing projections. In particular, decomposition enables separate projection of the more stable and less stable components of migration. Historical dependence models based on conditional probabilities or growth factors are therefore likely to be suitable for distributing projected levels or gross flows. In Section 8.4 age-disaggregated projections constructed using these models were compared alongside sets of projections generated using a simple rates approach and a doubly constrained spatial interaction model. The mean age-group deviation between 'observed' and projected flows for 1980–1 and 1981–2 is significantly larger for the spatial interaction model, whereas the other three methods produce projections which are similar in the magnitude and age-group pattern of deviation. One of the problems with these tests of projection is that the observed age-disaggregated data have been estimated and this renders the results less meaningful. Nevertheless, it can still be argued that the proportion of error attributable to the distribution process is still significantly lower in the case of the growth factor model, and an approach which distributes gross flows on the basis of the pattern of historical migration has the potential to produce more accurate projections.

Further work is clearly required to develop more advanced methods of gross flow projection which utilize the available time series data; to test alternative projection methods using more specific statistical indices; to explore the consequences of modelling age-aggregated flows, which can subsequently be deconsolidated; and to examine methods of incorporating non-demographic information.

9

Forecasting place-to-place migration with generalized linear models

FRANS WILLEKENS and NAZLI BAYDAR

9.1 Introduction

During the past two decades, with the drop of fertility to below replacement levels in most European countries and with the very low and nearly stabilized mortality levels, migration has emerged as the most important component of the population dynamics. The population sizes of subnational divisions and the population distribution at the national level are now to a large extent determined by migration behaviour. Therefore migration plays an increasingly critical rôle in subnational or regional population forecasts. The integration of migration in demographic projection models has been an issue for several years. An overview of classical approaches is presented by Pittenger (1976). A dominant feature of these approaches is that only net migration, that is, inmigration minus outmigration, is taken into account. More recently, the net migration component has been decomposed into gross inflows and outflows. In the multiregional approach the gross outflow of a particular region is further disaggregated by region of destination. The result is a set of place-to-place or origin-specific and destination-specific migration flows. The gross inflow of a region is obtained by summing the relevant destination-specific outflows.

The consideration of place-to-place migration flows for regional population projection leads to two basic issues. The first issue relates to the projection model and may be formulated as follows: how should the dependence of the population at a given time t on past migration patterns be modelled? Generally, some simplifying assumptions are introduced. The assumption that the migration pattern of persons in a given year is independent of the migration patterns in previous years implies that the population size and composition (by region) at time t only depends on the migration during the interval prior to t and on the population at $t - 1$. This simplified dependence may be described by a Markov model (Rogers 1968, 1975). The second issue

203

relates to the prediction of migration patterns. To forecast the population by region, migration must be predicted.

To clarify this issue and its implications we may adopt a systems perspective. Interregional migration may be considered as one of the realizations of linkages that exist between regions of a nation. The regions may therefore be treated as elements of a multiregional system and the linkages as the relationships between the elements. The system is situated in an environment. For multiregional demographic systems, the environment consists of the rest of the world and of non-demographic (e.g. economic, cultural, political) systems. In regional population forecasting, we are interested in forecasting the evolution of the system elements, in which the impact of the linkages has to be taken into account and the impact of the environment may be considered. In interregional migration forecasting, our interest is in the forecasting of the linkages. In order to forecast the linkages, we must understand their dynamics. The dynamics or pattern of change of the linkages may be attributed to two factors. The first factor is the inertia present in any system. In normal circumstances relations do not change rapidly. The second factor is the influence of the environment. The consequence of the inertia factor will be referred to as 'internal dynamics', the consequence of external factors will be referred to as 'external dynamics'. The systems approach to forecasting interrelated elements has been described elsewhere in more detail (Willekens & Baydar 1983a).

To predict migration or linkages between regions we need to understand both the internal and the external dynamics. The impact of economic and other factors on migration has been the subject of considerable research. Whether this explanatory approach, which focuses on the external dynamics only, can improve forecasts is not yet certain. Demographers have recently become increasingly sceptical about the forecasting powers of socio-demographic or demo-economic models. Frequently the prediction of the migration pattern is easier than the prediction of the explanatory variables. The study of the inertia in interregional migration patterns has received much less attention. However, a few authors have shown that a proper decomposition of the migration patterns leads to some components that exhibit a considerable degree of stability (Wolpert 1969, Wolpert & Yapa 1971, Van der Knaap & Sleegers 1982, Baydar 1983). The identification of the stable aspects of the migration patterns may further be enhanced if the proper decomposition of the migration pattern is supplemented by proper transformation and differencing of the component variables. The latter approach is basic to time-series analysis. Consequently, ideas of time-series analysis may fruitfully be used to study the dynamics of migration, even when the specific techniques for time-series analysis may not be suitable.

In this chapter we focus on the internal dynamics of the multiregional system, in particular on the identification of the inertia and stationarity in the linkages (migration). The data base consists of a time-series of place-to-place migration flows. To obtain an insight in the internal dynamics, we first decompose the migration flows. Three components are distinguished:

(1) the overall level of migration in the country;
(2) a generation component;
(3) a distribution component.

The latter two components are probabilities and give the relative weight of each migration flow within the system. The dynamics (time dependence or time heterogeneity) of each component are studied. The dynamics of migration are considered to be an outcome of the dynamics of the three components. To investigate the time dependence of a component, we propose a generalized linear model (GLM). A GLM is a statistical tool which decomposes the observed variations in the dependent variable into two components. The first component is the one which is accounted for by a linear combination of model parameters. The linearity may be ensured by transforming the original dependent variable through a link function. The second component is the random residual. The GLM removes the restrictions imposed on the random component by conventional regression models. Once the link function and the stochastic structure are fully specified the GLM parameters may be estimated by maximum likelihood procedures. The main lines of the estimation procedure are described in Section 9.3.1. The transformation considered in this chapter is the logit transformation of the generation and the distribution components. The parameters of the GLM represent the effects of origin, destination, and time and of their interactions on the transformed variable. The time dependencies of the overall level of migration, of the generation component and of the distribution component can thus readily be quantified by the parameters of the GLM. The GLMs also allow us to incorporate explanatory variables in the model, although this is not used here.

The remainder of the chapter consists of three main sections. Section 9.2 describes the data set used for the analysis, derives the three components to be considered and presents an exploratory analysis of the pattern of change of each of the components. In Section 9.3, we design GLMs for the time-series data on the components. These submodels are integrated in Section 9.4 and the use of the integrated model for forecasting purposes is evaluated.

9.2 Analysis of the time-series migration data for forecasting purposes

Migration has always been thought of as the most volatile component of demographic dynamics. However, recent research indicates otherwise. Once the overall level of migration is controlled for, spatial distribution patterns are found to be remarkably stable. In this section we express a migration flow in terms of the product of an overall level component, a generation probability and a distribution probability. Each component is analysed separately. The analysis consists of two parts, namely a general description of the pattern of change and a quantification of the degree of stability of the components. First, however, we describe the data that we work with in the following subsections.

9.2.1 Database

Since 1958 the Central Bureau of Statistics (CBS) of the Netherlands has classified municipalities by degree of urbanization (for full details see Central Bureau of Statistics 1958, 1964, 1983). Initially the classification was based on the characteristics of the municipalities as revealed by the 1947 population census and the 1956 housing census. In 1964 the municipalities were reclassified according to the results of the 1960 census. A further reclassification, on the basis of the 1971 census, was carried out in 1976. A total of 12 urbanization categories are distinguished, but for the present analysis they are combined into six categories:

(1) *Rural municipalities*: over 20% of the economically active male population works in agriculture; the population is less than 5000; the density of the built-up area is low (<300 inhabitants per square km).

(2) *Industrialized rural municipalities*: over 50% of the economically active male population works in manufacturing industry (in 1960 and in 1970 over 80% of the active population were outside agriculture); the population is less than x, where $x = 20\,000$ in the 1956 census and $30\,000$ in the 1960 and the 1971 censuses.

(3) *Commuter municipalities*: 30% or more of the active population works in another municipality; 60% or more of the resident commuters are born elsewhere; the proportion of salaried employees to wage earners is more than y% ($y = 60$ in 1947 and 1960 and 80 in 1971).

(4) *Small towns*: the population is 2000 to 30 000 in the built-up area.

(5) *Medium-sized towns*: the population is 30 000 to 100 000 in the built-up area.

(6) *Large towns*: there are more than 100 000 inhabitants in the built-up area.

In 1971, there were 269 rural municipalities (11% of total population), 347 industrialized rural municipalities (21% of population), 137 commuter municipalities (13% of population), 71 small towns, 35 medium-sized towns and 14 large towns.

The scheme of classification prior to 1964 was slightly different. An additional category was distinguished which included the municipalities (16 in total), characterized by the heterogeneity of their population composition, that is, those which could be included in more than one of the remaining categories. For the present analysis this category was aggregated with the category of industrial rural municipalities. Apart from this the data pose two other problems. The first is related to the updating of the categorization as the data from 1960 and 1971 censuses became available. Table 9.1 shows the number of reclassifications. The impact of the reclassification has been studied by Borchert (1979). The resulting shifts in the migration data are discussed in Section 9.2.2. The second data problem results from the division, abolition and amalgamation of the municipalities during the 1958—82 period. These changes undoubtedly cause distortions in the migration data; however in this study we do not deal with the problem of overcoming these distortions (see Van Engen & Van der Knaap 1980, Van der Erf *et al.* 1983). Finally, we should note that 1966 migration data have not been compiled by CBS due to some administrative problems. Therefore the 1966 migration matrix is missing from the time-series and we have 24 annual place-to-place flow matrices from 1958 to 1982. Table 9.2 provides an illustrative selection of these flow matrices.

9.2.2. Analysis of migration flows by components

We can express the number of migrations from origin i to destination j at year t, m_{ijt}, as

$$m_{ijt} = N_t w_{it} p_{ijt} \tag{9.1}$$

where

$N_t = m_{\cdot\cdot t} = $ the total number of migrations during year t;

$w_{it} = \dfrac{m_{i\cdot t}}{N_t} = $ the probability that a migration originates from region i during year t;

$p_{ijt} = \dfrac{m_{ijt}}{m_{i\cdot t}} = $ the probability that a migration originating from region i ends in region j during year t.

The dot ($\cdot$) denotes summation; hence $m_{i\cdot t} = \Sigma_j m_{ijt}$ and $m_{\cdot\cdot t} = \Sigma_{i,j} m_{ijt}$. Note that $\Sigma_i w_{it} = w_{\cdot t} = 1$ and $\Sigma_j p_{ijt} = p_{i\cdot t} = 1$.

For a system of n regions the same model for year t may be written in matrix form as

$$\underset{(n \times n)}{\mathbf{M}_t} = \underset{(1 \times 1)}{N_t} \underset{(n \times n)}{\mathbf{W}_t} \underset{(n \times n)}{\mathbf{P}_t} \tag{9.2}$$

where $\mathbf{W}_t$ is a diagonal matrix.

We now present the observed trends for each component of the

Table 9.1 Number of municipalities by urbanization category, 1961 and 1971.

Urbanization category in 1961	Urbanization category in 1971					
	Rural municipalities	Industrialized rural municipalities	Commuter municipalities	Small towns	Medium-sized towns	Large towns
rural (A1-4)	8	184	50	0	0	0
industrialized rural (B1-2)	0	134	36	3	3	0
commuter (B3)	0	0	49	0	1	0
small (C1-2)	0	4	0	62	4	0
medium (C3-4)	0	0	0	0	23	1
large (C5)	0	0	0	0	0	12

Table 9.2 The origin–destination-specific migration flows by the type of municipalities in the Netherlands, selected years.

Destination	Origin						
	Rural municipalities	Industrialized rural municipalities	Commuter municipalities	Small towns	Medium-sized towns	Large towns	Total
Year 1958							
rural municipalities	47 602	16 029	5 749	11 116	13 322	18 379	112 197
industrialized rural municipalities	19 896	17 081	4 639	7 365	13 266	20 304	82 551
commuter municipalities	6 077	4 132	7 142	2 581	7 882	23 133	50 947
small towns	15 197	7 348	2 769	5 762	6 755	10 541	48 372
medium-sized towns	15 833	12 590	7 314	7 457	12 862	24 864	80 920
large towns	19 154	16 538	15 923	10 264	23 495	29 701	115 075
total	123 759	73 718	43 536	44 545	77 582	126 922	490 062
Year 1970							
rural municipalities	44 333	18 843	11 010	17 858	18 870	33 149	144 063
industrialized rural municipalities	20 432	21 585	8 777	13 327	18 622	30 016	112 759
commuter municipalities	8 592	7 223	13 477	4 874	13 818	38 509	86 493
small towns	20 269	13 335	5 508	10 237	11 852	20 973	82 174
medium-sized towns	15 168	14 115	10 331	9 580	15 814	28 373	93 381
large towns	19 641	19 066	21 277	13 689	22 690	29 153	125 516
total	128 435	94 167	70 380	69 565	101 666	180 173	644 386
Year 1982							
rural municipalities	12 889	12 305	6 614	9 705	9 695	14 251	65 459
industrialized rural municipalities	12 227	29 549	12 300	13 021	18 542	24 794	110 433
commuter municipalities	5 751	10 877	22 513	8 723	17 573	47 607	113 044
small towns	10 410	13 972	8 213	8 320	9 215	17 737	67 867
medium-sized towns	9 582	18 628	14 663	9 012	13 779	20 114	85 778
large towns	8 536	21 393	30 036	12 178	20 523	22 957	115 623
total	59 395	106 724	94 339	60 959	89 327	147 460	558 204

Note: A full set of tables for all 24 years is available in Willekens and Baydar (1983c).

Netherlands migration data by the degree of urbanization of the municipalities for the years 1958–82.

9.2.2.1 TOTAL NUMBER OF INTERMUNICIPAL MIGRATIONS

The total number of migrations in the Netherlands follows the pattern which is seen in most of the Western European countries. The migration level rapidly increased from the early 1960s to a peak in 1973, but it declined thereafter reaching a low point in 1979. During the last three years, from 1979 to 1982, the migration level shows another increase. However, the extent to which this trend will persist remains to be confirmed (see Figure 9.1). Although this level component undoubtedly is of importance for forecasting the number of migrations between each group of municipalities, we focus here on the 'patterns' of migration which are given by the remaining two components of the model, namely the generation and the distribution components.

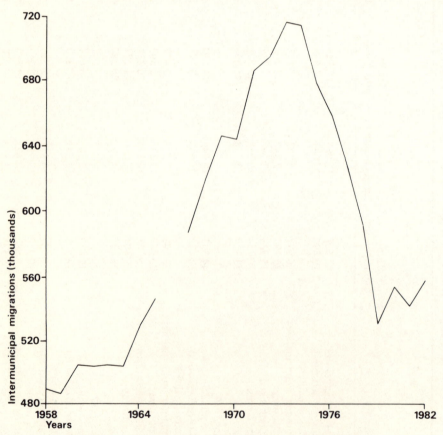

Figure 9.1 Total intermunicipal migrations (in thousands).

9.2.2.2 GENERATION COMPONENT

The generation components for the years 1958 to 1982 expressed as percentages are given in Figure 9.2. We observe jumps in the percentage shares of migration generation, especially at the years of reclassification, 1964 and 1976. The effect of reclassifications on the w_{it} component can be shown analytically.

Let K_{it} be the resident population in region i in the beginning of year t. The generation probability may be written as

$$w_{it} = \frac{m_{i \cdot t}}{N_t} = \frac{m_{i \cdot t}}{K_{it}} \frac{1}{N_t/K_{\cdot t}} \frac{K_{it}}{K_{\cdot t}} \tag{9.3}$$

The outmigration share of region i is a product of three components: risk of migration (migration rate) for the residents of region i; risk of migration in the country as a whole; the population share of region i. The national and the regional risks of migration definitely change over time, but they do

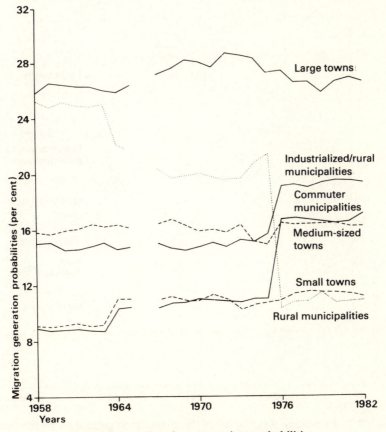

Figure 9.2 Migration generation probabilities.

211

not show drastic shifts and their trends may be considered gradual. Therefore a shift in w_{it} in 1964 and 1976 may, to a large extent, be attributed to the shifts in the relative shares of each type of municipality which are due to the reclassifications. This hypothesis is further supported by the comparison of Figure 9.2 which represents the generation component with Figure 9.3 which represents the population shares.

In 1958 the migrations out of the rural municipalities and out of large towns had approximately an equal share, and together they accounted for about 50% of the outmigrations. However, this picture changed gradually from 1958 to 1982. Large towns preserved their share, reached a maximum share of 28.6% in 1972, and declined a little afterwards to 26.4% until 1982. Rural municipalities on the other hand lost their share continuously, reaching 10.6% in 1982. The decline in their share is seen as an abrupt shift in the 1976 figure due to the reclassification mentioned in Section 9.2.1. This

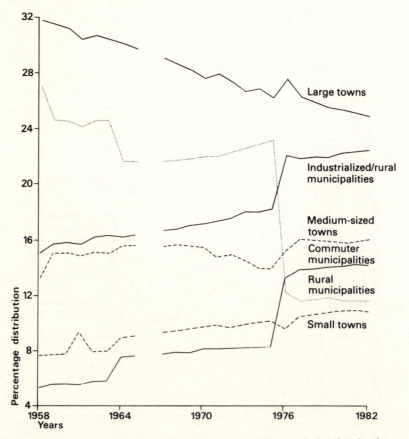

Figure 9.3 Percentage distribution of the Netherlands population by the degree of urbanization of the municipalities.

decline was compensated for by an increase in the shares of the industrialized rural municipalities and the commuter municipalities. The probability of outmigrating from industrialized rural municipalities, apart from a shift of level in 1976 seem to be quite stable. The commuter municipalities started with a 9% share in 1958, gradually increased their shares and, with a jump

Table 9.3 Distance measures for the migration generation vectors.

Intervals	Absolute deviation (AD)	Mean absolute deviation (MAD)	Information divergence A (IDA)	Information divergence B (IDB)
1958–59	0.014 809	0.075 562	0.000 144	0.000 143
1959–60	0.013 586	0.080 668	0.000 143	0.000 144
1960–61	0.007 501	0.051 065	0.000 039	0.000 039
1961–62	0.009 939	0.080 512	0.000 091	0.000 091
1962–63	0.010 973	0.069 372	0.000 073	0.000 073
1963–64	0.070 191	0.542 406	0.004 853	0.004 753
1964–65	0.015 082	0.079 486	0.000 132	0.000 132
1967–68	0.023 486	0.147 656	0.000 320	0.000 320
1968–69	0.016 356	0.092 034	0.000 177	0.000 178
1969–70	0.011 225	0.073 552	0.000 104	0.000 104
1970–71	0.015 214	0.097 217	0.000 142	0.000 141
1971–72	0.020 548	0.109 222	0.000 277	0.000 275
1972–73	0.020 783	0.152 518	0.000 413	0.000 416
1973–74	0.032 432	0.201 481	0.000 851	0.000 858
1974–75	0.025 645	0.132 218	0.000 400	0.000 400
1975–76	0.220 015	1.389 279	0.052 443	0.060 262
1976–77	0.019 975	0.127 896	0.000 312	0.000 312
1977–78	0.006 504	0.044 087	0.000 030	0.000 030
1978–79	0.019 824	0.123 897	0.000 335	0.000 333
1979–80	0.018 022	0.112 964	0.000 350	0.000 355
1980–81	0.007 931	0.044 323	0.000 042	0.000 042
1981–82	0.012 678	0.077 927	0.000 138	0.000 138
1958–82	0.292 267	1.984 306	0.089 564	0.101 555
1972–82	0.219 855	1.431 870	0.045 964	0.048 698

Notes:

$$AD = \sum_i \sum_j |m_{ijt} - m_{ijt+1}| \quad \text{where } |\ \ | = \text{absolute value of}$$

$$MAD = \sum_i \sum_j [\ |m_{ijt} - m_{ijt+1}|/m_{ijt}]$$

$$IDA = \sum_i \sum_j m_{ijt+1} \ln(m_{ijt+1}/m_{ijt})$$

$$IDB = \sum_i \sum_j m_{ijt} \ln(m_{ijt}/m_{ijt+1})$$

in 1976, reached a 17% share in 1982. The small and medium-sized towns constitute the stable components of the migration generation.

To summarize we may say that the migration generation patterns, except from the large shifts due to reclassifications, altered very little during the 25-year period. Migrations out of the large towns and migrations out of the rural municipalities have been the less stable elements of the migration generation.

The degree of stability may be quantified by the use of the distance measures between consecutive migration generation vectors given in Table 9.3. The distance measures between subsequent generation vectors are quite small, except for the distances between 1963–4 and 1975–6 vectors, referring to the years when the major reclassifications occurred. For instance, the information divergence due to the years 1975–6, accounts for about 86% of the total information divergence, and the mean absolute deviation due to the same period accounts for about 34% of the total mean absolute deviation observed over the 1958–82 period.

9.2.2.3 DISTRIBUTION COMPONENT

The distribution probabilities for the 1958–82 period are shown in Figures 9.4 to 9.9. The distribution components also show major shifts in the years of reclassification. The shifts cannot be attributed to changes in the population size of each category. Instead they are due to changes in the composition of the categories. For instance, in 1971, 234 rural municipalities were reclassified. A total of 184 became industrialized rural municipalities and 50 became commuter municipalities. If the migration pattern of the reclassified municipalities differed from the other municipalities, the distribution probabilities are affected.

Among the migrations originating from *rural municipalities*, until 1976 the largest flow has been towards rural municipalities. Thereafter the migrations to industrialized municipalities gained in their share whereas the share of the rural migrations to the large towns remained quite stable. For the migrations out of the rural municipalities, the least probable destinations are the commuter municipalities.

The distribution shares of the migrations out of the *industrialized rural municipalities* have been less stable, especially during the 1967–75 period. The most probable destinations of these migrations are the industrialized rural municipalities and the least probable destinations are the commuter municipalities. The probabilities of migrating to rural municipalities and to small towns increased until 1973 and decreased afterwards, whereas the probabilities of migrating to large and medium-sized towns have shown just the reverse trends.

From the *commuter municipalities* the largest flow by far is towards the large towns. Although before 1973 the probability of migrating to large

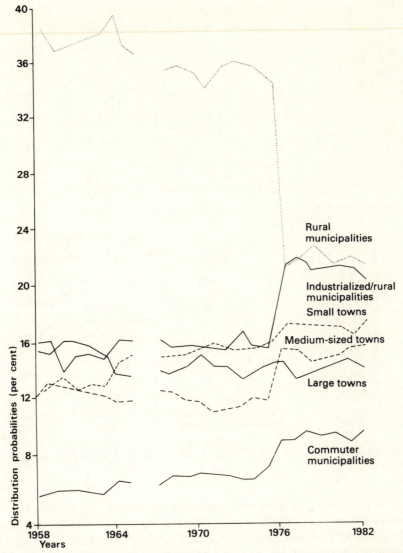

Figure 9.4 Distribution probabilities for the migration from rural municipalities.

towns was declining, in the last decade it showed a sharp turn and started to increase steadily, except for the reclassification year 1976. The migrations towards rural municipalities display the opposite trend. The migrations between commuter municipalities show an ever-increasing trend from about 1965 onwards. The least probable destination for the migrations out of the commuter municipalities was the small towns before 1976 and the rural municipalities from 1976 onwards.

215

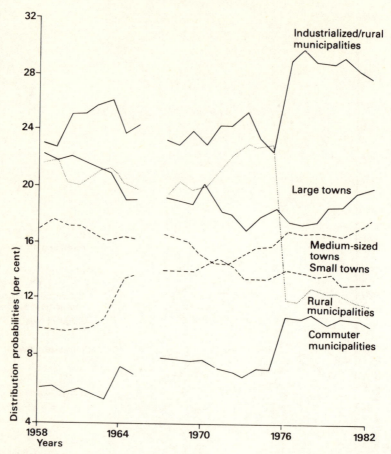

Figure 9.5 Distribution probabilities for the migration from industrialized rural municipalities.

Similarly, the probability of migrating from *small towns* to large and medium-sized towns declined until 1973 and increased afterwards, whereas the probability of migrating to rural municipalities had its peak in 1973. The commuter municipalities, although being the least probable destination for the migrations out of the small towns until 1981, definitely gained importance during the last decade and had a 14% share in 1982.

The migrations out of the *medium-sized towns* have very similar trends to the ones out of the small towns. However, the relative importance of the flows is quite different. The commuter municipalities constitute a much more important destination category, especially after 1976. During the last five years the most probable destination has been the large towns, whereas the least probable one has been the small towns.

Migrations originating from the *large towns*, although showing similar

216

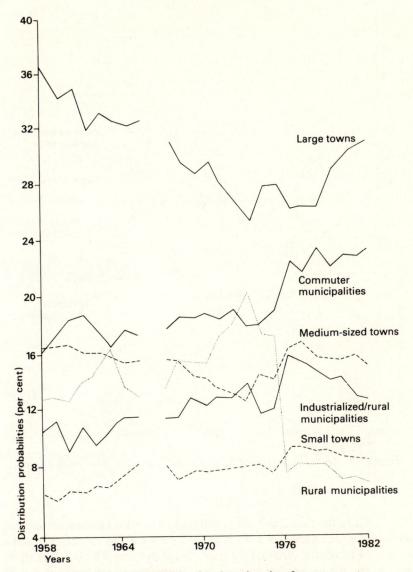

Figure 9.6 Distribution probabilities for the migration from commuter municipalities.

trends, have been much more volatile than the other flows. Apart from the major shifts due to the reclassifications of 1964 and 1976, large fluctuations have occurred, particularly for the flows towards the rural, industrialized rural, and commuter municipalities. Especially from 1976 onwards the commuter municipalities have been the most important category of destination, reaching a maximum share of 32% in 1982.

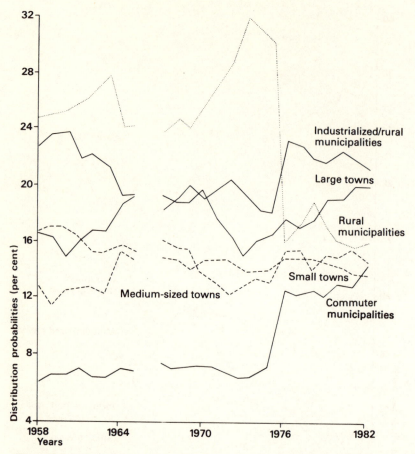

Figure 9.7 Distribution probabilities for the migration from small towns.

The changes in the distribution matrices may also be quantified. The summary distance measures are shown in Tables 9.4 and 9.5. Note that the distance measures for distribution matrices are in general higher than those observed for the generation component. The pattern of migrations out of large towns has been the most volatile component of migration distribution during the last 25 years. It accounts for 23% of the total information divergence. The shares of the other categories are: small towns 18%, medium-sized towns 17%, commuter municipalities 16%, industrialized rural municipalities 14% and rural municipalities 12%.

As a concluding note to the analysis of the components of migration we would like to make some summary remarks.

(a) The trends in the overall level of migrations have undergone a major

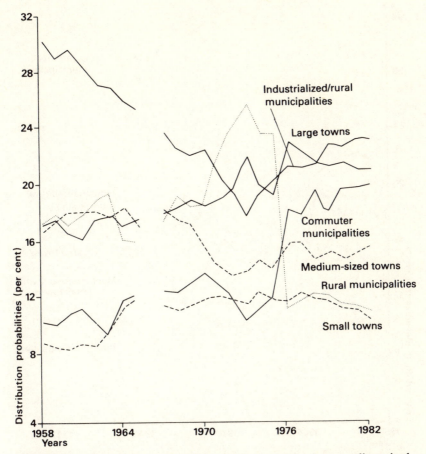

Figure 9.8 Distribution probabilities for the migration from medium-sized towns.

reversal, which was not only a reversal in size, but also a reversal of the structure of the distribution of migration.

(b) The generation component has remained remarkably stable over the last 25 years.

(c) The probabilities of migrating to large and medium-sized towns declined until 1973 and regained their importance after 1973.

(d) The probabilities of migrating to commuter municipalities have been increasing in magnitude, especially from the early 1960s onwards. In 1982 about one third of the migrants leaving large towns went to commuter municipalities. A large migration from commuter municipalities to large towns seems to indicate a considerable return migration.

(e) The probabilities of migrating to rural municipalities increased until 1973 and decreased afterwards.

219

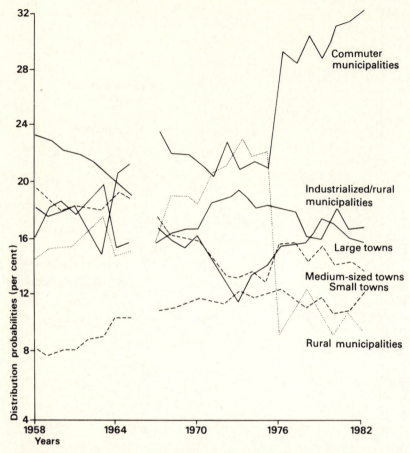

Figure 9.9 Distribution probabilities for the migration from large towns.

9.3 Modelling the components of migration

In this section we describe and illustrate an approach to modelling the components of interregional migration flows. The first subsection is an introduction to generalized linear models (GLMs) and an illustration of the models on a simple data set. The second subsection consists of the results of the analysis of the Netherlands time-series migration data for forecasting purposes. The data were processed by the GLIM program (Baker & Nelder 1978).

9.3.1 Introduction to the use of GLMs for modelling migration

In the previous section we described the representation of migration flows in terms of level, generation and distribution components. The generation

220

Table 9.4 Distance measures for the migration distribution matrices.

Intervals	Absolute deviation (AD)	Mean absolute deviation (MAD)	Information divergence A (IDA)	Information divergence B (IDB)
1958–59	0.221 830	1.451 790	0.006 496	0.006 471
1959–60	0.245 274	1.661 241	0.009 716	0.009 942
1960–61	0.211 930	1.355 994	0.007 223	0.007 144
1961–62	0.222 419	1.506 740	0.006 501	0.006 557
1962–63	0.218 042	1.431 978	0.006 429	0.006 429
1963–64	0.648 811	4.724 936	0.056 121	0.054 535
1964–65	0.139 248	0.911 676	0.002 488	0.002 496
1967–68	0.245 804	1.559 450	0.009 767	0.009 566
1968–69	0.146 073	0.940 066	0.003 014	0.002 992
1969–70	0.217 345	1.278 686	0.005 829	0.005 871
1970–71	0.371 030	2.128 332	0.015 917	0.015 748
1971–72	0.232 202	1.334 050	0.007 346	0.007 358
1972–73	0.369 690	2.234 802	0.014 979	0.015 004
1973–74	0.352 685	2.175 554	0.015 305	0.015 325
1974–75	0.148 600	1.058 543	0.003 183	0.003 159
1975–76	1.543 316	9.056 916	0.340 672	0.391 296
1976–77	0.161 665	1.088 011	0.004 662	0.004 578
1977–78	0.276 412	1.689 383	0.009 443	0.009 396
1978–79	0.246 426	1.451 398	0.009 021	0.009 053
1979–80	0.221 304	1.454 800	0.007 685	0.007 718
1980–81	0.193 613	1.209 932	0.005 430	0.005 414
1981–82	0.173 775	1.181 770	0.004 252	0.004 225
1958–82	1.801 847	12.777 560	0.399 961	0.392 548
1972–82	1.611 708	9.760 327	0.370 584	0.418 548

Note: see Table 9.3 for definitions of distance measures.

Table 9.5 Average percentage share of information divergence for each category of municipalities where migrations originate.

Rural municipalities	Industrialized rural municipalities	Commuter municipalities	Small towns	Medium-sized towns	Large towns
11.73	13.73	15.94	18.50	17.10	23.00

component represents the conditional probability of outmigration and the distribution component represents the conditional probability of going to a particular destination. These probabilities when displayed as an array would have a certain structure. The structure exhibited by the array of p_{ijt} elements may be made use of in forecasting. Because of the regularities, the data may be represented by means of parameters – which we call the effect parameters of origin i, destination j, time t – and their interactions. The segregation of time-dependent and time-independent components facilitates forecasting, which may be done by preserving the time-independent components and focusing attention on time-dependent components. In this section, we present a brief exposition of the specification of GLMs and of the estimation of the model parameters.

9.3.1.1 MODEL SPECIFICATION

For simplicity let us first consider a one-year migration matrix. As shown in Section 9.2, the number of migrations from i to j may be written as

$$m_{ij} = N w_i p_{ij} \qquad \text{where } N = m_{..} \tag{9.4}$$

Both the generation and the distribution probabilities may be modelled. To make sure that the probabilities predicted by a linear model lie between the boundaries zero and one and that they add to unity, we first transform the probabilities. The function by which we transform the dependent quantity is called the link function. We select a logit transformation. The logit transformation ensures that the predicted probabilities meet the desired properties. The model becomes linear in the parameters which describe the additive effects on logits of the probabilities. It may also be considered as a multiplicative model describing the probabilities. The model for the generation component is

$$\log \frac{w_i}{1 - w_i} = a + b_i \tag{9.5}$$

The model (Eqn 9.5) does not have an error term since the linear predictor describes the observed probabilities exactly. This is because w_i is a one-dimensional array so an overall effect and an origin effect are sufficient. Note that the number of terms in the model (Eqn 9.5) is more than the number of w_i observations. In this case only the first-order differences of the b_i parameters are estimable, which necessitates a normalization restriction on b_i parameters. The usual restrictions are

$$\sum_i b_i = 0 \quad \text{or} \quad b_1 = 0 \tag{9.6}$$

In this chapter we use the second alternative. However, once the b_i parameters are obtained for any normalization restriction they may be rescaled according to preference without affecting the predicted w_i probabilities. If no restrictions on b_i are imposed, the overall effect becomes redundant. The model becomes a non-hierarchical GLM.

The distribution probabilities, regarded as a two-dimensional array, would necessitate a more complicated linear predictor in order to be exactly described. The model which fully describes the p_{ij} probabilities, called a saturated model, is given as

$$\log \frac{p_{ij}}{1 - p_{ij}} = a + b_i + c_j + d_{ij} \qquad (9.7)$$

where a represents the overall effect, b_i the origin effect, c_j the destination effect and d_{ij} the effect of the interaction between origin and destination. Again the model has too many parameters and we need normalization restrictions on the b_i, c_j and d_{ij} parameters. The restrictions used in this chapter are $c_1 = 0$ and $d_{1j} = 0$. Since we do not restrict d_{i1}, we do not need the b_i term. Hence, b_i is set equal to zero for all i. This is done because the $p_{i\cdot} = 1$ for all i. The constraint $d_{i1} = 0$ can easily be introduced by letting $b_i = d_{i1}$ and subtracting d_{i1} from all interaction effects. Both models (Eqns 9.5 & 9.7) have zero degrees of freedom and have as many independent parameters as there are observations.

The p_{ij} probabilities may also be modelled by an unsaturated model that implies independence of origin i and destination j. The unsaturated model does not describe the p_{ij} terms exactly. The model becomes

$$\log \frac{\hat{p}_{ij}}{1 - \hat{p}_{ij}} = a + c_j \qquad (9.8)$$

where the $\hat{p}_{ij}$s are the predicted probabilities under the hypothesis of independence of the origin and destination. In the independence model, $b_i = 0$ for all i. We may also express the model in terms of the observed probabilities:

$$\log \frac{p_{ij}}{1 - p_{ij}} = a + c_j + \varepsilon_{ij} \qquad (9.9)$$

where ε_{ij} is the binomially distributed stochastic error term with mean zero. The c_j parameters in both models are subject to normalization restrictions. The unsaturated model implies that the migrations for i to j may be represented by a binomially distributed stochastic variable with a mean p_{ij}.

The models given by Equations 9.5, 9.7 and 9.9 are illustrated below for 1958 Netherlands migration data classified by urbanization categories. The data are given in Table 9.2 and Tables 9.6 and 9.7 display the results. The deviance or likelihood ratio statistic given in Table 9.6 may be used as a goodness-of-fit indicator. However, due to the fact that we have a very large number of cases —the whole population of migrants — and that the deviance is sensitive to the sample size, we do not perform any goodness-of-fit tests. Instead we try to select the appropriate model on the basis of inspection of the residuals, relative values of the deviance, and parsimony.

From Table 9.6 it is evident that the destination effect is not sufficient to represent the p_{ij} probabilities. The p_{ij} probabilities are therefore not independent of the region of origin i. The area of destination a migrant selects is affected by his or her area of origin. The dependence is fully taken into

Table 9.6 Parameters of the illustrative simple models.

Linear predictor	Deviance	Degrees of freedom	Grand mean	Region of destination	Region of origin (destination)					
					1	2	3	4	5	6
$\log \dfrac{w_i}{1-w_i} = a + b_i$	0	0	−1.085	—	0	−0.646	−1.243	−1.217	−0.586	0.034
$\log \dfrac{p_{ij}}{1-p_{ij}} = a + c_j + \varepsilon_{ij}$	60 120	30	−1.214	—	0	−0.382	−0.940	−0.992	−0.406	0.040
$\log \dfrac{p_{ij}}{1-p_{ij}} = a + c_j + d_{ij}$	0	0	−0.470	1	0	−1.183	−2.494	−1.497	−1.449	−1.228
				2	0	−0.811	−1.413	−0.631	−1.104	−1.306
				3	0	0.454	−0.474	0.034	0.074	−0.006
				4	0	0.140	1.335	0.175	0.784	1.462
				5	0	−0.235	−0.723	0.060	−0.384	−0.435
				6	0	0.339	0.320	0.315	0.304	0.507
					0	0.457	1.147	0.492	0.864	0.512
$\log \dfrac{p_{ij}}{1-p_{ij}} = a + c_j + d_{kj}$	7 932	15	−1.776	—	0	0.179	0.275	−0.436	0.155	0.590
				1	0	1.306	0.495	−0.107	0.675	0.202
				2	0	0	0	0	0	0
$k \begin{cases} = i, i = 1, 3, 6 \\ = 0, i = 2, 4, 5 \end{cases}$				3	0	−1.462	−1.323	−0.127	−1.288	−0.679
				4	0	0	0	0	0	0
				5	0	0	0	0	0	0
				6	0	−0.512	−0.055	0.635	−0.020	0.352

Note: the models are fitted to 1958 migration plans.

account in the saturated model. However, the saturated model requires many parameters, more than may be necessary to adequately represent the interaction pattern. Frequently, the data exhibit a simplified interaction pattern. For instance one may easily see that for the destination category 4 (small towns) and 5 (medium-sized towns) the probabilities are similar across all origins.

However, for the destination categories 1 (rural areas), 3 (commuter municipalities) and 6 (large towns), the probabilities show a larger variability among origins. Accordingly we may introduce interaction terms for these destinations only. We call such models – which have simplified patterns of interaction – hybrid models (Willekens & Baydar 1983b). Hybrid models provide a parsimonious alternative to traditional saturated models on the basis of *a priori* information. They are especially useful for modelling time-series data (see Sections 9.3.2 and 9.3.3), where the temporal variations exhibit a known pattern. For illustrative purposes, we display in Table 9.7 the results of the hybrid model mentioned above for the 1958 p_{ij} probabilities. Parameters are introduced to distinguish the destination selection of migrants from areas 1, 3 and 6. For the origins, 2, 4 and 5 a common set of destination parameters are postulated. The latter are set equal to zero in the normalization procedure.

Time-series of w_i or p_{ij} probabilities may easily be modelled by GLMs by extending the models given by Equations 9.5 and 9.7 appropriately. The saturated model for the w_{it} series is

$$\log \frac{w_{it}}{1 - w_{it}} = a + b_i + e_{it} \tag{9.10}$$

where the e_{it} parameters represent the dependence of effect of origin i and time t. These parameters are further restricted to generate the hybrid models in Section 9.3.2. The saturated model for the p_{ijt} series is more complicated:

$$\log \frac{p_{ijt}}{1 - p_{ijt}} = a + b_i + c_j + h_t + d_{ij} + f_{jt} + g_{ijt} \tag{9.11}$$

where h_t is the main effect of time, f_{jt} represents the time dependence of the effect of destination j, and g_{ijt} represents the time dependence of the origin–destination interaction. In Section 9.3.3 we generate hybrid models by imposing restrictions upon the time-dependent parameters of the model given by Equation 9.11, that is, f_{jt} and g_{ijt}. We do not attempt further restriction on the d_{ij} parameters since they are time independent and therefore do not enter the forecasting problem.

9.3.1.2 PARAMETER ESTIMATION

We mentioned above that we assume a binomial error structure for the logit model. For example, for the generation probabilities, the probability that

Table 9.7 Observed and fitted probabilities for the illustrative simple models.

| | | Observed and fitted values (%) | | | | | |
| | | Region of origin | | | | | |
Region of destination		1	2	3	4	5	6
$\log \dfrac{w_i}{1-w_i} = a + b_i$	—	25.25 (25.25)	15.04 (15.04)	8.88 (8.88)	9.09 (9.09)	15.83 (15.83)	25.90 (25.90)
$\log \dfrac{p_{ij}}{1-p_{ij}} = a + c_j + \varepsilon_{ij}$	1	38.46 (22.89)	21.74 (22.89)	13.21 (22.89)	24.95 (22.89)	17.17 (22.89)	14.48 (22.89)
	2	16.08 (16.85)	23.17 (16.85)	10.66 (16.85)	16.53 (16.85)	17.10 (16.85)	16.00 (16.85)
	3	4.91 (10.40)	5.61 (10.40)	16.40 (10.40)	5.79 (10.40)	10.16 (10.40)	18.23 (10.40)
	4	12.28 (9.87)	9.97 (9.87)	6.36 (9.87)	12.94 (9.87)	8.71 (9.87)	8.31 (9.87)
	5	12.79 (16.52)	17.08 (16.52)	16.80 (16.52)	16.74 (16.52)	16.58 (16.52)	19.59 (16.52)
	6	15.48 (23.48)	22.43 (23.48)	36.57 (23.48)	23.04 (23.48)	30.28 (23.48)	23.40 (23.48)

$$\log \frac{p_{ij}}{1-p_{ij}} = a + c_j + d_{ij}$$

	1	2	3	4	5	6
1	38.46 (38.46)	21.74 (21.74)	13.21 (13.21)	24.95 (24.95)	17.17 (17.17)	14.48 (14.48)
2	16.08 (16.08)	23.17 (23.17)	10.66 (10.66)	16.53 (16.53)	17.10 (17.10)	16.00 (16.00)
3	4.91 (4.91)	5.61 (5.61)	16.40 (16.40)	5.79 (5.79)	10.16 (10.16)	18.23 (18.23)
4	12.28 (12.28)	9.97 (9.97)	6.36 (6.36)	12.94 (12.94)	8.71 (8.71)	8.31 (8.31)
5	12.79 (12.79)	17.08 (17.08)	16.80 (16.80)	16.74 (16.74)	16.58 (16.58)	19.59 (19.59)
6	15.48 (15.48)	22.43 (22.43)	36.57 (36.57)	23.04 (23.04)	30.28 (30.28)	23.40 (23.40)

$$\log \frac{p_{ij}}{1-p_{ij}} = a + c_j + d_{kj} + \varepsilon_{ij}$$

$$k \begin{cases} = i \text{ for } i = 1, 3, 6 \\ = 0 \text{ for } i = 2, 4, 5 \end{cases}$$

	1	2	3	4	5	6
1	38.46 (38.46)	21.74 (21.74)	13.21 (13.21)	24.95 (24.95)	17.17 (17.17)	14.48 (14.48)
2	16.08 (16.85)	23.17 (16.85)	10.66 (16.85)	16.53 (16.85)	17.10 (16.85)	16.00 (16.85)
3	4.91 (4.91)	5.61 (5.61)	16.40 (16.40)	5.79 (5.79)	10.16 (10.16)	18.23 (18.23)
4	12.28 (9.87)	9.97 (9.87)	6.36 (9.87)	12.94 (9.87)	8.71 (9.87)	8.31 (9.87)
5	12.79 (16.52)	17.08 (16.52)	16.80 (16.52)	16.74 (16.52)	16.58 (16.52)	19.59 (16.52)
6	15.48 (15.48)	22.43 (22.43)	36.57 (36.57)	23.04 (23.04)	30.28 (30.28)	23.40 (23.40)

Note: the fitted values are in parentheses.

out of N migrations a migration occurs from origin i is assumed to follow a binomial distribution with a mean w_i. Similar assumptions apply to the distribution probabilities. Since the binomial distribution is a member of the exponential family, the maximum likelihood estimators of the parameters of a logit–linear model with binominal error structure may be found by an iterative weighted least squares procedure (Nelder & Wedderburn 1972). Below we present the basic equations.

Let

y   be the vector of the dependent variable to be modelled, with elements y_i,

η be the vector of expected values of the transformed dependent variables (in our example the expected logits of migration probabilities),

X   be the design matrix,

β be the vector of unknown parameters.

In matrix form the linear model may be written as

$$\eta = X\beta \tag{9.12}$$

and the maximum likelihood estimators for β may be found by iteration, provided that weights are known (or estimated on the basis of the observed variance of y_k) and X is of full column rank. In contingency table settings X is not usually of full rank since more parameters are considered than are strictly necessary for the description of the data. Therefore not the individual parameter values but their first-order differences are estimable. Normalization restrictions have to be imposed on the β_k parameters, which imply dropping columns of the design matrix until it becomes of full rank. However, some of the hybrid models do not allow the estimability of the first-order differences. In that case further restrictions on the β_k parameters are imposed until the design matrix becomes of full column rank. These restrictions which are needed to solve the second-order difference equations for β_k parameters are called identification specifications (Willekens & Baydar 1983b). The normalization restrictions arise because of the over-parametrized nature of the model. The identification specifications imply that the observations do not provide sufficient information to model all the independent variables included in the model. The identification specifications have an impact on all estimated first-order differences of the parameters. In other words, the inferences on the relative magnitude of the parameters can only be made conditional on the identification specifications. Neither normalization restrictions nor identification specifications have any effect on the predicted values of the dependent variable (η) and the goodness-of-fit measures.

9.3.2   Modelling the generation component

The trends and basic features of the migration generation component during the years 1958–82 have already been summarized in Section 9.2.2.1

(see also Figure 9.2). In this section we present general linear models of the generation component starting with an unsaturated model with an origin effect only, given as

$$\text{FIT 1: } \log \frac{w_{it}}{1 - w_{it}} = a + b_i + \varepsilon_{it} \tag{9.13}$$

The models are labelled FIT 1 ... FIT 6 for easy reference following GLIM nomenclature. FIT 1 serves as a base model with reference to which we compare the performance of more complicated models. The unsaturated model predicts a generation probability for each origin category which is independent of year of observation. The predicted w_{it} probabilities are displayed in Figures 9.10 to 9.15. The summary indices of goodness of fit are given in Table 9.8. Evidently the unsaturated model with only an origin parameter is not sufficient to describe the data. We therefore elaborate the model to take account of the large shifts due to the reclassification in the year 1976.

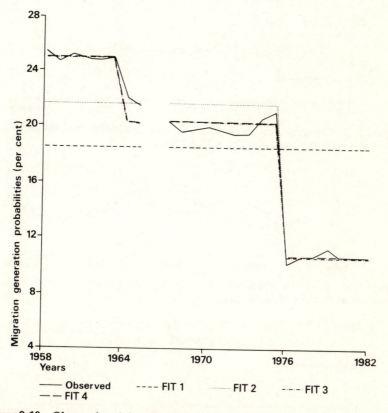

Figure 9.10 Observed and fitted values for the generation probabilities out of rural municipalities.

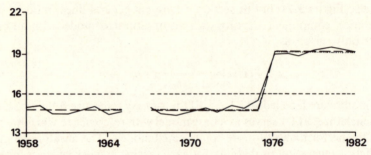

Figure 9.11 Observed and fitted values for the generation probabilities out of industrialized rural municipalities (see Fig. 9.10 for key).

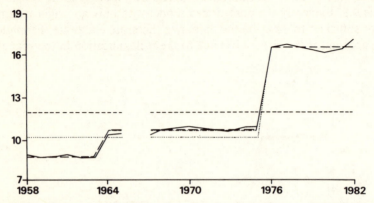

Figure 9.12 Observed and fitted values for the generation probabilities out of commuter municipalities (see Fig. 9.10 for key).

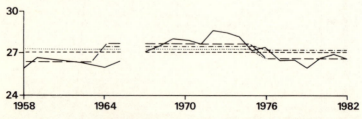

Figure 9.13 Observed and fitted values for the generation probabilities out of small towns (see Fig. 9.10 for key).

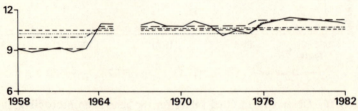

Figure 9.14 Observed and fitted values for the generation probabilities out of medium-sized towns (see Fig. 9.10 for key).

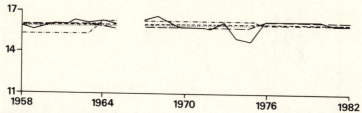

Figure 9.15 Observed and fitted values for the generation probabilities out of large towns (see Fig. 9.10 for key).

The model is

$$\text{FIT 2: } \log \frac{w_{it}}{1 - w_{it}} = a + b_i + h_{il} + \varepsilon_{it} \qquad (9.14)$$

$l = 1, 2$ with $l = 1$ for the years 1958 until 1975 ($t = 1, \ldots, 17$) and $l = 2$ for the years 1976 until 1982 ($t = 18, \ldots, 24$), where h_{il} represents the origin-specific shift parameter (interaction of the shift of 1976 with origin i). We may imagine a variable – a classification variable say, – with two levels only. The time periods before 1976 constitute the first level, and the time periods with and after 1976 constitute the second level. The parameter h_{il} represents the interaction of this classification variable with the origin. If $h_{i1} = 0$, then h_{i2} is the shift in the origin effects due to the reclassification in 1976. Its use is analogous to that of a dummy variable. The model shows a substantial improvement over FIT 1.

The model can be further elaborated to take account of the 1964 reclassification. Since the reclassifications affect certain origins more than others, we may restrict the interaction of origin and classification variables to zero for the unaffected origins. The reclassifications also affect some regions differently from other regions. We assume that the reclassification affects the small, medium-sized and large towns in the same way and allocate only one parameter to the three urbanization categories. The resulting model is

$$\text{FIT 3: } \log \frac{w_{it}}{1 - w_{it}} = a + b_i + h_{kl} + \varepsilon_{it} \qquad (9.15)$$

$$l = 1, 2, 3$$

$$k \begin{cases} = i \text{ for } i = 1, 2, 3 \\ = 4 \text{ for } i = 4, 5, 6 \end{cases}$$

This model allows the interaction of a three-level classification variable (1958–63, 1964–75, 1976–82) and the first three origin categories (namely the rural municipalities, the industrialized rural municipalities and the

231

Table 9.8 Summary indices for the models of the generation component.

Linear predictor	Deviance	Relative deviance as compared				Degrees of freedom
		FIT 1	FIT 2	FIT 3	FIT 4	
FIT 1: $\log \dfrac{w_{it}}{1-w_{it}} = a + b_i + \varepsilon_{it}$	457 400	100.0				138
FIT 2: $\log \dfrac{w_{it}}{1-w_{it}} = a + b_i + h_{il} + \varepsilon_{it}$ $l = 1,2$	53 450	11.7	100.0			132
FIT 3: $\log \dfrac{w_{it}}{1-w_{it}} = a + b_i + h_{kl} + \varepsilon_{it}$ $l = 1,2,3$ $k\begin{cases} = i, i = 1,2,3 \\ = 4, i = 4,5,6 \end{cases}$	16 990	3.7	31.8	100.0		130
FIT 4: $\log \dfrac{w_{it}}{1-w_{it}} = a + b_i + h_{il} + \varepsilon_{it}$ $l = 1,2,3$	9 939	2.2	18.6	58.5	100.0	126

commuter municipalities), which are the ones mostly affected by reclassifications. The fitted w_{it} probabilities are very close to the observed probabilities, especially for the three origins with which the classification variable is allowed to interact. Since the classification variable is not subject to forecasting, we may introduce interaction of the classification with all six origins without increasing the number of parameters to be forecast. We finally fit the model:

$$\text{FIT 4: } \log \frac{w_{it}}{1 - w_{it}} = a + b_i + h_{il} + \varepsilon_{it} \tag{9.16}$$

FIT 4 gives a very close fit, as can be seen from Figures 9.10 to 9.15 and Table 9.8. The model may be used for forecasting as estimated, provided that one is prepared to assume that no further reclassifications of the municipalities will be made and that no major structural changes in migration patterns will occur.

9.3.3 Modelling the distribution component

In Section 9.2.2.2 we summarized the major trends observed for the distribution component over the years 1958–82 and concluded that the distribution component has been less stable than the generation component. The changes in the level of migration have been accompanied by changes in the distribution structure, whereas the generation patterns have remained stable. This observation is further confirmed by the models of the distribution component (for summary indices see Table 9.9). As with generation probabilities, we start with a basic unsaturated model with only a main effect of destination:

$$\text{FIT 1: } \log \frac{p_{ijt}}{1 - p_{ijt}} = a + c_j + \varepsilon_{ijt} \tag{9.17}$$

The model assumes independence of the probability of migrating to j from the region of origin and time period of migration. In other words the model predicts one constant probability for destination j whatever the origin and year. The model is highly unrealistic, gives a very bad fit and creates convergence problems. The basic model may be elaborated by letting destination and time variables interact, or letting origin and destination variables interact, or both. The following three models try these alternatives respectively. FIT 2 predicts a destination and time-specific distribution probability irrespective of origin. In other words it models the time path of the destination effect. For each year t, a destination parameter is distinguished (d_{jt}). FIT 3 predicts an origin–destination-specific distribution probability which is constant over all years. FIT 4 combines FIT 2 and FIT 3. It considers the

Table 9.9 Summary indices for the models of the distribution component.

Linear predictor	Deviance	FIT 1	FIT 2	FIT 3	FIT 4	FIT 5	FIT 6	T-FIT 1	T-FIT 2	Degrees of freedom
FIT 1: $\log \dfrac{p_{ijt}}{1-p_{ijt}} = a + c_j + \varepsilon_{ijt}$	1 808 000 (n.c.)	100.00								858
FIT 2: $\log \dfrac{p_{ijt}}{1-p_{ijt}} = a + c_j + d_{jt} + \varepsilon_{ijt}$	1 329 000 (n.c.)	73.51	100.00							720
FIT 3: $\log \dfrac{p_{ijt}}{1-p_{ijt}} = a + c_j + e_{ij} + \varepsilon_{ijt}$	468 100	25.89	35.22	100.00						828
FIT 4: $\log \dfrac{p_{ijt}}{1-p_{ijt}} = a + c_j + d_{jt} + e_{ij} + \varepsilon_{ijt}$	68 440	3.79	5.15	14.62	100.00					680
FIT 5: $\log \dfrac{p_{ijt}}{1-p_{ijt}} = a + c_j + d_{jk} + e_{ij} + \varepsilon_{ijt}$	117 000	6.47	8.80	24.99	170.95	100.00				816
FIT 6: $\log \dfrac{p_{ijt}}{1-p_{ijt}} = a + c_j + d_{jk} + e_{ij} + f_{ijk} + \varepsilon_{ijt}$	77 570	4.29	5.84	16.57	113.34	66.30	100.00			756
T-FIT 1: $\log \dfrac{p_{ijt}}{1-p_{ijt}} = a + c_j + d_{jk} + e_{ij} + \beta_{I3}t + \beta_{iit}^{\delta}t + \varepsilon_{ijt}$	62 490	3.46	4.70	13.35	91.31	53.41	30.56	100.00		774
T-FIT 2: $\log \dfrac{p_{ijt}}{1-p_{ijt}} = a + c_j + d_{jk} + e_{ij} + \delta + c_j^{\delta} + e_{ij}^{\delta} + \beta_{I3}t + \beta_{iit}^{\delta}t + \varepsilon_{ijt}$	42 970	2.37	3.23	9.18	62.79	36.73	55.40	68.76	100.00	738

Note: n.c., no convergence has been obtained.

origin–destination interaction, averaged over the study period, and the time path of the destination effect. These three models are given as

$$\text{FIT 2: } \log \frac{p_{ijt}}{1 - p_{ijt}} = a + c_j + d_{jt} + \varepsilon_{ijt} \tag{9.18}$$

$$\text{FIT 3: } \log \frac{p_{ijt}}{1 - p_{ijt}} = a + c_j + e_{ij} + \varepsilon_{ijt} \tag{9.19}$$

$$\text{FIT 4: } \log \frac{p_{ijt}}{1 - p_{ijt}} = a + c_j + d_{jt} + e_{ij} + \varepsilon_{ijt} \tag{9.20}$$

FIT 2 gives very little improvement over FIT 1, yet creates convergence problems implying the unrealistic nature of the model. The limited contribution of d_{jt} demonstrates that the time dependence of the destination effect is relatively small compared to other interaction effects exhibited by the data but not considered in the model. A very important interaction exists between origin and destination. FIT 3 gives a large improvement over FIT 1, leading to the conclusion that the origin specificity of the destination effects of the migration flows among urbanization categories are more important than their time specificity. However, when we include both origin and time dependence of destination-specific probabilities we obtain a good fit (FIT 4). The time dependence of the destination effect is postulated in the model by associating a destination parameter with each year. Hence there are, in total, 144 parameters. We shall now investigate whether the number of parameters can be reduced without affecting the descriptive capacity of the model too much. First we shall see whether the time dependence is due to reclassifications. To this end, we shall consider three periods (1958–63, 1964–75, 1976–82) to see if the time dependence of directional migration probabilities are common within each period. We may consider two models. One assumes the dependence of reclassifications and destination, irrespective of the region of origin. The other assumes the dependence of each origin–destination-specific flow on reclassifications. These models are respectively given as

$$\text{FIT 5: } \log \frac{p_{ijt}}{1 - p_{ijt}} = a + c_j + d_{jk} + e_{ij} + \varepsilon_{ijt} \tag{9.21}$$

$$\text{FIT 6: } \log \frac{p_{ijt}}{1 - p_{ijt}} = a + c_j + d_{jk} + e_{ij} + f_{ijk} + \varepsilon_{ijt} \tag{9.22}$$

where
$$k = \begin{cases} 1 \text{ for } t = 1, \ldots, 6 \\ 2 \text{ for } t = 7, \ldots, 17 \\ 3 \text{ for } t = 18, \ldots, 24 \end{cases}$$

and f_{ijk} represents the origin–destination–reclassification interaction. The results of FIT 5 are not very encouraging. The destination–reclassification interaction does not absorb a large proportion of the destination–time interaction (compare FIT 5 with FIT 4). FIT 6 adds the origin–destination–reclassification interaction to the model and still does not reach the goodness of fit of FIT 4. It can be easily seen from Table 9.9 that among the first six models FIT 4 still stands as the best fit. The reason is that the reclassifications are not the only source of temporal shifts. Figures 9.4 to 9.9 clearly show non-negligible trends for the probabilities of migrating to large towns, medium-sized towns, commuter municipalities and rural areas. In order to be able to incorporate this information into the model without assigning one parameter to each destination-specific flow, we designed a GLM with parameters for the *discrete variables* origin, destination and reclassification, and the *continuous variable* time. The parameters of the discrete variables provide an intercept for each origin–destination and classification–period-specific probability, whereas the parameters of the continuous trend terms provide the slope of the time path within each period. The model thus becomes a mixture of a trend model and a hybrid contingency table model and incorporates the advantages of both:

(a) the trend component provides an easy framework for forecasting;
(b) the discrete variable component preserves the relational structure existing in the distribution component without complicating the forecasting procedure.

To distinguish between the models with discrete independent variables only and the ones with a continuous trend variable, we name the second type as trend-component models. For the distribution probabilities we propose two trend-component models. The first assigns a slope for each flow towards rural municipalities, commuter municipalities, medium-sized towns and large towns. The trends of migrations to industrialized rural municipalities and small towns are postulated to have zero slopes. Hence the trends of migrations to the first types of municipalities are expressed in relation to the trend of migrations to the latter municipalities. The 1958–73 and 1974–82 periods are treated separately, except for the flows towards commuter municipalities which have a smooth unidirectional trend during the 25 years. Therefore it is possible to have a negative slope for the 1958–73 period and a positive slope for the 1974–82 period. However, both periods have a common intercept in this model. The second trend-component model relaxes the assumption that both periods have a common intercept. We assign an intercept to each origin–destination-specific flow for the periods before and after 1973 for the destination regions mentioned above. This is achieved by postulating a dummy variable to denote the 1958–73 and 1974–82 periods and letting this dummy variable interact with the discrete component of the model as well as its trend component. Formally:

$$\text{T-FIT 1: } \log \frac{p_{ijt}}{1 - p_{ijt}} = a + c_j + d_{jk} + e_{ij} + \beta_{i3}t + \beta_{il}^{\delta}t + \varepsilon_{ijt} \qquad (9.23)$$

$$\text{T-FIT 2:} \quad \log \frac{p_{ijt}}{1 - p_{ijt}} = a + c_j + d_{jk} + e_{ij} + \delta + c_j^\delta + e_{ij}^\delta + \beta_{i3}t + \beta_{il}^\delta t + \varepsilon_{ijt}$$

$$(9.24)$$

where

$$k = \begin{cases} 1 \text{ for } t = 1, \ldots, 6 \\ 2 \text{ for } t = 7, \ldots, 17 \\ 3 \text{ for } t = 18, \ldots, 24 \end{cases}$$

$$l = \begin{cases} j \text{ for } j = 1, 5, 6 \\ 0 \text{ for } j = 2, 3, 4 \end{cases}$$

δ represents the dummy variable : $\delta = 0$ for $t = 1, \ldots, 15$ and $\delta = 1$ for $16, \ldots, 24$. When it appears as a superscript it denotes the interaction of the parameter with the dummy variable.

The second trend-component model provides a very good fit and meaningful parameter values for the slopes. Note that T-FIT 2 brings an improvement over FIT 4 which stood as the best model among the discrete models. The only improvement over FIT 4 in discrete variables would be the saturated model, which has an origin–destination–time interaction. The trend-component model, proposed by T-FIT 2 provides the best description of the observed p_{ijt} probabilities, and a framework for easily forecasting them. Furthermore it still preserves the interrelations displayed by the time-series of the distribution component (for full details of the parameters see Willekens & Baydar 1983c). The fitted p_{ijt} probabilities for two exemplary flows (from large towns to commuter municipalities and from medium-sized towns to large towns) are displayed in Figures 9.16 and 9.17. T-FIT 2 is the model on which forecasts of p_{ijt} probabilities may be based. The issue of relating these models in order to obtain forecasts of origin–destination-specific flows is discussed in the next section.

Because forecasting is the main theme of this chapter, we focus on the trend of the distribution component. We tried to identify which of the component effects (origin, destination or origin–destination) exhibited the largest time dependence (or time heterogeneity), and we tried to quantify the time dependence and to evaluate its significance for forecasting. However, it was also shown that the model specification is inadequate unless an origin–destination interaction term is included. The term considered in this chapter (e_{ij}) represents the average interaction during the period from 1958 to 1982. No real time dependence of the origin–destination interaction was assumed. The f_{ijk} term only accounts for the effects of reclassification of municipalities. The origin–destination interaction may also be approached from the perspective of spatial interaction models. Consider the gravity model

$$\hat{p}_{ij} = r_i s_j z_{ij} \qquad (9.25)$$

where z_{ij} represent the distribution function (spatial deterrence function)

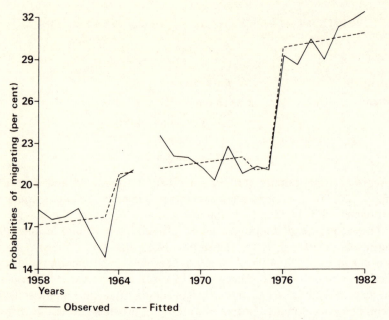

Figure 9.16 Observed and fitted values for the probabilities of migrating from large towns to commuter municipalities (T-FIT 2 model).

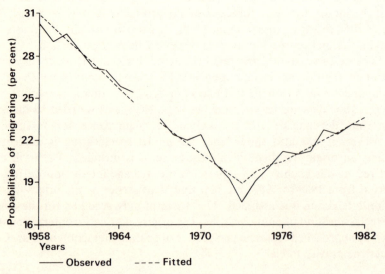

Figure 9.17 Observed and fitted values for the probabilities of migrating from medium-sized towns to large towns (T-FIT 2 model).

and r_i and s_j are balancing factors which assure that the $\hat{p}_{ij}$ matrix satisfies given marginal totals. The origin–destination interaction effects in the $\hat{p}_{ij}$ matrix are equal to those in the z_{ij} matrix (Willekens 1983). In estimating migration, the origin–destination interaction effect may hence be 'borrowed' from a known matrix.

9.4 Forecasting migration

In the previous sections we described and modelled the components of inter-regional gross migration flows. Each component was analysed separately. In Section 9.3 a model for the generation component and a model for the distribution component was developed to describe the observed trends adequately. In this section we develop a framework within which the results of the analysis in Sections 9.2 and 9.3 may be integrated. The basic model for an origin–destination-specific migration flow for year t is given as

$$m_{ijt} = N_t w_{it} p_{ijt} \qquad (9.26)$$

According to this model the forecasted migration flow from i to j may be obtained once each component is forecasted. The level component N_t, defined as the total number of migrations in a given year, is very responsive to the environmental variables as has been seen in Section 9.2.2.1. This feature of the level component calls for an explanatory model for forecasting. If one can predict the future behaviour of the exogenous variables, and assume that the relationship of the exogenous variables to the overall level of migration observed in the past will continue in the future, forecasts for N_t may be obtained.

Models for the migration generation component have been discussed in Section 9.3.2. In order to derive forecasts for migration generation it is important to note its stability. Unlike the migration level, migration genera-tion patterns show a considerable insensitivity to environmental variables. Our best model for migration generation (FIT 4, Section 9.3.2) does not have time-dependent parameters, except to account for the reclassifications in 1964 and 1976. The forecasts for migration generation, therefore, are easy to obtain under the assumptions:

(a) that the patterns of stability which persisted over the last 25 years will remain constant over the time horizon of the forecasts;
(b) that reclassifications will be absent or fully predictable.

The first assumption may be made with a reasonable confidence. However, the second needs further discussion. The reclassifications are made on the basis of some characteristics of the municipal populations. Until now the reclassifications were based on census data. Since in 1980 no census was held in the Netherlands, and since no census is planned, census data cannot provide a basis for reclassification of municipalities in urbanization categories. Although reclassification on the basis of registration and specialized survey data is feasible in principle, it is not envisaged. We may quite confidently assume no reclassifications for the next few years. The forecasted generation probabilities are easily derived from the parameters of FIT 4 (Eqn 9.16)

$$\log \frac{\hat{w}_{i,T+n}}{1 - \hat{w}_{i,T+n}} = a + b_i + h_{i3} \tag{9.27}$$

where $w_{i,T+n}$ represents the expected value of the generation probability for region i at year $T + n$. T is the year from which the forecast is made (base year) and $T + n$ is the year for which the forecast is made. The forecast is said to be an n-year ahead forecast made in year T. The forecasted value $w_{i,T+n}$ is obtained as follows:

$$\hat{w}_{i,T+n} = \frac{\exp(a + b_i + h_{i3})}{1 + \exp(a + b_i + h_{i3})} \tag{9.28}$$

Note that the forecast is independent of n and is a constant value. This stable pattern of the generation probabilities, observed in the past, is assumed to continue in the future.

The forecasts for the distribution probabilities involve more considerations since they are less stable than the generation probabilities. In order to obtain forecasts for p_{ijt} probabilities from the models developed in Section 9.3.3, three issues have to be considered:

(1) Will the patterns of redistribution of migration observed since 1973 pertain during the time horizon of the forecasts?
(2) If not, which new trends could be expected?
(3) If so, is it reasonable to assume the constancy of the observed trends?

The first issue relates to the reversal of the trends of suburbanization since 1973 discussed in Section 9.2.2.3. Probabilities of migrating towards medium-sized and large towns have been increasing since 1973, whereas the probabilities of migrating towards the rural municipalities have been declining. Although there seems to be no reason to assume another reversal of these trends for the time being, the possibility of new patterns of redistribution should be discussed. If we assume persistence of the overall patterns, then the third issue should be considered: whether the observed slopes for these trends will remain constant. The model designed in Section 9.3.3 has a continuous trend component which allows for the time dependency of the distribution probabilities. Whether the estimated slopes, that is, the time dependency of the probabilities, will remain constant is subject to the judgement of the forecaster. For the present purposes we assume that the estimated parameters of the model (T-FIT 2) will remain constant during the time horizon of the forecasts. Assuming again no reclassifications, we may derive the forecasted p_{ijt} values as follows:

$$\log \frac{\hat{p}_{ij,T+n}}{1-\hat{p}_{ij,T+n}} = a + c_j + e_{ij} + d_{j3} + \delta + c_j^\delta + e_{ij}^\delta + \beta_{i3}(T+n) + \beta_{il}^\delta(T+n) \qquad (9.29)$$

where
$$l = \begin{cases} j \text{ for } j = 1, 3, 5, 6 \\ 0 \text{ for } j = 2, 4 \end{cases}$$

and

$$\hat{p}_{ij,T+n} = \frac{\exp[\,a + c_j + e_{ij} + d_{j3} + \delta + c_j^\delta + e_{ij}^\delta + \beta_{i3}(T+n) + \beta_{il}^\delta(T+n)\,]}{1 + \exp[\,a + c_j + e_{ij} + d_{j3} + \delta + c_j^\delta + e_{ij}^\delta + \beta_{i3}(T+n) + \beta_{il}^\delta(T+n)\,]}$$

$$(9.30)$$

Finally, the forecasted place-to-place migration flows are obtained introducing Equations 9.28 and 9.30 into Equation 9.1:

$$\hat{m}_{ij,T+n} = \hat{N}_{T+n}\hat{w}_{i,T+n}\hat{p}_{ij,T+n} \qquad (9.31)$$

The total level of migration is forecasted separately. The generation component is assumed to remain constant and the distribution component changes according to a linear trend, with the trend factor being dependent on the origin and the destination of migration.

9.5 Conclusions

Migration is often the most important component of regional population change. The integration of migration into demographic projection models for subnational population has been a major concern in the past several years. Multiregional demographic models consider place-to-place migration and permit the evaluation of the impact of a change in migration from one place to another on the size and the regional distribution of the population. Multiregional demographic models are therefore the proper devices to study the demographic consequences of migration.

The dynamics of migration patterns are due to compositional changes in the population and can be studied only in part by demographic techniques. To fully appreciate the dynamics of migration patterns we need to augment the demographic analysis by an analysis of the spatial effects (effects of the origin, of the destination, and the interaction between origin and destination). Furthermore, we need to know the effects of the environment of the multiregional system, in particular the impact on migration of economic, social, cultural, political and environmental variables.

In this chapter an approach is proposed that allows an efficient integration of the spatial and temporal effects and of the explanatory variables in a forecasting model. In principle, the analysis consists of two steps. The first focuses on the internal dynamics of the system. It is a time-series analysis: the regularities in the time path are identified and modelled. The observed regularities express the presence of an inertia in the migration system. Changes do not occur abruptly unless shocks occur (reclassification of municipalities may be treated as a shock to the migration system). The second step focuses on the external dynamics. It is an explanatory analysis: the changes in migration components are related to explanatory variables external to the system that is being described. The second step is not considered here. The necessary and sufficient data set to carry out the first step is a time-series of migration data.

The strategy for the time-series analysis of migration data proposed in this chapter is as follows:

(a) Decompose place-to-place migration into three components:

    (i) a level component, the overall level of migration in the country;
    (ii) a generation component, the share of a particular area in the total number of outmigrations; and
    (iii) a distribution component, the distribution of the outmigrations of a particular area over all possible destinations.

(b) For each component perform an exploratory analysis to identify the major regularities and irregularities in the data structure. Plots may be very useful visual aids.

(c) Specify the link function and the error structure of the GLM.

(d) Design the model by assigning a parameter to each of the major determinants of the data structure. A distinction should be made between time-independent and time-dependent parameters.

(e) Select the proper normalization restrictions for the parameters. For each set of parameters that are restricted an additional parameter (lower-order interaction effect) must be added to the model.

(f) Evaluate the descriptive capacity of the model.

The outcome of the time-series analysis is a description of the internal dynamics of the migration system. The parameter values of the time-series model may further be related to contextual variables, which are part of the environment of the migration system but which may be introduced to explain variations in the parameters of the time-series model. Variations across space may be described by spatial interaction models, the parameters of which may be estimated from cross-sectional data (for example, distance). Variations in time, if present, may be described by dynamic econometric models. The need to combine spatial interaction models and econometric models to forecast migration has motivated the development of two-step procedures where first the parameters of the spatial interaction models are estimated for a time-series of migration data and then they are linked to exogenous variables at a second step (see Ledent 1985). However, the GLMs allow for the combination of both steps. Note that in this approach to designing a forecasting model the focus is on the understanding of the data structure and on the model identification. It contrasts with the traditional emphasis on model fitting (parameter estimation).

The data set used in this chapter consists of place-to-place migration flows among Dutch municipalities categorized by degree of urbanization from 1958 to 1982. To identify the regularities, it may be necessary to transform the variables representing the migration components. We adopted a logit transformation. To model the regularities, we propose a model of the transformed variables that is linear in the parameters. The terms (parameters) of the model represent the effects on migration of the area of origin, the area of destination, the interaction between origin and destination and the time dependencies of these effects. If a particular effect is stable, the time dependence term takes on a value close to zero and may therefore be omitted from the linear model. The outcome of the first step consists of models, the parameters of which describe and quantify the spatial effects on the migration components and the time dependencies of these effects if they are important enough.

Several models are presented. The parameters were estimated using the GLIM package. The major findings are:

(a) The reclassifications of the municipalities in 1964 and 1976 caused major shifts in the time-series of migration data. The shifts can be quantified by introducing special reclassification parameters. The approach is completely analogous to the introduction of dummy variables in classical regression models. Since the reclassifications have quite different effects on each of the urbanization categories, category-specific reclassification parameters must be distinguished. In the distribution component model the relevant category is the category of the area of destination.

(b) The level component has changed considerably over time. The total number of migrations in the Netherlands reached a peak in 1973 and declined by 25% between 1973 and 1979. Since 1979 there has been a slight recovery of the mobility. An explanatory model is called for to describe the pattern of change.

(c) The generation component remained remarkably constant in the study period, if controlled for the effect of the reclassifications of municipalities in 1964 and 1976. An adequate description of the generation component is given by model FIT 4 (Table 9.9). The model does not include any time dependence of the generation (except for the reclassification) and hence describes a constant generation component.

(d) To obtain an adequate representation of the distribution component we must include a term for the origin–destination interaction and an origin–destination-specific term for the reclassification (see model FIT 6, Table 9.9). However, the origin–destination interactions are not constant in time but show a linear trend. The change in each origin–destination interaction per unit time (slope of linear trend) is different in the period after 1973 from the period before 1973. We therefore introduced two trend-component terms for each origin–destination interaction together with two different slopes for each period. The model that results (T-FIT 2) gives a good description of the time-series of distribution probabilities from 1958 to 1982. The trend-component model combines discrete or categorical variables (origin, destination, reclassification period) and the continuous variable of time. It is therefore a truly generalized linear model (GLM).

(e) The GLM, the parameters of which denote the different spatial and temporal effects on migration, simplifies the task of forecasting place-to-place migration. Several of the parameters of the GLM (such as the origin–destination interaction term) do not include a time dimension. They do not require special attention in forecasting. The important parameters for forecasting are those that represent the time dependence of the spatial effects. If the time dependence of the spatial effects are expected to change in the future, the relevant parameter values should be adjusted. The time-related parameters present, therefore, a vehicle for the introduction of alternative hypotheses in the forecasts.

10

Demographic processes and household dynamics: a microsimulation approach

MARTIN CLARKE

10.1 Introduction

10.1.1 Scope of the chapter

This chapter addresses the problem of modelling household dynamics and producing regional forecasts of the number of different types of households over medium-term time spans (5–10 years) using microsimulation methods. The importance of producing these forecasts cannot be overemphasized. Whereas traditional population forecasts, disaggregated by age, sex and location, provide relevant information for certain planning issues – for instance education – there are a number of other areas where the production of household forecasts is more appropriate. For example, planning of the housing system is clearly concerned with ascertaining the demand for different types of houses which will largely be a function of household structure and income. Although this is the traditionally quoted area where households should be the unit of concern, other examples come readily to mind. For example, in the labour market many processes, such as female participation, income, taxation and benefit issues, are related to household structure. In the personal social services and health systems the form of care demanded and provided may be dependent on whether the household consists of a single person, a single parent with children, or otherwise. Policy on social security issues will need to account for the changing number of households of different kinds. Finally, the role of the family in society is at the centre of current political debate. To assess the implications of any policy proposals government needs to understand the dynamics of household structure over the next decade or so.

10.1.2 Household and population forecasting

The processes that form, change and dissolve households are complex and often interdependent. They are not always purely demographic processes

245

and often the consequence of one event may be to invoke a set of further transitions that affect household composition and hence structure. This is a point on which considerable emphasis will be placed in subsequent sections of this chapter. However, at the outset I would like to draw attention to some of the marked differences between population forecasting and household forecasting. These are summarized in Table 10.1.

First, it can be noted that the definition of the unit involved in population forecasting is the individual, this being an uncontentious matter, whereas with households we are faced with a number of alternative definitions. Furthermore, because of this there is never complete unanimity between different data sources. Secondly, while the number of alternative states an individual may exist in is potentially quite large, this number will be modest in comparison with the number of states a household may adopt; and once again in the type of applications for which household forecasts are developed it is extra pieces of information such as tenure, income bracket and employment characteristics that are relevant.

Table 10.1 Some differences between population and household forecasting.

Subject	Population forecasting	Household forecasting
state definition	individual – uncontentious	household – very contentious
no. of alternative states	relatively few – age, sex, marital status, race, location	many – age, sex, marital status, race of head, no. of adults and age, no. of children and age, location ...
transition between states	$x^t \rightarrow x^{t+1}$ conservation laws simple	$? \leftarrow x_t \rightarrow ?$ $\downarrow$ $?$ household may increase or decrease in size, its structure may completely dissolve or its component members may have to become parts of other households; therefore conservation laws complex
data availability	reasonable for most transitions	generally poor, often not available at all, e.g. leaving home

Partly as a consequence of the large number of potential states in which a household may exist, the number and nature of possible transitions are correspondingly large. To complicate matters further, the conservation laws that operate in household dynamics are not straightforward. For example, the dissolution of a household in a time period may be the result of death, divorce, a household becoming part of another household and so on. Household formation, correspondingly, shows similar traits. In comparison, the dynamics of individuals are underpinned by much clearer conservation laws.

Finally, as a result of the above complications the data required for models of household dynamics are substantial. To some extent this is due to the fact that several of the processes involved in household dynamics do not require statutory notification – for example, leaving home, groups of friends sharing accommodation. It was this lack of data that convinced Hetherington (1973) that it was impracticable to build a model for projection of households directly from household data.

10.1.3   Structure of the chapter

The rest of the chapter is organized as follows. In the next section the main principles behind a microsimulation approach to household dynamics are outlined, and previous work in the field is reviewed and compared with the more traditional method of headship rate analysis. Section 10.3 is devoted to a discussion of how to generate samples of individual and household data synthetically from published information, and an application for Yorkshire and Humberside is given. The full specification of a microsimulation model of household dynamics is the subject of Section 10.4, and some results for Yorkshire and Humberside are presented in Section 10.5. Some concluding remarks on the prospects for the methodology outlined are given in a final section.

10.2   Microsimulation: an outline of methodology and a review of practice

10.2.1   Introduction

Here the main features of the microsimulation methodology are introduced, and the justification and appropriateness of its use is examined; also some of the theoretical and practical problems of implementing these methods are discussed. In addition some of the applications of microsimulation methods to the problem of household forecasting are reviewed and the methods are briefly compared with the more traditional approach of headship rate analysis. Throughout this section the importance of the variability between different actors in socio-economic systems and the interdependence that exists between the attributes that characterize these individual units will be emphasized. It will be argued that as a consequence a greater amount of information is required to discriminate realistically between the actions and behaviour of individuals and households in particular contexts than is found in more conventional approaches. The focus is therefore concentrated on the high degree of heterogeneity that exists within a given population.

10.2.2 Microsimulation: principal features

As yet there is no coherent body of theory relating to the features, properties and applications of microsimulation methods. This is partly due to the fact that many of the advantages and principles of the approach have been recognized independently and dispersed over several disciplines. Much of the literature takes the form of 'in-house' publications and has failed to reach a wide audience. It may also be speculated that over the last two decades there has been little incentive to jettison conventional and easily accessible planning techniques. However, more recently there appears to have been a renewed and growing interest in microsimulation methods. Therefore the principle features of the approach will be examined briefly here, but for a more thorough presentation the reader is referred to Clarke and Williams (1986).

At the heart of any modelling exercise lies the state representation of the components of the system of interest. The microsimulation approach involves the microlevel representation of individuals and their associated households in terms of demographic, social and economic characteristics, together with any relevant spatial and activity attributes. This is achieved in the form of lists or samples of individuals and household attributes, an example of which is given in Table 10.2. More formally, let us define individuals, I, and households, H. Each individual and household will have an associated set of attributes which can be written as

$$x_I^i \quad \text{and} \quad x_H^h$$

where x_I^i is the vector of the s^i attributes associated with the ith individual on the list and x_H^h is the vector of the s^h attributes associated with the hth household on the list. The whole list of individuals can then be described by a matrix X_I^*, the components of which are the vectors associated with the N_I individuals in the sample

$$X_I^* = (x_I^1, \ldots, x_I^i, \ldots, x_I^{N_I}) \qquad (10.1)$$

and, in addition, a household matrix, X_H^* may be defined in a similar way:

$$X_H^* = (x_H^1, \ldots, x_H^h, \ldots, x_H^{N_H}) \qquad (10.2)$$

where N_H is the number of households in the sample.

Table 10.2 A list of individuals and their attributes: a microlevel specification.

Label 1	Age group 2	Specific age 3	Sex 4	Marital status 5	Race 6	Education 7	Occupation 8	Part or full-time job 10	No. of weeks worked in previous year 11	Wage earned in previous year 12	Multiple of wage median 13
1058.1	4	30	male	divorced	white	3	11	1	52	5110.11	1.40
2069.1	2	21	male	single	white	2	19	0	0	0.00	0.00
2187.1	3	25	male	married	white	4	16	1	52	4842.06	1.27
2187.2	2	23	female	married	white	4	3	1	52	3635.18	1.11
2206.1	8	54	male	married	white	4	3	1	52	8914.73	1.25
2206.2	9	55	female	married	white	2	3	1	52	7567.65	1.05
2206.3	3	28	female	single	white	2	21	0	52	0.00	0.00
2206.4	4	33	male	single	white	2	16	1	52	4069.80	0.98
2206.5	1	20	male	single	white	2	21	0	0	0.00	0.00
2728.1	7	46	male	married	white	4	11	1	52	3461.27	0.91
2728.2	6	41	female	married	white	2	18	1	52	4225.86	1.24
2728.3	2	21	female	single	white	2	6	1	52	3875.89	1.22
3031.1	11	69	male	married	white	4	20	0	0	0.00	0.00
3031.2	10	60	female	married	white	4	21	0	0	0.00	0.00
3039.1	7	46	male	married	white	2	14	1	52	6804.96	1.34
3039.2	6	42	female	married	white	3	7	1	52	5142.55	1.28
3039.3	1	12	female	single	white	1	0	0	0	0.00	0.00
4092.1	6	44	male	divorced	white	3	9	1	52	7495.00	1.33
4107.1	4	34	female	divorced	black	4	20	0	0	0.00	0.00
4107.2	1	7	male	single	black	1	0	0	0	0.00	0.00
4521.1	7	45	male	married	white	3	15	1	52	3693.00	0.91
4521.2	6	42	female	married	white	3	20	—	—	—	—
4521.2	1	11	female	single	white	1	0	—	—	—	—
4521.4	1	7	female	single	white	1	0	—	—	—	—

Note: see Table 10.3 for details of the attribute classifications.

The information pertaining to the individual and household vectors – the nature of which will of course depend on the type of application – will be stored in forms of lists and the successive updating of these lists is known as list processing. Several authors, including Orcutt *et al.* (1976), Wilson and Pownall (1976) and Kain *et al* (1978) have commented on the advantages of list processing for the efficient storage and retention of information, as compared with the more conventional aggregate approach of using an occupancy matrix. The number of elements in this matrix, denoted as E^1, will clearly be related to the number of attributes considered and the number of classes assigned to each attribute and is given by

$$E^1 = \prod_{\mu=1}^{M} \alpha^\mu \qquad (10.3)$$

where α^μ is the number of categories associated with the μth attribute. In comparison, the number of elements in a list processing representation, E^2, will simply consist of the number of individuals and households in the sample multiplied by the number of attributes considered, that is

$$E^2 = (s^i \times N_I) + (s^h \times N_H) \qquad (10.4)$$

Now, for most applications where a relatively large number of attributes is considered, E^2 will be much smaller than E^1. Furthermore, the occupancy matrix will typically be very sparse. A large proportion of states will not be occupied by any individual or household. This argument would apply if it was desired to record and process information on each member of a real population of individuals and examine the full individual information as output – for instance, for tax or health service purposes. However, for simulation models in which the aim is to represent and replicate real-world processes we are not interested in any particular individual but in information pertaining to samples, representative in terms of the joint distribution of characteristics over the population being considered. The key factor here is the interdependence that exists between the attributes being considered. If, for example, in an extreme case the attributes $x_1, \ldots, x_S$, were independent there would be no need to store the full occupancy matrix but simply the totals in each attribute vector. This would be much more efficient than a list-processing approach. Of course, the situation often lies between the two extremes of total independence or total interdependence and therefore each case must be considered on merit.

If it is deemed appropriate to adopt a microrepresentation the next step is to specify an initial population or sample of individuals and households along with their associated attributes. Ideally it would be desirable for a real sample to be used but very often this is not available and resort must be made to the production of a synthetic sample using contingency table analysis. This method is fully described in Section 10.3 of this chapter.

Given an initial population, the major task is to update the characteristics of the individuals and households in successive time periods. This is achieved through Monte Carlo sampling. For each potential transition (for example, migration) the conditional probability of an individual or household undergoing that event has to be given. A random number, r, in the interval $0-1$ is then drawn and compared with the conditional probability, p. If r is less than p then the event is deemed to occur, otherwise it is not. The attraction of the approach is that the interdependence between both individual and household attributes can be addressed in a consistent manner. For example, if a married male aged 46 dies, the marital status of his wife changes, and she now becomes eligible for remarriage; also the household size changes, the job the male had may be released into the supply pool and so on. In addition, the method in principle allows for a large number of attributes to be considered in the conditional probabilities, although in practice information limitations often prove restrictive. Another advantage relates to the aggregation of information. A micro-approach allows for flexible aggregation as the information may be cross-tabulated in any form. Compare this with an aggregate approach where the aggregation scheme is determined *a priori*.

However, the approach is not without its drawbacks. First of all in computational terms the processing of large lists of information can be expensive, although continuing developments in computer and information technology suggest that this will rapidly become a less significant issue. Secondly, the sequential ordering of events in list processing can be problematic because if one event is deemed to have occurred this may preclude others happening, as, for example, in the case of death being tested for before migration. Two methods for overcoming this exist. First, the simulation period could be reduced so as to make the possibility of multiple events very small; but this is a rather expensive solution computationally. Alternatively, a date or day at which each event occurs could be randomly assigned and the time structure and consequences of all events evaluated at the end of the processing of each individual and household. Another problem relates to Monte Carlo error generated through the sampling procedure. Clearly this will be related to the sample size used, the frequency of the events considered occurring, and to the number and interrelationship of these events. As yet not a great deal of analysis has been undertaken into the statistical properties of microsimulation models. Therefore resort must be made to simulation – running the model a number of times and checking means, standard deviations and the like. Of course, deriving statistical properties in this manner is not cheap computationally, but this is probably not a major obstacle.

Finally, mention must be made of the data requirements for micro-simulation models, particularly in the context of household dynamics. Although there is a growing move towards the collection of microdata sets, panel data and longitudinal studies, there is still a paucity of information relating to certain key processes (e.g. leaving home) that causes problems in the operationalization of micromodels. This remark will be elaborated upon in Section 10.4.

10.2.3 A survey of applications of microsimulation to household dynamics

This section includes a brief survey of the existing literature on the application of microsimulation methods for addressing the problem of modelling household dynamics. Reference will be made to the fact that the applications of microsimulation in general are spread across several disciplines and that on more than one occasion this has led to the approach being 'rediscovered'.

Applications related to socio-economic studies of the household can be traced back to the work of Guy Orcutt and his colleagues, first in Wisconsin and later at the Urban Institute in Washington DC. In their book *Microanalysis of socio-economic systems: a simulation study* (Orcutt *et al.* 1962) they presented the first results of their efforts towards developing a model of the US socio-economic system. Although most of their work was concentrated on household dynamics their intention was to model the economic sector as well. Despite this innovative work microsimulation techniques in the main lay dormant throughout the 1960s, although the work of Hyrenius and Adolfson (1964) and Ridley and Sheps (1966) related to micromodels of fertility deserves mention.

The 1970s, however, can be seen as a time of renewed interest in microsimulation methodology. A large-scale research project under the directorship of Orcutt at the Urban Institute resulted in the production of DYNASIM (Dynamic Simulation of Income, Orcutt *et al.* 1976), an extension of the previous work which was used to assess the effects of a large number of national policy options on processes such as female participation rates in the labour market and the effects of real equality in earnings between men and women. Operationalization of these models has been considerably aided by the availability of a large data base, specified at the microlevel and as a consequence the models are used to test federal policy alternatives in the United States.

The latest version of the NBER (National Bureau of Economic Research) housing model contains a microsimulation submodel to examine household dynamics, as reported in Kain and Apgar (1977). In the original NBER household dynamics model, which was used to study the housing systems of Detroit and Pittsburgh, a high level of disaggregation was sought in terms of household characteristics. It soom became apparent to the researchers that to include the characteristics they deemed important in the housing market a considerable dimensionality problem would be encountered. For example, in the Pittsburgh model the following household

252

categories were defined:

Category	Number of classes
workplace	20
residence zone	50
industry type	11
housing type	10
neighbourhood type	2
housing quality	2
education	2
income	4
life cycle	12

An occupancy matrix containing this cross-classified information contains 42 240 000 cells, the large majority with zero entries. When the NBER team wished to extend the attribute list to consider race, tenure and employment status this left them with a considerable computer storage problem and they resorted to a list representation.

What becomes noticeable when examining applications of microsimulation methods is that very often the model of household dynamics is not used as a means in itself but rather forms the driving mechanism behind models of the housing or labour systems. This is, of course, to be anticipated as household forecasts are clearly developed to be used in relation to other urban and regional subsystems. However, Nakamura and Nakamura (1978) have developed a microanalytic simulation model purely devoted to population dynamics. This work was motivated by a dissatisfaction with conventional, aggregate methods for making population projections stratified by a large number of variables. They constructed a model, based on list processing, for Alberta, Canada, and ran a series of historical simulations for the period 1961–71.

There are several other applications of microsimulation methods where household dynamics are not a central feature – for example, the work of Wilson and Pownall (1976) on activity analysis, Bonsall (1979) and Kreibich (1979) on individual choice in transport systems, Wegener (1982, 1983) on residential location and, in a very different vein, the work of Hammel *et al.* (1976) on kinship relations in small communities. A full review of these and other applications can be found in Clarke and Williams (1986).

10.2.4 Comparisons with headship rate analysis

The main similarities, differences and data requirements of a microsimulation approach compared with the more traditional headship rate analysis method of producing household forecasts are outlined in this section.

Very briefly, headship rate analysis can be considered to consist of three main stages. First, a conventional population forecasting exercise is undertaken at whatever level of disaggregation and spatial scale is deemed appropriate. Secondly, projected marital status rates, based on age and sex, are applied to this projected population. Finally, projected headship rates are applied on the basis of age, sex and marital status (see, for example, Stone 1971, Plessis-Fraissard 1976). The first and perhaps most important thing to note is that there is no attempt to reproduce the *processes* that contribute to a changing household structure. That is factors such as divorce, marriage, leaving home and so on are subsumed within the projections of marital status and headship rates, which tend to be based on extrapolations of past trends. The possible use of a transition matrix in which the probability of households in certain states becoming households in either the same or a different state over a certain time period has been rejected on the grounds of data availability, although in addition the dimensionality of this matrix would probably be very high and hence cumbersome computationally.

On the other hand a microsimulation approach attempts to model the various processes that together account for the dynamics of households. In terms of forecasting, assumptions can be made about how individual rates will change over time, which may be considered marginally better than making assumptions on how headship rates will change. The penalty we pay for focusing on processes is that information is often either not available at all or does not come in a form that is tailored to our needs. In addition the computational aspects of microsimulation are more complex than the relatively straightforward headship rate analysis.

10.2.5 Other approaches

Recently the use of the minimum information principle in household forecasting has attracted some attention by Swedish researchers (Harsman & Scheele 1982, Harsman & Snickars 1983). These applications are in principle extensions of the headship rate approach but allow for the incorporation of information relating to the transition of households between different states. In Sweden this information is collected by the census, but unfortunately this is not the case in Britain.

10.3 The generation of an initial population using synthetic sampling

10.3.1 Introduction

Here a method for synthetically generating a population of individuals and households, together with their associated attributes, is briefly outlined. In addition, an application of the method in relation to the Yorkshire and

Humberside region is presented. This population will form the starting point of the household dynamics model described below in Sections 10.3.2 and 10.3.3.

As has already been pointed out, the need to generate a population arises because a real sample obtained from a survey is not available. If this were available, recourse to synthetic sampling methods would be unnecessary.

10.3.2 Methodology

The basic idea behind the methodology consists of Monte Carlo sampling from a contingency table to produce individuals and households with a certain set of attributes. The theoretical basis for generating entries to a full contingency table consistent with available conditional and marginal probability distributions is long established (see, for example, McFadden *et al.* 1977). In principle the method is straightforward, but in practice it leads to some problems of inconsistency due to the lack of detailed conditional probabilities. The basic idea is to build up household and individual attribute lists on the basis of conditional probabilities obtained from published information such as the Census, the Family Expenditure Survey, the General Household Survey, and so on.

The procedure takes the form of producing a joint probability distribution $p(x)$ as a product of conditionals, as

$$p(x) = p(x_1)p(x_2 \mid x_1)p(x_3 \mid x_2, x_1) \dots$$

$$p(x_M \mid x_{m-1}, \dots, x_1)$$

(10.5)

and adopting approximations which impose a simplified structure on the conditional dependencies because of missing information. The estimation of missing information is the province of information theory and several well known techniques are available to assist us in this task, notably entropy maximizing and information minimizing (Shannon 1948). These techniques can be used for matrix infilling where row and column totals are known and where the matrix configuration may have to satisfy certain criteria. The scheme adopted here is based on Feinberg (1970) and takes the following form.

Assume it is wished to generate the probability matrix $p(x_1, x_2, x_3)$ such that all the known single and marginal probabilities are satisfied. These, say, are $p(x_1)$, $p(x_2)$, $p(x_2, x_3)$, $p(x_1, x_2)$. Let $p^i(x_1, x_2, x_3)$ be defined as the ith approximation of $p(x_1, x_2, x_3)$.

Step 1

$$\text{Set } p^1(x_1, x_2, x_3) = \frac{1}{c}$$

(10.6)

where c is the number of elements in the matrix. Let us assume all the probabilities are equally likely.

Step 2

$$p^2(x_1, x_2, x_3) = p^1(x_1, x_2, x_3) \frac{p(x_1)}{\displaystyle\sum_{x_2, x_3} p^1(x_1, x_2, x_3)} \tag{10.7}$$

Step 3

$$p^3(x_1, x_2, x_3) = p^2(x_1, x_2, x_3) \frac{p(x_2)}{\displaystyle\sum_{x_1, x_3} p^2(x_1, x_2, x_3)} \tag{10.8}$$

Step 4

$$p^4(x_1, x_2, x_3) = p^3(x_1, x_2, x_3) \frac{p(x_2, x_3)}{\displaystyle\sum_{x_1} p^3(x_1, x_2, x_3)} \tag{10.9}$$

Step 5

$$p^5(x_1, x_2, x_3) = p^4(x_1, x_2, x_3) \frac{p(x_1, x_2)}{\displaystyle\sum_{x_3} p^4(x_1, x_2\ x_3)} \tag{10.10}$$

Step 6

Return to step 2 with $p^2(x_1, x_2, x_3) = p^5(x_1, x_2, x_3)$ $\qquad$ (10.11)
until convergence.

Convergence, when $p^i(x_1, x_2, x_3) \simeq p^{i-1}(x_1, x_2, x_3)$, is typically very rapid – in the order of three or four iterations.

However, one rather important issue here that is often overlooked in microsimulation studies should here be pointed out. If the full contingency matrix for a given population were to be generated, the full occupancy matrix would in essence be reproduced. This would then negate all the arguments in favour of list processing as an efficient and compact way of storing information. Of course, the full contingency matrix is in practice decomposed into partial submatrices and the link between these matrices is achieved through the identification of relevant attributes. How this is achieved in relation to the application of the method for the Yorkshire and Humberside Region can now be described. One point to bear in mind in this example is that only a fairly hybrid selection of data sources is available and on several occasions it is necessary to resort to using, say, national information when its regional equivalent is not available.

In this application the aim is to derive two lists, one of households, the other containing the individuals who make up these households, taking our base year as 1975. The full set of attributes considered is given in Table 10.3. At the outset a matrix of probabilities pertaining to head of household characteristics is used, that is age, sex and marital status. This was obtained for Yorkshire and Humberside from the 1971 census and is shown in Table

Table 10.3 Attributes and their classifications as used in the microsimulation model.

Value of x^i	Description	Classification
Individual attributes		
1	label	unique to each individual
2	age group	0–15, 16–19, 20–24, then 5-year age groups until 75–79, 80 +
3	specific age	age in years
4	sex	male, female
5	marital status	single, married, widowed, divorced
6	race	white, black
7	education	left education at 16, at 16–18, 18–21 and 21–24
8	occupation	18 occupations, in education, unemployed, not in the labour force, retired
9	previous job	as above
10	part- or full-time job	part-time, full-time
11	number of weeks worked in previous year	0–52 weeks
12	wage earned in previous year	specific to each individual
13	multiple of wage median for appropriate occupation which is earned	value specific to each individual
Household attributes		
1	label	unique to household
2	age of head	unique to household
3	specific age of head	unique to household
4	sex of head	unique to household
5	marital status of head	unique to household
6	race of head	unique to household
7	number of children	0–9
8	number of people	0–9
9	socio-economic group	1–5
10	total income	amount in £–p

(Continued)

Table 10.3 (*Continued*)

Value of x^i	Description	Classification
11	tenure	owned outright, owned with mortgage, rented privately, rented from public sector
12	house size	1, 2, 3
13	location	30 wards of Leeds city area
14	structure	11 combinations of number of adults and children in household
15	retail expenditure	amount in £–p
16	on three types of	
17	goods	
18	retail location	900 potential supply points

10.4. Note that the probability of being a married female head of household is set to zero, even though there is a very small probability of this occurring, and the age-specific probabilities are added to the married male head probabilities. This procedure allows for a much more straightforward generation of additional members of the household but could be amended to include married female heads if deemed necessary.

This table of probabilities can now be multiplied by the household sample size, N^H, to produce the number of households with a head in each of the 64 categories. From this the appropriate number of individuals and households can be created and two lists can be formed. A label can be attached to each household (an integer number starting at 1 and ending with N^H). The head of household's individual number can also be defined as the household label plus 0.1. The individual, of course, takes the same age, sex and marital status attributes as a head of household.

By implication we are adopting the census definition of a household which, for 1971, was:

(a) any group of persons, whether related or not, who live together and benefit from common housekeeping; or
(b) any person living alone who is responsible for providing his or her own meals. (General Register Office 1968.)

The definition of households is a contentious issue and for a full discussion of the different approaches to this subject the reader is referred to Plessis-Fraissard (1976).

The first additional attribute to be allocated is race, and this is determined on the basis of age. This information is obtained from national data in the 1975 General Household Survey (GHS) (OPCS, Social Survey Division,

Table 10.4 The probability of sex, marital status and age categories for heads of household, Yorkshire and Humberside, 1971.

Marital status	Age groups							
	16–19	20–24	25–29	30–39	40–54	55–64	65–74	75+
Male								
single	0.016 70	0.007 25	0.023 85	0.014 98	0.003 85	0.002 50	0.001 64	0.001 33
married	0.042 80	0.067 01	0.218 50	0.230 20	0.064 10	0.041 60	0.033 72	0.013 40
widowed	0.000 01	0.000 05	0.000 86	0.005 33	0.003 83	0.004 54	0.006 13	0.007 76
divorced	0.000 11	0.000 64	0.003 20	0.003 09	0.000 64	0.000 32	0.000 24	0.000 12
Female								
single	0.008 50	0.002 85	0.007 77	0.012 41	0.005 50	0.006 02	0.006 80	0.006 67
married	0.000 00	0.000 00	0.000 00	0.000 00	0.000 00	0.000 00	0.000 00	0.000 00
widowed	0.000 05	0.000 15	0.002 36	0.016 19	0.014 41	0.020 54	0.039 64	0.029 86
divorced	0.000 30	0.000 94	0.004 15	0.003 73	0.000 77	0.000 58	0.000 43	0.000 09

Source: computed from OPCS (1975a, Table 19, p. 13).

1978, Table 4.2(a), p.106). The head of household is now given an occupation, based on age and sex and derived from regional data for Yorkshire and Humberside given in the 1975 New Earnings Survey (NES) (Department of Employment 1975a, Tables 122, 123 and 138). If the individual is of retirement age the occupation label is changed to that of retired. We can also test whether the individual is unemployed by applying occupation-specific unemployment probabilities, again derived from the NES for the base year 1975 at the regional level (Department of Employment 1975b, Table 2, pp. 685–7). On the basis of the occupation category assigned to the individual we can allocate an education attribute, this being obtained from the GHS.

We now proceed to create a wife for the married males who are heads of households. It is assumed that several attributes follow automatically, namely her label, sex, marital status; and her race is assumed to be the same as that of her husband. Her age is generated on the basis of her husband's age, as is her educational status. Her occupation is not determined until the number of children, if any, has been allocated, unless she is above retirement age.

The number and type of any other members of the household are based on the marital status and age of the head. This set of conditional probabilities is derived from the 1971 census (OPCS 1975b, Table 38, p. 57). From the same report we can identify the number of these members that are children and allocate them an age on the basis of the age of the mother (from the GHS national data given in OPCS, Social Survey Division 1978, Table 4.11, p. 99) and an educational status based on the child's age and the occupation of the head of the household, taken from the same source (Table 7.3, p. 207). If the family is a lone male parent one we allocate the child's age on the basis of the father's age. The occupation of the child, if not in education, is obtained on the basis of the educational status and sex of the child. Marital status is assumed to be single, and race is that of the father (or mother in lone-parent families). Sex is determined randomly.

The occupation of the wife (if any) can now be determined and this is done on the basis of the age of the wife, the age of the youngest child in the household and the educational status of the wife. These data derive from a special tabulation (Table 755v) of the Qualified Manpower Tables of the 1971 census (see OPCS, London and General Register Office, Edinburgh 1976, p. xvi). Unemployment is attributed in the same manner as for males.

Other attributes, both relating to individuals and households, could also be generated. In the application studied by Clarke *et al.* (1981a) a full income model was attached to the initial population routine. This considered earned income, state benefits and taxation. A spatial label was also generated, again using 1971 census data, together with the matrix-infilling methodology described above.

10.3.3 Some comparative results

In comparing the results of the synthetic sampling exercise two points should be borne in mind. First, information used in the exercise consisted both of regional and national data for both 1971 and 1975. Secondly, the comparative data used also come from a variety of sources, and we must be careful that we are always comparing like with like.

Table 10.5 compares the model-derived age and sex distributions with OPCS 1975 population estimates. It should be remembered that the distributions are for private households only whereas the population estimates are for the whole population. In 1971, 3.3% of the population of England and Wales was not in private households. This probably explains why there is some discrepancy at the upper and lower ends of the distribution. It is children and elderly who are most likely to reside in non-private households.

For comparative purposes the distribution of household structure is taken from the 1974–5 Family Expenditure Survey (FES) (Department of Employment 1976, Table 64, p.122). Table 10.6 compares the modelled and observed household structures adopting the FES household classification, and Table 10.7 compares the household size distributions. Again the observed data are taken from the FES (Department of Employment 1976). In general, these results are encouraging, with close fits between model outputs and observed data.

All these distributions were obtained by calculating the mean of five

Table 10.5 Population age and sex structure, Yorkshire and Humberside, 1975: model and observed distributions.

Age groups	Males		Females	
	Model	Observed	Model	Observed
0–14	11.45	12.05	11.02	11.51
15–19	3.42	3.73	3.39	3.54
20–24	3.67	3.48	3.48	3.30
25–29	4.01	3.71	3.82	3.61
30–34	3.38	3.08	3.20	3.01
35–39	3.09	2.92	3.22	2.85
40–44	3.19	2.82	2.91	2.79
45–49	3.21	2.97	3.14	2.94
50–54	3.30	3.19	3.41	3.24
55–59	2.89	2.63	2.98	2.82
60–64	2.68	2.70	2.90	3.04
65 +	4.97	5.07	7.27	8.59
Total	49.26	48.75	50.74	51.25

Source of observed population: OPCS (1977b, Table 3, pp. 10–11).

Table 10.6 Household structure, Yorkshire and Humberside, 1975: model and observed distributions.

Household type	Percentage distributions	
	Model	Observed
one man or one woman	21.0	19.5
one adult, one child	1.1	1.0
one adult, two or more children	1.6	1.5
two adults	29.6	31.5
one man, one woman, one child	11.4	11.1
one man, one woman, two children	14.1	13.9
one man, one woman, three children	5.0	5.0
two adults, four or more children	2.8	2.7
three adults	5.9	5.8
three adults, plus children	4.9	4.8
four or more adults	1.1	1.2
four or more adults, plus children	1.5	1.6
all other households without children	0.0	0.0
all other households with children	0.0	0.5

Source: Department of Employment (1976, Table 64, p. 122).

simulations for each entry and for a sample size of 5000 households representing 13 650 individuals. The average number of individuals per household is therefore 2.73 compared with an observed average of 2.72 (Department of Employment 1976, Table 56, p.118).

An attraction of the microsimulation approach is that one can perform any cross-tabulation of attributes one desires – although for comparative purposes many of these will not be available in published form. For examples of these the reader is referred to either Clarke (1985) or Clarke and Williams (1986).

Table 10.7 Household size, Yorkshire and Humberside, 1975: model and observed distributions.

Household type	Percentage distributions	
	Model	Observed
one person	21.0	19.5
two persons	30.6	32.5
three persons	18.9	18.5
four persons	17.3	17.4
five persons	7.2	7.6
six persons	2.9	2.6
seven or more persons	2.1	1.9

Source: Department of Employment (1976, Table 63, p.122).

10.4 A microsimulation model of household dynamics

10.4.1 Introduction

Here a description is given of how the attributes of the individuals and households in the initial population are successively updated over the simulation period. In particular attention is paid to each of the main demographic processes and how these are interrelated with other social and economic events. As already stated, it is often this linkage that is of interest to planners. One point worth making at this stage is that the functional specification of the model used is not particularly easy or elegant. Instead resort is made to the use of flow diagrams which give an impression of the detailed structure of the model.

Each component of the demographic model is described in turn. Attention is paid to the attribute dependence used and the data sources used as inputs. The overall structure of the model is given in Figure 10.1 and the description follows this flow diagram.

10.4.2 Model specification: death

The probability of an individual dying within the simulation period is taken as a function of age and sex. Five-year age cohorts are used and the data are obtained from both *Mortality statistics for England and Wales, 1975,* and Table 4 and Table 2 of *Mortality statistics by area* (OPCS 1978a, 1977a). The socio-economic implications of an individual dying are detailed on the left-hand side of Figure 10.1. A single-person household would be dissolved and the dwelling unit released into the supply side. Death in a multiperson household would involve a change in household size and income, as well as a marital status change for the remaining spouse. All these changes at the microlevel imply adjustments to the total stock of various factors and these are all accounted for by positive or negative increments to the relevant totals as they occur.

10.4.3 Model specification: fertility

Fertility is a difficult process to model at the very detailed level, partly because fertility rates show a great deal of variation between different groups of females but also because fertility rates fluctuate markedly over time (see Cartwright 1976). In the model presented here three groups are distinguished: New Commonwealth and Pakistan (NCWP) females, married non-NCWP females and non-married non-NCWP females. These groups have different fertility characteristics, so their differentiation is important. Data for NCWP fertility rates for England and Wales were obtained from OPCS, Immigrant Statistics Unit, Population Statistics

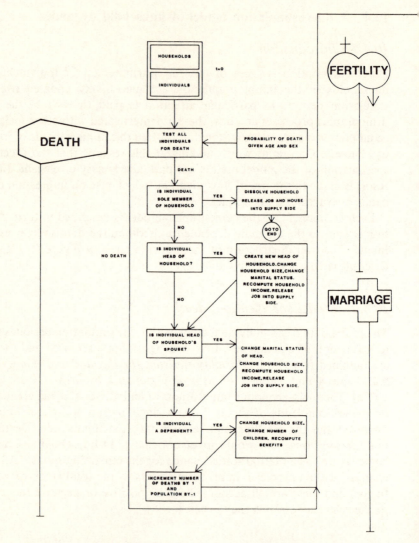

Figure 10.1 The detailed structure of the demographic model.

Division (1978), and the other two rates were derived from *Birth statistics, 1975* (OPCS 1978b). Five-year age groups in the range 15–44 years were used in these sources.

If a birth is deemed to occur we must 'create' a new individual (or two, in the case of twins) as well as adjusting the household size. The new individual's attributes are derived as follows: age is zero, sex is determined probabilistically, marital status is single and race is taken as that of the mother. Other consequences of a birth, such as labour-force participation

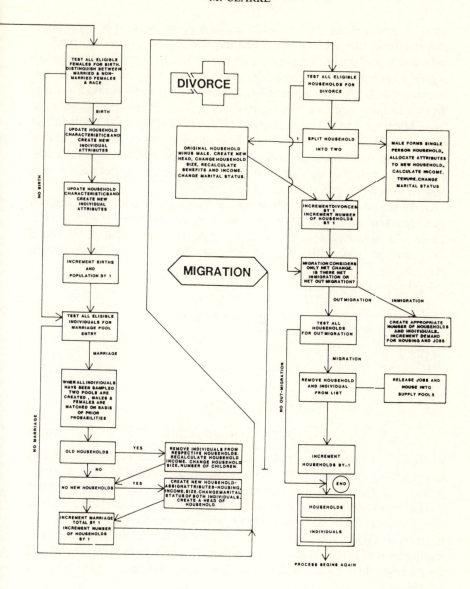

of the female, income and benefit changes, are also accounted for (see Clarke 1985).

10.4.4   Model specification: marriage

Unlike the previous two processes, which both involve events occurring to an established household, marriage involves the fusion of two individuals from different households (at least usually) to form a new household. As such, it involves the matching of males and females with appropriate characteristics. To achieve this in the micromodel we create two pools of individuals, males and females, which are sampled from all those who are eligible (considered to be single, divorced and widowed males and females over the age of 15). The probability of entering these pools is taken as being dependent upon age, sex and marital status. This information is obtained from *Marriage and divorce statistics, 1975* (OPCS 1978c) for England and Wales (Tables 3.3 (a) and 3.3 (c)). This process creates two lists, one of females and one of males, and both lists include age and marital status attributes. These two lists are then aggregated into appropriate age groups and an allocation procedure is carried out.

Given a known or prior allocation of marriage partners, Z_{ij}, obtained and modified from the *Marriage and divorce statistics*, (OPCS 1978c, Table 3.7) for the sample size used, the problem is to calculate the actual or *posterior* allocation, P_{ij}, by solving the following mathematical programme.

Find the values of P_{ij} by

minimizing
$$X = \sum_{ij} P_{ij} \ln(P_{ij}/Z_{ij}) \qquad (10.12)$$

subject to:

$$\sum_{i} P_{ij} = C_j \qquad \text{for all } j \qquad (10.13)$$

$$\sum_{j} P_{ij} = S_i \qquad \text{for all } i \qquad (10.14)$$

$$P_{ij} > 0 \qquad \text{for all } i \text{ and } j \qquad (10.15)$$

where C_j is the number of males in age group j, S_i the number of females in age group i, and Z_{ij} is the prior allocation of females of age i to males of age j. Simple division of the resultant allocation P_{ij} by the appropriate total gives the probability p_{ij} of a female in age group i marrying a male in age group j. This is then used to allocate marriage partners at the microlevel. Again this is achieved through Monte Carlo sampling. The implications of marriage are quite complex. A new household is formed and the households from which the partners originated are adjusted accordingly.

10.4.5 Model specification: divorce

The probability of divorce is taken simply as a function of age and sex of the head of household, taken from *Marriage and divorce statistics*, Table 4.1 (OPCS 1978c). Although length of marriage should be taken into account (it is readily available from published information), it is not one of the household attributes generated here. The following set of assumptions were made about the outcome of a divorce transition.

(a) The former husband becomes a single person household and has a probability of entering any of the three tenure sectors.
(b) The former wife and any children remain in their present dwelling unit, but with updated attributes reflecting their new circumstances.
(c) Both former partners now become eligible for remarriage, for which significantly higher age-specific probabilities exist than for first marriage.

10.4.6 Model specification: migration

For simplicity only net-migration is considered, either in or out of the region of interest. The relatively crude assumption is made that, apart from net change, outmigrants are replaced by equivalent inmigrants or vice versa. This simplification is largely a consequence of the paucity of data on migration at the household level as opposed to individual data.

In Yorkshire and Humberside there is – and will probably continue to be – net outmigration from the region, assumed by OPCS (1981b) to remain at about 3.5 per thousand until 1991. Data on migration by households were derived from the *1971 Census Migration Regional Report for Yorkshire and Humberside,* Parts I, II and III (OPCS 1975–7). From these reports it was possible to generate the probability of (net) outmigration by age of the head of household.

The usual Monte Carlo sampling exercise was undertaken for each household. If migration out of the region was deemed to occur, then the household is dissolved, jobs held by various members of the household released and the dwelling unit released into the housing supply pool. Relevant stocks and totals are, of course, adjusted.

10.4.7 Model specification: other demographic processes

Under this category retirement, leaving home, and ageing are considered. Retirement from employment or from seeking a job is mandatory in our model at the ages of 65 for males and 60 for females. Jobs that are occupied are vacated and enter the pool of vacant jobs. Individual members of a household who leave home are a difficult phenomenon to model. For example, they may leave home to get married, in which case they have already been dealt with in Section 10.4.4. However information on individuals leaving home to form new households – or to become members of other households – is difficult to come by. If they migrate out of the region then they may be picked up in the census data, but otherwise there is unlikely to be any specific information pertaining to this group of people. This is an unfortunate state of affairs as they probably constitute an important component in the changing nature of the household size distribution, as well as significantly contributing to housing demand (Department of the Environment 1977). This being the case, we are forced into making some assumption about the rate at which leaving home occurs. In the model runs performed in the next section it is assumed that the probability of someone (excluding the head of household and his spouse) between the ages of 18 and 30 leaving home is 0.1 per year and that the probability of their doing so between the ages of 31 and 60 is 0.025 per year. This is clearly an area where the use of sensitivity analysis is a priority.

In addition, at the end of each simulation period all individuals in the sample population have their age incremented by 1.

10.5 Results of numerical simulations

10.5.1 Introduction

Here a set of results is presented from the simulation work on the household structure of Yorkshire and Humberside carried out at the University of Leeds. In presenting these results a number of issues relating to the implementation of microsimulation models, such as sample size, sources of error and computational issues, are examined. It should be re-emphasized that the most typical use of this type of model would not be solely for demographic forecasts but to relate the demographic subsystem to other subsystems such as the labour, housing and service systems (see Clarke & Williams 1986).

10.5.2 Sample size

The first task in model implementation is the generation of an initial population consisting of a sample of individuals and households and their relevant attributes for the Yorkshire and Humberside region. One issue, therefore, is to decide what is an appropriate population sample size for the task at hand. When modellers traditionally face this problem they resort to standard statistical theory relating to confidence limits associated with particular sample sizes. In the case of this study however, the structure of the model makes this rather difficult (for a technical discussion of this problem see Clarke & Williams 1986). Instead a more pragmatic approach is adopted which takes into account the availability of computer resources and experience in running the set of models. The results presented below were obtained using a sample of 10 000 households containing approximately 26 000 individuals, representing about a 0.5% sample of the Yorkshire and Humberside population.

10.5.3 Computational issues

In the implementation of the micro-simulation models on a computer there are a number of issues that emerge that relate to how efficiently the models run. The majority of the computing time is devoted to list processing – that is the successive updating of the individual records. A considerable amount of this time is taken up by input–output operations, and it is therefore important that this is undertaken efficiently. Much time can be saved by the use of unformatted READ and WRITE statements and by paying careful attention to file manipulation. There is no denying that when these models are run for realistic sample sizes – say for a ten-year period – they consume a significant amount of computer resources, but this is likely to become less of a problem in the future.

10.5.4 Sources of error

Apart from model mis-specification and data problems there are two related sources of potential error in the model outputs. The first, which has already been discussed, is the sample size used; the second is Monte Carlo variation. Monte Carlo variation is attributable to the fact that Monte Carlo sampling involves the generation of a string of random numbers and testing for transitions on the basis of these numbers. If different random number strings are used, it is very likely that a different number of a given type of transition (for example, birth) will occur. The amount of variation that will occur is directly related to the probability of a particular event happening and to the sample size used, or, more specifically, the number of individuals in the sample who are eligible for that transition. Hence the more unlikely a certain event or set of events is, the more likely it is that there will be variation between model runs. In the particular example given the majority of demographic events are sufficiently common not to involve a great deal of variation in aggregate outputs (for example, births or deaths per 1000 population). However, when we begin to disaggregate the outputs we are likely to obtain variations between runs.

10.5.5 Model results

Here a set of results are given relating to household dynamics in Yorkshire and Humberside in the period 1975–86. These results are not intended as definitive forecasts of change but rather as illustrations of the potential of the approach. There still remain a number of problems that need to be resolved. These will be discussed later.

The results were obtained in the following manner. The data for demographic transitions were obtained as outlined in Section 10.4. All rates were assumed to remain constant over the simulation period (1975–86). The model was run three times and all results presented are the average of these three runs. This was done to reduce the amount of error introduced through Monte Carlo variation.

A set of tabulations of the output obtained from the model runs are now presented. It should be remembered that in principle any cross-tabulation of attributes can be produced. Here we restrict ourselves to a limited number of results and, where possible, provide comparative tabulations obtained from other sources.

Table 10.8 gives the age distribution for 1981 and 1986. The comparisons are with 1981 census data and 1986 OPCS projections. The 1986 projections were made before the 1981 data were available and will inevitably be revised in due course. Although the overall projected total population is close to the 1981 data, in the 1986 projection the distribution by age groups shows some discrepancies. It should be pointed out that there were some small errors in the synthetically generated population, and these will be reflected in the updated populations. Furthermore, the assumption was also made that all transition rates would remain constant over the period. This will not be the case in practice and certain assumptions as to their direction of change could be made.

Table 10.9 presents a set of projections for household size. The comparisons provided for 1974–5 and 1980 are from the Family Expenditure Survey (Department of Employment 1976, 1981). The model output suggests that average household size will continue to decline in the simulation

Table 10.8 Age distribution of population, Yorkshire and Humberside, 1981 and 1986.

Age groups	1981		1986	
	Model	Observed[a]	Model	OPCS[b]
0–14	1 006 130	1 013 871	987 188	958 400
15–19	400 823	403 531	386 973	394 400
20–24	337 889	350 618	398 785	412 000
25–29	320 169	317 404	333 611	353 200
30–34	361 107	356 741	317 929	325 800
35–39	301 839	296 139	354 997	353 100
40–44	279 027	275 883	295 729	299 500
45–49	289 007	266 110	283 509	267 300
50–54	286 156	274 698	275 973	257 600
55–59	296 340	287 925	274 547	263 600
60–64	260 087	251 730	277 806	267 100
65–69	239 312	241 098	230 351	229 600
70–74	200 411	203 607	198 375	200 400
75–79	136 459	143 826	148 882	152 900
80–84	73 118	80 620	81 468	91 600
85 +	40 938	46 673	47 862	57 100
Totals	4 828 812	4 810 474	4 893 985	4 883 500

Sources:
[a] 1981 census data: OPCS (1983a, Table 3, p.8).
[b] 1986 OPCS projections: OPCS (1981b, Appendix Table 1, p. 19).

Table 10.9 Household size, Yorkshire and Humberside, 1974–5, 1980 and 1986.

Number of persons in household	Percentage distributions				
	1974–5		1980		1986
	Model	Observed[a]	Model	Observed[b]	Model
1	21.0	19.5	23.0	22.5	23.7
2	30.6	32.5	33.2	34.0	32.9
3	18.9	18.5	17.7	16.2	17.4
4	17.3	17.4	17.0	16.2	16.8
5	7.2	7.6	6.9	7.3	6.3
6	2.9	2.6	2.1	2.3	2.1
7+	2.1	1.9	0.5	1.5	0.8
average household size	2.73	2.72	2.66	2.65	2.64

Sources:
[a] Department of Employment (1976, Table 63, p. 122).
[b] Department of Employment (1981, Table 49, p. 123).

period, although it will gradually stabilize. This is due largely to the increase in single-person households and suggests an increase in the demand for dwelling units. These projections must be treated with some caution due to the difficulty of modelling the single person leaving home.

Table 10.10 extends the analysis of household dynamics to the distribution of household type. The categories of households correspond to

Table 10.10 Household type, Yorkshire and Humberside, 1974–5 and 1986.

Household type	Percentages	
	1974–5	1986
one man, one woman	21.0	23.7
one adult, one child	1.1	1.2
one adult, two + children	1.6	1.9
two adults	29.6	31.7
one man, one woman, one child	11.4	10.4
one man, one woman, two children	14.1	13.8
one man, one woman, three children	5.0	4.6
two adults, four + children	2.8	2.2
three adults	5.9	5.1
three adults plus children	4.9	3.9
four or more adults	1.2	0.9
four or more adults plus children	1.5	0.6
all other households without children	0.0	0.0
all other households with children	0.0	0.0

Source: model runs.

those used by the Family Expenditure Survey. The results suggest that the largest change will take place in one- and two-adult households, with a corresponding decline in larger households with children.

These results give a flavour of the potential of the methodology to produce interesting and useful information. As already noted, the range of possible outputs is very large. However, there are still a number of problems and limitations that prevent the full potential being realized. Some of these are discussed in the next and final section.

10.6 Concluding comments: present problems and future priorities

The growing interest in microsimulation methods suggests that their potential contribution to the modelling of complex systems is being recognized. Certainly the approach appears to be attractive on a number of grounds, not least that it is conceptually simple. However, there are a number of problems in implementation that prevent the full effectiveness of the approach from being adequately demonstrated. Many of these relate to problems of data availability. It would seem that, although we know a great deal about the structure of households at any one time, we still know relatively little about their dynamics. Because of their complexity, household dynamics require further analysis as an aid to understanding and forecasting. The majority of the attention that regional scientists, geographers and spatial demographers have given to population dynamics has focused on the individual or groups of individuals, not on the household. As Rees (1983) has recently noted, this is a situation that needs rectifying.

One of the major contributions a particular set of models can make is to point out areas where there is a lack of understanding and to highlight where the main data deficiencies lie. Indeed a model framework that offers the planner crucially useful information provides the rationale and scheme for collecting the missing data on household formation.

So let us conclude on an optimistic note. In an age of information technology with the availability of computer resources on a scale unimaginable several years ago, perhaps we can look forward to the day when it is the lack of ingenuity of modellers rather than the lack of appropriate information that proves to be the stumbling block in the development and application of these types of models.

11

A demographic–economic model of a metropolis

MOSS MADDEN and PETER BATEY

11.1 Introduction

An important activity in most regional planning exercises is the analysis and forecasting of population and the economy. Although these elements of urban and regional systems each present their own distinct problems, there is a further area of concern associated with the linkages between demographic and economic subsystems. However, recent evidence suggests that in practice these linkages are largely ignored (Long 1977, Breheny & Roberts 1980, Barras & Broadbent 1982). Reviewing the forecasting methods used in the British structure plans of the 1970s, Breheny and Roberts (1981, p. 85) point to the serious consequences of this general failure to integrate the analysis of the various components of urban and regional systems and conclude that

> ...a lot of effort is put into technical work on individual methods. Little [effort] appears to go into using these methods in combination in producing integrated forecasts. ... At times the neglect of such [integration] has produced literally nonsensical results in plans whose forecasts aim to set out the framework for long-term land-use policies.

Population analysis and forecasting cannot be expected to produce accurate results if demographic systems are modelled on their own with no relationship to other components of the overall socio-economic system of which they are a part. In particular, changes in demographic structure and size in any region or subregion are affected by changes in the economy of that region, and by changes in the economies of exogenous regions. Similarly, regional economic analysis must consider the effects changes in the population size and structure of a region will have on that region's economy, both in terms of personal consumption and in terms of labour supply.

The integration of demographic and economic models presents problems of two main kinds: those relating to demographic–economic linkages – the effect that population has on the economy; and those related to the mirror image of this, economic–demographic linkages – or the effect that the economy has on population. These linkages are illustrated in Figure 11.1. Here the upper part of the diagram shows demographic–economic linkages, including the effects of population upon industrial output (through household consumption of goods and services, for example) and upon the size and composition of the labour force (through labour-force participation rates). In contrast the lower part of the diagram deals with economic–demographic linkages, particularly the effect of wage levels, employment and unemployment upon demographic factors, including migration and fertility.

Techniques for the analysis and forecasting of demographic and economic systems separately are well developed: in the demographic sphere a number of variations of the cohort survival model of Rogers (1968, 1975), for example, are available, or demographic accounts of the type developed by Stone (1971) and Rees and Wilson (1977) may be employed. Such methods are considered in greater detail elsewhere in this volume (Chapter

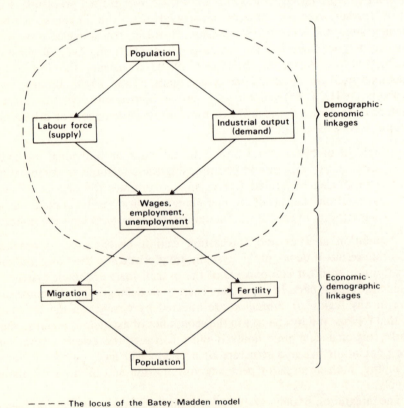

– – – – The locus of the Batey · Madden model

Figure 11.1 The linkages between demographic and economic subsystems.

7). Economic analysis and forecasting may be carried out using the equally well established techniques of, for example, export base analysis or input–output analysis (Hewings 1977). At the national scale the use of such methods may be expected to produce forecasts that have a reasonable chance of being accurate without too much attention being paid to the exact specification of the links between the demographic and economic sub-systems (Luptacik & Schmoranz 1980). However, at the regional level factors such as migration, unemployment and differential labour-force participation rates assume greater importance in relation to the sizes of the economy and population under consideration, and so exact specification of the linkages becomes necessary. Indeed, below the regional level a third element, the supply and consumption of housing, becomes critical in deter-mining migration rates and headship rates and must be modelled in at least as much detail as the population and the economy.

During the last ten years several different approaches have been developed in order to improve the representation of demographic–economic linkages in regional models. Ledent (1982b), for example, has shown how demographic and economic models can be combined in an econometric modelling scheme to provide what he terms a 'minimal demoeconomic model'. The recently developed ECESIS model (Beaumont *et al.* 1985) is a further attempt to model demographic–economic linkages using econometric techniques – in this case in an interregional model designed to forecast population for the fifty states in the US. In other work more concerned with evaluating policy impacts than forecasting, microsimulation techniques have been employed (Orcutt *et al.* 1976, Clarke *et al.* 1981b, see also Chapter 9). Such techniques have the advantage of handling linkages at a high degree of detail. There have also been efforts within the field of strategic land-use planning to develop simple accounting schemes which permit integrated forecasting of population, employment and housing demand (Breheny & Roberts 1978) and to set these accounts within a policy-making context in which sources of uncertainty are explicitly recognized (Bracken 1982).

The approach that is of special concern in this chapter takes as its starting point the input–output modelling system first developed by Leontief as a tool in inter-industry analysis (Leontief 1951). Many authors have suggested ways in which the input–output model can be extended and generalized to include elements of the wider socio-economic system. Schinnar (1976) and Stone (1971), for example, have demonstrated the value of input–output analysis as a framework for studying the interrelationships between demographic and economic variables.

In the next section we consider the various choices that are available in extending an input–output model to include demographic variables. Among these extensions is a form of input–output model in which employ-ment, unemployment and industrial output are all treated endogenously.

275

This model, developed by the present authors, is the subject of the following section. Here applications are discussed: an operational version of the model is presented and examples are described of its use in impact analysis and forecasting in the Merseyside metropolitan area in North-West England. In the final section in this chapter some of the ways in which this model can be further refined and extended are examined.

11.2   An input–output approach to demographic–economic modelling

11.2.1   Introduction

In input–output analysis it is sometimes useful to make a basic distinction between household exogenous and household endogenous models, depending on whether households are assumed to form one component of final demand or to function in a similar manner to other industrial sectors within the matrix of technical coefficients. Such models are known as Type I and Type II models, respectively, and may be represented in matrix form as follows:

$$\text{Type I:}\quad [I - A]\ [x_I] = [d_I] \tag{11.1}$$

$$\text{Type II:}\quad \begin{bmatrix} I - A & -h_c \\ -h_w & 1 \end{bmatrix} \begin{bmatrix} x_I \\ x_H \end{bmatrix} = \begin{bmatrix} d_I \\ d_H \end{bmatrix} \tag{11.2}$$

where A is a square matrix of inter-industry technical coefficients;

I is an identity matrix;

h_w is a row vector of income from employment coefficients;

h_c is a column vector of household consumption coefficients;

x_I is a column vector of industrial gross output;

x_H is a scalar representing household gross output;

d_I is a column vector of industrial final demand;

d_H is a scalar representing household final demand.

Both models can be viewed as systems of simultaneous equations and, provided the matrix of coefficients is square, these will yield determinate solutions. In each case the solution (gross output) is obtained by post-multiplying the inverse of the matrix of coefficients by the vector of inputs (final demand).

Because it embodies household income and consumption, the Type II input–output model can be seen as a rudimentary form of demographic–economic model: economic (industrial) activities consume demographic (household) commodities and a demographic activity (household purchases) consumes economic commodities. The Type II model also shows economic commodities produced and consumed by economic activities $(I - A)$ (Madden & Batey 1983). The same distinctions between demographic and

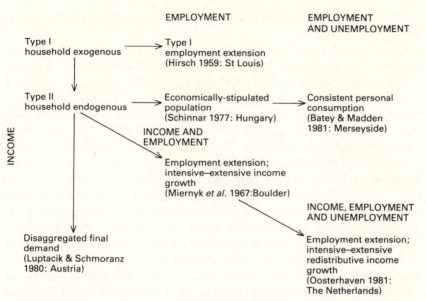

Figure 11.2 Extensions of the input–output model to include demographic variables.

economic activities and commodities can be applied to a whole family of extended input–output models, most of which stem from the basic Type II model. Structural similarities and differences between these models are analysed in detail in Batey (1985). Here it will be sufficient to point out the main distinguishing characteristics of the various members of this family of models. This can be done with the aid of Figure 11.2.

11.2.2 A classification of extended input–output models

In Figure 11.2 we classify input–output models according to their treatment of income, employment and unemployment and give examples of studies in which the models concerned have been made operational. The diagram shows that the Type II model is an extension of the Type I model and that most of the other models are developments of the Type II model. The only exception to this is Hirsch's St Louis model (Hirsch 1959) in which employment production functions are combined with the basic Type I model, so that forecasts of industrial gross output can be translated into employment forecasts.

The simplest extension of the Type II model involves disaggregation of the household sector to represent more than one income group of households. This approach has been followed in a number of studies, among them Artle's (1965) work on Hawaii and Sadler *et al.*'s (1970) work on Anglesey. Its theoretical implications are fully explored by Miyazawa (1976).

Other extensions of the Type II model can be classified according to whether they involve the addition of income and employment variables. Luptacik and Schmoranz's (1980) demo-economic model of Austria is interesting because it assumes that a component of final demand is determined by the size and structure of the population. However, at the same time household income and consumption are treated in the characteristic Type II manner described earlier. Two other models, due to Schinnar (1976) and Batey and Madden (1981), are notable in that household income is not modelled explicitly. Instead both models focus upon employment and its relationship with industrial gross output. The fundamental difference between these two models lies in their treatment of unemployment. In Schinnar's model unemployment (and consumption by unemployed workers) is a fixed *a priori* assumption and the employed population emerges as an output from the model. On the other hand, in the Batey–Madden model, the levels of employment and unemployment are both determined endogenously, given an input assumption about the size of the labour force. Formal mathematical relationships between the two models are derived in Batey (1985).

The two remaining models may both be regarded as hybrid in the sense that they each combine a representation of employment–production functions with an explicit treatment of income change. Miernyk *et al.*'s (1967) model was originally designed to evaluate the impact of the US space programme upon Boulder, Colorado, and takes account of two distinct kinds of income growth: intensive income growth reflecting a per capita growth in the incomes of existing residents and extensive income growth due to the inmigration of workers who are successful in obtaining employment in the study region. The second of these models, constructed by Oosterhaven (1981), takes the representation of income a step further by including the redistributive effect created when locally based workers move from a dependence on income derived from unemployment benefit to income from employment, and vice versa. An interregional version of this model has been used to estimate the effects of some features of regional policy in the Netherlands.

11.3 Methodological developments and empirical applications

11.3.1 The personal and household consumption frameworks

We shall now examine the Batey–Madden model more closely. We shall show that a better understanding of the effects of demographic and economic change can be obtained by interpreting the inverse of this model as a multiplier matrix. The various kinds of impact multiplier that can be derived from this inverse will be illustrated by reference to a model constructed using data for the Merseyside metropolitan area. We will then describe how this model can be linked with a multiregional population forecasting model in order to give estimates of future population and employment levels.

In its simplest form the Batey–Madden model can be expressed as

$$\mathbf{A}^*\mathbf{x} = \mathbf{b} \tag{11.3}$$

or as a system of three blocks of simultaneous equations:

$$\begin{bmatrix} \mathbf{I} - \mathbf{A} & -\beta & -\alpha \\ -\mathbf{l} & \mathbf{I} & \mathbf{0} \\ \mathbf{0} & \mathbf{I} & \mathbf{I} \end{bmatrix} \begin{bmatrix} \mathbf{x}_I \\ \mathbf{e} \\ \mathbf{u} \end{bmatrix} = \begin{bmatrix} \mathbf{d}_I \\ \mathbf{0} \\ \mathbf{p} \end{bmatrix} \tag{11.4}$$

where $\mathbf{A}^*$ is a (square) matrix of coefficients;

$\mathbf{A}$ is a (square) matrix of technical inter-industry coefficients;

β is a matrix of consumption coefficients: employed workers;

α is a matrix of consumption coefficients: unemployed workers;

$\mathbf{l}$ is a matrix of labour demand coefficients expressing employment per unit of sectoral gross output;

$\mathbf{I}$ is an identity matrix;

$\mathbf{x}$ is a vector of activity levels;

$\mathbf{x}_I$ is a vector of industrial gross output;

$\mathbf{e}$ is a vector of employed workers, by type of worker;

$\mathbf{u}$ is a vector of unemployed workers, by type of worker;

$\mathbf{b}$ is a vector of input variables;

$\mathbf{d}_I$ is a vector of industrial final demand;

$\mathbf{p}$ is a vector of labour supply.

The first block of equations sets gross output equal to the sum of intermediate and final demand:

$$(\mathbf{I} - \mathbf{A})\mathbf{x}_I - \beta\mathbf{e} - \alpha\mathbf{u} = \mathbf{d}_I \tag{11.5}$$

which, in rearranged form, gives

$$\mathbf{x}_I = \mathbf{A}\mathbf{x}_I + \beta\mathbf{e} + \alpha\mathbf{u} + \mathbf{d}_I \tag{11.6}$$

We note here that intermediate demand due to the consumption of employed and unemployed workers ($\beta\mathbf{e}$ and $\alpha\mathbf{u}$, respectively) is determined endogenously in that its magnitude depends on the solution of the simultaneous equations. The second block translates industrial gross output into labour demand:

$$\mathbf{e} = \mathbf{l}\mathbf{x}_I \tag{11.7}$$

if necessary by skill-type or income group of worker (otherwise $\mathbf{e}$ will be a scalar). In the final block labour demand and unemployment are summed and the result set equal to labour supply:

$$\mathbf{p} = \mathbf{e} + \mathbf{u} \tag{11.8}$$

Again it is possible to specify more than one type of worker. Net commuting between the study region and the surrounding area can be taken into account by appropriate entries in the input vector of the second block of equations.

The model in the form in which it is described here can be regarded as a consistent personal consumption framework: consistent because, unlike in other input–output models, there is no conflict between *a priori* and *a posteriori* measures of employment and unemployment; and personal because it represents consumption at the individual level, rather than for household units. As an alternative, a consistent household consumption framework may be put forward:

$$\begin{bmatrix} \mathbf{I} - \mathbf{A} & -\boldsymbol{\beta}_h & -\boldsymbol{\alpha}_h \\ -1 & \hat{\mathbf{W}} & \hat{0} \\ 0 & \mathbf{I} & \mathbf{I} \end{bmatrix} \begin{bmatrix} \mathbf{x}_I \\ \mathbf{h}_e \\ \mathbf{h}_u \end{bmatrix} = \begin{bmatrix} \mathbf{d}_I \\ 0 \\ \mathbf{h} \end{bmatrix} \tag{11.9}$$

In this case $\boldsymbol{\beta}_h$ and $\boldsymbol{\alpha}_h$ denote matrices of consumption coefficients for employed and unemployed households, respectively, while $\mathbf{h}_e$ and $\mathbf{h}_u$ are the numbers of households with employed (e) and unemployed (u) workers. Households are assigned to the employed category if they contain at least one employed worker; otherwise they are regarded as unemployed. $\hat{\mathbf{W}}$ is a diagonal matrix containing ratios of workers to households, each ratio applying to a different type of worker. This assumes that each household contains only one type of worker and, to allow for cases where a household has several different types of worker, $\hat{\mathbf{W}}$ can be replaced by $\mathbf{W}$ which has off-diagonal entries denoting the incidence of mixed composition households. Apart from these relatively minor differences, the household consumption framework follows the same structure as the personal consumption framework.

Inspecting the block equation structure of each of these models, we find that it is possible to partition the matrix of coefficients and the vectors of activity levels and inputs in order to separate the economic and demographic characteristics of the system. Thus, for example, $(\mathbf{I} - \mathbf{A})$ can be regarded as the interaction between economic activities and commodities,

$$\begin{bmatrix} 1 \\ 0 \end{bmatrix}$$

as the interaction between economic activities and demographic commodities, $[-\boldsymbol{\beta} - \boldsymbol{\alpha}]$ (or $[-\boldsymbol{\beta}_h - \boldsymbol{\alpha}_h]$) as the interaction between demographic activities and economic commodities and

$$\begin{bmatrix} \mathbf{I} & \mathbf{0} \\ \mathbf{I} & \mathbf{I} \end{bmatrix} \left(\text{or} \begin{bmatrix} \hat{\mathbf{W}} & \mathbf{0} \\ \mathbf{I} & \mathbf{I} \end{bmatrix} \right)$$

as the interaction between demographic activities and commodities. Partitioning the frameworks and their related inverses in this manner enables the main causal factors underlying forecasts of activity levels to be analysed (Batey & Madden 1981, 1983). It establishes, for example, how much of the shift in a sector's gross output can be attributed to economic change, how much to demographic change and how much to the interaction between economic and demographic variables.

In both models the inverse of the matrix of coefficients provides the basis for the construction of impact multipliers – analogous to the multipliers obtained from a conventional Leontief model – which indicate the effects on activity levels (gross output, employment and unemployment) of unit relaxations in the input variables (final demand, population or number of households). Here for the sake of simplicity we will focus on the interpretation of the personal consumption framework. Supposing that we denote the inverse by the following matrix:

$$(\mathbf{A}^*)^{-1} = \begin{bmatrix} \Delta & \Lambda \\ \Pi & \Gamma \end{bmatrix} \tag{11.10}$$

Like the earlier matrices of coefficients the inverse has been partitioned, so that Δ is $n \times n$, Λ is $n \times m$, Π is $m \times n$ and Γ is $m \times m$, where n is the number of economic activities and m the number of demographic activities. Submatrix Δ represents the effects on gross output of unit changes in final demand, a single entry Δ_{ij} denoting the effect on sector i's gross output of a unit change in sector j's final demand. If columns in Δ are summed, we are able to obtain a production or output multiplier, ϕ_j:

$$\phi_j = \sum_{i=1}^{n} \Delta_{ij} \tag{11.11}$$

Sub-matrix Π contains information about the direct, indirect and induced effects upon employment and unemployment of a unit change in final demand. In the most straightforward case where only one type of worker is identified, the first row of Π denotes employment effects and the second row unemployment effects. Because an increase in employment is matched by a corresponding decrease in unemployment the second row merely repeats the entries in the first row, with signs reversed. In fact the entries in the first row of Π are of particular interest in that when they are divided by the appropriate entry from $\mathbf{l}$ in the matrix of coefficients an employment multiplier is obtained which is comparable but not identical to that from a

Type II input–output model (Richardson 1972, Batey & Madden 1983):

$$\psi_j = \frac{\Pi_{1j}}{l_j} \qquad (11.12)$$

where ψ_j is the employment multiplier for sector j

Π_{1j} is the jth entry in row 1 of Π, and

l_j is the jth entry in l.

Turning now to submatrix Λ, we find information about the effects on gross output of unit changes in demographic input variables. This information relates to two distinct kinds of change. The first $m/2$ columns of Λ indicate the impact on gross output of a unit increase in net outcommuting; in other words, the effect of a locally resident unemployed worker taking a job outside the study area but continuing to live within that area. The second m_2 columns of Λ have a more straightforward interpretation and show the impact on gross output of a unit increase in the size of the labour force, either as a result of net inmigration or because of a change in the age structure of the population or a change in labour-force participation rates. By summing columns in Λ we can obtain demographic–economic production multipliers which complement the economic production multipliers derived from Δ.

The final submatrix to be interpreted is Γ, the bottom right-hand quadrant of the inverse. The simplest version of Γ is 2×2, although when there is more than one type of worker its size increases substantially: $2k \times 2k$, where k is the number of types of worker. When $k = 1$ it can be shown (Batey & Madden 1983) that

$$\Gamma_{11} = \frac{1}{1 - \gamma + \delta} \qquad (11.13)$$

$$\Gamma_{12} = \frac{\delta}{1 - \gamma + \delta} \qquad (11.14)$$

$$\Gamma_{21} = \frac{-1}{1 - \gamma + \delta} \qquad (11.15)$$

$$\Gamma_{22} = \frac{1 - \gamma}{1 - \gamma + \delta} \qquad (11.16)$$

where γ and δ are defined as

$$\gamma = l(I - A)^{-1}\beta \qquad (11.17)$$

and

$$\delta = l(I - A)^{-1}\alpha \qquad (11.18)$$

the direct and indirect effects upon employment of the consumption of an employed or an unemployed worker, respectively.

Element Γ_{11} is of particular interest since it can be interpreted as a multisector employment multiplier, analogous to the Keynesian multisector income multiplier obtainable from the inverse of a conventional Type II input–output model (Bradley & Gander 1969, Miyazawa 1976). Γ_{11} can be seen as the effect on the study region's employment level of an exogenous unit increase in employment. The mirror image of this effect upon unemployment in the region is given by Γ_{21}. The two remaining elements, Γ_{12} and Γ_{22}, demonstrate the effects upon employment and unemployment, respectively, of unit increases in the size of the labour force. Because all new additions to the labour force must either become employed or unemployed, it is possible to interpret element Γ_{12} and Γ_{22} as probabilities: in the former case the probability of gaining employment, and in the latter case the probability of remaining unemployed, assuming that all other factors (particularly final demand) remain constant. Since Γ_{12} and Γ_{22} are probabilities and together they exhaust the range of possible outcomes their sum is unity.

11.3.2 Impact multipliers for Merseyside

To illustrate the various types of impact multipliers that can be obtained we draw upon a consistent personal consumption framework constructed for the county of Merseyside in North-West England. Merseyside is a metropolitan area with a population of approximately 1.5 million and an industrial base that has experienced a sharp decline in the last fifteen years. The unemployment rate for the county has remained consistently above the national average for more than 50 years.

The Merseyside personal consumption framework consists of 32 simultaneous equations. It includes an input–output model with 15 sectors based on the non-survey input–output table of de Kanter and Morrison (1978), a demographic component in which twelve groups are identified according to age, sex and marital status, and two types of worker defined according to occupational skills (manual and non-manual). This framework differs slightly from that described earlier in this chapter in that labour-force participation rates and headship rates are absorbed into the matrix of coefficients. This enables the multiplier effects of unit changes in each of the twelve demographic categories to be traced within the framework.

The results obtained from the inverse of the Merseyside framework can be presented most effectively by reference to the four quadrants defined earlier: Δ, Π, Λ and Γ. These results are shown in Tables 11.1 to 11.4 for a selection of demographic categories and economic sectors.

Table 11.1 shows that in Merseyside the largest effects upon industrial output are obtained when final demand changes are made in the public administration, the oils and fats sector and the textiles and transport sectors, reflecting the strong pattern of local inter-industry linkages associated with each of these sectors. Table 11.2 summarizes the impact on local

Table 11.1 Quadrant Δ: economic production multipliers.

Sector	Multiplier
agriculture	1.216
oils and fats	1.431
food	1.391
textiles	1.418
chemicals	1.404
paper	1.278
engineering	1.354
vehicles	1.268
construction	1.073
energy	1.325
transport	1.415
port	1.233
distributive trades	1.173
miscellaneous services	1.210
public administration	2.139

Note: economic production multiplier = the effects upon total gross output of a unit change in a given sector's final demand.

Table 11.2 Quadrant Π: employment multipliers.

Sector	Multiplier	
	Non-manual	Manual
agriculture	1.186	1.242
oils and fats	2.154	1.954
food	1.653	1.315
textiles	1.660	1.186
chemicals	1.567	1.256
paper	1.379	1.233
engineering	1.411	1.217
vehicles	1.209	1.203
construction	1.278	1.360
energy	1.345	1.114
transport	1.757	1.315
port	1.214	1.189
distributive trades	1.126	1.467
miscellaneous services	1.175	1.467
public administration	1.757	2.010

Note: employment multiplier = the direct, indirect and induced effects upon employment of a unit change in final demand divided by the direct effects of that same change.

Table 11.3 Quadrant Λ: demographic–economic multipliers.

Sector	Male population			
	0–19	20–39	40–59	60 +
agriculture	0	0	0	0
oils and fats	1	1	1	0
food	4	4	4	2
textiles	3	3	3	1
chemicals	6	7	7	3
paper	13	16	15	6
engineering	8	10	10	4
vehicles	7	9	9	4
construction	8	9	9	4
energy	85	103	101	48
transport	42	51	50	18
port	3	4	4	2
distributive trades	583	707	695	289
miscellaneous services	452	549	538	227
public administration	47	56	55	23

Note: demographic–economic multipliers = effects upon sectoral gross output of a unit change in a given demographic category (effect is measured in £ sterling at 1970 prices).

employment of changes in final demand, the employment multiplier measuring the ratio between direct, indirect and induced effects and direct effects. It is clear that for most sectors employment multiplier impacts are stronger for non-manual jobs than manual jobs. Again, oils and fats and public administration are the sectors most affected. In Table 11.3 the effects of demographic change can be seen. Here we see that when the population aged 20–59 changes this has massive repercussions for the distributive trades and miscellaneous services sectors, but only a very limited effect upon the manufacturing sectors. Finally in Table 11.4 we present a series of multisector multipliers. Γ_{11} provides an indication of how local employment would benefit if an unemployed Merseyside resident were to obtain a job outside the region: in addition to his own job, a further 0.0714 jobs would be generated locally because the resident's shift from an unemployed to an employed status means a higher rate of personal consumption. The mirror image of this effect – upon unemployment – is given by Γ_{21}. Cells Γ_{12} and Γ_{22} are probabilities showing the likelihood of a new Merseyside resident obtaining employment or remaining unemployed, respectively. From this evidence, a new resident has a one in four chance of obtaining employment, although it must be emphasized that this is an average probability and the actual rate would vary considerably depending on the worker's age and skills.

Table 11.4 Quadrant Γ: multisector multipliers.

Multiplier	Definition	Numerical value
Γ_{11}	multisector employment multiplier: the direct, indirect and induced effects upon local employment of an exogenous unit change in employment	$\dfrac{1}{1 - \gamma + \delta} = 1.0714$
Γ_{21}	multisector unemployment multiplier: the direct, indirect and induced effects upon local unemployment of an exogenous unit change in employment	$\dfrac{-1}{1 - \gamma + \delta} = -1.0714$
Γ_{12}	probability of a new entrant to the labour force obtaining employment	$\dfrac{\delta}{1 - \gamma + \delta} = 0.2538$
Γ_{22}	probability of a new entrant to the labour force remaining unemployed	$\dfrac{1 - \gamma}{1 - \gamma + \delta} = 0.7462$
γ	direct and indirect effects upon employment of the consumption of one employed worker	0.3035
δ	direct and indirect effects upon employment of the consumption of one unemployed worker	0.2369

11.4 The household consumption framework as a forecasting device

11.4.1 Linkages in the forecasting framework

We have seen in the previous section how an extended input–output model can be used as a device for the analysis of impacts on the demographic–economic system. It should also be apparent that like a conventional input–output model these models can also be used as forecasting devices, either to produce projections of a system under study or to simulate through time the results of the application of different policies. Although the models we have described here are static in that there is no internal, endogenous mechanism for altering the values of coefficients, it is a reasonable assumption to make that over fairly short periods of time the input coefficients, the labour demand coefficients and the patterns of household consumption will remain stable.

In a demographic–economic system any attempt at forecasting must involve the projection of population growth or decline, the projection of economic growth or decline and the linking of these two components of change. We focus here upon the household consumption model which requires as inputs levels of active population and final demand. We shall assume that final demand is an exogenously determined quantity and demonstrate here how the model can be integrated with a purely demographic model to produce forecasts. We can expect the outputs from such an exercise to include labour demand, labour supply and unemployment forecasts.

We shall explore the problems involved with linking the household consumption model with a multiregional cohort survival model by drawing upon previous work (Madden & Batey 1980, Madden *et al.* 1981, Batey & Madden 1983) which has attempted to apply such a conjoint modelling system to the Merseyside metropolitan area. We can start the exploration with a Rogers-type multiregional model (Rogers 1968, 1975). Let us assume that our area of study is one region within a set of regions, identified by the subscript i. Then

$$\mathbf{k}_{t+n} = \mathbf{G}^* \mathbf{k}_t \qquad (11.19)$$

where $\mathbf{k}$ is the multiregional vector of population and $\mathbf{G}^*$ is the characteristic Rogers multiregional growth operator. Within $\mathbf{G}^*$ of course we can locate $\mathbf{G}^{*ii}$, the regional growth operator of our study area, and a set of matrices $\mathbf{G}^{*ji}$, $j = 1 \ldots n$ where n is the number of regions, representing migration from the study area to all other regions, $\mathbf{G}^{*ij}$ representing migration into the study area from all other regions and $\mathbf{G}^{*kj}$, $j, k \neq i$, $j \neq k$, representing migration among the other regions (see Rees & Wilson 1977). Assuming that we can establish from other sources the necessary survival and fertility rates for the age-specific and sex-specific components of the regional populations, in order to fill the appropriate cells in the $\mathbf{G}^{*ii}$ we are faced with the problem of establishing the entries for the $\mathbf{G}^{*ji}$, $i \neq j$.

As far as the base year is concerned let us further assume that we have census or survey data on migration between the regions and thus can establish the migration rates for the population, including neonates, by appropriate manipulation of the migration and population figures and the known survival and fertility rates. We recognize that there are errors and inaccuracies involved in crude exercises of this sort, but acknowledge their precise documentation in Rees and Wilson (1977) and ignore them for the purposes of our argument. We can then fill $\mathbf{G}^{*ji}$, $i \neq j$ for the base year using these rates. However, in order to fill these submatrices of the growth operator in future years we need to model migration in those years. We can choose any multiregional migration model, provided that it is possible from its output to create $\mathbf{G}^{*ji}$, $i \neq j$ entries and that its inputs are available as exogenous or endogenous forecasts.

In order to demonstrate the linking of the models let us adopt a migration model that depends upon, among other input variables, the unemployment rates in the regions under consideration (for a specification of the model used in the Merseyside study see Madden 1977). We can then represent the forecasting process by Figure 11.3. Matrix $\mathbf{G}^{*ji}$, $i \neq j$, representing migration flows from the base year to the end of the first time period, can be

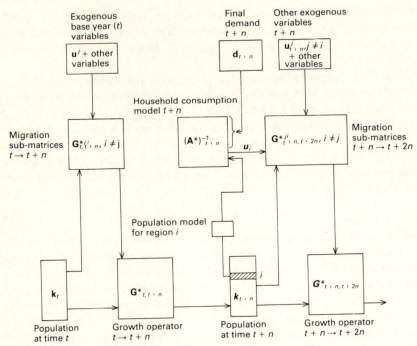

Figure 11.3 The forecasting framework.

constructed using the migration model with a knowledge of the base year variables relevant to the model for all regions, and $\mathbf{k}_t$ and $\mathbf{G}^*_{t,t+n}$ can be created in the usual way. $\mathbf{k}_{t+n}$ is then derived and the subvector $\mathbf{k}^i_{t,t+n}$ extracted to provide an input to $(\mathbf{A}^*)^{-1}_{t+n}$ after suitable attenuation to produce economically active from 'raw' population. Let us identify this subvector as $\mathbf{p}^i_{t+n}$. Together with the exogenously determined $\mathbf{d}_{t+n}$, this subvector drives the household consumption framework which distributes active population between employed and unemployed. Some measure of unemployment $\mathbf{u}^i$ is an output of $(\mathbf{A}^*)^{-1}_{t+n}$, which then, together with other information about region i and sets of information including $\mathbf{u}^j_{t+n}$, $j \neq i$ for the other regions in the system, provides an input to the migration model. The output from this in turn, together with $\mathbf{k}_{t+n}$, provides input for $\mathbf{G}^{*ji}_{t+n, t+2n}$, $i \neq j$. The process is recursive.

In this forecasting ensemble the household consumption model is acting as an employment distribution device. Alternative outcomes and scenarios will be determined by the exogenous inputs, in this case the successive (in time) vectors $\mathbf{d}$ of final demand and the information $\mathbf{u}^j$, $j \neq i$ and other variables relating to the study area and other regions, as well as any changes made to the coefficients inside the growth operator matrices $\mathbf{G}^*$, the model $\mathbf{A}^*$, and the attenuation process between $\mathbf{k}^i$ and $\mathbf{A}^*$.

11.4.2 *The marital state population model*

Obviously the relationship between $\mathbf{K}^i$ and $\mathbf{P}^i$ is crucially important for the establishment of $\mathbf{u}^i$. In the Merseyside study we have applied a model developed from earlier work by Masser (1972) and Spohr (1974), which takes explicit account of marital state mix. This is a particularly important component in determining female activity rates, and is also highly significant in determining household formation rates.

The model follows the usual conventions of accounting and of cohort survival technique: the population is aged, and its marital status simultaneously changed, by shifting members of the population among the categories single, married, widowed and divorced. Figure 11.4 demonstrates the feasible changes. Note that several of the transitions imply more than one move between marital states. For a person in the widowed state at the start of the time period to appear in the divorced state at the end means that he or she married again during the period and subsequently got divorced. Column headings represent marital state at the beginning of the time period and row headings status at the end of the period. For reasons which will become clear it is necessary to treat the transitions differently, first to simulate reality as closely as possible and secondly to ensure consistency.

The basis of the method is to apply sets of probabilities to the population which determine the survival of age-, sex- and marital state-specific cohorts, as well as the movement among marital states. This is carried out by deriving a set of marital status change rates for each age-specific and sex-specific cohort, and a separate set of survival rates. Cohorts can then be aged, and changes in their marital status projected, by application of the sets of survival rates and marital status rates. We ignore the finer details of whether survival rates vary during a period as a person changes marital status and adopt the survival rate of their status at the beginning of the cohort. In principle, following Masser, we can develop a model for a single region and single sex.

$$\mathbf{k}_{t+n}^M = \mathbf{M}^s \mathbf{k}_t^M \tag{11.20}$$

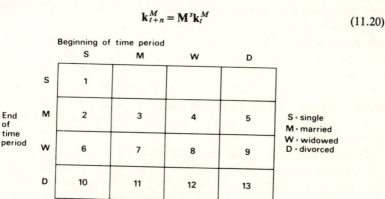

Figure 11.4 The marital state transitions.

where $\mathbf{k}^M$ is a vector of age-specific and marital status-specific population of the form

$$\begin{bmatrix} \mathbf{k}_1^s \\ \mathbf{k}_2^s \\ \cdot \\ \cdot \\ \cdot \\ \mathbf{k}_m^s \end{bmatrix}$$

where $\mathbf{k}_l^s$ is a vector of numbers of people in age group l disaggregated by marital status. $\mathbf{M}^s$ is a square growth operator matrix consisting of the subdiagonal of age-specific submatrices of the form of Figure 11.4, attenuated for survival, with a set of birth rates for the female population along the top row. In effect this model is the single-region cohort survival model with each survivorship entry disaggregated to a 4×4 matrix, and with age-specific birth rates similarly disaggregated into four.

However, the model cannot be operated in this structurally simple format because of errors of consistency which occur. Let us inspect each transition in Figure 11.4 in turn. Transition 1, people remaining single, presents little difficulty. Population at time t is aged and the proportion remaining single calculated to give the number of people still alive and single at time $t + n$. Transitions 2, 4 and 5, involving people of non-married status who become married, require different treatment to ensure that the number of new male marriages is equal to the number of new female marriages. The method adopted is due to Spohr (1974). Marriage rates 2, 4 and 5 are multiplied by a factor ρ, and a set of 'primary' marriages obtained for men and for women in each age group. We followed Spohr in adopting a ρ of 0.5. The difference between the notional total marriages in each age group applying the rates before multiplication by ρ and the 'primary' marriages is designated as 'secondary' marriages. Since $\rho = 0.5$, primary and secondary marriages for each sex are equal in number. Secondary marriages are specified by applying an age distribution of spouses to the number of secondary marriages for each sex and identifying this distribution as new marriages for the other sex. Formally, if m_l is the number of men in a particular age group who are expected to marry and f_l the equivalent number of female marriages, we can specify primary marriages of ρm_l and ρf_l. We can then distribute ρf_l 'secondary' husbands across a range of male ages and ρm_l equivalent wives. This process applied across $l = a, b, \ldots, m$ ensures that consistency is achieved between total new male and female marriages. Here we age the population before applying marriage rates and distribution probabilities.

Transition 3 presents different problems. Consistency must be achieved here between the total number of men remaining alive and married and the total number of women in the same condition. We achieve this by the very crude method of scaling each set of married survivors to the mean of the unscaled totals. Transitions 6, 7 and 9 are treated in the same way as new marriages. Male and female deaths in each age group are calculated, and age distributions of widows and widowers are respectively applied to the figures for each age group. These new widows and widowers are then aged. Transitions 10, 11 and 12, relating to new divorces and divorcees are executed by ageing and divorcing the population and then scaling so that total male divorces equal total female divorces. Transitions 8 and 13 are not susceptible to errors of inconsistency of the type described here.

Clearly this model involves a great deal of explicit manipulation to avoid inconsistencies. Experience has shown that the actual size of the inconsistencies is not large and that the manipulations in any one time period do not normally involve changes in the outputs of more than about 3% for the larger flows in the system (such as new marriages). New divorces have tended to demonstrate a greater inconsistency, but since the numbers are (historically) so small this has proved a minor error. There are other inconsistencies which are not taken account of. For example, our figures for widows and widowers in the Merseyside study were taken from projections of married male and female deaths. No account was taken of those single or divorced people who married and then died during a time period.

The model described here is a hybrid formulation: marriages, for example, are determined by transition rates, whereas widows and widowers are created by applying distributions to the numbers of male and female deaths. Transitions 6, 7 and 9 are not therefore modelled in the same way as the other transitions, and there are a number of error corrections necessary in other transitions.

In order to fit a model of this sort into the framework shown in Figure 11.3, it is necessary to override the output in k_{t+n} for the study area and in a sense to run a parallel modelling of the study area alongside the Rogers multiregional cohort survival model. Migration into and out of the study area can be taken account of by either simply scaling the marital state disaggregated population to ensure that each age group is consistent in total with the cohort survival projections as a control, or by incorporating inmigration and outmigration probabilities into the survival rates used in the marital status model. In either case, there will be a difference between the method of modelling the population in the study area and that in other regions. The advantage of this approach is the greater accuracy obtained in the forecasting of active population and household formation for input to the $(A^*)^{-1}$ matrix model. In the empirical results presented in the next section we scaled the marital state-specific population so that the male and female total populations were equal to those projected by the cohort survival model.

11.4.3 Forecasting the Merseyside demographic–economic system

The household consumption framework used in the case study has at its centre an input–output model for the county of Merseyside developed by consultants for the County Council using the RAS non-survey technique for a base year of 1970 (de Kanter & Morrison 1978). This is the same input–output model as that used in the impact multiplier study. Full details of the procedures used in setting up the data for the household consumption framework are given in Madden *et al.* (1981). Sources included the Family Expenditure Survey 1970 (Department of Employment 1971), the Annual Census of Employment 1971 (Department of Employment 1973), the 1971 census at national and local level and the national input–output table for 1970.

The multiregional cohort survival model was developed to encompass a system of four regions: Merseyside, the rest of the North-West region, Clwyd and the rest of Great Britain. The two local regions were considered important as areas where inmigration and outmigration to and from Merseyside were likely to occur and as likely sources and sinks of any commuting across the county boundary. This commuting was assumed constant and was derived from census journey-to-work tables. Survival rates for the populations in the four regions were obtained from Part I of the Registrar General's statistical review for 1971 (OPCS 1973); transition probabilities between the marital states and the distributions of spouses and widows and widowers were obtained from Part II of the review (OPCS 1973). Migration rates for the period t to $t + n$ were derived from known base year variables, the migration model, a regression-based gross migration formulation, and the base year population vectors.

The method of operation was straightforward. In the first instance the multiregional cohort survival model was implemented, transforming the base year population vectors $\mathbf{k}_t$ into the end-of-period vectors $\mathbf{k}_{t+n}$. The marital state model was then operated for the study area alone, producing output vectors $\mathbf{k}_{t+n}^M$. Each of these (male and female) vectors was then scaled within each age group to bring the distribution into line with that of the $\mathbf{k}_{t+n}$ vectors, and the activity rates and household information rates were applied to each scaled vector to obtain the total active workforce and the total number of households. These were then used as inputs, along with the regional-specific final demand by sector, to the Merseyside $(\mathbf{A}^*)^{-1}$ household consumption framework. Output from this model showed the industrial activity levels, the number of employed and unemployed households and unemployed non-heads of households. From these figures an unemployment rate was derived, which was used as one of the input variables, u_i, to the migration model in the next round. This process was iterated for three quinquennial time periods, producing forecasts of the Merseyside demographic–economic system from 1976 to 1986. Variation in the forecasts are made possible by altering the final demand vectors used in each time period and altering the values of the exogenous variables used in the migration model (in this case u^j, $j \neq i$).

Table 11.5 Merseyside demographic–economic forecasts.

	1971	1976	1981	1986	1971–6	1976–81	1981–6
total population	1 657 115	1 596 423	1 534 206	1 501 367	− 60 692	− 62 217	− 32 839
number of households:							
active	481 635	492 129	456 356	429 024	10 494	− 35 773	− 27 332
inactive	63 586	63 297	86 924	111 036	− 289	23 627	24 112
average household size	3.039	2.870	2.824	2.780	0.169	0.046	0.044
economically active	711 301	702 163	687 152	668 425	− 9 138	− 15 011	− 18 727
net commuting	− 1 615	− 1 615	− 1 615	− 1 615	0	0	0
unemployment	46 867	61 252	92 438	125 062	14 385	31 186	32 624
unemployment rate	6.59%	8.72%	13.45%	18.71%	2.13	4.73	5.26
labour demand	664 434	640 911	596 714	543 363	− 23 523	− 44 197	− 53 351

In Table 11.5 we present some selected data from our fifteen-year forecast exercise. The changes in marital status of the Merseyside population aged 15 and over are shown in Table 11.6.

In Table 11.5 we can see a substantial decrease in the county population between 1971 and 1986; it is rapid at first and then begins to slow down towards the end of the period. However within this overall decrease there are interesting shifts in numbers of households and numbers of economically active ones. Active households show an initial increase in number caused by the increase in household formation rates and the initially young population. After 1976, however, this increase in numbers reverses, until by 1986 the number of active households has dropped considerably. This contrasts with an initial decrease in numbers of inactive households, followed by a dramatic increase towards the end of the time period as the population ages. The number of economically active households, as a function particularly of the age of the population, decreases throughout the period, although not as rapidly as the fall-off in labour demand, which reflects the decline in the economy of Merseyside, coupled with rationalization by local firms. This of course produces the rapid increase in unemployment.

In Table 11.6 we can observe the changes in marital state of the population aged over fifteen. As the population ages the proportion of single people decreases relative to the population as a whole and the proportion of married people increases. This change is so pronounced that there is actually an increase in married population from 1981–6 despite a decrease in the total population. The number of widowed males similarly increases, although widowed females actually decrease in number. We might expect the latter as the overall population declines; the former can be explained in part by the converging of male and female death rates. Divorced population increases throughout the period, although less so for men than for women because of the greater tendency for men to remarry after divorce than for women to do so.

Table 11.6 Population aged 15 + in different marital states.

		Single	Married	Widowed	Divorced
1971	male	160 314	387 070	22 858	5 737
	female	151 119	391 087	100 802	9 116
1976	male	152 821	387 078	23 430	10 402
	female	146 247	390 917	99 582	14 776
1981	male	148 779	385 107	24 227	11 394
	female	138 323	388 759	96 922	16 984
1986	male	146 725	387 548	25 523	12 998
	female	133 905	390 821	95 336	20 091

It should be stressed here that we do not present these results as actual forecasts. Clearly there are discrepancies between the 1981 results shown here and the reality of 1981 as recorded in the Census of Population. Our intention is merely to indicate typical outputs from the forecasting framework and to demonstrate the breadth of its coverage. The economic assumptions (in terms of final demand) and the exogenous inputs of employment rates in surrounding regions were chosen for this exercise to accord as closely as possible with our assumptions as to what was reasonable and to recorded information. Alternative scenarios for 1986 could obviously be developed. Elsewhere (Batey & Madden 1981) we present and discuss alternative scenarios of this sort.

11.5 Conclusions

11.5.1 The Batey–Madden model

We have demonstrated in this chapter the relationship between a Leontief-type input–output model and the Batey–Madden model. This relationship involves the addition of three quadrants to the interindustrial sector of the Leontief model (see Eqn 11.4). The top right-hand quadrant contains a disaggregated set of personal household consumption vectors representing consumption by employed persons (households) and unemployed persons (households). Further disaggregation can distinguish between workers of different income or skill types (Batey & Madden 1981). The bottom left-hand quadrant identifies labour demand through the introduction of a labour coefficient vector or vectors, each element of which refers to one industrial sector. Again disaggregation can take place to explicitly represent demand for different types of labour.

The bottom right-hand quadrant then contains an allocation matrix which relates economically active population to labour demand. This matrix contains the most significant innovation in the model, the balancing of labour demand and supply with an explicit recognition of the importance of the difference in consumption between employed and unemployed workers. The unemployment level is endogenized in this model, and the feedback relationships between industrial output, labour demand and consumption treated consistently.

The inverse of the $\mathbf{A}^*$ matrix as we have seen contains a range of useful and informative multipliers, which can be used to identify the effects of changes in population and of final demand upon output and, more importantly, employment. In forecasting, the model can be linked easily with more orthodox demographic modelling systems and provides outputs which are of direct relevance to the assessment of migration flows between regions.

295

11.5.2 Future directions

There are a number of areas in which we intend to refine our model. Two of the most fruitful are in terms of further disaggregation of the demographic side of the labour supply and demand equation and of an explicit introduction of spatial disaggregation into the model. At the moment the labour force in the system can be disaggregated by type, but not by age. We model differential household consumption by type of worker, but not by age of worker. It is evident that the aggregate consumption of a household must have some relation to the age of the principal worker. We intend therefore to disaggregate the household sector of the model by age into, say, three or four relevantly spaced cohorts, and to identify the different consumption totals and patterns that will occur. This is more important when dealing with consumption of employed households.

At the same time it will be necessary to model age-disaggregated labour demand, so that any mismatches will occur differentially with age groups. However, there are problems with making labour demand age-specific. In principle it may not matter what the age of a worker is in many jobs, and we have fixed coefficients of labour demand and, by implication, fixed wage bills. If we age the labour force, for example, our *a priori* assumption is that, unemployment remaining equal, household consumption will increase. Ignoring knock-on effects, this implies an increase in the wage bill with fixed labour demand, which our model cannot currently deal with. However, if we assume a constant age distribution of employment within each sector such a circumstance would create an increase in unemployment in the older workers and a decrease in unemployment in younger workers. This is not an entirely unrealistic scenario to suggest.

The introduction of space is also of interest. So far we have talked of a single-region model. By expansion of the whole system we can develop a multiregional formulation, which enables interregional multipliers to be calculated where the effects of changes in employment or population in one region spill over into the other areas of the system through both direct economic linkages and interactional phenomena such as crossing regional boundaries to consume. If we identify three interactive matrices, one each for journey to work, journey to shop by employed consumers and journey to shop by unemployed consumers, we can locate these within the bottom right-hand quadrant to model interregional interaction. At the same time we can develop differential, region-specific consumption patterns and set up a separate group of labour demand vectors for each region. The Leontief portion of the model can be dealt with in two ways. We can either retain one Leontief model to represent the economy of the whole system of regions, or we can develop a separate input–output table for each region and locate these down the diagonal of the $\mathbf{A}^*$ matrix. Given the difficulty of creating input–output matrices it is likely that the first approach will be the easier to implement. We are then in a position to introduce a set of regions within one A^* matrix and to produce a whole range of multipliers with a great deal of information in them concerning the effects of changes in the demographic and economic characteristics of regions on all other regions within a system.

We anticipate that the development of these two areas of the model will be the first task we undertake and that the realization of these developments will greatly aid our capacity to understand and predict the structure of shifts in employment and unemployment within a multiregional system.

PART III

Reconstruction, estimation and evaluation of demographic patterns

12

Demographic estimation: problems, methods and examples

PHILIP REES and ROBERT WOODS

In seeking to describe the spatial and temporal patterns that characterize human populations (Part I of this volume) or in wishing to organize that description in ways that make some predictions possible and testable (Part II), the researcher faces the question: Are there data of sufficient reliability and of the right kind to enable me to provide an adequate description or to make operational my model of the population? The answer to that question is rarely in the affirmative.

The reason is that students of population are seldom able to specify and control what data are gathered on populations of millions of persons. It is simply too expensive for the individual researcher — or for the research institute — to mount surveys of the whole population. Reliance must therefore be placed on the agencies of national governments charged with collecting demographic statistics to provide the necessary information.

In the long run pioneering efforts by academic researchers and the resulting reports will persuade official statisticians to extend or to improve the kind of statistics that are gathered. Most influential in this respect are those customers of official demographic agencies with the financial resources to pay for improved data (in the United Kingdom these have largely been central government departments or local authorities rather than institutions of higher education). In the short run the research scholar must resort to estimating the necessary missing information from the available scraps at his or her disposal. Some of these data problems are most acute where the statistical system is newly developed, in Western nations prior to the 20th century, and in contemporary Latin America, Africa and Asia.

In the following sections we emphasize the need for making regional demographic estimates and discuss the problems encountered in the process, but we use illustrations that are intended to highlight the value of estimation methods in the relatively sophisticated statistical context of

America and Europe compared with that in most developing countries. We use India to represent the latter. The former is treated in a more theoretical fashion since several of the issues involved, together with the necessity for estimation, have already been raised in passing in Part II. We begin with some definitions in Section 12.1 before developing conceptual frameworks in Sections 12.2 to 12.5. In Section 12.6 we illustrate the use of the frameworks by estimating external migration flows for a set of developed country regions. In Section 12.7 we introduce a particular case study for a developing country. By these means we not only look back to Parts I and II, but also introduce Chapters 13 and 14.

12.1 A definition of estimation

Estimation is the process of transforming the available or raw demographic data for a population into the information required in a descriptive framework or analytical model (Fig. 12.1a). Sometimes that estimation is merely the adding up of data items to form the model variables; more

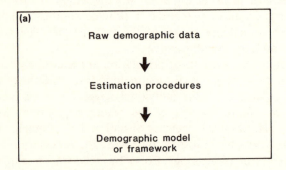

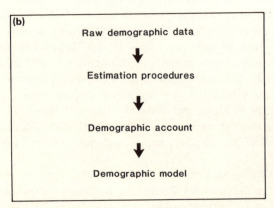

Figure 12.1 Estimation procedures as the interface between data and model.

usually the data items need to be broken down into the required model variables. In some applications an additional interface is also present (Fig. 12.1b): that of the demographic account, a representation of state-to-state population changes from which the researcher may build his or her population model.

What elements are necessary in the estimation of variables for spatial population models? We need to consider

(a) the concepts used in defining the population stocks and flows;
(b) the age–time frameworks adopted;
(c) the spatial frameworks used; and
(d) the temporal and accounting frameworks employed.

These elements should not be neglected in any spatial population analysis. The first two considerations are treated in some depth in many demographic texts (for example, Shryock & Siegel 1976), but the third and fourth have received less attention.

12.2 The concepts used in defining the population stocks and flows

Traditionally in demographic models it is the *de facto* or usually resident population that is counted at points in time, and the events associated with population change are related to that usually resident population. Usual residence is defined using some minimum length of stay (1 month, 6 months, 1 year) in an area. It is the place at which a person customarily resides. Mobile persons, particularly those moving between one family stage and another, cause problems. Vagrants, students and members of the armed forces fall into this category. Detailed knowledge of the definitions used in the statistical sources employed is needed, and an attempt should be made to match these most closely with the concept required in the model or descriptive framework.

However, for many planning applications, it is important to assess the actual numbers of people present in an area, rather than just the permanently resident population. For example, both public and private (for example, retailing) planning in resorts requires knowledge of the numbers of people staying in the town, including visitors, month by month. The traditional components of change model

$$P^i(t+i) = P^i(t) + B^i - D^i + M^{Oi} - M^{iO} \qquad (12.1)$$

must be extended to read

$$P^i(t+1) = P^i(t) + B^i - D^i + M^{Oi} - M^{iO} + V^{Oi} - V^{iO} \qquad (12.2)$$

where the superscript i refers to the area in question, P to population, B to births, D to deaths, M to migration, and V to visitors. The superscripts iO refer to moves from area i to the outside world, and Oi moves from the outside world to area i. The terms t and $t + 1$ refer to successive points in time one interval apart. Visitor statistics are rarely collected and must be estimated through a survey of the registers of places of stay.

Equation 12.1 still focuses on population stocks. Person–time may, in certain circumstances, be a more useful concept. To compute person–time, coefficients that measure length of stay would be applied to each of the terms in the population change equation. However, the person–time concept can only be derived from a person or transition version of the components of growth equation

$$P^i(t + 1) = K^{..si} = K^{eisi} + \sum_{j \neq i} K^{ejsi} + K^{bisi} + \sum_{j \neq i} K^{bjsi} \tag{12.3}$$

where K is a count of persons, and the superscripts indicate the transition in a time period characteristic of this count: e represents existence at time t; i,j are labels for locations; s represents survival at time $t + 1$. This is linked back to the initial population by substituting for the surviving stayer and infant surviving stayer terms. The person–time measure is then simply a weighted sum of the terms in the component equation, where the weights are proportional to the length of residence of the persons represented by the terms for the areas being studied (for details see Rees & Wilson 1977).

This discussion serves to show that there are important differences in the way components of change are measured. In Equation 12.1 they are represented as counts of events or moves; in Equation 12.3 they are person or transition counts. This distinction is crucial in spatial demography. The data used must match in concept those required in the models employed, and the appropriate equation should be used in estimating the model rates. Table 12.1 outlines the differences between the inputs to the movement and the transition approaches to spatial population analysis. Although the distinction has been known for some time (Courgeau 1973, Rees 1977,

Table 12.1 The two approaches to spatial population analysis.

Component	Movement approach	Transition approach
stocks	initial population final population in a time interval	initial population final population in a time interval
flows	births deaths inmigrations outmigrations	persons born persons dying inmigrants outmigrants

Ledent 1980), the full implications of the distinction for discrete population models are still being worked out. The Chapter 7 projections for United Kingdom zones are all carried out using movement data, as are the analyses of Netherlands migration in Chapter 9. In Chapter 8 Stillwell employs transition data for 1966–71 and movement data for 1976–81, and this restricts the amount of cross-temporal comparison of the level of migration activity that he can carry out.

It should be noted that there are methods of measuring migration such as the last residence census question or the place of births question for which adequate models of population change in a fixed time interval have yet to be developed (for a discussion of the issues see Rees 1984a).

12.3   The age–time frameworks adopted

12.3.1   Age–time observation plans

Although the device for analysing the rôle of age and time in discrete population models – the Lexis diagram – has existed for over a 100 years, and although it has been frequently applied in the French, German and East European demographic literature, it has been relatively neglected in the English language literature. A careful exposition is therefore required.

Figure 12.2 outlines the four age–time observation plans which describe how demographic data can be organized. Initially attention is confined to situations where the age and time intervals are equal. Events (such as births, deaths, migrations, marriages) can be counted in any one of these plans; transitions (migrants) are in practice counted using only plan II, although plan III is also theoretically employable. Plan I is the one normally employed in English-speaking countries; plan IV is used elsewhere in Europe. Plans II and III are associated with two classical demographic models, plan II with the cohort survival model and plan III with the life-table model.

Under plan I events are counted in period–age groups which are squares in the diagram. Examples might be deaths in age group 70–74 in West Yorkshire over the period 1976–81 (data used in Ch. 7) or births in Bradford to Indian mothers over the period 1979–83 in six age groups (Ram & Rees 1985). No sensible population models can be built with data in this form. The data must be deconsolidated in one way or another to yield variables appropriate for models using plans II or III.

Events counted using plan IV are gathered under a double classification, that of age at time of event and that of birth cohort. The events are located in the pecked triangles in the diagram. Events can be reassembled into either plan II or plan III parallelograms, depending on which model is of interest.

Under plan II the focus is on how a cohort evolves between two exact points in time. Two age groups are involved.

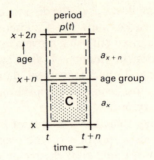

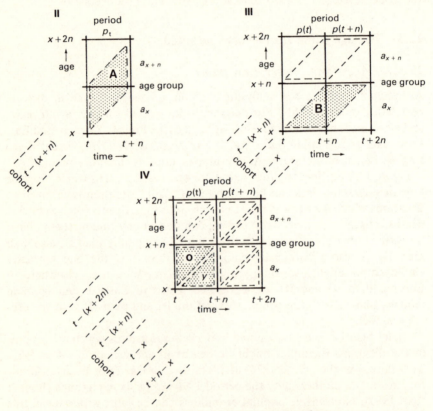

Figure 12.2 Age–time observation plans.

From Figure 12.3 we can see that there are several ways in which event rates or transition rates could be estimated. Statistics on events gathered using plan I must be disaggregated first to a plan IV framework, and then aggregated to yield plan II or plan III counts (Fig. 12.3). Plan IV counts are similarly aggregated. Statistics on transitions (for example, the number of migrants recorded in a census at location i who n years earlier were at

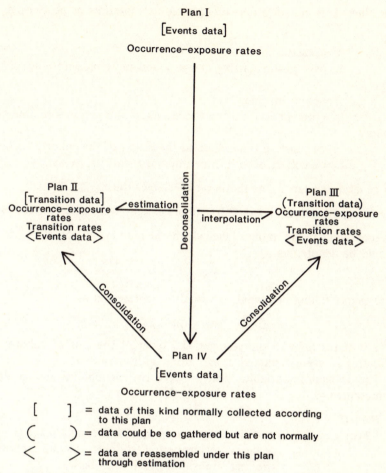

Figure 12.3 Routes between the age–time observation plans.

location *j*) gathered normally using only plan II and not plan III, can be used directly to measure the transition rates required in projection or life-table models. Note that if the researcher has access to information systems that yield the full migration histories of populations then data can be extracted easily under any of the age–time plans as required.

12.3.2 Notation

To outline these diagrammatic notions more precisely we need to define a detailed notation. We adopt the two general variables:

E = a count of demographic events,
T = a count of demographic transitions,

and then three classifications represented as subscripts or postscripts:

age

x = exact age,

a_x = age group starting at age x and finishing before age $x + n$.

time

t = point in time,

p_t = time period starting at time t and finishing before time $t + n$.

cohort

$t - x$ = a point in time marking the origin of the cohort,

c_{t-x} = a cohort born in time interval $t - x$ to $t - x + n$.

In general, we can define the *events* variables thus:

$E(c, a, p)$ = events classified by cohort c, age group a and period p.

Events falling in the triangle labelled y in the plan IV portion of Figure 12.2 would be denoted as

$$E(c_{t-x}, \ a, p)$$

and events falling in triangle o would be represented as

$$E(c_{t-(x+n)}, \ a, p)$$

The y and o refer to the younger and older of the pair of cohorts contributing to events counted in age group a_x in period p_t.

The transition variables always refer to one cohort and could be represented as:

Plan II

$T(a_1, t_1, a_2, t_2)$ = persons in age group a_1 at time t_1 and in age group a_2 at the end of the period, at time t_2, having experienced the 'net' transition involved in between,

Plan III

$T(x_1, \ p_1, x_2, p_2)$ = persons attaining age x_1 in period p_1 and age x_2 in period p_2, having experienced the net transition involved in between.

The cohort to which the persons belong would be defined automatically. Transitions falling in parallelogram A in Figure 12.2 would be denoted as

$$T(a_x, t, a_{x+n}, t + n)$$

and those falling in parallelogram B as

$$T(x, p_t, x + n, p_{t+n})$$

In these specific variables and the equivalents for events the classifications are linked together by the age and time subscripts attached to cohort, age and time labels.

12.3.3   Estimation methods

Plan I events can be represented at $E(\cdot, a, p)$ where the $(\cdot)$ represents summation over the subscript replaced (the cohort subscript). Specifically, events in area C in Figure 12.2 are denoted as

$$E(\cdot, a, p) = \sum_{c} E(c, a, p)$$

$$= E(c_{t-(x+n)}, a_x, p_t) + E(c_{t-x}, a_x, p_t) \tag{12.4}$$

At its simplest, the problem of estimation is to divide the variable into its two right-hand side components and to reassemble these components as plan II or plan III variables, for example,

$$E(c_{t-(x+n)}, \cdot, p_t) = E(c_{t-(x+n)}, a_x, p_t) + E(c_{t-(x+n)}, a_{x+n}, p_t) \tag{12.5}$$

In principle, we need only specify the relevant deconsolidation proportions, $e(c, a, p)$ to achieve this:

$$E(c, a, p) = e(c, a, p)E(\cdot, a, p) \tag{12.6}$$

where

$$\sum_{c} e(c, a, p) = 1 \tag{12.7}$$

In practice, we only require two deconsolidation proportions, $e(y, a, p)$ and $e(o, a, p)$ for the younger and older cohorts respectively.

Where do the values of e come from? Either we can assume that events are equally distributed within the age group–period by cohort, or we can use information about the regional populations at risk of the events and assume that the same rates apply to each cohort or we can use more detailed information for a larger area (commonly the nation) that contains the spatial unit being studied. Figure 12.4 shows examples of each method applied to a period–age group count of 100 events in a region. In the first example, the events are simply multiplied by a half:

$$e(o, a_x, p_t) = \tfrac{1}{2} \tag{12.8}$$

$$e(y, a_x, p_t) = \tfrac{1}{2} \tag{12.9}$$

In the middle example, the deconsolidation coefficients are defined using the regional populations at risk for each cohort:

$$e(o, a_x, p_t) = \frac{\hat{P}(o, a_x, p_t)}{[\hat{P}(o, a_x, p_t) + \hat{P}(y, a_x, p_t)]} \tag{12.10}$$

$$e(y, a_x, p_t) = \frac{\hat{P}(y, a_x, p_t)}{[\hat{P}(o, a_x, p_t) + \hat{P}(y, a_x, p_t)]} \tag{12.11}$$

The populations at risk are most conveniently defined as those involved in

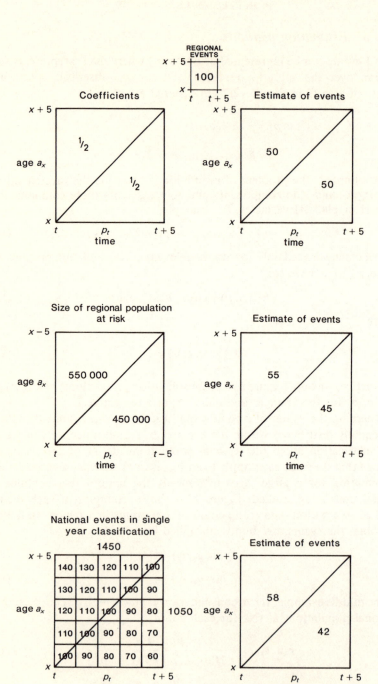

Figure 12.4 Methods of deconsolidation.

the definition of occurrence–exposure rates

$$\hat{P}(o, a_x, p_t) = \tfrac{1}{2}[P(a_{x-n}, t) + P(a_x, t+n)] \tag{12.12}$$

and

$$\hat{P}(y, a_x, p_t) = \tfrac{1}{2}[P(a_x, t) + P(a_{x+n}, t+n)] \tag{12.13}$$

In the third example in Figure 12.4 national events in a more detailed single year of age classification are used to estimate the deconsolidation proportions by adding together events in each triangle, having applied method one to the events along the cohort dividing line.

All of these methods make crude assumptions. A method which combines elements of the second and third improves on both. Event rates are defined

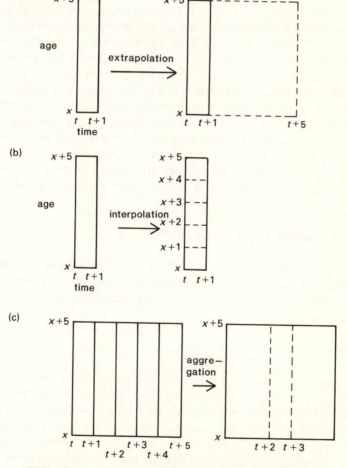

Figure 12.5 Methods to equalize age and time intervals.

for the system (national) for which the most detailed information is available and these are then applied to regional populations at risk. Let r^N represent the occurrence–exposure rate for events in the nation:

$$r^N(c, a, p) = \frac{E^N(c, a, p)}{\hat{P}^N(c, a, p)} \qquad (12.14)$$

These are then used to estimate regional events, E:

$$E^i(c, a, p) = r^N(c, a, p)\hat{P}(c, a, p) \qquad (12.15)$$

Where national rates are unavailable, appropriate rates may be selected from banks of rates constructed by demographic researchers for countries (Keyfitz & Flieger 1971, Rogers & Castro 1981) or for families of model schedules (Coale & Demeny 1966, Clairin *et al.* 1980).

Although the age–time framework has been treated at length here, we have only scratched the surface of the concepts and issues involved because we have assumed throughout that the age and time intervals are equal in the data. Very often they are not. A typical situation is that the data are available for time periods of a year in length but only for five-year age groups. Typical solutions to this problem are shown in Figure 12.5. In solution (a) the statistics are extrapolated to a five-year period by multiplication by 5. In solution (b) the single time interval is retained and the statistics for five-year age groups are broken down to figures for one-year age groups using methods of deconsolidation similar to those described earlier (see Fig. 12.4). In solution (c) the events data for five single years are aggregated to a five-year period. This is particularly appropriate if the only available population at risk is for a central year in which a census was taken.

12.4 The spatial frameworks adopted

A spatial population analysis is carried out for a set of regions. In defining the regions for study two considerations are important. Are the regions defined appropriately for the processes being studied? Are they defined consistently over time?

12.4.1 Regional systems selected

Geographers have long been interested in defining the proper regions for studying the evolution of settlement systems. Objective algorithms for the definition of functional urban regions have been developed by the Centre for Urban and Regional Development Studies at Newcastle University (see Coombes *et al.* 1980, Champion *et al.* 1984). The problem with such systems for spatial population analysis is that demographic statistics are not regularly reported on such a basis.

The alternative of using administrative units for which demographic statistics are more readily available was adopted by Rees and Stillwell (1984) and in Chapters 7 and 8 of this volume. However, administrative units pose different difficulties: their boundaries change over time with local government reform and reorganization. In studying regional population change in the United Kingdom over the 1960s and 1970s the researcher has to contend with two major boundary revisions (1965 and 1974–5).

12.4.2 Changes in the boundaries of units

Both functional urban regions and administrative units suffer from changes in the boundaries of the units. In the former case the change comes about through the spread or contraction of cities and their constituent parts (core, suburban ring, outer ring, rural periphery); in the latter case it comes about because of definitional changes.

To examine population change the researcher must focus on a fixed set of boundaries. Usually the most recent set is adopted and the estimation problem is then to convert statistics for previous points or periods to this new base. The methods used are sketched in Figure 12.6. This usually involves careful cartographic analysis and assembly of population statistics for basic spatial units that can be classified by both 'old' region (current when the data were first collected) and the 'new' region used in the analysis. The population falling in the intersection of the old and new system is counted by summing the populations of the basic spatial units:

$$P(i, j, \cdot) = \sum_k P(i, j, k) \qquad (12.16)$$

where i is the label for a 'new' region, j is the label for an 'old' region and k is the label for the basic spatial units involved. From the population matrix so counted can be worked out the regional conversion matrices which, in the absence of better alternative information, can be used to convert the flow data (events or transitions).

Let $\mathbf{C}$ be the matrix containing regional conversion coefficients, $\mathbf{e}$ a vector of events by region, and $\mathbf{T}$ a matrix of interregional transitions. Then the conversion is effected thus (Stillwell 1976):

$$\mathbf{e}_{new} = \mathbf{C}\mathbf{e}_{old} \qquad (12.17)$$

and

$$\mathbf{T}_{new} = \mathbf{C}\mathbf{T}_{old}\mathbf{C}' \qquad (12.18)$$

The same conversion techniques can be used if the spatial units employed are functional urban regions, although in that case it may be of interest to trace population change for each element of the population matrix separ-

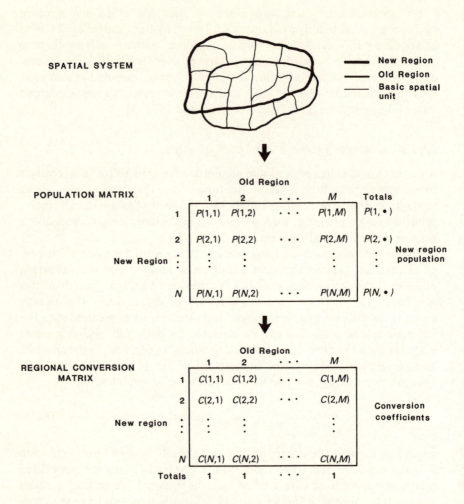

Figure 12.6 Methods of estimating a spatially consistent time-series.

ately when that matrix looks like this:

$$\mathbf{P} = \text{old definitions}$$

		core	inner ring	outer ring	periphery
		C	I	O	P
	C	P(C, C)	P(C, I)	P(C, O)	P(C, P)
new	I	P(I, C)	P(I, I)	P(I, O)	P(I, P)
definitions	O	P(O, C)	P(O, I)	P(O, O)	P(O, P)
	P	P(P, C)	P(P, I)	P(P, O)	P(P, P)

(12.19)

These techniques for coercing a time series of spatial data into consistency are fairly rough and ready. Attempts have been made to define fixed basic spatial units which can be aggregated to any regional definition but the ultimate solution is that suggested by Rhind (1984). All population statistics would be available in individual case form (person, family, household) and could be aggregated by the researcher in any way needed. The data would reside on a secure national computer and would be accessed by an efficient, common-use software package which would have built into it a set of secure rules to prevent privacy violation. Each case would have a unique location code (Ordnance Survey National Grid Coordinates in the UK) so that another software package could aggregate the data to match sets of boundary coordinates for the units being studied.

12.4.3 Estimation of migration arrays

One estimation problem faced by users of multiregional population models exemplified in Chapter 7 is that, very often, information on the full region-by-region-by-age array is not provided. The range of estimation problems and their solution has been outlined by Willekens (1977) and Willekens *et al.* (1979, 1981). Here we summarize their approach in a simplified fashion (see also Rees 1979a).

The target array to be estimated contains elements $M(i, j, a)$ = migration between region i and region j at age a. The migration variable could be of either the movement or transition variety and the age–time framework of either the plan I or plan II kind. This array can be aggregated into three matrices with elements

$$M(i, j, \cdot) = \sum_a M(i, j, a) \tag{12.20}$$

$$M(i, \cdot, a) = \sum_j M(i, j, a) \tag{12.21}$$

$$M(\cdot, j, a) = \sum_i M(i, j, a) \tag{12.22}$$

315

respectively, and into three vectors with elements

$$M(i, \cdot, \cdot) = \sum_j \sum_a M(i, j, a) \qquad (12.23)$$

$$M(\cdot, j, \cdot) = \sum_i \sum_a M(i, j, a) \qquad (12.24)$$

$$M(\cdot, \cdot, a) = \sum_i \sum_j M(i, j, a) \qquad (12.25)$$

The array, matrices and vectors are represented as a cube, three faces and three edges in geometric form in Figure 12.7. There are then some 8 possible estimation problems requiring solution.

(1)   The most information rich involves knowledge of the three faces, that is, variables $M(i, j, \cdot)$, $M(i, \cdot, a)$ and $M(\cdot, j, a)$.
Three problems involve knowledge of two faces:

(2) $M(i, j, \cdot)$ and $M(i, \cdot, a)$
(3) $M(i, j, \cdot)$ and $M(\cdot, j, a)$
(4) $M(i, \cdot, a)$ and $M(\cdot, j, a)$

Another three involve knowledge of one face and one edge:

(5) $M(i, j, \cdot)$ and $M(\cdot, \cdot, a)$
(6) $M(i, \cdot, a)$ and $M(\cdot, j, \cdot)$
(7) $M(\cdot, j, a)$ and $M(i, \cdot, \cdot)$

and a final problem involves knowledge of three edges only:

(8) $M(i, \cdot, \cdot)$, $M(\cdot, j, \cdot)$ and $M(\cdot, \cdot, a)$.

This knowledge is used to estimate the full three-dimensional array, either with or without a prior expectation.

The commonest problem faced in practice is the three face problem. Here demographic agencies provide the aggregate interzonal migration matrix and disaggregations of outmigration totals and inmigration totals by age. The technique is to adjust an initial three-dimensional array to the two-dimensional matrix constraints by iterative proportional fitting:

Step 0

$$\text{Set all } M^0(i, j, a) = 1 \qquad (12.26)$$

Step 1

$$M^1(i, j, a) = M^0(i, j, a) \frac{M(i, j, \cdot)}{\sum_a M^0(i, j, a)} \qquad (12.27)$$

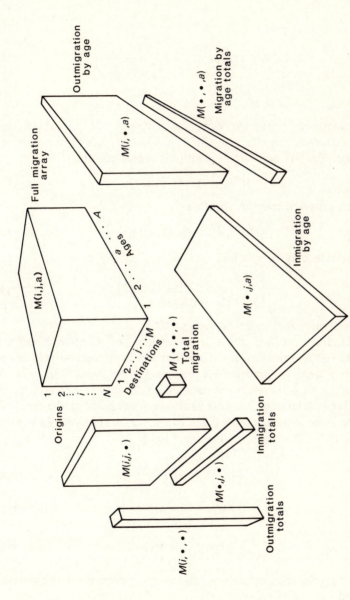

Figure 12.7 The migration array, its faces and edges.

Step 2

$$M^2(i, j, a) = M^1(i, j, a) \frac{M(i, \cdot, a)}{\sum_j M^1(i, j, a)} \qquad (12.28)$$

Step 3

$$M^3(i, j, a) = M^2(i, j, a) \frac{M(\cdot, j, a)}{\sum_i M^2(i, j, a)} \qquad (12.29)$$

Step 4

The estimates are tested for convergence. Are all $M(i, j, a)$ at iteration p of the procedure not significantly different from $M(i, j, a)$ at iteration $p - 1$ of the procedure? If not, the procedure is repeated setting

$$M^0(i, j, a) = M^3(i, j, a) \qquad (12.30)$$

The testing criterion may be absolute:

$$| M_p^3(i, j, a) - M_{p-1}^3(i, j, a) | \overset{?}{\lessgtr} \tfrac{1}{2} \qquad (12.31)$$

or the criterion may be relative:

$$\left| \frac{M_p^3(i, j, a) - M_{p-1}^3(i, j, a)}{M_{p-1}^3(i, j, a) \overset{?}{\lessgtr} x} \right| \qquad (12.32)$$

where x is a very small number such as 10^{-6}.

The technique outlined above is an example of iterative proportional fitting. The initial estimates of the array elements are successively adjusted so that they total to pre-specified marginal constraints. The process is repeated until all constraints are satisfied. Note that before multiproportional fitting is attempted the user must always check that the constraints sum to the same total or convergence can never be achieved. In the three-faced case the following equalities must hold:

$$\sum_a M(i, j, \cdot) = M(T) \qquad (12.33)$$

$$\sum_j M(i, \cdot, a) = M(T) \qquad (12.34)$$

$$\sum_i M(\cdot, j, a) = M(T) \qquad (12.35)$$

where $M(T)$ is the total number of migrations or migrants in the system being studied.

In the example above we had no prior knowledge of the migration flows. All were held to be equally likely and therefore all were given the initial value 1. However, in the migration case we know from the previous studies that the distances between zones can affect (reduce) the migration between them. So we could set the initial migration estimate as

$$M^0(i, j, a) = \Pr(i)\Pr(j)f[d(i, j)] \tag{12.36}$$

where $\Pr(i)$, the probability of outmigration from region i, might be given as

$$\Pr(i) = \frac{M(i, \cdot, \cdot)}{M(\cdot, \cdot, \cdot)} \tag{12.37}$$

and the probability of inmigration to region j, $\Pr(j)$ might be given as

$$\Pr(j) = \frac{M(\cdot, j, \cdot)}{M(\cdot, \cdot, \cdot)} \tag{12.38}$$

and $f[d(i, j)]$ is some function of the distance between i and j, for example

$$f[d(i, j)] = d(i, j)^{-\beta} \tag{12.39}$$

However care must be taken not to try to use the same model to predict migration flows as the one used to estimate them. These models and issues are discussed in depth in Chapter 8.

Prior estimates of demographic data for use in such estimation come in a variety of guises. They will usually be introduced as rates. If regional rates are not available, national rates may be used; if national rates are unavailable, those from a country with a similar demographic structure and history may be used; or rates may be selected from a set of standard or model schedules.

12.5 The temporal and accounting frameworks adopted

12.5.1 Temporal frameworks for assembling the components of change

In discussing the age–time frameworks within which demographic statistics are assembled it was implicitly assumed that when these were put together they would match temporally. In other words, we assumed that it would be possible to assemble statistics for births, deaths and migrations (internal and external), whether of the movement or transition variety, for the same time period (as in Figure 12.8a), together with the appropriate population at risk.

In practice this is not always possible. Four examples taken from recent multiregional population analyses are shown in Figure 12.8b, c, d and e.

In the study of the population dynamics of Finland's 12 Lääni, Rikkinen (1979) was able to assemble all the components of internal population change for a single calendar year on a consistent basis (Fig. 12.8b). Method (a) in Figure 12.5 was used to bring age (5-year) and time (1-year) intervals into equality.

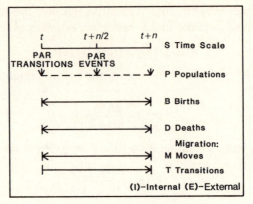

(a) General framework for assembling the components of population change.

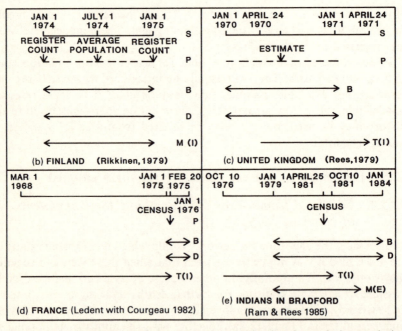

Figure 12.8 Selected time frameworks for multiregional population analysis.

The temporal framework for the equivalent study of ten United Kingdom regions by Rees (1979a) was less exact. The migration data referred to a slightly different period (1 year prior to 24 April 1971) from that for births and deaths (calendar year 1970). Since the migration data are transitions the mid-year estimated population used in the multiregional population was a second best to an estimate based at the start of the migration year.

The variation between the time periods used for the components is even greater in the French analysis (Fig. 12.8d) of Ledent with Courgeau (1982). Births and deaths are for calendar year 1975, but the migration data are transitions over the period between successive censuses. This period is almost seven years in length. The migration rates are converted by Ledent to a five-year time interval by working out the 5/7ths power of the rates matrix.

In the final example (Fig. 12.8e), the components of change for one ethnic group in a city are put together (Ram & Rees 1985) in an eclectic fashion from available birth and death statistics which cover the period 1979–83, external migration statistics (1979–82), and internal migration statistics which derive from a household survey which measures migration over a five-year period from October 1976 to October 1981. The 1981 census population is used as the at-risk population because no other source provides a good estimate of numbers in an ethnic group.

12.5.2 Accounting frameworks

The difficulty of putting together the component statistics perhaps explains why the accounting frameworks (discussed earlier in Chapter 6 and used in Chapter 7) have not been adopted very often. Using an accounting framework demands that all components be estimated for the same time interval, and that consistency checks be built into the accounts estimation. That is, both initial and final populations are input and the accounts matrices adjusted to ensure that the components of change do, in fact, generate the final from the initial populations (for details see Rees 1979b, 1981a and 1984b).

There are many alternative ways in which population constraints can be introduced (Fig. 12.9). In the first (Fig. 12.9a) census populations, independently taken, are available both for the start and end of the accounting period. In practice, the time interval involved is usually 10 years. Changes in the way statistics are measured – because boundaries or definitions differ – make it difficult to link decennial censuses effectively. Some countries, such as Canada or Australia, have quinquennial censuses, which, coupled with a five-year migration question, enable the population researcher to construct very precise accounting systems. Situations in which census populations are available at one end of the five-year period (Figs 12.8b or c) are commoner. At the other end there will be either official population estimates or register counts. For periods not bounded by a census the situation in Figure 12.8d applies. The consistency check in this case is merely on the method of arriving at the estimates or in linking successive register counts. Finally, the situation in which only one population estimate is available (Fig. 12.8e) allows for no consistency checks, but the previous situation can usually be restored if successive periods are linked.

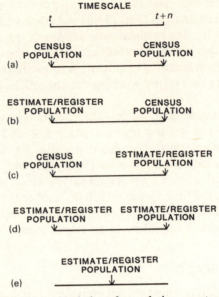

Figure 12.9 Varieties of population constraint.

12.5.3 *Forecasting scenarios*

Although the term 'estimation' has traditionally been restricted to periods in the past and the terms 'forecasting' or 'projection' reserved for periods in the future, it is relevant to observe briefly that many types of forecasting scenario (future temporal frameworks) are possible for demographic models. Four of the commonest are depicted in Figure 12.10. The demographer has been most interested in the long-run impact of fixed rate

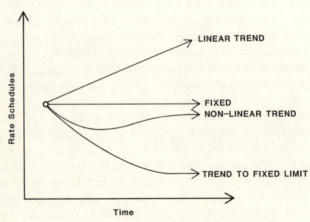

Figure 12.10 Types of forecasting scenarios.

schedules. Planners and official forecasters have been more concerned with taking into account trends in demographic rates (this presupposes a good time-series of all component rates): linear extrapolation, trended extrapolation to a fixed limit and non-linear trending (linked to exogenous variables) have all been applied.

In reality, the problems of estimation faced by population researchers are never quite as simple as we have suggested in the chapter so far. Even in data-rich situations quite complicated estimation techniques may be needed (see, for example, Rees 1984a, Appendix, for the techniques required to make a good estimate of regional deaths by single year of age for the Netherlands). However, even in data-poor situations, the ideal frameworks outlined here will serve to guide the researcher through the estimation problems. An awareness of concepts used in defining the population stocks and flows, of the age–time frameworks adopted, of the spatial system used and of the temporal and accounting framework employed is essential.

We illustrate the practical application of these principles in two examples. The first concerns the population flow – emigration – about which least is usually known in developed countries. Some national demographic agencies appear even to deny its existence. The example involves the estimation of external migration flows for 20 United Kingdom regions. The estimates are used in the analyses of Chapter 7.

The second example concerns regional demographic variation and change in a developing country, India. This example illustrates how the principles outlined so far in this chapter must be adapted to deal with a variety of new problems; also it gives a foretaste of Chapter 13 in which an account of how an integrated data base was constructed for Thailand is given.

12.6   Example 1: external migration flows from a set of United Kingdom zones, 1976–81

Essential inputs to spatial population models are estimates of migration between regions internal to the system of interest and those external to it. These are normally international migration flows. Here we describe the procedures needed to estimate such flows for the 20-zone system covering the United Kingdom employed in Chapters 7 and 8. The reader may well ask at the end of this description: Why does it require such complicated ingenuity to generate a set of estimates that are absolutely necessary for local area population projections? Answers, please, from the Office of Population Censuses and Surveys (OPCS).

12.6.1   The problem

The task before us is to estimate the migration flows over the period 1976–81 (mid-year to mid-year) to and from 20 zones in the UK consisting

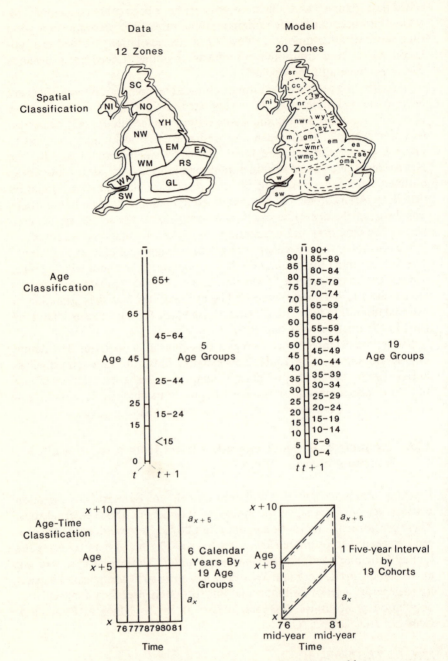

Figure 12.11 The external migration estimation problem.

of a mixture of metropolitan counties or their equivalents, region remainders and regions, disaggregated by 19 plan II cohorts (Fig. 12.11).

The problem can be divided into three stages. The first involves spatial adjustment, the second concerns age-group deconsolidation, and the third consists of temporal aggregation and cohort estimation. The solutions to the first and second problems were combined in one algorithm which was applied to each calendar year. Then the data for the six calendar years covering the 1976–81 period were combined.

Immigration and emigration data are available from the International Passenger Survey (reported in OPCS's MN series and in the migration tables of *Population trends*) for some 12 regions in the UK and for 5 broad age groups. Table 12.2 gives the figures for 1976. To estimate immigration and emigration flows for 20 regions and for 19 age transitions the basic hypothesis is adopted that the corresponding patterns of internal inmigration and outmigration, already estimated using a three-face technique (see

Table 12.2 External migration: information for 1976.

(a) External migration flows by regions.

Region	Emigration	Immigration
Wales (WA)	6 400	2 900
Scotland (SC)	18 700	12 100
Northern Ireland (NI)	4 200	600
North (NO)	7 000	5 300
Yorkshire and Humberside (YH)	12 000	12 900
East Midlands (EM)	8 500	6 900
East Anglia (EA)	6 200	3 800
Rest of South East (RS)	48 500	40 000
Greater London (GL)	56 600	62 100
South West (SW)	12 700	12 900
West Midlands (WM)	11 600	17 000
North West (NW)	18 200	15 000

(b) External migration flows by age group.

Age group	United Kingdom Emigration	United Kingdom Immigration	England and Wales Emigration	England and Wales Immigration
0–14	40 300	31 400	35 100	29 400
15–24	51 700	64 000	46 700	60 400
25–44	97 200	77 100	86 600	72 100
45–64	15 400	12 800	13 800	12 200
65 +	5 800	5 100	5 400	4 600

Source: OPCS (1983b, Tables 2.7, 2.8 and 2.9).

Chapter 8), will tell us how external migrations are distributed within the 12 regions and by detailed five-year age groups within the 5 broader age groups.

The problem is thus to estimate the target variable $E(i, a)$ where

$E(i, a)$ = external migration to or from zone i in five-year age group a

subject to the constraints $E(I, \cdot)$ and $E(\cdot, A)$ where

$E(I, \cdot)$ = external migration to or from region I over all ages, and

$E(\cdot, A)$ = external migration to or from the UK in broad age group A.

12.6.2   The solution: stages 1 and 2

We begin with the hypothesis that $M(i, a)$ provides an initial estimate for $E(i, a)$ where

$M(i, a)$ = the total internal outmigration from and inmigration to region i in age group a.

The solution to this problem is therefore as follows.

Step 1: the initial estimate

$$E(i, a)[1] = M(i, a) \tag{12.40}$$

Step 2: the estimates are adjusted to regional constraints

$$E(i, a)[2] = E(i, a)[1]$$

$$\times \left[\frac{E(I, \cdot)}{\sum_{i \in I} \sum_a E(i, a)[1]} \right] \tag{12.41}$$

Step 3: the estimates are adjusted to age constraints

$$E(i, a)[3] = E(i, a)[2]$$

$$\times \left[\frac{E(\cdot, A)}{\sum_{a \in A} \sum_i E(i, a)[2]} \right] \tag{12.42}$$

Step 4: the estimates are tested for convergence

If for all zones i and age groups a

$$| E(i, a)[3] - E(i, a)[0] | < k \tag{12.43}$$

where k is a small constant, say $1/2$. Then the iterative procedure is stopped, otherwise

$$E(i, a)[1] = E(i, a)[3] \tag{12.44}$$

and the process returns to step 2 again.

Figure 12.12 shows that this solution is a nested version of the more usual

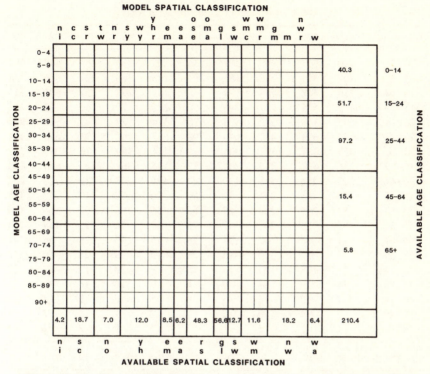

Figure 12.12 The constraints in the external migration estimation problem.

adjustment of a matrix to its row and column constraints. Table 12.3 shows the final emigration estimates for 1976.

12.6.3 The solution: stage 3

The third stage in estimating external migration is to deconsolidate the $E(i,a)$ estimates from plan I to plan IV and then reassemble them in a plan II framework.

Coefficients are used that reflect which calendar year the data refer to. These are based on the geometry of the age–time framework and are shown in Figure 12.13. Thus

$$E(i, c_{t-x}) = \sum_{y=1}^{6} \{ f1 \times E(i, a_x)[y] + f2 \times E(i, a_{x-n})[y] \} \qquad (12.45)$$

where y is an index referring to calendar years 1976 to 1981.

Stages 1 and 2 of the estimation system described above can be applied to any calendar year and any spatial system which aggregates to the 12 regions and for which internal migration estimates are available (via the NHSCR). It thus constitutes an essential ingredient for any UK spatial population analysis.

Table 12.3 Emigration flows for 1976.

Age group	ni	cc	sr	tw	nr	sy	wy	yhr	em	ea
0–4	490	757	990	201	336	209	363	341	660	504
5–9	307	595	778	155	294	173	340	321	606	424
10–14	250	448	587	134	236	137	293	251	501	357
15–19	419	579	757	249	556	271	527	552	923	654
20–24	595	1148	1502	528	636	524	824	687	1346	964
25–29	794	1695	2218	646	799	557	968	773	1650	1224
30–34	459	1067	1397	305	519	314	589	476	1065	777
35–39	286	639	836	164	312	185	362	326	614	460
40–44	225	426	558	130	224	136	271	212	426	292
45–49	94	215	281	66	100	70	132	117	210	139
50–54	84	205	268	67	82	56	106	92	165	134
55–59	98	154	201	42	73	41	76	72	149	114
60–64	21	48	62	17	23	16	29	26	56	41
65–69	23	31	40	15	25	12	29	28	50	42
70–74	13	25	33	10	15	9	20	17	32	29
75–79	14	19	24	9	16	9	16	16	26	24
80–84	7	10	13	5	8	5	8	9	14	14
85–89	3	4	6	2	3	2	4	4	7	7
90 +	1	1	2	1	1	1	1	2	2	3

Age group	ose	oma	gl	sw	wmc	wmr	gm	m	nwr	w
0–4	1428	2090	3732	981	487	452	520	346	565	470
5–9	1306	1912	2837	835	392	406	446	278	519	401
10–14	1184	1733	2227	763	297	343	341	219	421	335
15–19	2044	2993	3658	1509	523	618	613	423	855	805
20–24	2705	3961	9091	1956	1088	748	1026	773	999	1068
25–29	3858	5649	13932	2379	1285	1036	1475	868	1328	1242
30–34	2454	3594	7565	1464	755	729	829	502	885	738
35–39	1462	2141	4258	846	439	415	503	275	551	431
40–44	1055	1545	2859	627	296	295	350	186	389	334
45–49	540	790	1580	331	165	138	176	100	187	149
50–54	515	754	1557	301	131	104	167	100	168	142
55–59	463	677	1468	287	121	98	143	73	144	128
60–64	179	262	628	106	46	35	51	34	53	41
65–69	154	225	560	114	36	32	49	26	51	40
70–74	102	149	288	78	19	21	25	21	36	29
75–79	82	120	201	65	14	16	21	17	29	27
80–84	48	70	115	38	7	9	11	9	15	15
85–89	24	35	56	18	3	4	5	4	6	6
90 +	9	13	21	7	1	1	2	1	2	2

Source: as described in text.

Notes to Table 12.3
Zone abbreviations:

ni	Northern Ireland	ose	Outer South East
cc	Clydeside Conurbation	oma	Outer Metropolitan Area
sr	Scotland Remainder	gl	Greater London
tw	Tyne and Wear	sw	South West
nr	North Remainder	wmc	West Midlands County
sy	South Yorkshire	wmr	West Midlands Remainder
wy	West Yorkshire	gm	Greater Manchester
yhr	Yorkshire and Humberside Remainder	m	Merseyside
em	East Midlands	nwr	North West Remainder
ea	East Anglia	w	Wales

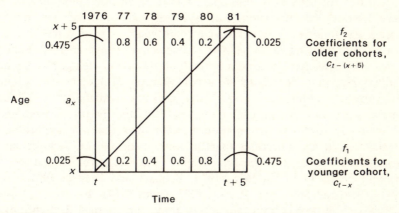

Figure 12.13 Factors used in the deconsolidation and aggregation of external migration data.

12.7 Example 2: India's spatial demography

12.7.1 Context

In this second example we present a critical review of our work on the spatial demography of India with particular reference to the general estimation framework outlined earlier in Chapter 12. We also place that work in context by discussing briefly some of the main problems to be faced in reconstructing the spatial demographies of countries with limited vital data, but for which population censuses are available. We conclude our consideration of the Indian example by referring back to the issues first outlined in Chapter 2 by reviewing the possible fertility variation amongst Indian states.

The need for demographic estimation in much of the world is still all too obvious, for although regular censuses are held the system of vital registration is often woefully inadequate. In India the Sample Registration System

(SRS) was commenced in the late 1960s. It was designed using the 1961 census as a framework and by the 1970s comprised 3700 sample units in which the enumerator produced a continuous record of births and deaths – with some periodic checking (see Bhat *et al.* 1984). Since the Indian SRS framework has not been changed it is likely that the extent to which it reflects national trends will have become distorted. Nevertheless, results from the SRS provide a valuable standard against which to check census-based estimates (Preston & Bhat 1984).

The case of China is different again. There the censuses have been irregular (1953, 1964 and 1982 in the period since 1949); the vital registration system has not been fully developed; and those demographic surveys that have been carried out have not always been fully reported. Yet the 1982 census was followed by an extensive fertility survey so that the results of census and survey may now be linked (Caldwell & Srinivasan 1984, Banister 1984). The considerable growth in the literature on contemporary Chinese demography may be related to a combination of factors: the Chinese government's population policy, the growing availability of Chinese demographic data in both China and the West, and the prior development of relatively sophisticated estimation techniques that are applicable to census-derived age structures together with birth and death information from partial surveys (for the demography of contemporary China see, for example, Aird 1978, Yu 1978, 1979, Banister and Preston 1981, Coale 1981a, b, Goodstadt 1982, Pressat 1983, Calot 1984a, b).

Relatively little has been said so far about the regional demography of China, yet it is clear from Banister (1984, Table 3, p. 250) that fertility did vary considerably between provinces in 1981 (TFR ranged from 1.32 to 4.36 and was 2.69 in China as a whole) as well as between urban and rural populations. Regional patterns are also obvious in Africa where the work of Brass *et al.* (1968), Adegbola (1977), Page and Lesthaeghe (1981) and Bongaarts *et al.* (1984) has shown the extent to which sterility and age at marriage may vary and thus affect total fertility rates. India, our principal example in this section, also displays particularly interesting regional demographic patterns over and above those one would expect to result from differences between urban and rural environments. But how are we to discern such patterns?

12.7.2 *Forecasting the population of India and subnational areas with minimal information*

Rees (1984b) provides a simple guide to the models that might be used to project the population of the subnational areas of India with minimal information to hand. It describes a standard cohort survival model for two sexes that allows inputs of survival and fertility rates that can be changed in an ordered fashion by the user. How were the initial sets of survival and fertility rates arrived at and how much were they forecast?

Survival rates were estimated by interpolation between two model schedules given in the Coale and Demeny (1966) tables (listed in Table 12.4). The North model life table set was chosen because work by Woods (1982a, Ch. 2, Table 2.9, p. 77) indicated that this was the model that most often fitted the Indian data best. The two schedules in Table 12.4 combine, in terms of life expectancy, e_0, current Indian experience and that likely in the long term. Interpolation between the two schedules for a forecasting period was accomplished in the following way.

A forecast life expectancy value for the projection period was determined (see later). Then survival rates were computed as follows.

Survival rate (s.r.) for the current forecasting period is

$$\text{s.r. at lower } e_0 + \left[\frac{\text{forecast } e_0 - \text{lower } e_0}{\text{higher } e_0 - \text{lower } e_0} \right] \times (\text{higher s.r.} - \text{lower s.r.})$$

(12.46)

For example, assume e_0 was forecast to be 60 years at some time in the future. The survival rate for age group 30–34 surviving into age group 35–39 would be forecast as

$$\text{s.r.} = 0.962\ 35 + \left[\frac{(60-50)}{(70-50)} \right] \times (0.988\ 39 - 0.962\ 35)$$

$$= 0.962\ 35 + 0.5(0.026\ 04) = 0.975\ 37 \qquad (12.47)$$

A similar technique was used to interpolate fertility rates using age-specific fertility rates for India in 1972 estimated from SRS data reported in Visaria and Visaria (1981) as the high fertility level and a schedule for the United Kingdom in 1975 to represent the lowest likely level of fertility. These schedules are listed in Table 12.4. The total fertility rate per woman was forecast (see later) and then the following interpolation was carried out.

The age-specific fertility rate (f.r.) for the current forecasting period is

$$\text{f.r.} = \begin{array}{c} \text{f.r. at} \\ \text{higher} \\ \text{TFR} \end{array} + \left[\frac{\text{forecast TFR} - \text{higher TFR}}{\text{lower TFR} - \text{higher TFR}} \right] \times \begin{array}{c} \text{(f.r. at lower} \\ \text{TFR} - \text{f.r.} \\ \text{at higher TFR)} \end{array}$$

(12.48)

So, if total fertility for a state population was forecast to be three children per woman, the fertility rate for women aged 25–29 would be estimated as follows:

$$\text{f.r. at age } 25\text{--}29 = 275.9 + \left[\frac{3 - 5.387}{1.822 - 5.387} \right] \times (124.9 - 275.5)$$

$$= 275.9 + (0.669\ 57)(-150.6) = 175.1 \qquad (12.49)$$

Table 12.4 Survival and fertility rates for projecting Indian populations.

(a) Survival rates.

Age transition	Male		Female	
	Level 14	Level 23	Level 13	Level 21
Birth to 0–4	0.861 65	0.974 68	0.864 86	0.962 92
0–4 to 5–9	0.934 71	0.994 72	0.928 78	0.988 94
5–9 to 10–14	0.973 92	0.996 85	0.971 25	0.994 90
10–14 to 15–19	0.979 58	0.995 64	0.978 60	0.994 78
15–19 to 20–24	0.972 65	0.992 73	0.975 58	0.992 75
20–24 to 25–29	0.967 04	0.991 32	0.971 48	0.990 98
25–29 to 30–34	0.965 15	0.990 75	0.967 14	0.989 79
30–34 to 35–39	0.961 74	0.989 57	0.962 35	0.988 39
35–39 to 40–44	0.955 39	0.987 33	0.957 27	0.985 24
40–44 to 45–49	0.946 17	0.983 12	0.952 35	0.980 92
45–49 to 50–54	0.932 14	0.974 30	0.943 45	0.973 83
50–54 to 55–59	0.911 93	0.962 31	0.926 38	0.963 39
55–59 to 60–64	0.880 77	0.943 23	0.897 06	0.945 92
60–64 to 65–69	0.831 02	0.909 36	0.848 25	0.912 94
65–69 to 70–74	0.756 34	0.858 09	0.774 69	0.858 65
70–74 to 75–79	0.652 66	0.778 51	0.674 98	0.775 36
75 + to 80 +	0.401 99	0.512 40	0.416 80	0.508 83
e_0	49.1	71.6	50.0	70.0

(b) Fertility rates (per 1000 women).

Age group	India 1972	UK 1975
15–19	87.5	36.8
20–24	261.9	116.5
25–29	275.5	124.9
30–34	215.4	59.8
35–39	141.7	20.9
40–44	74.0	5.2
45–49	21.3	0.3
TFR	5.387	1.822

Sources:
Survival rates (North model life tables):
Coale and Demeny (1966, pp. 232–3, 240, 242).
Fertility rates (births per 1000 women in age group in year):
India, 1972 – Visaria and Visaria (1981, Table 13);
UK, 1975 – Rees (1979a, Table 13, p. 42).

12.7.3   Trends in and forecasts of life expectancy, e_0

These methods use life expectancy (e_0) and total fertility rate (TFR) as leading indicators. Base levels for the states of India and trends were established by consulting secondary sources. Table 12.5 gathers together life expectancy figures for India and for selected states. Substantial improvement has been effected in the past three decades: 10.6 years have been added to male e_0 (0.42 years per year) and 10.7 to female e_0 (0.43 years per year).

Table 12.5 reports two views as to future trends. The United Nations in its 1980-based medium variant projections (United Nations 1981a) sees the rate of improvement increasing to 2000 but decreasing thereafter. The rate of improvement in female e_0 is greater than that of males: women's e_0, currently lower than that of men, overtakes male e_0 in 2005–10. The

Table 12.5   Life expectancy (e_0) trends for India.

Years	UN estimates[a] Male	Female	Years	Other sources Male		Female	
1950–5	39.4	38.0					
1955–60	41.4	40.0					
1960–5	44.3	43.0	1961–70[b]	46.4		44.7	
			1961–70[c]	47.1		45.6	
1965–70	46.8	45.5	1966–70[d]	48.0		46.0	
			1966–71[e]	49.2		47.1	
1970–5	49.0	47.7	1971–6[e]	51.7		49.7	
			1976–7[f]	50.8		50.0	
1975–80	50.0	48.7	1976–81[e]	53.7		53.1	
Forecasts				M1	M2	M3	M4
1980–5	52.0	51.0	1981–5[g]	51.2	58.4	49.6	57.6
1985–90	54.1	53.4	1986–90	52.3	61.6	50.8	61.2
1990–5	56.4	55.8	1991–5	53.4	64.6	52.0	64.5
1995–2000	58.8	58.0	1996–2000	54.4	67.4	53.2	67.4
2000–05	61.0	61.0	2001–5	55.5	70.0	54.4	70.0
2005–10	62.9	63.1	2006–10	56.5	70.0	55.5	70.0
2010–15	64.6	65.3	2011–15	57.5	70.0	56.6	70.0
2015–20	66.1	67.3	2016–20	58.5	70.0	57.6	70.0
2020–5	67.3	69.1					

Sources:
a   United Nations (1981a, Table A-15, pp. 84–5).
b   United Nations (1983, Table 16).
c   Government of India quoted in Cassen (1978, Table 2.11, p. 116).
d   Cassen (1978, Table 2.11, p. 116).
e   Preston and Bhat (1984, p. 498).
f   United Nations (1981b, Table 4, p. 184).
g   Cassen (1978, Table 2.18, p. 133).

average rates of improvement over the 1980–2020 period (0.38 and 0.45 years per year for men and women respectively) are assumed to be quite close to the experience of the 30 years to 1980.

Other authorities are more pessimistic about the rate of improvement. Cassen (1978) includes a series of projections (labelled M1) that assume an improvement rate of only 0.2 years per year, and another series (labelled M4) that assumes a faster rate of improvement of 0.7 years per year up to a limit of 70 years. Cassen regards the former rate as much more likely.

To estimate life expectancies for the states Rees (1984c) uses Woods's (1982a) estimates for 1961–71 to derive the ratios between state and national life expectancies. Selected figures are presented in Table 12.6. Andhra Pradesh has lower life expectancy (e_0) values for both men and women than All India, and Kerala has higher ones. Uttar Pradesh has marginally higher life expectancies for men but much lower ones for women.

The life expectancy (e_0) for a state population for a forecasting period is computed as follows.

(a) The All India life expectancy (e_0) values for the first forecasting period (1981–5) are set at 52 for males and 51 for females (following the UN estimates).

(b) The following ratios to national life expectancy are used:

	Males	Females
Andhra Pradesh	0.92	0.97
Kerala	1.17	1.22
Uttar Pradesh	1.02	0.85
Rest of India	1.00	1.07

Table 12.6 Life expectancy (e_0) estimates for selected Indian states, 1961–71.

State	Male		Female	
	e_0	Ratio	e_0	Ratio
Andhra Pradesh	44.3	92	40.0	97
Kerala	56.3	117	50.0	122
Uttar Pradesh	49.1	102	35.0	85
Rest of India	48.2	100	43.8	107
India	48.2	100	41.1	100

Source: Woods (1982a, Table 2.10, p. 78).
Note: The Rest of India figures are an unweighted average of the remaining states in the table. The India figures are population-weighted averages for 13 states.

(c) The state life expectancies (e_0) are computed by multiplying the state ratios by the All India e_0:

	Males	Females
Andhra Pradesh	47.8	49.5
Kerala	60.8	62.2
Uttar Pradesh	53.0	43.4
Rest of India	52.0	54.6

(d) In each period these life expectancies are increased by the rates of change adopted for the particular projection. For example, in 1996–2001 Kerala's female e_0 climbs to $62.2 + 0.4 \times 15 = 68.2$ years, assuming an improvement of 0.4 years per year.

12.7.4 Trends in and forecasts of total fertility (TFR)

Similar difficulties were involved in forecasting total fertility rates (TFR) for the selected states, and similar methods were employed to overcome them. Estimates for All India total fertility were first gathered together (Table 12.7). For the early 1970s the consensus of estimates based on the SRS is that the TFR was 5.3–5.4 children per family with the UN estimates about 5% higher to allow for under-reporting. In the late 1970s the rate had dropped to 4.3–4.6 with the UN suggesting about 5.05 (a 10% under-reporting).

A variety of future forecasts are put forward by Cassen (1978), ranging from a decline of 0.060 of a child per year to 0.122. The UN medium variant forecast begins with an annual decline of 0.124 children per woman per year between the first and second half of the 1980s, falling steadily to a rate of 0.02 children per woman per year in the 2015–20 to 2020–5 time interval. Over the late 1960s and 1970s the decline rate averaged about 0.1 of a child per woman per year, although there were substantial variations from year to year, reflecting the state of the family planning programme (Visaria & Visaria 1981, pp. 35–43).

Fertility levels for the selected states were derived using the ratio of the crude birth rate of the state to the national average (Table 12.8).

Thus the TFR for a state population for a projection period is computed as follows.

(a) The United Nations estimate for All India for 1980–5 of 4.54 children per woman is adopted for the base period.
(b) The state values are computed by applying the 1976–8 ratios in decimal

fraction form to yield:

	TFR
Andhra Pradesh	4.54
Kerala	3.59
Uttar Pradesh	5.49
Rest of India	4.36

(c) In each period these TFRs are decreased by the rate of decline adopted for the particular projection. For example, in 1996–2001 Kerala's TFR is projected to be $3.58 - 0.06 \times 15 = 2.69$, assuming a decline of 0.06 of a child per year.

Rees (1984b) also presents an interactive computer program for carrying out

Table 12.7 Total fertility rates (TFR) in India, past and future.

Years	UN estimates[a]		Years	Other estimates TFR		
	GRR	GRR $\times 1/0.485$		Total	Urban	Rural
1950–5	3.11	6.41	1966–71[b]	5.67		
1955–60	3.15	6.49	1972[c]	5.387	4.290	5.696
1960–5	3.07	6.33	1971–6[b]	5.37		
1965–70	2.93	6.04	1976[d]	4.685		
1970–5	2.75	5.67	1976–81[b]	4.69		
1975–80	2.45	5.05	1978[c]	4.278	3.294	4.556
			1980[e]	4.900		
Forecasts				F1	F6	
1980–5	2.20	4.54	1981–5[f]	4.879	3.203	
1985–90	1.90	3.92	1986–90	4.530	2.500	
1990–5	1.70	3.51	1991–5	4.206	2.500	
1995–2000	1.50	3.09	1996–2000	3.904	2.500	
2000–5	1.30	2.68	2001–5	3.624	2.500	
2005–10	1.20	2.47	2006–10	3.364	2.500	
2010–15	1.10	2.27	2011–15	3.123	2.500	
2015–20	1.05	2.16	2016–20	2.899	2.500	
2020–5	1.00	2.06				

Notes: GRR, gross reproduction rate; TFR, total fertility rate.
Sources:
a United Nations (1981a).
b Preston and Bhat, (1984, p. 496).
c Visaria and Visaria (1981, Table 7, p. 26).
d Population Reference Bureau (1982).
e World Bank (1982, Table 18, p. 144).
f Cassen (1978, Table 2.18, p. 133).

Table 12.8 Regional differentials in crude birth rates.

State	Ratio to national average (= 100)	
	1970–2	1976–8
Andhra Pradesh	95	100
Kerala	84	79
Uttar Pradesh	119	121
Rest of India	97	96

Source: Visaria and Visaria (1981, Table 6).

these projections in which the user selects the life expectancy improvement rate and the fertility decline rate per five-year time interval.

12.7.5 Evaluation

How does this pedagogic model stand in relation to the conceptual, age–time, spatial, temporal and accounting frameworks discussed earlier? The main flaw is clearly lack of a data-base specific to the spatial units being studied. The estimated rates employed in the model are only flimsily connected to observations of events in the particular areas. Direct use of the SRS, both to establish base-period rates and trends around those rates is indicated for a fuller study of India's population. The spatial framework of 'isolated states' is also clearly inadequate: migration data must be incorporated.

Woods (1982a, Ch. 2) shows how mortality levels (e_0) for Indian states can be estimated using model schedules of survival rates from the Coale and Demeny (1966) tabulations and population data for the states from the 1961 and 1971 censuses. The method involves the application of model survival rates to the 1961 population and its projection to 1971. Projected 1971 populations are then compared with census observed populations. Direct adjustment, or computation, of survival rates is not possible because of under-reporting and age mis-specifications in the census population. Instead comparisons are made between projected and observed populations cumulated over wide age ranges – when at least age mis-specifications cancel out. The model survival rates are chosen which overall give the best fit and the nearest life expectancy estimates for states selected (for details see Woods 1982a, Chapter 2). This analysis makes use of more 'local' data than the forecasting model of Rees (1984b), but in common with that model still involves the assumption that the contribution of migration to state population growth is negligible.

Some of these state-specific estimates of crude birth and death rates for 1961–71 (CBR and CDR in parts per thousand) are shown in Table 12.9 where they are also compared with Dyson's CBR estimates for 1961–71 and

Table 12.9 Estimates of crude birth and death rates for Indian states, 1961–71 and 1971–81.

| | 1961–71 | | | |
| | Woods[a] | | Dyson[b] | 1971–81[c] |
States	CBR	CDR	CBR	CBR
Andhra Pradesh	40.7	21.6	38.4	33.2
Bihar	39.2	21.9	41.0	39.1
Gujarat	41.1	15.5	41.4	36.4
Haryana, Himachal Pradesh and Punjab	39.2	16.7	39.5	34.4
Karnataka	40.5	17.8	39.3	33.1
Kerala	38.0	14.0	34.8	28.1
Madhya Pradesh	43.2	18.7	45.0	36.4
Maharashtra	38.8	16.1	39.1	31.2
Orissa	43.3	21.7	42.3	33.2
Rajasthan	43.6	17.8	43.8	40.9
Tamil Nadu	39.7	19.8	36.8	30.2
Uttar Pradesh	41.5	22.1	44.0	40.4
West Bengal	46.9	22.6	40.5	37.5

Sources:
[a] Woods (1982a, Table 2.10, p. 78).
[b] Dyson's estimates in Bhat *et al.* (1984).
[c] Preston and Bhat (1984, Table 7, p. 500).

others for 1971–81 (see Bhat *et al.* 1984). Table 12.9 effectively demonstrates that estimates are bound to vary depending on the techniques employed as well as on the assumptions made about the quality of data and the influence of net migration, since both Woods and Dyson have used population data by age groups from the 1961 and 1971 censuses as their starting points.

Nair (1982b) has, however, shown that the assumption regarding the negligible influence of net migration on state population structures can be relaxed by employing migration data from the 1971 Census of India that measure migration over the period 1966–71. Nair applies the methodology of multiregional demographic analysis, developed in the 1970s by Rogers, Willekens and Ledent (see Rogers 1975, Ledent 1978a, Willekens & Rogers 1978, Rogers & Willekens 1986), to a four-region aggregation of India's states. The analysis is concerned with the estimation of multiregional life expectancies and the state of the multiregional population system at stability.

The results of this analysis incorporating migration confirm the assumption that migration plays a relatively unimportant part in the short-term future of India's regional populations. Only 6.4% of the e_0s of the populations of the five regions is likely, on the basis of 1966–71 migration patterns, to be spent outside the region of birth.

To carry out the multiregional analysis Nair had to estimate the full migration array disaggregated by origin, destination and age from an aggregate interregional flow matrix and estimates of the age structure of inmigration and outmigration (for details see Nair 1982a, pp. 5–12). The entropy maximization technique (the algorithm and computer program are described in Willekens *et al.* 1979) was used to solve this three-face problem and estimate the detailed age categories of the five-year migration flow matrix. A simplified discussion of this technique has been presented in Section 12.4.

Nair's analysis takes our understanding of the dynamics of India's spatial populations much further than that of Rees or Woods. However, he works with a one-sex population at a more spatially aggregate level (5 regions rather than 18 states), whereas both Rees and Woods work with both sexes – which are uniquely different in their mortality experience in India – and at the state level. The investigations of both Woods and Nair are restricted to stationary and stable population analysis – that is, the consequences of current vital and mobility rates only are explored; Rees, on the other hand, builds in the possibility of change in vital rates into his projections.

Thus there is room for much further exploration of the patterns in India's demography, an exploration that should encompass the future populations of India's states, distinguished by sex and by urban and rural residence, undergoing evolution in mortality, fertility and mobility rates. Only then would the full variety of India's spatial population processes be captured.

However, before such an analysis could be successfully carried out a method would need to be developed to overcome a problem addressed neither by Nair nor by the Rogers–Willekens methodology. This problem is that the method of migration measurement employed in the Indian census (the last migration question) provides biased estimates of the migration variables required in either the movement version (Willekens & Rogers 1978) or the transition version (Ledent & Rees 1980, 1986) of the multiregional population models. The problem, though not a full solution, is explained in Rees (1985).

What we have available (summarized, for example, in Tables 12.5 to 12.9) does provide, none the less, an interesting insight into the varying rates of population growth, mortality, fertility and urbanization among the Indian states. It suggests that there are distinctive differences between the north and the south of India in terms of both mortality and fertility with the southern states, such as Kerala and Tamil Nadu, having lower fertility and mortality in the 1960s and 1970s, and the larger northern states, especially Uttar Pradesh, having higher than average levels.

One way to explore these patterns has already been discussed in Section

Table 12.10 Socio-economic variables for Indian states, 1961.

State	Urban X_1	Single X_2	Muslim X_3	Literate X_4	M'f'g X_5	BC X_6	CBR1 Y_1	CBR2 Y_2
Andhra Pradesh	17.44	11.07	7.55	34.98	3.43	14.4	38.4	33.2
Bihar	8.43	8.82	12.45	35.19	2.97	6.3	41.0	39.1
Gujarat	25.77	22.81	8.46	48.73	8.80	18.1	41.4	36.4
H, HP and P	20.13	28.85	1.94	38.92	5.88	21.0	39.5	34.4
Karnataka	22.33	18.80	9.87	42.29	5.11	10.0	39.3	33.1
Kerala	15.11	45.99	17.91	64.89	9.96	18.6	34.8	28.1
Madhya Pradesh	14.29	6.77	4.07	32.18	3.03	10.6	45.0	36.4
Maharashtra	28.22	15.13	7.67	49.26	10.22	19.2	39.1	31.2
Orissa	6.32	17.30	1.23	40.26	1.37	16.9	42.3	33.2
Rajasthan	16.28	8.00	6.52	28.08	2.46	6.0	43.8	40.9
Tamil Nadu	26.69	32.26	4.63	51.59	7.43	16.1	36.8	30.2
Uttar Pradesh	12.85	9.23	14.63	31.89	3.42	6.5	44.0	40.4
West Bengal	24.45	16.03	20.00	46.57	12.39	9.7	40.5	37.5

Sources:
X_1–X_5 from Bose (1967) for 1961.
X_6 from figures quoted in Blaikie (1975, p. 19) for 1972.
Y_1 and Y_2 from Table 12.9.

Definitions:
X_1 % population in urban areas.
X_2 % single females aged 15–24.
X_3 % Muslim.
X_4 % males, literate.
X_5 % male workers in manufacturing.
X_6 % couples using birth control, 1972.
Y_1 crude birth rate (per 1000), 1961–71.
Y_2 crude birth rate (per 1000), 1971–81.
H, HP and P: Haryana, Himachal Pradesh and Punjab.

2.3 and illustrated in Chapters 3 and 4. Causal modelling via multiple regression analysis could provide a means of isolating some of the hypothetical associations that one would expect to be at work. Table 12.10 lists a small number of socio-economic variables which reflect some of the aspects of variation apparent among Indian states in the 1960s. It captures urbanization and industrialization (X_1, X_5), nuptiality (X_2), religious heterogeneity (X_3), literacy and thus, to an extent, the level of educational provision (X_4) and the success of the various family planning programmes (X_6). Dyson's estimates of CBR for 1961–71 (Y_1) and the equivalent estimates for 1971–81 (Y_2) are also reproduced from Table 12.9.

Examination of Table 12.10 reveals that literacy was higher in the south and that women married later there, but that Kerala and Tamil Nadu were not necessarily more urbanized or industrialized than many other states. Dyson and Moore (1983) have argued that some of the differences in inter-state fertility patterns have a basis in Indian culture. For example, female social status is relatively higher in the south than in the north, and this degree of autonomy among wives in family matters is reflected in the response to family planning programmes and the greater use of health care services.

However, Srinivasan *et al.* (1984) stress the importance of modernization in accounting for variations in the use of birth control. Their argument runs as follows: a higher level of socio-economic modernization provides the motivation for family limitation; such levels may be achieved where increased education leads not only to a reduction in ideal family size, but also through reduced lactational amenorrhea, to higher natural fertility and higher child survival. The last to be mentioned are also affected by improved public health. In these circumstances the mismatch between the reduced demand for children and the increased supply is exacerbated in a way that, according to the Easterlin (1978, p.106) model, is most likely to generate family limitation, once the costs of birth control have been reduced.

Our attempts to examine some of these notions, albeit in a tangential fashion, using the variables in Table 12.10 have largely been thwarted by the high degree of multicollinearity among the independent variables and the relatively small number of observations. For, although we are able to achieve a coefficient of determination (R^2) of 76% with Y_1 and $X_1, \ldots, X_6$, none of the individual variables makes a significant contribution in its own right since all but X_5 are inversely related to Y_1 and positively associated with one another. For Y_2 the level of R^2 is increased to 84% with X_4 now making a significant contribution – X_2 and X_5 are now the only variables positively associated with Y_2.

The failure to develop a fuller causal model of India's spatial fertility variation at this time leads us to re-emphasize three important points. The first is that there are inherent limitations in exploring demographic patterns with traditional multivariate methods. The second is that such an exercise requires more reliable data and better measures (for example, TFRs) so that the estimation of crude demographic indices, such as CBRs, becomes unnecessary. The third point is that we need to appreciate the extreme complexity of demographic relationships in which politics, economics and sociology condition but do not determine human behaviour within a context fixed by environment and culture (see Fig. 3.1).

12.8 Lessons

In this chapter we have attempted to outline some of the issues the demographic researcher has to confront when investigating populations that vary over space, as well as some of the techniques that may be employed in estimating the data needed for such investigations. The examples have served to show that the general techniques always need elaboration and adjustment in specific application. From this account we can extract a set of general principles to be followed in spatial demographic estimation.

The most general principle must be that the researcher needs to understand and describe in formal terms the variables both in his or her model and in the available information bank. If this description is carried out well, the solutions to the estimation problems posed may suggest themselves. An aid to such description is a formal notation. This notation may be verbal, logical, geometric, algebraic, that of a programming language, or that of another branch of mathematics.

The formal description of the model and the data should include four dimensions – concept, age–time, space and time account. This is not to suggest that any particular concept, age–time plan, spatial system or temporal accounting framework is ideal. Ultimately the best choice in these four dimensions will depend on the purpose of the analysis and the available resources. However, if all four dimensions are explicitly considered – they are always implicit – new and better solutions to estimation problems may become apparent.

It is clear that there is a hierarchy present in most information systems. More information is available – that is, published in printed or machine-readable form – at the more aggregate scales in the hierarchy. National patterns have to be used to estimate regional ones, and regional estimates can be adjusted to be consistent with national totals. This adjustment technique can be used with any classification of the population. In the first example concerned with the estimation of external migration flows this method was used with both regional and age classifications.

The hierarchy of information availability is not, however, an inherent feature of the information itself. It is merely a feature of the ways in which data collection agencies work. As Rhind (1984) has observed, most population data are collected for individual units, but all that is published – even in electronic form – are statistical aggregates of these data for individuals. It would be very easy, Rhind pointed out, to substitute a computer-held information system in which the data files would be processed (and guarded) by a software system that would enable users to design their own statistical aggregations (subject to confidentiality rules). The technology and software techniques already exist to handle such information. The data-set of individuals by characteristics would be no bigger than existing small-area statistics; the software package would be no more complicated than, say, the existing SASPAC (Small Area Statistics Package) or SPSS (Statistical Package for the Social Sciences) packages. All that is required to implement such a system is the political will. It would probably cost less than current processing and tabulation and publication methods.

Until the suggestions of Rhind are implemented, however, the estimation methods outlined in this chapter will still be needed and will require refinement and extension. The possibility of creating a database even for a developing country should not be overlooked. Chapter 13 tackles such a task for Thailand and by so doing reveals new applications for estimation, modelling and planning. The final chapter in Part III is also concerned with data problems, and with methods of estimating the changing level of urbanization. Chapter 14 presents a critique of recent United Nations (1980c) attempts to project urbanization for the Asian Pacific.

In short, Part III presents a variety of examples of the ingenious techniques that have been developed to facilitate demographic estimation, projection and modelling in circumstances in which data are inadequate. It emphasizes the problems, but also reflects an overwhelming need for reliable estimates where, as Chapter 5 demonstrates, the demographic system has been destabilized and population growth and redistribution are substantial.

13

Regional population analysis in developing countries: the creation of a database for Thailand

WIM DOEVE

13.1 Introduction

The populations of almost all developing countries are currently undergoing rapid transformations; rates of growth, for example, are unprecedented. A growth rate of 3% annually, which is not uncommon, implies a population of twice the current size in less than twenty-five years. The human mind has difficulties in grasping such exponential developments, let alone foreseeing their consequences accurately. It is here that the body of formal knowledge known as mathematical demography comes to our aid. As a body of science it is comparatively well developed, and it has greatly added to the degree of understanding of the structure and dynamics of population-related aspects of societies. In this respect it compares favourably with any of the sciences which are concerned with other aspects of societies, such as economics or econometrics.

The relevance of a thorough understanding of the population aspects of developing countries is apparent, and can perhaps be summarized in two points. First, in the time perspective one deals with in planning and policy making – usually up to five years – population structure and dynamics are to a large extent given and uninfluenceable. Because of this relatively fixed character, as compared with other socio-economic characteristics, population statistics are an important standard against which the performances of other aspects of society may be evaluated. Only too often one finds quantitative (mostly economic) targets in development plans lacking any reference to standards, and this renders such targets meaningless. Secondly, it takes a long time to radically change the structure and dynamics that currently characterize a given population; in other words, the fact that a population has an important momentum requires that early action must be taken if the long-term path of estimated population differs from one's goals and objectives. The influenceability of long-term population developments is a matter of continuous debate and argument. Yet the character of such developments hardly admits delay. Mathematical demography offers us models of population dynamics with the help of which the effect of changes may be gauged; such sensitivity analysis can thus be used to single out more and less important fields for direct action.

It should be noted that the rapid transformations mentioned above are far from uniform over most developing countries, and that the turbulent character of many Third World populations is frequently concealed by quoting national averages only. The differences between regions, between urban and rural populations, or between several socio-economic sectors of the population are usually far more striking. However, in such subnational analyses we face considerable methodological difficulties. These relate to the formal representation of subnational population systems on the one hand, and to the availability and quality of the necessary population data on the other. Until recently mathematical demography, well developed as it was in dealing with closed national populations, left the researcher with little more than some tools from descriptive statistics, such as ratios, when it came to representing open (sub-) populations that interact with one another through migration. For regional population projections the best method available has long been to first make individual projections for each of the regions separately, under the assumption of no interregional migration, and then to apply a series of corrections to account for the net effect of interregional migration. Another method still widely used is to make a national population projection first, then to disaggregate the result according to assumed future trends in the shares of the total population in each of the regions. Substituting socio-economic groups for regional populations gives the traditional procedures for projections of subgroups within the school-going population or the labour force.

Recently, however, mathematical demography has been expanded and generalized. Multistate mathematical demography is the multidimensional equivalent of its one-dimensional predecessor in the sense that it allows members of a population, after being born, not only to either survive or die but also to further change state as well, whether it be region or socio-economic group. These changes of state are achieved not by applying correction factors nor by disaggregating totals with ratios, but in a manner fully consistent with the way in which the only change in state recognized in 'classical' mathematical demography, that of survival, is dealt with. To date, most attention has focused on regional disaggregation (Rogers 1975, Rees & Wilson 1977, Willekens & Rogers 1978). Obviously this development in demographic theory seems attractive for developing countries. These are the very areas where demographic developments are most rapid and where population questions are most pressing. Our knowledge of the structure and dynamics of the population should increase in quality when it is based on a sound and consistent body of demographic theory, instead of on simple statistical disaggregations; and, in addition, by employing results that derive from the body of multistate demographic theory we would be able to answer questions analytically which hitherto could only be answered in an approximate and inconsistent fashion. Finally, a sound theoretical framework offers a more reasonable reference base when dealing with questions to which demographic data are relevant and, furthermore, it enables us to determine how these data should be collected and made available for subsequent use.

This aspect of data is of fundamental importance since new developments in theory imply new requirements with regard to the kind and quality of population data; but it is not a one way relationship between demographic theory and demographic data. In developing countries this becomes clear as one realizes how much effort has been put into the development of demographic estimation theory in response to the kind and quality of available population data. It is no exaggeration to argue that there would not be any scope for the application of established demographic models – such as the cohort-survival projection model – in Third World countries without the help of demographic estimation theory in establishing an adequate database. In the case of regional disaggregation, data must be available to answer such questions as: How many children just born in one region will migrate to another and survive there into the next age group? If such questions cannot be answered adequately, the generalization of demographic theory is of little use to Third World countries. There will then be no other choice but to continue using means which, from a theoretical viewpoint, are second best.

This fundamental issue for the regional case is discussed in this chapter. In Section 13.2 a number of criteria for the establishment of an adequate database are briefly described, and then a possible way in which these criteria can be satisfactorily put into operation is outlined. In Section 13.3 some empirical results of the application of generalized multistate demographic theory to Thailand are highlighted.

13.2 Problems of creating a database

In the previous section it was pointed out that multistate mathematical demography would be of great value in population research in developing countries if only an adequate database could be established. This discussion will be limited to states in the sense of regions, as it is the dynamics of the differential geographical population developments which are a major source of concern in many Third World countries. Although the example given below, Thailand, employs 'geographical regions' (or 'homogeneous regions'), the same approach can be followed with other types of regional classification, such as urban and rural.

Regional multistate demographic theory, or multiregional demography, can be put into operation perfectly well in Western countries where a virtually complete and highly accurate system of population registration exists. The only problem one faces under such circumstances is the collection of the available data in the appropriate format. However, in developing countries this source of population data is frequently non-existent; and where it exists it is usually of rather unreliable quality. Sometimes demographic surveys are conducted, but the only source generally available is the population census. Apart from flaws such as underenumeration and inaccurate answers, the census itself does not provide information on a number of essential subjects, mainly because it is an operation *ex post*. For example, no direct mortality data follow from a census. To fill in such gaps in our knowledge a specific branch of demography, demographic estimation theory, has come into existence in recent years. It aims at making the best of the limited and often defective information available in Third World countries by exploiting the regularities exhibited by human populations. Approaches have been designed to adjust defects in reported data, and to estimate unavailable data using information that is generally at the disposal of researchers; but there are some important limitations in its application to the present context. They relate to the fact that demographic estimation theory is not an integrated body of knowledge. Various strains of theory have been developed independently from one another in response to different questions raised as to the characteristics of Third World populations. Consequently, the various strains require different and sometimes contradictory conditions and assumptions to be valid. Many approaches may therefore only be applied when strict conditions are fulfilled, such as that of the stability of the population under study. It follows that the interpretation of the outcomes of any such approach is conditional upon the validity of the relevant assumptions. In the present context two particular aspects of consistent and valid integration merit attention. [1]

First, it requires careful consideration to select suitable approaches for the adjustment and estimation of age distributions, fertility schedules, mortality schedules, and migration schedules at the same time. The problem of the properly timed and consistent complete picture is the first aspect of the problem of arriving at an 'integrated' database. Secondly, demographic estimation theory is essentially concerned with closed populations. Obviously this observation does not hold true for the comparatively limited results achieved in the field of the estimation of migration data. A common procedure is to infer mortality from an age distribution given an estimated population growth rate, or from an age distribution at two points in time. Clearly, in the multiregional case, methods such as these are ruled out. Age distributions are not now the resultant of 'local' mortality and fertility but of interregional migration as well. To those who are aware of what demographic estimation theory has to offer it will become clear that an open, multiregional population system forms a serious constraint to the choice between the available well-established and robust avenues. This issue of interaction among demographic states (regions) I would call the second aspect of the problem of arriving at an integrated database.

13.2.1 Database framework

Before embarking upon the listing of some of the criteria for database establishment, two background issues merit attention. They are that of framework and that of generality.

As mentioned in the introduction, there exists a strong mutual interaction between the formal approach used in analysing and forecasting a country's regional population system on the one hand, and the collection, structuring and making available of appropriate population data on the other. The operation and use of multistate demographic analysis thus takes place within a given context or framework. Ideally this framework is part of a wider context in which population issues are considered in their relationship with other socio-economic facets. This may be a purely descriptive–analytic context, but it may also include active and prospective elements as is the case in development planning (Doeve 1981a). Whatever the specific situation, one can invariably distinguish three phases in putting multistate demographic theory into operation in developing countries. First an appropriate 'benchmark integrated' database has to be established; one has to 'get things going'. The basic source of information will usually be a recent population census. If one has been successful, there will then follow a continuous cycle where two phases alternate, that is the intercensal period and the period in which the results from a subsequent census gradually become available. In the intercensal period one would use the results from the analysis of the benchmark database as a standard for the evaluation of alternatives – sensitivity analysis of intervention, feasibility analysis of policy goals and objectives, and so on. Also the benchmark database may be employed in the monitoring of changes and deviations from the time path that follows from the assumption of no change from the dynamics implicit in the benchmark database. Such deviations become apparent from subsidiary sources, such as periodic surveys, and sometimes from continuous population registration, that is when the latter is available, and when its information can be adequately corrected to provide an answer to the specific question posed. If and when such deviations are convincing the benchmark database may be adjusted pending more definite information from the census to follow. Thus one would adopt a preliminary revised benchmark integrated database. When the results from the subsequent population census gradually become available the validity of the database used to date can be thoroughly examined. This may well lead to the adoption of a revised benchmark integrated database for use in future research. Typically there is a continuous alternation of phases of adjustments made to the database. These enable estimates to be made of the size and trends in errors in the estimated database. Using this information on errors in the estimates so far derived, the quality of the database can be improved. This allows for some degree of uncertainty with respect to the benchmark estimates that are first used to put multistate demographic theory in phase one into operation.

13.2.2 Database generality

In the remainder of this chapter emphasis will be upon this first phase, since it is a fundamental one and relates to the issue of generality. It is possible to design a first phase which, as will be shown below, is general in kind and can hence be used in any Third World country, provided the results of at least one modern population census are available. In practice the approach suggested would obviously need to be refined – or perhaps even totally deviated from – in order to make use of the unique advantages offered by the information available in the country under study. Such refinements and deviations are more likely once the cycle has gone round once. Furthermore, demographic estimation theory is not a stationary subject. Hence references to a distant and yet unknown future are likely to be less relevant methodologically.

13.2.3 Criteria in the establishment of a benchmark integrated database

Bearing the above considerations in mind, what are the general criteria that should be met in order to guarantee that one arrives at a benchmark integrated database which is adequate for the purpose? They are summarized below.[2]

First, the approach must be based on information collected through one population census only. To date most developing countries have the outcomes of at least one modern population census. Thus the general applicability of the approach is not restricted by the absence of the relevant data. Furthermore, in a number of developing countries that have taken more than one census the operation still lacks a routine character. This may seriously hinder comparability between censuses taken in the recent past. Successive censuses are usually some ten years apart, so causing three types of difficulties: such long intervals conceal much of the detail of the rapid changes in regional demographic characteristics that are currently taking place; the benchmark database would inevitably pertain, at least in part, to a rather distant past (it is thus likely to be outdated before any analysis has even started); and serious data problems of a technical nature would also arise. Multiple moves will cause migration to be underestimated if the further analysis is in the common five-year intervals. Boundary changes between regions are more likely to have occurred and the effect of emigration, unrecorded by censuses, increases. However, when due care is taken a prior census may help to improve the quality of some of the estimates. It could prove particularly helpful in providing consistency checks on the procedures adopted and the assumptions made.

Secondly, the information to be used must consist of commonly tabulated and published basic data.

Thirdly, the methods used for adjusting and estimating must have been firmly established and validated. Relative parsimony with respect to theoretical framework, assumptions and information needed is a distinct advantage. The methods must be robust, efficient and unbiased under the conditions of use. As far as theoretical underpinnings and assumptions are concerned, methods must be mutually compatible within the overall integrated database adjustment and estimation frame. The accumulation of estimates (estimate upon estimate) should be minimized. One particular assumption needs special attention. That is, no use should be made of approaches involving the assumption that the population under study is stable or quasi-stable. In many developing countries mortality decline started over some forty years ago. So the use of the well known adjustment factors for deviations from stability due to a recent onset of mortality decline (quasi-stable populations) is ruled out. There is also mounting evidence on the decline of fertility in more and more regions of the Third World (see Ch. 5). Under the present circumstances in most developing countries migration schedules, the characteristic ingredient in a multiregional approach, are rarely stable. These conditions will render the use of stable population theory invalid in the years to come for many parts of the Third World. From the point of view of demographic estimation this is unfortunate because stable population analysis forms the essential backbone of an important and powerful part of that theory.

Fourthly, whenever possible consistency checks must be made using current and previous outcomes of the adjustment and estimation approaches, other sources (parallel strains of research, sources on the present and historical socio-economic structure of the regions under study), and validated social science theory.

Fifthly, in addition to checking and validating outcomes of the integrated database establishment approach adopted (fourth criterion) it is particularly helpful to record as completely as possible all reasons for the choice of individual procedures, their underlying assumptions, their advantages and disadvantages as compared to possible alternative procedures when designing the overall approach. By these means comparability can be checked far more easily. Tracing the extent to which design influences outcome will not be limited to rough guesses and in future the consistency of changes and additions to the overall approach need to be ascertained unambiguously.

Sixthly, having established a database, the procedures used should allow the determination of the degree of accuracy of the results obtained.[3] Here one can distinguish three levels. Some procedures themselves implicitly produce an indication of their accuracy. In many cases carefully designed sets of simulations may produce valuable insights into the question of accuracy.

Finally, thorough theoretical and empirical knowledge may help in establishing upper and lower bounds of the estimates. This criterion is discussed at length by Doeve (1981a).

13.2.4 Procedures

I shall only outline the procedure developed for database establishment in general terms since a detailed description falls outside the scope of this chapter because the proper juxtaposition of the guiding methodological principles on the one hand, and the elements within the consistent set of adjustment and estimation methods on the other, unavoidably involves many minutiae (see Doeve 1984). In summary, it will suffice to bear in mind that the basic assumption underlying the benchmark integrated database establishment approach is the Markovian assumption of multistate demographic theory: demographic behaviour depends on the region of residence at the beginning of each time interval of analysis. Hence the problem facing the analyst is to derive from the census a local and well–timed database that contains estimates of region-specific age distributions, mortality schedules and fertility schedules, and of inter-regional gross migration schedules, all at the beginning of the first time interval of analysis, which is usually the date of census taking. The age–time reference specification of this database must match that of the demographic models to be used. Each of the estimates, it should be stressed, must be purely local, which is to say free from bias due to interregional interaction. There are two avenues open to the analyst. Apart from the regional age distributions, multistate demographic theory makes use of fertility data in the form of rates, and mortality and migration data either in the form of life-table mortality and migration proportions or in the form of state-specific life-table survivorship ratios as its basic inputs for subsequent analysis. Earlier formulations of the present database strategy have therefore always been in such terms (see Doeve 1981a). However, in the demographic literature increasing attention is paid to the concept of population accounting (Rees & Wilson 1977). Furthermore, and in a sense related to this, above I emphasized the relevance of demographic theory as a meaningful framework for collecting, making available and studying demographic data. These considerations have influenced me to add to, and slightly modify, procedures so as to be able to produce fertility, mortality and migration data in absolute numbers as well.

13.2.5 Benchmark integrated database establishment procedure

Based upon these considerations, the procedure can be summarized as follows.

Age distribution for the individual regions as they follow from reported ages may well suffer from the 'standard' errors, such as global and age–specific underenumeration and global and age–specific age shifting. The first may be related to census-taking practice – for instance, mapping procedures – as well as to differential characteristics of the persons missed out, who may, for example, be recent migrants. The latter finds its origin in matters such as the kind and quality of the people's frame of reference regarding time scales, or as digit preferences. Consequentially regional age distributions may be characterized by an insufficient total area under the curve as well as by erroneous peaks and dips. In the case of national population analysis there exist a whole range of well known diagnostic and remedial aids. Their use is considered appropriate when national populations can be considered to be closed. Without evidence of major upheavals it is then assumed that they ought to exhibit certain regular features. But in the regional case matters are completely different: the effects of births and deaths on age distributions are modified by migration. Although these effects are difficult to disentangle it is very likely that the resultant regional age distributions will be characterized by very real peaks and dips. The tools designed for the analysis of closed national age distributions in general obviously fail to distinguish between such real irregularities and the erroneous ones mentioned above. The ultimate solution is rather straightforward and consists of two elements which derive from the distinction between erroneous and real irregularities. First, careful investigation is required into the respects in which the census coverage failed to be complete and into the biases to which this has given rise. The reported versus the real timing of events, which relates to cultural and educational circumstances, requires investigation as well so that sound empirically based adjustments can be made. Secondly, real irregularities will become apparent from simulations of the dynamics of the multiregional population system; for instance, by tracing regional cohorts over a ten-year interval and comparing the outcomes with the following decennial census. Other sources of information on the history of regions can sometimes yield invaluable insights as well.

Neither of the above avenues offers an immediate solution when establishing a first benchmark integrated database. Possibly the best provisional approach is a partial one, namely to correct at least the regional age distributions for real errors which are apparent in the national age distribution. These latter errors follow from 'traditional' national analysis. It does not seem logical to leave errors which would have been corrected in a national analysis. On the other hand, the empirical basis for making region-specific adjustments will in general be insufficient at this stage instead of rectifying them. This is likely to hold true since the stronger the case for a multistate demographic approach the more age distributions will be influenced by interregional migration.

Regional mortality experience is estimated by fitting appropriate model life tables. Attention must be paid to the general methodological considerations mentioned above; for instance, life tables should be local and free from the disturbing effects of interregional migration and properly timed. On the basis of an evaluation of these requirements, Doeve (1984) shows that the best suited model life tables are those designed by Ledermann (1969) whose *reseau* 101 variant is particularly convenient in the present context. It is estimated on the basis of the proportion of newly born male and female babies dying before reaching age five ($_5q_0$). The latter value of the so-called entry parameter for the model life tables can be estimated using a number of well known and robust procedures locally for each of the regions. The information needed is generally collected in censuses in developing countries. The procedure by Brass (Brass 1975, Brass *et al.* 1968) is used for this purpose; it employs the parity ratio of women aged 20–24 and 25–29 (P_2/P_3) for fitting. This ratio follows from the analysis of regional fertility described below. There is one complication in using the $_5q_0$ entry parameter thus estimated. That is, it pertains to the regional mortality experience some time before census taking. When regional mortality is declining the force of mortality at the time of the census is slightly overestimated. However, it is not difficult to estimate the trend in the entry parameter or the consequential regional mortality schedule. Two approaches can be followed. First, there are now procedures available which are modifications of the line of thinking originally developed by Brass and which give an indication of the trend in time in mortality at young ages. Secondly, the point in time before census taking to which estimated $_5q_0$ values pertain can be established accurately. As soon as the following census is available the trend in regional $_5q_0$ values can be re-established. The second procedure is likely to be the more robust; but the first procedure can be used for provisional adjustment until the new census has been processed.

Regional fertility estimation is based on information on current fertility. This may either be in the form of children born in the previous twelve months (usually but not necessarily), or in the form of living own children of zero to one year of age (again, usually but not necessarily). In the second case, backsurvival to births is achieved in a two-step closed cyclic procedure with mortality estimation (Doeve 1984). The estimation procedure is based on the principles outlined by Brass (Brass *et al.* 1968). Doeve (1981b, 1984) shows that among the several methods available it suits the relevant criteria best. Particularly, Doeve (1981b) shows its robustness under the most common patterns of fertility decline, provided the fertility experience of women aged 20–24, that is the P_2/F_2 multiplier, is used to make the adjustments.

New interpolation equations for the evaluation of the reconstructed parity values (F_1) from Barclay *et al.* (1976) are used. Given the assumption that although a woman might migrate when she is still pregnant she is not likely to do so shortly after she has given birth to a baby, the estimates of regional fertility are local under the Markovian assumption. The translation suggested by Brass (Brass *et al.* 1968) is used to interpolate the estimates at the common five-year age groups, as recorded data on average pertain to a point in time half a year before the date of census taking when women were on average half a year younger. Once a subsequent census is available the trend in time in regional fertility over the intercensal period can be established, which will enable interpolation of estimated regional fertility exactly at the time of the first census (instead of at one half year before the census). By extrapolating, properly timed estimates for that subsequent census can then be found as well. Finally, it may be noted that the estimation of regional $_5q_0$ values uses the parity ratio of women in age groups 20–24 and 25–29 (P_2/P_3) for fitting only after adjustment of the latter, that is F_2/F_3, so as to achieve consistency between procedures employed in the estimation of mortality and fertility. Generally, adjusted parity values are found by multiplying the corresponding reconstructed parity values (F_1) by the chosen P/F fertility adjustment multiplier.

The distinguishing mark of multistate demographic theory is the treatment of interregional migration in a consistent fashion within the overall regional framework. Consequently, in the establishment of the database the estimation of migration data should be dealt with accordingly. Conceptually, migration is probably the most difficult element in establishing a benchmark integrated database, when the relevant methodological considerations such as 'localness' and 'timeliness' have to be met. Empirically, migrants, notably recent ones, are an elusive group to enumerate. Compared with the fields of mortality and fertility, demographic estimation theory has relatively little to offer in the field of migration. There exist, for example, a number of indirect methods based on data that are not derived from direct questions on migration behaviour, but only net migration estimates can be derived from them, whereas region-by-region gross out-migration estimates are required. Furthermore, such procedures are generally based on the comparison of two or more censuses. In Section 13.2.3 under the first criterion some of the fundamental problems to which this gives rise – especially in the case of the study of migration – have already been mentioned briefly. Under certain circumstances they may be used to check the outcomes of alternative procedures.

Direct methods, that is methods that do use data derived from answers to questions on migration behaviour, are arguably least well developed of all (Doeve 1984). Model migration schedules are the subject of study, but they are not operational yet in the present context. A second method is available which uses place of birth data cross-classified by place of residence; this yields region-by-region gross migration flows and is based on the comparison of two successive censuses. A third kind of direct method is well established, namely the entropy maximizing and other related approaches. They aim at recovering the statistically most probable detailed matrix of interregional migration flows, given limited aggregate information; for example, the combination of total numbers of inmigrants by region of inmigration, total numbers of outmigrants by region of outmigration, and the age distribution of the grand total number of migrants. In the present context of first benchmark integrated database establishment, I would suggest the following application in situations where one has no more knowledge than regional net migration from a suitable indirect method. Under these circumstances, the most probable pattern of net region-by-region flows can be recovered (see Doeve 1984). Although the underlying gross interregional flows – of which the recovered net interregional flows are the balances – themselves remain unknown, the resulting outcomes of projections and other simulations, for example, will be correct. It seems that this latter combination of indirect with direct (entropy maximization type) methods holds considerable promise in cases with poor data, so that at least a provisional benchmark database can be established, pending the collection of more adequate migration data in a subsequent census.

When direct questions on migration behaviour are asked, one on place of previous residence and one on duration of residence are usually included. A common way of producing outcomes from these census questions is in the form of numbers that have inmigrated into the present region of residence within a five-year period prior to the census by region of previous residence. This information is frequently used by analysis of interregional migration. Notwithstanding the efforts to arrive at proper estimates of fertility and mortality, these migration data are usually taken for granted without any critical study regarding format or quality. However, the time reference of the reported census migration data – on average 2.5 years before the date of census taking when dealing with five-year migration data – does not coincide with the timing of age distributions and of mortality and fertility schedules derived from the same census. Furthermore, the age–time reference specification of census migration data is based on a comparison along cohort lines of the place of residence at two points in time. Is this in agreement with the age–time reference specification of the demographic models to be used, or are the latter perhaps of the kind that require period (transversal) data on events (moves instead of migrants)? Frequently data on children born during the five years prior to the census who migrated during that period (that is, migrants aged 0–4 at the time of the census) are not available and, as far as quality is concerned, it is well known that recent migrants are usually grossly underenumerated. It should also be noted that reported census migration data only relate to surviving inmigrants; some migrants will have died in the five years prior to the census. Finally, an important issue relating to 'localness', which is usually ignored by analysts, will be taken up again at the end of this section on interregional migration.

A set of procedures has been developed to perform the necessary adjustments and estimations in order to arrive at the data required on the basis of the census information outlined above. It is fully integrated within, and consistent with, the overall benchmark database establishment approach outlined so far. This coherent set of adjustment and estimation procedures incorporates features such as facilities for the correction of underenumeration of recent and other migrants, matrix shrinking procedures, in-line cubic spline interpolation facilities, and multiregional backward population projections. It is designed to handle the raw input data as they are usually tabulated — for example, with the possibility of distributing the omnipresent category 'other regions of previous residence' according to optional criteria. The advantage is that special census tabulations can therefore be avoided when desired, thus enhancing general applicability. The procedures are organized in a modular form allowing for flexible adjustment to varying circumstances (Doeve 1984).

One final remark relating to 'localness' must be made. Given only the raw reported census migration data described above, one cannot but assume that the place of previous residence is the same as the place of residence five years before the date of census taking. Because of multiple moves this assumption is likely to be invalid; but the kind and degree of error involved cannot be established without further information. Two solutions to this problem are possible. First, one may substitute a question in the census on the place of residence five years prior to the census. To some extent, memory lapses and errors in the reference period are likely to detract from the value of the answers, although the character and extent of such memory lapses and errors in the reference period can be studied in a carefully designed set of longitudinal pilot surveys, for example. These surveys should result in adequate insights to permit the adjustment of raw reported census migration data that follow from such questions on place of residence at a fixed date prior to the census for the effects of such memory lapses and reference period errors. Secondly, there is the situation in which a question is asked on the place of previous residence without any indication of the place of residence, say five years prior to the census. In this instance the solution is to investigate the character and extent of the phenomenon of multiple moves. This may also be done through a similar set of longitudinal pilot surveys. These surveys should then result in adequate insights to allow the adjustment of available raw reported census migration data for the effects of such multiple moves.

A number of conclusions emerge from the discussion above. First of all, it was shown that putting multistate demographic theory into operation requires a carefully designed methodological framework. Secondly, within such a framework it was described how a benchmark integrated database could be established and further developed. Obviously, given the availability and quality of demographic data, minor flaws cannot always be avoided – at least initially. Some have been mentioned already, but usually remedies can be indicated that will improve the future quality of the database. Two cases still need raising. The value of $_5q_0$ in mortality estimation is determined by events that happened some time prior to census taking. The current procedure takes all women, including those who inmigrated only recently, to represent the experience of the region of residence at the time of the census. A similar observation holds true for parity data. Only when cross-tabulations by migratory status are available can these cases be handled adequately. Given the possibilities of eliminating such minor flaws in the future, database considerations do not form an obstacle to the implementation of multistate demographic theory in regional population analysis in Third World countries. In addition, it should be noted that use is made not only of very limited basic data but also of basic data that are nowadays generally available in developing countries and are readily available from existing sources. This obviously results in a very high degree of cost-effectiveness for any applications. In summary, the attractiveness of the multistate demographic framework which is powerful, internally consistent, unifies database establishment, and is comparable externally – that is, in space (other countries) and in time (historical continuity) – coupled with an integrated database establishment procedure which is geared to this theoretical framework, generally applicable and cost-effective, seems to hold great promise for population analysis in developing countries.

The final section of this chapter contains some preliminary results from an application of this approach to Thailand.

13.3 The establishment of a benchmark integrated database for Thailand

A first benchmark integrated database has been developed for Thailand using the guidelines set out in the previous section. In this final section some of the preliminary results are presented by way of illustration. It should be stressed that what follow are merely one or two illustrative examples and by no means a full discussion of the case with an analysis of the results.

The Thai database has been established with selected results from the 1970 Population and Housing Census, conducted and published by the National Statistical Office (NSO) of the Kingdom. The database allows analyses to be performed for both sexes individually, as well as for males and females together. Only results for males and females together will be given below. The database is in common five-year age groups, with additional information on mortality among infants aged 0–1. The highest age group is an open-ended one arbitrarily chosen as 70 + . The date of reference of the database is the date of census taking − 1 April 1970. The regionalization is in conformity with the NSO practice at the time of the census. There are four regions which for the sake of convenience are commonly referred to by their geographical location within the country as North, North-east, Central and South (see Fig. 13.1). There is one exception. Intraregional migration in each of the regions is set equal to zero, except for Central. Anticipating the recent decision by the NSO to single out the five *changwat* (province) region of Greater Bangkok Metropolitan Area from the rest of Central, the migrants moving between these two new regions (but only these migrants) will be found in the category 'internal migrants' for the old Central region. (Central in the present database still pertains to the 1970 definition of that region, as stated above.) Table 13.1 gives the summary account of the estimates for males and females combined

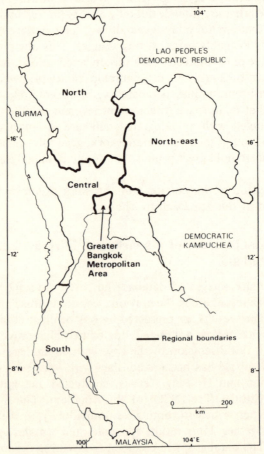

Figure 13.1 The regions of Thailand used in the construction of a database.

by region. Migrants in both tables are measured over five years whereas mortality and fertility data are measured annually. It should be understood that these tables represent summary results only, which is to say that they are the final product *after* the full procedure outlined in the previous sections had been completed.

It is obvious that the database itself is the first object of analysis throughout the full procedure of its establishment. First, this is of methodological importance since it may well be that a particular country or region is characterized by features which require modifications from the general procedures either because the standard procedures do not fit, or because they produce results which are suboptimal in quality as compared with alternative procedures. Secondly, valuable empirical insights may be acquired by carefully monitoring the process of transforming the raw input data into the final benchmark integrated database. Interesting similarities and differences between the regions will usually become apparent. Consider, for example, the summary results in Table 13.1. The young age distribution of North-east, coupled with a mortality regime characterized by relatively high child mortality, forces the mean age at death down. Or, taking migration, compare the striking differences in shape of the age–specific curves. Those differences most likely represent the different character of the interregional flows. For instance, the presence of many young children probably represents moves of families as opposed to individuals. All such preliminary hypotheses are important guides in determining what further investigation can best be aimed at. This can be research within the multistate demographic framework as well as economic, geographical, sociological and other work aimed at analysing causes and consequences from disciplinary points of view.

Multistate demographic theory offers a wide variety of analytical tools in the fields of fertility, mortality and mobility analysis. One example is the multistate life table which is an expansion of the classical life table, in the sense that all life-table functions are disaggregated by state (region in our case). For instance, the well known life expectation function gives life expectancies beyond each exact age x of persons who are living in each of the four regions at that age (e_x). Table 13.2 not only indicates e_x but also shows how many years of the total will be spent in each of the four regions. For example, a person of exact age 10 and currently living in North-east has a remaining expectancy of life of about 53.7 years. Only 47.0 of those are expected to be spent in the region of current residence. The remainder of 6.7 years is expected to be spent mainly (4.5 years) in Central. A person of the same age, but currently living in Central, is expected to live almost 3 years longer ($e_{10} - 56.4$). However, he or she is expected to spend no more than 2.7 years of this total in North-east. Expectancies such as these are thus one way of conveniently summarizing regional mortality and migration characteristics that are implicit in the benchmark database.

Table 13.1 Integrated benchmark database derived from selected information in the 1970 Population and Housing Census of Thailand.

North (N)

Age groups	Total population	Births	Deaths	Migration from North to:		
				NE	C	S
0–4	1 274 700	0	37 414	6 140	11 787	420
5–9	1 179 500	0	3 531	5 880	18 649	602
10–14	1 033 500	0	2 196	3 778	19 332	623
15–19	857 700	33 347	2 942	4 578	19 985	723
20–24	661 800	80 074	3 155	4 702	16 536	651
25–29	509 300	62 320	2 600	3 427	9 749	405
30–34	432 800	47 600	2 406	2 185	5 130	228
35–39	424 000	36 306	2 720	1 768	4 038	188
40–44	365 000	10 832	2 851	1 239	2 981	138
45–49	304 000	1 340	3 041	893	2 349	93
50–54	223 900	0	3 047	511	1 469	48
55–59	182 400	0	3 479	377	1 091	37
60–64	142 600	0	4 021	278	785	33
65–69	106 400	0	4 553	200	544	27
70 +	137 200	0	15 758	137	331	27
Total	7 834 800	271 819	93 714	36 100	114 756	4 243

North-east (NE)

Age groups	Total population	Births	Deaths	Migration from North-east to:		
				N	C	S
0–4	2 511 100	0	82 485	11 528	15 038	1 201
5–9	1 924 400	0	6 456	11 519	31 503	1 751
10–14	1 547 800	0	3 617	7 548	35 603	2 209
15–19	1 328 400	53 163	4 948	6 859	32 843	2 977
20–24	1 200 300	178 242	6 209	7 535	30 858	3 603
25–29	897 100	146 862	4 965	5 979	17 621	2 555
30–34	659 200	97 800	3 910	3 455	6 410	1 127
35–39	603 100	76 072	4 164	2 937	4 569	683
40–44	504 700	32 631	4 204	2 072	3 098	350
45–49	442 300	3 972	4 662	1 659	2 288	246
50–54	323 000	0	4 592	975	1 230	137
55–59	261 100	0	5 174	779	975	106
60–64	185 000	0	5 395	550	713	74
65–69	126 800	0	5 587	377	512	48
70 +	156 200	0	18 114	225	349	25
Total	12 661 500	588 742	164 482	63 997	183 610	17 092

Central (C)

Age groups	Total population	Births	Deaths	Migration from Central to:			
				N	NE	C	S
0–4	1 732 000	0	33 126	14 340	14 272	29 528	4 562
5–9	1 589 900	0	3 065	14 665	12 535	46 304	5 043
10–14	1 398 300	0	2 060	10 652	8 621	49 293	4 237
15–19	1 260 500	38 163	3 140	13 962	14 447	58 350	5 851
20–24	1 066 200	98 989	3 710	15 985	17 956	57 191	6 722
25–29	795 400	97 720	2 976	10 841	11 945	30 882	4 522
30–34	648 000	62 243	2 658	6 938	7 163	15 328	2 828
35–39	560 300	43 348	2 706	4 751	4 415	10 515	1 853
40–44	485 000	21 834	2 954	3 436	2 801	8 198	1 252
45–49	406 300	3 418	3 321	2 640	1 945	6 300	889
50–54	327 600	0	3 764	1 875	1 288	4 461	597
55–59	275 400	0	4 531	1 497	998	3 756	475
60–64	207 600	0	5 145	1 027	671	2 786	333
65–69	154 500	0	5 910	687	435	2 086	229
70 +	219 700	0	24 362	376	209	1 561	138
Total	11 126 700	365 715	103 428	103 672	99 701	326 539	39 531

South (S)

Age groups	Total population	Births	Deaths	Migration from South to:		
				N	NE	C
0–4	791 500	0	15 835	606	1 033	5 201
5–9	676 100	0	1 366	647	926	11 062
10–14	538 000	0	824	528	546	11 942
15–19	462 100	22 122	1 191	777	805	12 069
20–24	380 200	45 925	1 368	791	906	9 527
25–29	305 700	39 223	1 182	489	689	4 875
30–34	252 400	32 254	1 069	250	431	2 001
35–39	226 300	23 729	1 127	184	275	1 535
40–44	201 600	9 422	1 261	153	185	1 427
45–49	161 900	784	1 352	103	117	995
50–54	128 400	0	1 502	66	75	631
55–59	105 300	0	1 760	49	57	431
60–64	90 600	0	2 276	48	54	370
65–69	64 600	0	2 500	40	44	267
70 +	91 800	0	10 216	36	40	180
Total	4 476 500	173 459	44 829	4 767	6 183	62 513

Table 13.2 Life expectation (e_x, sexes combined) by region of residence at age x and future possible residence, Thailand 1970.

North (N)

Age	Total	N	NE	C	S
0	55.17	48.32	1.66	4.90	0.29
5	58.49	51.31	1.68	5.20	0.30
10	54.30	48.06	1.44	4.54	0.26
20	45.59	41.50	1.04	2.88	0.16
30	37.56	35.64	0.53	1.32	0.06

Northeast (NE)

Age	Total	NE	N	C	S
0	53.68	46.66	1.77	4.70	0.55
5	51.80	50.12	1.83	5.23	0.62
10	53.68	47.01	1.55	4.55	0.57
20	45.02	40.89	1.11	2.64	0.39
30	37.09	35.30	0.63	1.00	0.15

Central (C)

Age	Total	C	N	NE	S
0	59.93	52.28	3.25	3.08	1.32
5	60.77	53.24	3.19	3.01	1.32
10	56.38	49.68	2.80	2.70	1.19
20	47.47	42.43	2.10	2.06	0.87
30	39.16	36.60	1.14	0.98	0.44

South (S)

Age	Total	S	N	NE	C
0	59.75	53.47	0.62	0.70	5.00
5	60.79	54.28	0.62	0.69	5.20
10	56.39	50.77	0.54	0.60	4.48
20	47.46	44.22	0.45	0.39	2.51
30	39.08	37.77	0.33	0.17	1.01

One of the most useful multistate demographic tools for population analysis is the multiregional population projection. An example is given in Table 13.3. The total population by age and region is projected forward from 1970 to 2005 in five-year periods. Intermediate results can be obtained by interpolation. The example given assumes that the 1970 fertility, mortality and migration schedules remain unchanged over the projection period. In other words we shall be concerned with the analysis of the consequences

Table 13.3 Multiregional population projections for Thailand, 1970–2005. (Constant change at 1970 levels is assumed.)

Year	North	North-east	Central	South
1970	7 834 800	12 661 500	11 126 700	4 476 500
1975	8 867 424	14 852 890	12 745 262	5 174 608
1980	10 121 877	17 401 464	14 704 052	6 007 235
1985	11 619 984	20 373 565	17 020 033	6 986 593
1990	13 324 563	23 810 271	19 662 906	8 145 059
1995	15 225 582	27 829 894	22 660 249	9 487 244
2000	17 310 620	32 471 031	26 031 190	11 033 057
2005	19 671 724	37 930 943	29 883 844	12 810 638

of the persistence of the regional population dynamics as of 1970, assuming no change in these 1970 dynamics over time (constant derivatives scenario). Other scenarios are equally plausible.

During the establishment of the database it became clear that the fertility adjustment procedure did indeed reveal tendencies for fertility to decline in North and Central. Thus the findings of other researchers that in the mid-1960s fertility started to show a downward trend in both these regions were reaffirmed. There is very little variation in the proportion of women in the childbearing ages among the regions in 1970, despite the fact that North and Central are both regions of net inmigration; and, although Central is characterized by somewhat lower mortality, lower regional fertility easily offsets the positive effect of net inmigration and lower mortality on population growth in either region. This follows from the annual growth rate for the period 1970–5, which was 2.48% for North and 2.72% for Central, compared with a national average of 2.86% and a figure for North-east of 3.19%. What may seem odd at first sight is that this effect of comparatively low regional fertility, with its consequences for regional growth, does not produce greater disparities in the course of time; instead regional disparities in growth rate diminish. Fertility is high in one part of the country, North-east, which is a region with rather high outmigration but is also a region with high inmigration. This enables the region not only to maintain its population but even to increase it at a substantial rate. As a region with high outmigration proportions, notably to North and Central, it continues to be the origin of an ever-increasing flow of migrants to these regions. This phenomenon becomes fully evident when one pursues the projection process to multiregional population stability. Table 13.4 gives the stable equivalent population. North-east now has over 50% of the national population and the growth rate is 3.01% which is even higher than the national average over the 1970–5 period.

A final point is worth noting at this stage. In discussing the third criterion for first benchmark integrated database establishment in Section 13.2.3 it

Table 13.4 Regional population structures for Thailand, 1970, compared with the stable age structures. (Percentage distributions with sexes combined.)

1970

Age groups	North	North-east	Central	South
0–4	16.27	19.83	15.57	17.68
5–9	15.05	15.20	14.29	15.10
10–14	13.19	12.22	12.57	12.02
15–19	10.95	10.49	11.33	10.32
20–24	8.45	9.48	9.58	8.49
25–29	6.50	7.09	7.15	6.83
30–34	5.52	5.14	5.82	5.64
35–39	5.41	4.76	5.04	5.06
40–44	4.66	3.99	4.36	4.50
45–49	3.88	3.49	3.65	3.62
50–54	2.86	2.55	2.94	2.87
55–59	2.33	2.06	2.48	2.35
60–64	1.82	1.46	1.87	2.02
65–69	1.35	1.00	1.39	1.44
70 +	1.75	1.23	1.97	2.05

Stable age distribution

Age groups	Total	North	North-east	Central	South
0–4	18.03	16.35	19.69	15.46	17.75
5–9	14.33	13.34	15.22	12.88	14.36
10–14	12.18	11.61	12.63	11.52	12.12
15–19	10.34	10.06	10.44	10.34	10.21
20–24	8.73	8.70	8.57	9.14	8.59
25–29	7.34	7.55	7.02	7.94	7.26
30–34	6.16	6.53	5.79	6.76	6.15
35–39	5.15	5.60	4.78	5.69	5.20
40–44	4.29	4.75	3.93	4.77	4.35
45–49	3.53	3.98	3.21	3.97	3.61
50–54	2.87	3.28	2.58	3.26	2.95
55–59	2.29	2.64	2.03	2.61	2.37
60–64	1.76	2.05	1.54	2.03	1.84
65–69	1.28	1.50	1.10	1.50	1.35
70 +	1.73	2.04	1.45	2.11	1.88

was argued that no procedures should be used that rely on the assumption that regional populations are stable or quasi-stable. Table 13.4 illustrates this argument. Perhaps it is helpful to recall what the stable equivalent population is. Projecting our actual multiregional population system forwards from 1970 by applying the same multiregional growth matrix over n time intervals we shall ultimately achieve stability. The relative age–specific multiregional population distribution will remain constant, as will the growth rate for all regions. The (hypothetical) multiregional population of the same relative distribution by age and region, which, by applying the multiregional growth matrix, would be growing at the same rate and would achieve the same size after n time intervals as the actual multiregional population at stability, is called the stable equivalent population. Its relative distribution is that of the characteristic vector associated with the dominant characteristic root of the growth matrix. Hence it is the 1970 stable multiregional population that is consistent with the multiregional growth matrix, that is, consistent with the fertility, mortality and migration elements of the benchmark integrated database.

In the population analysis of single regions the determination of whether or not a given population is approximately stable is usually done on the basis of a comparison of the relative distribution of the actual population with an appropriate stable population. It is not difficult to see that this would give a rather false impression in the present case as the relative 1970 regional age distributions each individually conform quite closely to the relative stable regional distributions. The considerable deviations only become clear by comparing the actual 1970 multiregional population with its stable equivalent population. Compare, for example, the absolute sizes, or the shares of each region in the country's total. The deviations are confirmed by the differential regional growth rates that follow from the projections over 1970–5, 1975–80, and so on. Even if regional mortality and fertility were 'locally' stable, age distributions might not conform because of interregional migration which is unlikely to have been stable for considerable periods in the past.

13.4 Discussion

From the above examples of the application of multistate demographic analysis to Thailand as an operational case some methodological and empirical issues emerge. First, the adoption of multistate demographic theory as a consistent and unifying framework for regional population analysis is attractive because it makes a range of powerful analytical tools available to the population analyst. These cover the entire field of mortality, fertility and migration. Secondly, it has been shown in a number of cases how such tools might be employed to help clarify methodological as well as empirical questions. One example of a methodological question was the discussion on the stability assumption in the database establishment procedure. An example of an empirical matter was the question regarding the trends in differential growth rates among the regions in the course of time.

Here multiregional stable population analysis was used as a sort of magnifying glass to trace what the long-term implications of the dynamics implicit in the benchmark integrated database would be with respect to these growth rates, so assisting the understanding and explanation of the short-term trends. An important conclusion for policy makers in the field of population planning can be drawn from the study of this latter issue. If one aims at curbing population growth, the reduction in fertility in North and Central will only be a short-term success, unless similar results are achieved in North-east, which is the origin of sizeable outmigration. Finally, and perhaps most important of all, this study of differential regional growth rates could not have been carried out, and the conclusion that was relevant for population policy makers and planners could not have been reached if the regional population projections had been carried out in the traditional way by disaggregating a national projection according to estimated future trends in regional shares in the total population, where those trends in regional shares in turn are based on estimated growth rates of the individual regions.

Notes

1 In addition, Doeve (1984) discusses a third aspect, namely that of the consistency between the specification of the age–time reference of the database on the one hand and that of the demographic model used on the other.
2 As was pointed out before, these criteria relate to the establishment of a first multiregional benchmark integrated database (phase 1). This represents the situation, typically in Third World countries, where one starts from scratch, or with only limited groundwork already available to build upon. The criteria do not necessarily all pertain to the process of further investigation, analysis, monitoring and updating which is characteristic of phases 2 and 3.
3 This more or less *ex post facto* criterion follows naturally from the *ex ante facto* third criterion, which stresses among other things robustness, efficiency and unbiasedness of the adjustment and estimation methods.

14

Assessing the United Nations urbanization projections for the Asian Pacific

JACQUES LEDENT and ANDREI ROGERS

14.1 Introduction

The fundamental question addressed in this chapter is the reasonableness of available projections of urbanization, such as those recently published by the United Nations (1980c). In studying this question we follow Keyfitz's (1977, pp. 4–5) advice for developing a better appreciation of population projections:

> One way of enabling clients to understand the model they are to buy is to compare its results with alternative forms simple enough to be called transparent... With much consideration of detail, the United Nations in 1968 arrived at 6.5 billion for the world in the year 2000; in 1972 they gave the figure as 6.2 billion. Can we judge such totals by formulas simple enought to be worked out on a hand calculator?

Drawing on simple models of urban and rural population dynamics, we propose two alternative methods for assessing projected urbanization paths in terms of their underlying assumptions. One focuses on the implied rural–urban migration flows, whereas the other emphasizes the association between urbanization and economic development. Both methods are introduced with the help of an illustration from those nations in East Asia and South Asia that border on the Pacific Ocean, a region that we shall call the Asian Pacific. Our definition of the Asian Pacific includes nine countries and two city–states: Cambodia, China, Hong Kong, Indonesia, Japan, Korea (North and South), Malaysia, the Philippines, Singapore, Thailand, Vietnam.

14.2 Projected population growth and urbanization in the Asian Pacific

The population of the Asian Pacific in 1975 numbered about 1.3 billion and was growing at a rate of just under 2% a year. Continued growth at this

Table 14.1 Population estimates and projections (in thousands) and average annual rates of growth (per thousand): Asian Pacific, urban and rural, 1950–2000.

Area		1950 P	1960 g	1960 P	1970 g	1970 P	1975 g	1975 P	1980 g	1980 P	1990 g	1990 P	2000 g	2000 P
Asian Pacific	T	826 304	16.9	978 640	18.4	1 176 853	18.8	1 293 139	18.3	1 416 811	15.8	1 659 317	13.4	1 896 622
	U	135 021	52.3	227 690	32.2	314 187	32.1	368 931	32.5	433 927	31.3	593 464	30.3	803 762
	R	691 283	8.3	750 950	13.9	862 666	13.8	924 208	12.3	982 884	8.1	1 065 853	2.5	1 092 860
China	T	558 190	15.9	654 488	16.5	771 840	16.6	838 803	15.8	907 609	12.8	1 031 142	10.7	1 147 987
	U	61 393	68.4	121 716	31.5	166 710	31.7	195 355	33.2	230 652	32.9	320 393	32.5	443 213
	R	496 797	7.0	532 772	12.7	605 130	12.3	643 448	10.2	676 957	4.9	710 749	−8.4	704 774
Japan	T	83 625	11.8	94 096	10.3	104 331	12.6	111 120	11.2	117 546	7.1	126 213	5.2	132 929
	U	41 977	33.6	58 712	23.7	74 386	22.9	83 424	19.5	91 970	12.9	104 668	8.7	114 128
	R	41 648	−16.3	35 384	−16.7	29 945	−15.6	27 696	−15.9	25 576	−17.2	21 545	−13.6	18 801
Rest of Asian Pacific	T	184 489	22.1	230 056	26.8	300 682	26.5	343 216	26.4	391 656	24.8	501 962	20.4	615 706
	U	31 651	40.1	47 262	43.6	73 091	42.0	90 152	42.2	111 305	41.4	168 403	38.1	246 421
	R	152 838	17.9	182 794	21.9	227 591	21.2	253 064	20.5	280 351	17.4	333 559	10.2	369 285
Cambodia	T	4 163	25.3	5 364	27.5	7 060	27.7	8 110	29.7	9 409	28.3	12 491	23.6	15 619
	U	425	30.1	574	36.4	826	43.2	1 025	48.9	1 309	52.5	2 213	52.7	3 749
	R	3 738	24.0	4 790	26.3	6 234	25.6	7 085	26.8	8 100	23.8	10 278	16.1	12 070
Hong Kong	T	1 974	44.3	3 075	24.8	3 942	13.9	4 225	13.6	4 522	12.9	5 147	8.9	5 625
	U	1 747	45.0	2 739	25.5	3 534	14.5	3 800	14.5	4 085	14.1	4 703	10.2	5 210
	R	227	39.2	336	19.4	408	8.2	425	5.6	437	1.6	444	−6.8	415

Indonesia	T	75 449	20.6	92 701	25.4	119 467	26.0	136 044	25.9	154 869	23.8	196 576	18.9	237 507
	U	9 362	36.8	13 522	41.1	20 395	41.3	25 079	44.3	31 293	45.8	49 477	43.7	76 612
	R	66 087	18.1	79 179	22.4	99 072	22.7	110 965	21.5	123 576	17.4	147 099	9.0	160 895
Korea	T	30 096	15.7	35 221	25.1	45 257	22.0	50 515	21.0	56 111	19.9	68 486	16.1	80 448
	U	7 371	40.7	11 074	57.7	19 723	50.7	25 412	43.7	31 621	35.6	45 132	24.8	57 813
	R	22 725	6.1	24 147	5.6	25 534	-3.4	25 103	-4.9	24 490	-4.7	23 354	-3.1	22 635
Malaysia	T	6 187	24.5	7 908	28.0	10 466	28.9	12 093	29.3	13 998	26.6	18 260	18.9	22 054
	U	1 260	45.9	1 994	34.8	2 823	35.5	3 371	39.6	4 110	41.8	6 244	38.5	9 172
	R	4 927	18.3	5 914	25.6	7 643	26.4	8 722	25.1	9 888	19.5	12 016	7.0	12 882
Philippines	T	20 988	27.2	27 561	31.0	37 564	33.6	44 437	32.2	52 203	29.5	70 119	24.6	89 707
	U	5 695	38.3	8 350	39.1	12 387	42.2	15 244	43.0	18 902	43.5	29 198	41.8	43 988
	R	15 293	22.8	19 211	27.2	25 217	29.3	29 193	26.3	33 301	20.6	40 921	11.1	45 719
Singapore	T	1 022	46.9	1 634	23.9	2 075	16.0	2 248	16.1	2 437	14.9	2 829	10.0	3 126
	U	815	44.2	1 268	20.9	1 562	12.8	1 665	16.1	1 805	16.2	2 123	14.4	2 453
	R	207	57.0	366	33.8	513	25.6	583	16.1	632	11.1	706	-4.8	673
Thailand	T	20 010	27.7	26 392	30.3	35 745	32.7	42 093	32.3	49 473	30.0	66 752	24.9	85 618
	U	2 096	45.4	3 302	35.8	4 725	38.2	5 718	43.6	7 110	49.4	11 650	53.3	19 850
	R	17 914	25.4	23 090	29.5	31 020	31.8	36 375	30.5	42 363	26.3	55 102	17.7	65 768
Vietnam	T	24 600	20.5	30 200	25.8	39 106	21.1	43 451	22.5	48 634	23.1	61 302	21.2	75 802
	U	2 880	43.3	4 439	47.8	7 156	42.2	8 838	45.0	11 070	46.7	17 663	44.5	27 574
	R	21 720	17.1	25 761	21.5	31 950	16.0	34 613	16.4	37 564	15.0	43 639	10.0	48 228

Source: United Nations (1980c, Annex II, Tables 48 and 49).

Notes:
P, population estimate (1950–75) or projection (1980–2000).
g, growth rate (per 1000 per year) in period between population estimates or projections.

rate would double the region's population in roughly 35 years and would raise the region's total population to almost two billion by the end of this century.

Urban populations in the Asian Pacific are growing much more rapidly than the total populations of which they are a part. Between 1950 and 1970 the total population of the Asian Pacific region increased by 42%; its urban population, however, increased by 133%. Roughly 400 million people — almost 30% of the region's population — live in urban areas today. Recent United Nations projections indicate that this urban population will more than double by the year 2000 (United Nations 1980c).

Table 14.1 presents urban and rural population estimates and projections and average annual rates of growth for the nine countries and two city–states of the Asian Pacific region from 1950 to 2000 as assessed by the United Nations in 1980. The corresponding degrees of urbanization, as measured by percentage urban (that is, percentage of population in urban areas) appear in Table 14.2. The urban population of the Asian Pacific is expected to continue to grow at a relatively steady rate of just over 3% per annum until the year 2000. The rural population on the other hand is expected to slow its rate of increase dramatically, dropping from its current 1.2% rate to roughly one-fifth of that value in the course of the next two decades. The current percentage urban figure of roughly 30% is expected to grow to 42% by that time.

The aggregate totals for the Asian Pacific region conceal large differences in subregional patterns of population growth and urbanization. Japan's rural population, for example, is expected to continue to exhibit a negative

Table 14.2 Estimated and projected percentage of population in urban areas: Asian Pacific, 1950–2000.

Area	1950	1960	1970	1975	1980	1990	2000
Asian Pacific	16.34	23.27	26.70	28.53	30.63	35.77	42.38
China	11.00	18.60	21.60	23.29	25.41	31.07	38.61
Japan	50.20	62.40	71.30	75.08	78.24	82.93	85.86
Rest of Asian Pacific	17.16	20.54	24.31	26.27	28.42	35.55	40.02
Cambodia	10.21	10.70	11.70	12.64	13.91	17.72	23.70
Hong Kong	88.50	89.07	89.65	89.94	90.34	91.37	92.62
Indonesia	12.41	14.59	17.07	18.43	20.21	25.17	32.26
Korea	24.49	31.44	43.58	50.31	56.35	65.90	71.86
Malaysia	20.37	25.21	26.97	27.88	29.36	34.19	41.59
Philippines	27.13	30.30	32.87	34.30	36.21	41.64	49.04
Singapore	79.95	77.60	75.28	74.07	74.07	75.08	78.47
Thailand	10.47	12.51	13.22	13.58	14.37	17.45	23.18
Vietnam	11.71	14.70	18.30	20.34	22.76	28.81	36.38

Source: United Nations (1980c, Table 50) and the authors' computations from Table 14.1.

Table 14.3 The tempo of urbanization: Asian Pacific, 1950–2000.

Area	1950–60	1960–70	1970–5	1975–80	1980–90	1990–2000
Asian Pacific	35.34	13.76	13.28	14.19	15.51	16.97
China	52.52	14.96	15.07	17.45	20.10	21.72
Japan	21.75	13.34	10.33	8.26	5.82	3.47
Rest of Asian Pacific	18.02	16.83	15.50	15.75	16.59	17.64
Cambodia	4.71	8.92	15.44	19.20	24.17	29.09
Hong Kong	0.64	0.65	0.65	0.88	1.14	1.36
Indonesia	16.17	15.73	15.36	18.35	21.96	24.81
Korea	24.98	32.65	28.70	22.71	15.65	8.66
Malaysia	21.36	6.74	6.58	10.39	15.24	19.58
Philippines	11.02	8.15	8.55	10.80	13.98	16.35
Singapore	− 2.73	− 3.04	− 3.24	0.00	1.31	4.47
Thailand	17.77	5.50	5.46	11.27	19.42	28.40
Vietnam	22.75	21.91	21.15	22.50	23.57	23.31

Source: Table 14.1.

growth rate in excess of 1% per annum by the year 2000; China's, on the other hand, will be almost stationary by then, and the population of the Rest of the Asian Pacific should still be increasing at the rate of about 1% a year. Japan's degree of urbanization in the year 2000 is expected to stand at roughly 85% urban; China and the Rest of the Asian Pacific are projected to show less than half that level. Further disaggregation of the latter region reveals, of course, a much wider range of differences in expected patterns of growth and urbanization.

It can be demonstrated that the difference between the urban and total annual growth rates, $r_u - r_T$, is a rough indicator of the 'tempo' of urbanization (Arriaga 1975). 'Tempo' here is defined as the rate of change, with respect to time, of the percentage of the population residing in urban areas. Table 14.3 sets out these differences over time for the eleven Asian Pacific nations. Note that if natural increase differentials between urban and rural areas are negligible, these differences also reflect the values of the urban net migration rate. They indicate that the tempo of urbanization is expected to continue to decline for Japan, to increase slightly for China and to hold steady for the Rest of the Asian Pacific.

14.3 The components of growth

Further insights into the changing patterns of urbanization may be obtained by disaggregating growth rates into their principal components: natural increase and rural–urban migration. Our rural–urban migration component includes area reclassification.

Let n_u and m_u denote the natural increase and net inmigration components of the urban growth rate r_u, then

$$r_u = n_u + m_u \qquad (14.1)$$

Similarly, in the case of the rural population:

$$r_r = n_r + m_r \qquad (14.2)$$

Assume that natural increase rates in urban and rural regions are equal, that is, $n_u = n_r = n_T$, where n_T is the rate of natural increase of the total national population. Assume that the country is undisturbed by immigration and emigration and therefore that n_T is equal to the national rate of growth r_T. Then the rural net outmigration rate is given by

$$\hat{m}_r = r_r - r_T \qquad (14.3)$$

Because the assumption that natural increase rates are the same in urban and rural areas is probably incorrect, we shall now test the sensitivity of this assumption. First, differentiating between urban and rural rates of natural increase gives

$$m_r = r_r - n_r \qquad (14.4)$$

and the error introduced by assuming those rates to be identical is

$$\hat{m}_r - m_r = n_r - r_T \qquad (14.5)$$

By definition, the national rate of growth is the weighted sum of the urban and rural rates of natural increase:

$$r_T = \frac{n_r + n_u S(t)}{1 + S(t)} \qquad (14.6)$$

where $S(t)$ denotes the ratio of the urban to rural population at time t. Setting $n_u/n_r = k$ gives

$$r_T = n_r \frac{1 + k\, S(t)}{1 + S(t)} \qquad (14.7)$$

whence

$$\hat{m}_r - m_r = \left[\frac{1 + S(t)}{1 + k\, S(t)} - 1 \right] r_T$$

$$= \left[\frac{(1 - k)S(t)}{1 + k\, S(t)} \right] r_T$$

$$\simeq [\alpha(t)(1 - k)] r_T \qquad \text{for } k \neq 1 \qquad (14.8)$$

where $\alpha(t)$ denotes the proportion of the national population that is urban at time t. Thus if $k = 0.95$, the error is less than 5% of the value of the national rate of growth (since $\alpha(t) < 1$).

Table 14.4 Estimates of rural net migration rates (per 1000): Asian Pacific, 1950–2000.

Area	1950–60	1960–70	1970–5	1975–80	1980–90	1990–2000
Asian Pacific	−8.64	−4.57	−5.06	−5.96	−7.70	−10.86
China	−8.92	−3.76	−4.36	−5.61	−7.89	−11.58
Japan	−28.10	−27.02	−28.22	−27.17	−24.27	−18.81
Rest of Asian Pacific	−4.18	−4.85	−5.24	−5.92	−7.44	−10.25
Cambodia	−0.55	−1.12	−2.14	−2.94	−4.52	−7.55
Hong Kong	−5.11	−5.42	−5.70	−8.02	−11.36	−15.64
Indonesia	−2.52	−2.95	−3.31	−4.39	−6.42	−9.95
Korea	−9.66	−19.49	−25.39	−25.96	−24.68	−19.23
Malaysia	−6.28	−2.38	−2.49	−4.16	−7.09	−11.92
Philippines	−4.44	−3.76	−4.32	−5.88	−8.90	−13.55
Singapore	10.06	9.87	9.57	−0.00	−3.84	−14.77
Thailand	−2.30	−0.81	−0.84	−1.83	−3.66	−7.20
Vietnam	−3.45	−4.31	−5.06	−6.17	−8.16	−11.23

Source: authors' estimates.

Table 14.4 presents our estimates of rural net migration rates, $\hat{m}_r$, for the Asian Pacific nations during the period 1950 to 2000, taking the data in Table 14.1 as given.

Dividing minus the rural net migration rates, $-m_r$, in Table 14.4 by the urban–rural population ratio, S, gives the corresponding urban net migration rates, m_u. Subtracting these from the urban growth rate, r_u, gives n_u,

Table 14.5 Percentage of urban growth due to natural increase: Asian Pacific, 1950–2000.

Area	1950–60	1960–70	1970–5	1975–80	1980–90	1990–2000
Asian Pacific	32.38	57.28	58.67	56.29	50.46	44.07
China	23.25	52.43	52.47	47.47	38.83	33.08
Japan	35.16	43.64	54.98	57.64	55.01	59.92
Rest of Asian Pacific	55.05	61.41	63.07	62.64	59.92	53.65
Cambodia	84.34	75.48	64.23	60.75	53.96	44.81
Hong Kong	98.57	97.47	95.54	93.94	91.89	86.74
Indonesia	56.01	61.72	62.85	58.55	52.05	43.26
Korea	38.63	43.44	43.37	48.06	56.02	65.01
Malaysia	53.47	80.61	81.45	73.80	63.56	49.09
Philippines	71.20	79.16	79.72	74.89	67.85	60.11
Singapore	106.17	114.58	125.40	99.99	91.92	69.10
Thailand	60.91	84.65	85.70	74.14	60.66	46.71
Vietnam	47.41	54.12	49.91	50.04	49.54	47.67

Source: authors' estimates.

Table 14.6 Alternative population projections (runs 1 and 2), in thousands, and average annual rates of growth (per thousand): Asian Pacific, urban and rural, 1975–2000.

Area		Run 1 1975 P	g	1980 P	g	1990 P	g	2000 P	Run 2 g	1980 P	g	1990 P	g	2000 P
Asian	T	1 293 139	18.3	1 416 811	15.8	1 659 317	13.4	1 896 622	18.3	1 416 811	15.8	1 659 317	13.4	1 896 622
Pacific	U	368 931	29.8	428 234	25.4	552 012	21.3	682 954	35.2	440 018	36.0	630 535	34.4	889 449
	R	924 208	13.5	988 577	11.3	1 107 305	9.2	1 213 668	11.2	976 794	5.2	1 028 782	-2.1	1 007 173
China	T	838 803	15.8	907 609	12.8	1 031 142	10.7	1 147 987	15.8	907 609	12.8	1 031 142	10.7	1 147 987
	U	195 355	29.5	226 394	24.8	290 227	21.1	358 308	37.1	235 147	38.5	345 548	36.5	497 560
	R	643 448	11.4	681 215	8.4	740 914	6.4	789 679	8.8	672 462	1.9	685 594	-5.3	650 427
Japan	T	111 120	11.2	117 546	7.1	126 213	5.2	132 929	11.2	117 546	7.1	126 213	5.2	132 929
	U	83 424	19.8	92 104	13.7	105 613	9.9	116 568	19.0	91 756	12.4	103 864	8.3	112 871
	R	27 696	-17.0	25 442	-21.1	20 600	-23.0	16 361	-14.3	25 790	-14.3	22 349	-10.8	20 058
Rest of	T	343 216	26.4	391 656	24.8	501 962	20.4	615 706	26.4	391 656	24.8	501 962	20.4	615 706
Asian	U	90 152	39.3	109 736	35.3	156 172	28.7	208 078	45.4	113 114	47.1	181 123	43.2	279 018
Pacific	R	253 064	21.6	281 920	20.4	345 790	16.5	407 628	19.2	278 542	14.1	320 839	4.8	336 688
Cambodia	T	8 110	29.7	9 409	28.3	12 491	23.6	15 819	29.7	9 409	28.3	12 491	23.6	15 819
	U	1 025	43.9	1 277	41.0	1 923	34.6	2 719	62.5	1 401	71.2	2 856	64.1	5 421
	R	7 085	27.6	8 132	26.2	10 568	21.5	13 100	24.5	8 008	18.5	9 635	7.6	10 398

Hong Kong	T	4 225	13.6	4 522	12.9	5 147	8.9	5 625	13.6	4 522	12.9	5 147	8.9	5 625
	U	3 800	14.2	4 080	13.5	4 672	9.4	5 134	14.5	4 085	14.1	4 703	10.3	5 212
	R	425	7.9	442	7.2	475	3.2	491	5.6	437	1.5	444	-7.1	413
Indonesia	T	136 044	25.9	154 869	23.8	196 576	18.9	237 507	25.9	154 869	23.8	196 576	18.9	237 507
	U	25 079	40.0	30 625	36.3	44 013	29.6	59 186	51.0	32 364	55.5	56 386	50.2	93 170
	R	110 965	22.6	124 244	20.5	152 563	15.6	178 321	19.8	122 505	13.5	140 190	2.9	144 337
Korea	T	50 515	21.0	56 111	19.9	68 486	16.1	80 448	21.0	56 111	19.9	68 486	16.1	80 448
	U	25 412	43.3	31 551	36.0	45 231	27.0	59 256	41.6	31 294	33.5	43 729	24.1	55 666
	R	25 103	-4.4	24 560	-5.5	23 255	-9.3	21 192	-2.3	24 817	-0.2	24 757	0.1	24 782
Malaysia	T	12 093	29.3	13 998	26.6	18 260	18.9	22 054	29.3	13 998	26.6	18 260	18.9	22 054
	U	3 371	35.6	4 027	32.5	5 572	24.3	7 107	42.8	4 175	46.8	6 665	41.8	10 121
	R	8 722	26.8	9 971	24.1	12 688	16.4	14 947	23.8	9 823	16.6	11 595	2.9	11 933
Philippines	T	44 437	32.2	52 203	29.5	70 119	24.6	89 707	32.2	52 203	29.5	70 119	24.6	89 707
	U	15 244	40.2	18 641	36.8	26 947	31.2	36 811	44.8	19 074	45.9	30 180	42.5	46 166
	R	29 193	27.9	33 562	25.2	43 172	20.3	52 896	25.3	33 129	18.7	39 939	8.6	43 541
Singapore	T	2 248	16.1	2 437	14.9	2 829	10.0	3 126	16.1	2 437	14.9	2 829	10.0	3 126
	U	1 665	12.7	1 774	11.1	1 982	5.6	2 096	14.8	1 793	16.5	2 115	14.9	2 454
	R	583	25.7	663	24.5	847	19.5	1 030	20.0	644	10.3	714	-6.0	672
Thailand	T	42 093	32.3	49 473	30.0	66 752	24.9	85 618	32.3	49 473	30.0	66 752	24.9	85 618
	U	5 718	37.6	6 901	35.0	9 794	29.7	13 176	57.2	7 612	69.6	15 267	65.3	29 346
	R	36 375	31.5	42 572	29.1	56 958	24.0	72 442	28.1	41 861	20.7	51 485	8.9	56 272
Vietnam	T	43 451	22.5	48 634	23.1	61 302	21.2	75 802	22.5	48 634	23.1	61 302	21.2	75 802
	U	8 838	41.2	10 860	39.0	16 038	34.3	22 594	49.4	11 317	53.0	19 222	49.3	31 462
	R	34 613	17.5	37 774	18.1	45 264	16.2	53 208	15.0	37 317	12.0	42 080	5.2	44 340

Source: authors' estimates.

the urban annual rate of natural increase. Dividing the latter by the former, and multiplying by 100, indicates the percentage of urban growth that is attributable to natural increase. Table 14.5 sets out these percentages for the Asian Pacific data. One intuitively feels that the results are plausible. The Asian Pacific's urban population recently has been growing more because of urban natural increase than because of net rural-to-urban migration. However, the relative contribution of the latter component to China's urban growth is expected to increase dramatically by the end of the century.

14.4 Urbanization dynamics

Given a set of estimated natural increase and net migration rates for the eleven Asian Pacific nations, what can we then say about the reasonableness of the expected urban and rural population totals set out in Table 14.1? The following simple model of urbanization dynamics will be used to assist us in this assessment. Let $P_T(t)$, $P_u(t)$ and $P_r(t)$ denote, respectively, the total, the urban and the rural populations of a region at time t. Assume that

$$P_T(t) = P_T(0) \exp(r_T t) \tag{14.9}$$

$$P_r(t) = P_r(0) \exp[(r_T + m_r)t] \tag{14.10}$$

and

$$P_u(t) = P_T(t) - P_r(t) \tag{14.11}$$

The urban and rural populations are assumed to have natural rates of increase equal to the national growth rate r_T. Such a simple model has been used by Keyfitz (1980) and Ledent (1978b) to examine a number of interesting dimensions of urbanization. We shall use it here only to project the 1975 Asian Pacific population forward to the year 2000 using two variants. In both variants the national growth rates r_T are assumed to follow the paths set out in Table 14.1. In run 1 the rates of rural net (in)migration are fixed at levels exhibited in 1970–5 as presented in Table 14.4; in run 2 they are all forced to converge linearly over time from 1970–5 onwards to the same rate of $m_r = -0.016$ in 1990–2000. The latter rate was selected after an examination of migration data for a number of countries and represents, in our judgement, a reasonable assumption against which to assess the UN projections.

The projections generated by the two alternatives are presented in Tables 14.6, 14.7, 14.8, 14.9 and 14.10; they are the 'transparent-model' counterparts to the UN results in Tables 14.1, 14.2, 14.3, 14.4 and 14.5, respectively. Table 14.11 brings together summary results of all three sets of projections for purposes of comparison.

It appears that the UN projections fall roughly midway between our two alternative 'transparent' projections. As suggested by a comparison of

Table 14.7 Alternative projections of percentages of population in urban areas (runs 1 and 2): Asian Pacific, 1975–2000.

Area	1975	Run 1			Run 2		
		1980	1990	2000	1980	1990	2000
Asian Pacific	28.53	30.23	33.27	36.01	31.06	38.00	46.90
China	23.29	24.94	28.15	31.21	25.91	33.51	43.34
Japan	75.08	78.36	83.68	87.69	78.06	82.29	84.91
Rest of Asian Pacific	26.27	28.02	31.11	33.80	28.88	36.08	45.32
Cambodia	12.64	13.57	15.40	17.19	14.89	22.86	34.27
Hong Kong	89.94	90.22	90.77	91.28	90.33	91.38	92.65
Indonesia	18.43	19.77	22.39	24.92	20.90	28.68	39.23
Korea	50.31	56.23	66.04	73.66	55.77	63.85	69.20
Malaysia	27.88	28.77	30.52	32.22	29.63	36.50	45.89
Philippines	34.30	35.71	38.43	41.03	36.54	43.04	51.46
Singapore	74.07	72.80	70.06	67.06	73.56	74.76	78.49
Thailand	13.58	13.95	14.67	15.39	15.39	22.87	34.28
Vietnam	20.34	22.33	26.16	29.81	23.27	31.36	41.51

Source: Table 14.6.

Table 14.8 Alternative tempos of urbanization (runs 1 and 2): Asian Pacific, 1975–2000.

Area	Run 1			Run 2		
	1975–80	1980–90	1990–2000	1975–80	1980–90	1990–2000
Asian Pacific	11.54	9.59	7.92	16.97	20.18	21.04
China	13.72	12.08	10.34	21.31	25.73	25.72
Japan	8.55	6.57	4.68	7.80	5.28	3.13
Rest of Asian Pacific	12.91	10.47	8.27	18.97	22.26	22.79
Cambodia	14.19	12.64	11.00	32.77	42.90	40.47
Hong Kong	0.63	0.60	0.56	0.87	1.15	1.39
Indonesia	14.04	12.42	10.71	25.08	31.67	31.31
Korea	22.27	16.09	10.91	20.63	13.53	8.04
Malaysia	6.30	5.91	5.44	13.54	20.19	22.89
Philippines	8.03	7.34	6.56	12.62	16.38	17.87
Singapore	− 3.46	− 3.82	− 4.38	− 1.38	1.62	4.87
Thailand	5.29	5.06	4.77	24.90	39.65	40.45
Vietnam	18.67	15.84	13.04	26.90	29.83	28.04

Source: authors' estimates.

Tables 14.4 and 14.9, they generally assume a level of rural–urban migration that is higher than the level observed in 1970–5, but one that is lower than is implied by a convergence of migration rates to the level of $m_r = - 0.016$ by the period 1900–2000. Exceptions occur in the case of the

Table 14.9 Alternative rural net migration rates (runs 1 and 2), per thousand: Asian Pacific, 1975–2000.

Area	Run 1			Run 2		
	1975–80	1980–90	1990–2000	1975–80	1980–90	1990–2000
Asian Pacific	−4.80	−4.46	−4.20	−7.20	−10.61	−15.49
China	−4.36	−4.36	−4.36	−6.95	−10.83	−16.00
Japan	−28.22	−28.22	−28.22	−25.51	−21.43	−16.00
Rest of Asian Pacific	−4.81	−4.39	−3.97	−7.22	−10.68	−15.60
Cambodia	−2.14	−2.14	−2.14	−5.22	−9.84	−16.00
Hong Kong	−5.70	−5.70	−5.70	−7.99	−11.42	−16.00
Indonesia	−3.31	−3.31	−3.31	−6.13	−10.36	−16.00
Korea	−25.39	−25.39	−25.39	−23.30	−20.17	−16.00
Malaysia	−2.49	−2.49	−2.49	−5.49	−9.99	−16.00
Philippines	−4.32	−4.32	−4.32	−6.92	−10.81	−16.00
Singapore	9.57	9.57	9.57	3.88	−4.64	−16.00
Thailand	−0.84	−0.84	−0.84	−4.21	−9.26	−16.00
Vietnam	−5.06	−5.06	−5.06	−7.49	−11.14	−16.00

Note:
In both runs the population projections for the Asian Pacific and the Rest of the Asian Pacific were obtained by consolidating the separate projections made for the component countries; hence the apparent non-constancy of the rural net migration rate in run 1 and the convergence of this rate to a value different from −16 per thousand in run 2.

Table 14.10 Alternative percentages of urban growth due to natural increase (runs 1 and 2): Asian Pacific, 1975–2000.

Area	Run 1			Run 2		
	1975–80	1980–90	1990–2000	1975–80	1980–90	1990–2000
Asian Pacific	61.27	62.23	62.80	51.84	43.92	38.85
China	53.46	51.37	50.94	42.52	33.15	29.44
Japan	56.80	51.98	52.53	59.05	57.40	62.34
Rest of Asian Pacific	67.16	70.32	71.18	58.19	52.71	47.27
Cambodia	67.69	69.15	68.23	47.56	39.78	36.86
Hong Kong	95.58	95.58	94.05	93.96	91.85	86.50
Indonesia	64.87	65.75	63.86	50.82	42.96	37.66
Korea	48.55	55.34	59.60	50.46	59.56	66.69
Malaysia	82.29	81.82	77.62	68.36	56.83	45.20
Philippines	80.05	80.08	78.97	71.86	64.30	57.96
Singapore	127.28	134.47	178.29	109.33	90.23	67.20
Thailand	85.93	85.56	83.91	56.48	43.04	38.09
Vietnam	54.69	59.37	61.95	45.59	43.69	43.09

Table 14.11 Summary of alternative projections to the year 2000 (in thousands): Asian Pacific, 1950–2000.

Area		1950 No.	1950–75 % change	1975 No.	Run 1		UN		Run 2	
					1975–2000 % change	2000 No.	1975–2000 % change	2000 No.	1975–2000 % change	2000 No.
Asian Pacific	T	826 304	17.9	1 293 139	15.3	1 896 622	15.3	1 896 622	15.3	1 896 622
	U	135 021	40.2	368 931	24.6	682 954	31.1	803 762	35.2	889 449
	R	691 283	11.6	924 208	10.9	1 213 668	6.7	1 092 860	3.4	1 007 173
	PU	16.34	22.3	28.53	9.3	36.01	15.8	42.38	19.9	46.90
China	T	558 190	16.3	838 803	12.6	1 147 987	12.6	1 147 987	12.6	1 147 987
	U	61 393	46.3	195 355	24.3	358 308	32.8	443 213	37.4	497 560
	R	496 797	10.3	643 448	8.2	789 679	3.6	704 774	0.4	650 427
	PU	11.00	30.0	23.29	11.7	31.21	20.2	38.61	24.8	43.34
Japan	T	83 625	11.4	111 120	7.2	132 929	7.2	132 929	7.2	132 929
	U	41 977	27.5	83 424	13.4	116 568	12.1	114 128	12.5	112 871
	R	41 648	−16.3	27 696	−21.1	16 361	−15.5	18 801	−12.9	20 058
	PU	50.20	16.1	75.08	6.2	87.69	5.4	85.86	4.9	84.91
Rest of Asian Pacific	T	184 489	24.8	343 216	23.4	615 706	23.4	615 706	23.4	615 706
	U	31 651	41.9	90 152	33.5	208 078	40.2	246 421	45.2	279 018
	R	152 838	20.2	253 064	19.1	407 628	15.1	369 285	11.4	336 688
	PU	17.16	17.0	26.27	10.1	33.80	16.8	40.02	21.8	45.32

Source: Tables 14.1 and 14.6.
Note:
T, total population; U, urban population; R, rural population; PU, percentage of population urban.

already highly urbanized countries, Japan and Korea, for which the order of the migration levels implied by the two transparent projections is reversed.

The simple transparent models of urbanization dynamics used here allow us to gauge the reasonableness of the UN projections with respect to the implied levels of future patterns of net migration. But net migration patterns in turn are associated with patterns of economic development as reflected, for example, in changes in levels of per capita income and other indicators of a nation's structural transformation. To incorporate this association we next consider how a widely observed regularity along this dimension of change may be used to create yet another 'transparent' model of urbanization.

14.5 Urbanization and development

In developed countries high levels of urbanization and high rates of urban growth have been associated historically with high and increasing national per capita income and production. This positive correlation is usually attributed to factors such as rapid industrialization, increases in productivity, widespread literacy, improved nutrition and advances in health care. But, although high proportions of national populations in urban areas are positively associated with high levels of per capita income, this does not mean that rapid urbanization automatically fosters rapid increases in a nation's wealth or productivity. Nevertheless, a strong association between a nation's degree of urbanization and its level of per capita GNP is a commonly observed 'fact' in the economic development literature (International Bank for Reconstruction and Development 1972, Berry 1973, Chenery & Syrquin 1975).

From an applied viewpoint this association can be depicted by attenuated S-shaped curves and a logistic relationship is often indicated by the data. For example, in fitting a logistic equation to the 88 cross-sectional observations in the scatter diagram of Figure 14.1, Ledent (1982a) finds the following relationship between per capital GNP, y, and percentage urban, $\alpha(y)$:

$$\alpha(y) = 0.61 + \frac{73.32}{1 + 1615.8 \exp(-1.352 \ln y)} \qquad (14.12)$$

This function describes a trajectory of urbanization that shows 8.6% for a per capita GNP of 50 US (1964) dollars, 50% for y slightly higher than 500 dollars, 70% for y approximately equal to 2000 dollars and an ultimate asymptotic values of 73.9%.

The above function suggests an alternative transparent model for assessing the reasonableness of the UN projections – one that introduces an economic dimension to the purely demographic variables considered earlier. The fundamental idea is to combine the estimated relationship between per capita GNP and percentage urban with the urbanization projections set out in Table 14.2 in such a way as to obtain a corresponding set of expectations for per capita GNP. The resulting transparent model asks the question: What growth path of per capita GNP is implied by the projected pace of urbanization if the historical association between the two variables continues as before?

An obvious difficulty in implementing this model arises from the observation that, in a given nation, the evolution of the association between urbanization and economic development generally does not coincide with the corresponding evolution in the 'representative' country, that is, the hypothetical country depicted by the curve in Figure 14.1. Therefore, to infer the growth path of per capita GNP implied by a projected pace of urbanization, an additional assumption, linking a nation's growth in per

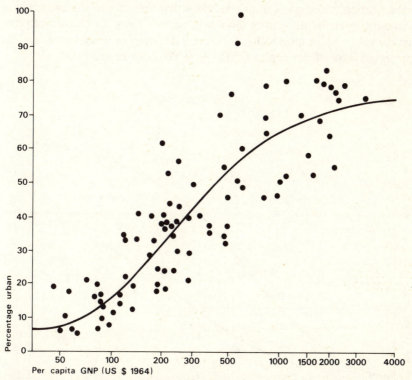

Figure 14.1 The association of the degree of urbanization with per capita GNP: scatter for 88 non-centrally planned countries in 1965 and logistic evolution pertaining to the 'representative' country.
(*Sources:* scatter of points, Chenery and Syrquin 1975; estimated logistic, Ledent, 1982a).

381

capita GNP with that of the representative country, appears to be necessary.

We make our transparent model operational with two alternative assumptions made with reference to the historical data. One relies on a single observation of per capita GNP and percentage urban, whereas the other is made on the basis of several such observations. They give rise to two alternative procedures, labelled method A and method B, respectively.

To illustrate these two models, suppose that a nation has, in a given year, achieved a level of urbanization with a higher level of per capita GNP than is indicated by the logistic standard of Figure 14.1. On this dimension, therefore, this country may be said to be 'underurbanized'. Such a situation is illustrated in Figure 14.2, where point j describes the nation's current position and point s the 'representative' country's position corresponding to an identical urbanization level, α.

On the reasonable presumption that the nation's future trajectory of the urbanization–development relationship will continue to exhibit 'under-urbanization', method A simply assumes that the ratio of the projected to standard levels of per capita GNP will remain equal to its currently observed value. More specifically, for a projected level of urbanization α', the projected level of per capita GNP, $y_{j_1'}$ is taken to be such that

$$\frac{y_{j_1'}}{y_{s'}} = \frac{y_j}{y_s} \qquad (14.13)$$

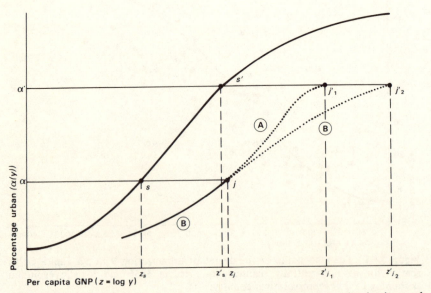

Figure 14.2 Alternative trajectories of the association between urbanization and development.

where $y_{s'}$ is the corresponding level of the standard and y_j and y_s are the observed and standard per capita GNP associated with the observed urbanization level, α.

This relationship can be written equivalently as

$$\ln y_{j\{} - \ln y_{s'} = \ln y_j - \ln y_s \tag{14.14}$$

or

$$z_{j\{} - z_{s'} = z_j - z_s \tag{14.15}$$

In other words, the absolute difference between observed and standard per capita levels of GNP (in logarithmic terms) associated with the observed urbanization level remains constant: $s' j\{ = sj$ in Figure 14.2.

Method A hypothesizes that as the level of urbanization increases the degree of 'underurbanization' remains unchanged. By contrast, method B allows this degree of 'underurbanization' to vary according to the historically observed trend. Specifically, this alternative method assumes that the projected and standard levels of per capita GNP, $y_{j\}}$ and $y_{s'}$, respectively, associated with the projected level of urbanization α' are linked by the relationship

$$\ln y_{j\}} - \ln y_{s'} = z_{j\}} - z_{s'} = a + b\alpha' \tag{14.16}$$

where b is statistically estimated and a is adjusted so that the corresponding curve passes through the last observation (point j). Thus

$$z_{j\}} - z_{s'} = z_j - z_s + b(\alpha' - \alpha) \tag{14.17}$$

so that the absolute difference between projected and standard per capita levels of GNP (in logarithmic terms) associated with the projected level of urbanization α' is equal to the corresponding difference between observed and standard values associated with the observed urbanization level α, plus a quantity proportional to the change in the urban percentage: $s' j\} = s' j\{ + j\{ j\}$ where $j\{ j\}$ is a linear function of the level of urbanization (see Fig. 14.2).

Naturally, the sign of the estimated coefficient b reflects the past trend of variation in the degree of 'underurbanization'; thus a positive sign indicates an increasing 'underurbanization', whereas a negative sign shows it to be decreasing.

Below we apply both methods A and B to the alternative urbanization projections set out in Tables 14.2 and 14.7 for the following five countries: Cambodia, Indonesia, Malaysia, the Philippines, and Thailand. Before presenting and discussing the results obtained, a description of the recent urbanization–development association in those countries is in order.

Table 14.12 suggests that in 1975 Cambodia, having higher levels of urbanization than its per capita GNP would imply, was 'overurbanized', whereas Malaysia and Thailand, having a level of urbanization substantially

Table 14.12 Urbanization and per capita GNP: selected Asian Pacific countries, 1975.

	Urban percentage[a]	Observed per capita GNP[b]	Per capita GNP of standard[c]
Cambodia	12.6	45	71
Indonesia	18.4	101	102
Malaysia	27.9	429	160
Philippines	34.3	210	209
Thailand	13.6	208	76

Sources:
[a] Table 14.2.
[b] Logistic curve in Figure 14.1. Expressed in 1964 US dollars.
[c] International Bank for Reconstruction and Development (1976). Expressed in 1964 US dollars.

smaller than their per capita GNP would imply, were 'underurbanized'. Indonesia and the Philippines showed a per capita GNP quite similar to the standard level and therefore may be said to exhibit a normal pattern of urbanization.

Such was the situation in 1975. A question that immediately comes to mind is whether this situation has been a stable one in the recent past? Drawing on data available for selected years from 1950 to 1975, Figure 14.3 shows that 'overurbanization' in Cambodia and 'underurbanization' in Malaysia and Thailand persisted during the third quarter of this century. However, in Indonesia and the Philippines the situation observed in 1975 apparently was a transient one: between 1950 and 1975 these two countries exhibited a definite tendency to switch from being 'overurbanized' to being 'underurbanized', with the actual switch occurring around 1975.

Another and perhaps more interesting observation suggested by Figure 14.3 is that in four of the five countries (Cambodia being the exception) urbanization has, between 1950 and 1975, taken place less rapidly than in the 'representative' country described by the cross-sectional data of Figure 14.1. This observation is confirmed by the result that the estimated value of the b-coefficient required for the implementation of method B is positive in these four countries. Of course, the higher the value of b the slower the urbanization process with regard to the standard evolution indicated by Figure 14.1. Thus the substandard pace of urbanization just described was slowest in Malaysia ($b = 0.017$) and fastest in Thailand ($b = 0.211$) with intermediate values in Indonesia ($b = 0.028$) and the Philippines ($b = 0.055$).

Turning now from the past to future we present, in Tables 14.13 and 14.14, the increases in per capita GNP that are implied by the UN projection and our two alternative projections of urbanization (runs 1 and 2): annual per capita growth rates for three intervals are set out in Table 14.13, whereas relative changes over the extended period 1975–2000 appear in

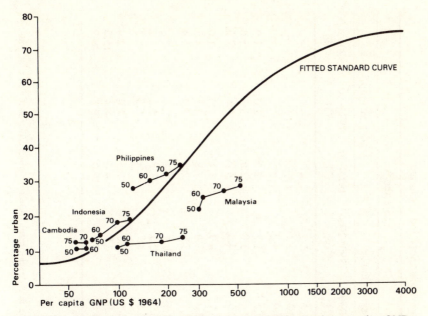

Figure 14.3 Historical association between urbanization and per capita GNP. (*Sources:* urban percentages, Table 14.2; per capita GNP, International Bank for Reconstruction and Development 1976; logistic curve, Fig. 14.1.)

Table 14.14. The results of both methods of inference, methods A and B are included for all countries except Cambodia.

We begin the discussion of these results with an examination of those obtained by the use of method B, a method which relies on a projection of the historical positions of the urbanization–development trajectory in the country under examination and the 'representative' country. The UN projection for the Philippines, for example, implies an average annual rate of growth in per capita GNP of 3.6% during 1975–80, 5.2% during 1980–90 and 7.2% during 1990–2000. These percentages lie above those implied by our first alternative projection, run 1 (2.7, 2.6 and 2.5%, respectively) and below those implied by our second alternative projection, run 2 (4.3, 6.2 and 8.3%, respectively).

Compounding these percentages over the 1975–2000 study period yields a level of per capita GNP in the year 2000 which is equal to 4.1 times the 1975 level in the case of the UN projection and to 1.9 and 5.3 times the level in the case of our two alternative projections, runs 1 and 2, respectively. Since the level of per capita GNP in 1975 was equal to 2.0 times the 1950 level, we see that the 1975–2000 increase in per capita GNP 'consistent' with the projected level of urbanization is similar to the actual 1950–75 increase in the case of run 1, but it is substantially higher in the case of the UN projection and in run 2.

Table 14.13 Annual per capita GNP growth rates: historical and projected.

Area	Historical			Run	Projected					
					Under assumption A			Under assumption B		
	1950–60 (1)	1960–70 (2)	1970–3 (3)		1975–80 (4)	1980–90 (5)	1990–2000 (6)	1975–80 (7)	1980–90 (8)	1990–2000 (9)
Cambodia	1.7	0.3	−5.2	Run 1	1.3	1.2	1.1	—	—	—
				UN	1.8	2.3	3.1	—	—	—
				Run 2	3.1	4.4	4.9	—	—	—
Indonesia	1.6	1.9	4.5	Run 1	1.4	1.3	1.2	2.2	2.0	1.9
				UN	1.9	2.4	3.0	2.9	3.8	5.0
				Run 2	2.6	3.6	4.3	4.0	5.8	7.3
Malaysia	0.8	2.9	3.0	Run 1	0.8	0.7	0.7	1.1	1.0	1.0
				UN	1.3	2.0	3.0	1.8	2.8	4.2
				Run 2	1.7	2.7	3.9	2.3	3.9	5.4
Philippines	3.2	2.4	2.7	Run 1	1.1	1.1	1.1	2.7	2.6	2.5
				UN	1.5	2.2	3.1	3.6	5.2	7.2
				Run 2	1.8	2.6	3.7	4.3	6.2	8.3
Thailand	2.6	4.8	4.2	Run 1	0.5	0.5	0.5	0.5	2.0	2.0
				UN	1.1	1.9	3.0	4.4	8.4	15.0
				Run 2	2.4	4.0	4.9	10.0	19.8	28.9

Sources:
Columns (1)–(3): International Bank for Reconstruction and Development (1976).
Columns (4)–(9): projected by the authors.
Note:
Method 2 was not applied to the Cambodian case because of the peculiar urbanization and development trajectory observed recently in that country.

Table 14.14 Changes in per capita GNP over two quarter-centuries: historical and projected.

Area	1950	1975				1975	2000	
		Under assumption A (1)	Actual (2)				Under assumption A (3)	Under assumption B (4)
Cambodia	100	122	94	Run 1	100		134	—
				UN	100		188	—
				Run 2	100		295	—
Indonesia	100	146	178	Run 1	100		138	166
				UN	100		189	279
				Run 2	100		251	450
Malaysia	100	142	168	Run 1	100		120	129
				UN	100		176	221
				Run 2	100		210	284
Philippines	100	135	200	Run 1	100		131	190
				UN	100		184	414
				Run 2	100		206	529
Thailand	100	127	259	Run 1	100		113	165
				UN	100		171	1 292
				Run 2	100		276	21 536

Sources:
Column (2): International Bank for Reconstruction and Development (1976).
Columns (1), (3), (4): estimated or projected by authors.

Note:
Column (1) results obtained by ex-post application of method 1. Method 2 was not applied to the Cambodian case because of the peculiar urbanization–development trajectory observed recently in that country.

Thus, should the recent 'substandard' pace of urbanization persist during the remainder of this century, the deviation from the standard pace would have to diminish significantly according to most projections (including the UN's). In fact, as suggested by the result obtained with run 1, the historical deviation from the standard pace could be maintained only if the rural net outmigration rate were to remain at the level it exhibited during the early 1970s. A similar conclusion arises in the case of Indonesia, Malaysia, and Thailand.

The above conclusion suggests the following question: How large will be the future reduction in the deviation from the standard pace of urbanization in our four countries? Could this deviation vanish or even shift in such a way as to lead to an 'above standard' pace of urbanization?

To answer this question we turn to an examination of the results of method A, a method that fixes the urbanization–development association between the country under study and the 'representative' country. The UN projection for the Philippines, for example, implies (a) an average annual rate of growth in per capita GNP of 1.5% during 1975–80, 2.2% during 1980–90 and 3.1% during 1990–2000, and (b) a level of per capita GNP in the year 2000 that is 1.8 times its 1975 level compared to the 1.3 and 2.1 times this level in the case of runs 1 and 2, respectively. Recalling that the level of per capita GNP in 1975 was equal to 2.0 times the 1950 level, we conclude that the UN projection – and any other projection that implies a more rapid increase in the rural net outmigration rate – will extrapolate the substandard pace of urbanization observed in the recent past.

This conclusion, derived for the case of the Philippines, also applies to Thailand. For Indonesia and Malaysia we note that the UN projection implies a standard pace of urbanization until the year 2000, and any projection based on higher rural net outmigration rates would cause urbanization to occur at a rate above the standard.

Recapitulating the above results obtained using methods A and B, we conclude that in four Asian Pacific countries (Indonesia, Malaysia, the Philippines, and Thailand) the UN projection implies an increase in per capita GNP for the period 1975–2000 that is comparable to the increase observed during the period 1950–75, and therefore that the projection implies a continuation of the substandard pace of urbanization observed in the third quarter of this century. However, this continuation of past trends should produce a smaller deviation from the standard than in the past, especially in the case of Malaysia and Indonesia where this deviation should vanish altogether. In all four countries the deviation can be maintained only if the rural net outmigration rates do not increase substantially above their early 1970s values.

Finally, we note (see Tables 14.13 and 14.14) that for Cambodia (somewhat neglected in the above discussion) an above standard pace of urbanization arises from any projection that assumes a constant or an increasing rural net outmigration rate (including the UN projection).

14.6 Conclusion

Our understanding of urbanization dynamics is heavily based on the historical experience of the presently more developed nations. A key element of the historical model is internal migration from rural to urban areas, a response to structural imbalances between spatial distributions of labour demand and labour supply arising during the course of industrialization. The end result of this massive transfer of people from rural to urban communities is, of course, a rise in the proportion of the national population residing in urban areas, a proportion which increases from a low of 5 to 10% urban to a high of over 75% urban.

A number of researchers have observed that this basic model may contribute little to the understanding of urbanization in today's less developed nations because in many instances urbanization in these nations seems to be occurring independently of economic development. Not wishing to join either side of this debate, we have nevertheless sought to infer and judge the reasonableness of the future paths of rural-to-urban migration implied by recent UN projections of urbanization in the Asian Pacific. The reasonableness of these paths was assessed with respect to past trends in patterns of net migration, and with respect to past patterns of association between urbanization and development. Each assessment was conducted using a simple transparent model of urbanization dynamics, and both led to the conclusion that the UN projections appear to be reasonable ones in the light of historical experience. Highly urbanized countries like Japan and Korea are expected to continue urbanizing, though at a much decreased rate. Primarily rural nations such as China, Indonesia, and Thailand are expected to exhibit a moderate rise in urbanization and the rate is expected to increase. Net rural to urban migration rates are likely to continue to be high for the former and low for the latter.

Finally, a number of countries are apparently increasing their per capita incomes without significantly increasing their pace of urbanization. Our investigations seem to indicate that the process of urbanization in the Asian Pacific has been and will continue to be slower than the historical pattern of today's more developed nations, and that the association between this process and economic growth seems to have been running counter to the one posited by the 'overurbanization' theorists.

Bibliography

Adegbola, O. 1977. New estimates of fertility and child mortality in Africa, south of the Sahara. *Population Studies* **31**, 467–86.

Aird, J. S. 1978. Fertility decline and birth control in the People's Republic of China. *Population and Development Review* **4**, 225–53.

Aird, J. S. 1982. Population studies and population policy in China. *Population and Development Review* **8**, 267–97.

Akkerman, A. 1980. On the relationship between household composition and population age distribution. *Population Studies* **34**, 525–34.

Akkerman, A. 1983. *Structural foundations for a single-region analysis of household population growth*. Unpublished PhD dissertation, School of Urban and Regional Planning, University of Waterloo, Waterloo, Canada.

Alexander, S. 1983. A model of population change with new and return migration. *Environment and Planning A* **15**, 1231–57.

Algeria 1981. *Annuaire statistique de l'Algerie, 1980*. Algiers: Direction Generale des Statistiques.

Alonso, W. 1980. Population as a system in regional development. *American Economic Review* **70**, 405–9.

Andorka, R. 1978. *Determinants of fertility in advanced societies*. London: Methuen.

Arriaga, E. 1975. Selected measures of urbanization. In *Measurement of urbanization and projection of urban population,* S. Goldstein and D. Sly (eds), 79–87. Dolhain, Belgium: Ordina Editions for the International Union for the Scientific Study of Population.

Artle, R. 1965. External trade, industrial structure, employment mix, and the distribution of incomes: a simple model of planning growth. *Swedish Journal of Economics* **67**, 1–23.

Askham, J. 1976. *Fertility and deprivation*. Cambridge: Cambridge University Press.

Baker, R. J. and J. A. Nelder 1978. *The GLIM system, release 3*. Oxford: Numerical Algorithms Group.

Balakrishnan, T., G. Ebanks and C. Grindstaff 1980. A multivariate analysis of 1971 Canadian Census fertility data. *Canadian Studies in Population* **7**, 81–98.

Balkaran, S. 1982. *Evaluation of the Guyana Fertility Survey 1975*. Scientific report no. 26, World Fertility Survey, London.

Banister, J. 1984. An analysis of recent data on the population of China. *Population and Development Review* **10**, 241–71.

Banister, J. and S. H. Preston 1981. Mortality in China. *Population and Development Review* **7**, 98–110.

Banks, J. A. 1972. Historical sociology and the study of population. In *Population and social change,* D. V. Glass and R. Revelle (eds), 55–70. London: Edward Arnold.

Barclay, G. W., A. J. Coale, M. A. Stoto and T. J. Trussell 1976. A reassessment of the demography of traditional rural China. *Population Index* 42, 606–35.

Barras, R. and T. A. Broadbent 1982. A review of operational methods in structure Planning. *Progress in Planning* 17, 55–268.

Batey, P. W. J. 1985. Input–output models for regional demographic–economic analysis: some structural comparisons. *Environment and Planning A* 17, 73–99.

Batey, P. W. J. and M. Madden 1981. Demographic–economic forecasting within an activity–commodity framework: some theoretical considerations and empirical results. *Environment and Planning A* 13, 1067–83.

Batey, P. W. J. and M. Madden 1983. The modelling of demographic–economic change within the context of regional decline. *Socio-Economic Planning Sciences* 17, 315–28.

Baydar, N. 1983. *Analysis of the temporal stability of migration patterns in the context of multiregional forecasting.* Working paper no. 38, Netherlands Interuniversity Demographic Institute, Voorburg, The Netherlands.

Beaumont, P., A. Isserman, D. McMillen, D. Plane and P. Rogerson 1985. The ECESIS economic–demographic interregional model of the United States. In *Population and the economy: theory and models*, A. Isserman (ed.). Boston: Kluwer Nijhoff.

Beaver, S. E. 1975. *Demographic transition theory reinterpreted: an application to recent natality trends in Latin America.* Lexington: Lexington Books.

Bennett, R. J. 1979. *Spatial time series.* London: Pion.

Berry, B. 1973. *The human consequences of urbanization.* London: Macmillan.

Bhat, M., S. H. Preston and T. Dyson 1984. *Vital rates in India, 1961–81.* Report no. 24, Panel on India, Committee on Population and Demography. Washington, DC: National Academy Press.

Blaikie, P. 1975. *Family planning in India: diffusion and policy.* London: Edward Arnold.

Blalock, H. M. 1961. *Causal inferences in nonexperimental research.* Chapel Hill, NC: University of North Carolina Press.

Blalock, H. M. 1969. *Theory construction.* Englewood Cliffs, NJ: Prentice Hall.

Bogue, D. J. and J. A. Palmore 1964. Some empirical and analytical relations among demographic fertility measures and regression models for fertility estimation. *Demography* 1, 316–38.

Bongaarts, J., O. Frank and R. J. Lesthaeghe 1984. The proximate determinants of fertility in sub-Saharan Africa. *Population and Development Review* 10, 511–37.

Bonsall, P. 1979. Micro-simulation of mode choice: a model of organized car sharing. In *Planning and Transportation Research Conference Proceedings*, Summer Annual Meeting, University of Warwick.

Boonstra, O. W. A. and A. M. van der Woude 1984. Demographic transition in the Netherlands. A statistical analysis of regional differences in the level of development of the birth rate and fertility, 1850–1890. *Afdeling Agrarische Geschiedenie Bijdragen* 24, 1–57.

Borchert, J. G. 1979. Urbanisatie in Nederland (Urbanization in the Netherlands). *Kartografisch Tijdschrift* 4, 30–3.

Bose, A. (ed.) 1967. *Patterns of population change in India, 1951–61.* Bombay: Allied Publishers.

Bourgeois-Pichat, J. 1965. The general development of the population of France since the eighteenth century. In *Population in history*, D. V. Glass and D. E. C. Eversley (eds), 474–506. London: Edward Arnold.

Bourgeois-Pichat, J. 1973. *Main trends in demography.* London: George Allen & Unwin.

Bracken, I. 1982. New directions in key activity forecasting. *Town Planning Review* **53**, 51–64.

Bradley, I. E. and J. P. Gander 1969. Input–output multipliers: some theoretical comments. *Journal of Regional Science* **9**, 309–17.

Brass, W. 1975. *Methods of estimating fertility and mortality from limited and defective data.* Occasional publication, Laboratories for Population Statistics, University of North Carolina, Chapel Hill, NC.

Brass, W., A. J. Coale, P. Demeny, D. F. Heisel, F. Lorimer, A. Romaniuk and E. van de Walle 1968. *The demography of Tropical Africa.* Princeton, NJ: Princeton University Press.

Breheny, M. J. and A. J. Roberts 1978. An integrated forecasting system for structure planning. *Town Planning Review* **49**, 306–18.

Breheny, M. J. and A. J. Roberts 1980. Forecasting methodologies in strategic planning: a review. *Papers of the Regional Science Association* **44**, 75–90.

Breheny, M. J. and A. J. Roberts 1981. The forecasts in structure plans. *The Planner* **67**, 102–4.

Bulatao, R. A. and R. D. Lee (eds) 1983. *Determinants of fertility in developing countries.* Vol. 1. *Supply and demand for children.* New York: Academic Press.

Burns, A. and W. C. Mitchell 1946. *Measuring business cycles.* New York: National Bureau of Economic Research.

Cadwallader, M. 1985. Structural-equation models of migration: an example from the Upper Midwest USA. *Environment and Planning A* **17**, 101–13.

Caldwell, J. C. 1976. Toward a restatement of demographic transition theory. *Population and Development Review* **2**, 321–66.

Caldwell, J. C. 1982a. The failure of theories of social and economic change to explain demographic change: puzzles of modernization or westernization. *Research in Population Economics* **4**, 297–332.

Caldwell, J. C. 1982b. *Theory of fertility decline.* London: Academic Press.

Caldwell, J. C. and K. Srinivasan 1984. New data on nuptiality and fertility in China. *Population and Development Review* **10**, 71–79.

Calot, G. 1984a. Données nouvelles sur l'évolution démographique Chinoise I. Les recensements de 1953, 1964 et 1982 et l'évolution des taux bruts depuis 1950. *Population* **39**, 807–36.

Calot, G. 1984b. Données nouvelles sur l'évolution démographique Chinoise II. L'évolution de la fécondité, de la nuptialité, de l'espérance de vie à la naissance et de la répartition urbaine/rurale de la population. *Population* **39**, 1045–62.

Cartwright, A. 1976. *How many children?* London: Routledge & Kegan Paul.

Carvalho, J. A. M. 1974. Regional trends in fertility and mortality in Brazil. *Population Studies* **28**, 401–21.

Cassedy, J. H. 1984. *American medicine and statistical thinking, 1800–1860.* Cambridge, Mass.: Harvard University Press.

Cassen, R. H. 1978. *India: population, economy and society.* London: Macmillan.

Central Bureau of Statistics 1958. *Typologie van de Nederlandse gemeenten naar urbanisatie-graad 31 mei 1947 en 30 juni 1956.* (Typology of the Netherlands municipalities according to degree of urbanization, May 31st 1947 and June 30th 1956.) Zeist: de Haan.

Central Bureau of Statistics 1964. *Typologie van de Nederlandse gemeenten naar urbanisatie-graad 31 mei 1960.* (Typology of the Netherlands municipalities according to degree of urbanization, May 31st 1960.) Zeist: de Haan.

Central Bureau of Statistics 1983. *Typologie van de Nederlandse gemeenten naar urbanisatie-graad 31 mei 1971.* (Typology of the Netherlands municipalities according to degree of urbanization, May 31st 1971.) Zeist: de Haan.

Central Policy Review Staff 1976. *Population and the social services*. London: Central Statistical Office.

Central Statistical Office 1984. *Social trends 1984*. London: HMSO.

Cespedes, Y. 1982. *Evaluation of the Peru National Fertility Survey, 1977–78*. Scientific report no. 33, World Fertility Survey, London.

Champion, A., M. Coombes and S. Openshaw 1984. New regions for a new Britain. *Geographical Magazine* **LVI** (4), 187–90.

Chang, C. 1979. Fertility transition of the Chinese in Singapore. In *Fertility transition of the East Asian population*, L.-J. Cho and K. Kobayashi (eds), 222–46. Honolulu: University Press of Hawaii.

Chen, P. and M. A. Kols 1982. *Population and birth planning in the People's Republic of China*. Population report no. 25, Population Information Program, Johns Hopkins University, Baltimore.

Chenery, H. and M. Syrquin 1975. *Patterns of development 1950–70*. London: Oxford University Press for World Bank.

Chilver, C. 1978. Regional mortality, 1969–73. *Population Trends* **11**, 16–20.

Cho, L.-J., S. Suharto, G. McNicoll and S. G. Made Mamas 1980. *Population growth of Indonesia*. Honolulu: University Press of Hawaii.

Clairin, R., J. Conde, M. Fleury-Brousse, D. Waltisperger and G. Wunsch 1980. *New model life tables for use in developing countries. Tome III, Vol. V/Vol. VI: Mortality in developing countries*. Paris: Development Centre of the Organization for Economic Cooperation and Development.

Clarke, M. 1985. *Integrating dynamic models of urban and regional retailing systems*. Unpublished PhD thesis, University of Leeds.

Clarke, M. and H. C. W. L. Williams 1986. *Micro-analysis and simulation in urban and regional systems*. Cambridge: Cambridge University Press. Forthcoming.

Clarke, M., P. Keys and H. C. W. L. Williams 1981a. Micro-simulation. In *Quantitative geography*, N. Wrigley and R. J. Bennett (eds), 248–56. London: Routledge & Kegan Paul.

Clarke, M., P. Keys and H. C. W. L. Williams 1981b. Microsimulation in socioeconomic and public policy analysis. In *Strategic planning in a dynamic society*, H. Voogd (ed.), 115–26. Delft: Delftsche Uitgever smaatschappij.

Cleland, J. and J. N. Hobcraft (eds), 1985. *Reproductive change in developing countries: insights from the World Fertility Survey*. Oxford: Oxford University Press.

Cliff, A. D. and J. K. Ord 1973. *Spatial autocorrelation*. London: Pion.

Coale, A. J. 1967. Factors associated with the development of low fertility: an historic summary. In *Proceedings of the World Population Conference, 1965*, **2**, 205–9. New York: United Nations.

Coale, A. J. 1969. The decline of fertility in Europe from the French Revolution to World War II. In *Fertility and family planning: a world view*, S. J. Behrman, L. Corsa and R. Freedman (eds), 3–24. Ann Arbor, Mich.: Michigan University Press.

Coale, A. J. 1973. The demographic transition. In *International Population Conference*, **1**, 53–72. Liège: International Union for the Scientific Study of Population.

Coale, A. J. 1981a. Population trends, population policy and population studies in China. *Population and Development Review* **7**, 85–97.

Coale, A. J. 1981b. A further note on Chinese population statistics. *Population and Development Review* **7**, 512–18.

Coale, A. J. 1982. Preface. In *The estimation of recent trends in fertility and mortality in Egypt*. Report no. 9, Panel on Egypt, Committee on Population and Demography. Washington, DC: National Academy of Sciences.

Coale, A. J. 1984. Fertility in prerevolutionary China: defense of a reassessment. *Population and Development Review* **10**, 471–80.

Coale, A. J. and P. Demeny 1966. *Regional model life tables and stable populations*. Princeton, NJ: Princeton University Press. 2nd edn, 1983. New York: Academic Press.

Coale, A. J., B. Anderson and E. Härm 1979. *Human fertility in Russia since the nineteenth century*. Princeton, NJ: Princeton University Press.

Coale, A. J., L.-J. Cho, and N. Goldman 1980. *Estimation of recent trends in fertility and mortality in the Republic of Korea*. Report no. 1, Committee on Population and Demography. Washington, DC: National Academy of Sciences.

Coale, A. J. and S. C. Watkins (eds) 1986. *The decline of fertility in Europe*. Princeton, NJ: Princeton University Press.

Cochrane-Hill, S. 1979. *Fertility and education: what do we really know?* New York: World Bank.

Compton, P. 1978. Fertility differentials and their impact on population distribution and composition in Northern Ireland. *Environment and Planning A* **10**, 1397–411.

Compton, P. 1982. The changing population. In *The changing geography of the United Kingdom*, R. J. Johnston and J. Doornkamp (eds), 37–74. London: Methuen.

Cook, N. D. 1981. *Demographic collapse: Indian Peru, 1520–1620*. Cambridge: Cambridge University Press.

Coombes, M., J. S. Dixon, J. B. Goddard, P. J. Taylor and S. Openshaw 1980. *Functional regions for the 1981 census of Britain: a user's guide to the CURDS definitions*. Discussion paper 30, Centre for Urban and Regional Development Studies, University of Newcastle upon Tyne, Newcastle upon Tyne.

Cordey-Hayes, M. and D. Gleave 1974. Migration movements and the differential growth of city regions in England and Wales. *Papers of the Regional Science Association* **33**, 99–123.

Courgeau, D. 1973. Migrants et migrations. *Population* **28**, 95–129.

Coward, J. 1978. Changes in the pattern of fertility in the Republic of Ireland. *Tjidschrift voor Economische en Sociale Geografie* **69**, 353–61.

Coward J. 1980. Variations in family size in the Republic of Ireland. *Journal of Biosocial Science* **12**, 1–14.

Coward, J. 1982a. Fertility changes in the Republic of Ireland during the 1970s. *Area* **14**, 109–117.

Coward, J. 1982b. Birth under-registration in the Republic of Ireland. *Economic and Social Review* **14**, 1–27.

Craig, J. 1981. Migration patterns of Surrey, Devon and South Yorkshire. *Population Trends* **23**, 16–21.

Craig, J. 1983. The growth of the elderly population. *Population Trends* **32**, 28–33.

Cullen, J. 1975. *The statistical movement in early Victorian Britain: the foundation of empirical social science*. Brighton: Hassocks.

Davis, K. 1951. *The population of India and Pakistan*. Princeton, NJ: Princeton University Press.

de Kanter, J. and W. I. Morrison 1978. The Merseyside input–output study and its application in structure planning. In *Theory and method in urban and regional analysis*, P. W. J. Batey (ed.), 120–49. London: Pion.

Department of Employment 1971. *Family expenditure survey. Report for 1970*. London: HMSO.

Department of Employment 1973. *Employment Gazette*. London: HMSO.

Department of Employment 1975a. *New earnings survey*. Part E: *Analysis by region and age group*. London: HMSO.

Department of Employment 1975b. *Department of Employment Gazette, July 1975*. London: HMSO.

Department of Employment 1976. *Family expenditure survey. Report for 1975*. London: HMSO.

Department of Employment 1981. *Family expenditure survey. Report for 1980*. London: HMSO.

Department of the Environment 1971. *Long term population distribution in Great Britain – a study*. London: HMSO.

Department of the Environment 1977. *Housing policy*. Part 1: *Technical volume*. London: HMSO.

Department of the Environment, Yorkshire and Humberside Regional Office 1979. *A study of migration in Yorkshire and Humberside, 1966–71*. Unpublished report, Department of the Environment, Leeds.

Desbarats, J. M. 1983. Constrained choice and migration. *Geografiska Annaler* **65B**, 11–22.

Doeve, W. L. J. 1981a. Demographic models for Third World countries: towards operational planning tools. In *Urban problems and economic development*, L. Chatterjee and P. Nijkamp (eds), 221–41. Alphen aan dén Rijn: Sijthoff and Noordhoff.

Doeve, W. L. J. 1981b. Fertility estimation for population projections in developing countries currently experiencing fertility decline. In *Perspectives de population d'emploi et de croissance urbaine*, Departément de Démographie, Université Catholique de Louvain, Chaire Quetelet, 1980, 171–94. Liège: Ordina Editions.

Doeve, W. L. J. 1984. *Operational multiregional demography in developing countries: an application to Thailand*. Working paper no. 48, Netherlands Interuniversity Demographic Institute, Voorburg, The Netherlands.

Duncan, O. D. 1975. *Introduction to structural equation models*. New York: Academic Press.

Dyson, T. and M. Moore 1983. Kinship structure, female autonomy, and demographic behaviour in India. *Population and Development Review* **9**, 35–60.

Dyson, T. and N. Crook (eds) 1984. *India's demography: essays on the contemporary population*. New Delhi: South Asia Publishers.

Dyson, T. and G. Somawat 1983. An assessment of fertility trends in India. In *Dynamics of population and family welfare, 1983*, K. Srinivasan and S. Mukerji (eds), 73–90. Bombay: Himalaya Publishing House.

Easterlin, R. A. 1978. The economics and sociology of fertility: a synthesis. In *Historical studies of changing fertility*, C. Tilly (ed.), 57–133. Princeton, NJ: Princeton University Press.

Easterlin, R. A. 1980. *Birth and fortune*. London: Grant McIntyre.

Economic and Social Commission for Asia and the Pacific 1976. *Population of Sri Lanka*. Country monograph series no. 4, Economic and Social Commission for Asia and the Pacific, Bangkok.

Edwards, S. L. and M. Pender 1976. Migration within Great Britain. *Statistical News* **34**, 17–19.

El-Badry, M. A. 1965. Trends in the components of population growth in the Arab countries of the Middle East. *Demography* **2**, 140–86.

Elias, P. and I. Molho 1982. *Regional labour supply: an economic/demographic model. Occasional paper 28*, Office of Population Censuses and Surveys, London.

Ermisch, J. 1983. *Political economy and demographic change*. London: Heinemann.

Espenshade, T. J., L. Bouvier and W. B. Arthur 1982. Immigration and the stable population model. *Demography* **19**, 125–33.

Eversley, D. 1982. Demographic change and regional policy in the United Kingdom. In *Population change and social planning*, D. Eversley and W. Köllmann (eds), 349–73. London: Edward Arnold.

Eyler, J. M. 1979. *Victorian social medicine: the ideas and methods of William Farr*. Baltimore, Md: Johns Hopkins University Press.

Feinberg, S. E. 1970. An iterative procedure for estimation in contingency tables. *Annals of Mathematical Statistics* **41**, 907–17.

Figueroa, B. 1980. *El problema del registro tardio de naciminentos*. Mexico City: Segunda Reunion Nacional sobre la Investigacion Demografica en Mexico.

Flinn, M. W. 1981. *The European demographic system, 1500–1820*. Brighton: Harvester Press.

Fonaroff, L. 1968. Man and malaria in Trinidad. *Annals of the Association of American Geographers* **58**, 526–56.

Fox, A. and P. Goldblatt 1982. *Longitudinal study: socio-demographic mortality differentials*. Series LS no. 1, Office of Population Censuses and Surveys, London.

Frey, W. 1983. A multiregional population-projection framework that incorporates both migration and residential mobility streams: application to metropolitan city–suburb redistribution. *Environment and Planning A* **15**, 1613–32.

Fuller, G. 1974. On the spatial diffusion of fertility decline: the distance to clinic variable in a Chilean community. *Economic Geography,* **50**, 324–32.

Fuller, G. and M. Khan 1978. *Spatial fertility analysis in a limited data situation: the case of Pakistan*. Paper no. 56, East–West Population Institute, Honolulu, Hawaii.

General Register Office 1968. *Household composition tables, sample census 1966, England and Wales*. London: HMSO.

General Register Office, Northern Ireland 1975. *Migration tables*. Belfast: HMSO.

Gilje, E. and R. Campbell 1973. *A new model for projecting the population of the Greater London boroughs*. Research memorandum 408, Greater London Council, London.

Glass, D. V. 1938. Changes in fertility in England and Wales, 1851–1931. In *Political arithmetic,* L. Hogben (ed.), 161–212. London: George Allen & Unwin.

Goldman, N. and J. N. Hobcraft 1982. *Birth histories*. Comparative studies no. 17, World Fertility Survey, London.

Goldman, N., A. J. Coale and M. Weinstein 1979. *The quality of data in the Nepal Fertility Survey*. Scientific report no. 6, World Fertility Survey, London.

Goodstadt, L. F. 1982. China's one-child family: policy and public response. *Population and Development Review* **8**, 37–58.

Gordon, I. 1982. The analysis of motivation-specific migration streams. *Environment and Planning A* **14**, 5–20.

Gottfried, R. S. 1978. *Epidemic disease in fifteenth century England: the medical response and the demographic consequences*. Leicester: Leicester University Press.

Greenwood, M. J. 1981. *Migration and economic growth in the United States*. New York: Academic Press.

Grigg, D. B. 1977. E. G. Ravenstein and the 'Laws of migration'. *Journal of Historical Geography* **3**, 41–54.

Grigg, D. B. 1982. Modern population growth in historical perspective. *Geography* **67**, 97–108.

Guzman, J. M. 1980. *Evaluation of the Dominican Republic National Fertility Survey, 1975*. Scientific report no. 14, World Fertility Survey, London.

Haines, M. R. 1979. *Occupation and fertility: population patterns in industrialization*. New York: Academic Press.

Hajnal, J. 1982. Two kinds of preindustrial household formation system. *Population and Development Review* **8**, 449–94.

Hajnal, J. 1983. Two kinds of pre-industrial household formation system. In *Family forms in historic Europe*, R. Wall, J. Robin and P. Laslett (eds), 65–104. Cambridge: Cambridge University Press.

Hammel, E. A., D. W. Hutchinson, K. W. Wachter, R. T. Lundy and R. Z. Devel 1976. *The SOCISM demographic–sociological micro-simulation program: operating manual*. Research series no. 27, Institute of International Studies, University of California, Berkeley.

Harewood, J. 1975. *The population of Trinidad and Tobago*. Paris: Comité International de Coordination des Recherches Nationales en Démographie.

Harewood, J. 1978. *Female fertility and family planning in Trinidad and Tobago*. Kingston, Jamaica: Institute of Social and Economic Research, University of West Indies.

Harsman, B. and B. Marksjo 1977. Modelling household changes by efficient information adding. In *Demographic, economic and social interaction*, A. Andersson and I. Holmberg (eds), Ch. 14, 307–24. Cambridge, Mass.: Ballinger.

Harsman, B. and S. Scheele 1982. *Household projections with a reconciliation of demographic and economic factors*. Paper presented at the Demographic Symposium in Kungalir, June 1982.

Harsman, B. and F. Snickars 1983. A method for disaggregate household forecasts. *Tjidschrift voor Economische en Sociale Geografie* **74**, 282–90.

Henin, R. A., A. Korten and L. H. Werner 1982. *Evaluation of birth histories: a case study of Kenya*. Scientific report no. 36, World Fertility Survey, London.

Hermalin, A. 1975. Regression analysis of areal data. In *Measuring the effect of family planning programs on fertility*, C. Chandrasekhan and A. Hermalin (eds), 245–99. Dolhain, Belgium: Ordina Editions for the International Union for the Scientific Study of Population.

Hetherington, M. F. 1973. *A consideration of a household based projection model for Greater London*. Research memorandum 371, Greater London Council, London.

Hewings, G. J. D. 1977. *Regional industrial analysis and development*. London: Methuen.

Hill, A. 1983. The Palestinian population of the Middle East. *Population and Development Review* **9**, 293–316.

Hinde, P. R. A. and R. I. Woods 1984. Variations in historical natural fertility patterns and the measurement of fertility control. *Journal of Biosocial Science* **16**, 309–21.

Hirsch, W. Z. 1959. Inter-industry relations of a metropolitan area. *Review of Economics and Statistics* **41**, 360–69.

Hobcraft, J.N. 1980. *Illustrative analysis: evaluating fertility levels and trends in Colombia*. Scientific report no. 15, World Fertility Survey, London.

Hofsten, E. and H. Lundström 1976. *Swedish population history: Main trends from 1750 to 1970*. Stockholm: Liber Folag.

Hollerbach, P. E. 1980. *Recent trends in fertility, abortion and contraception in Cuba*. Working paper no. 61, Center for Policy Studies, The Population Council, New York.

Hyman, G,. and D. Gleave 1978. A reasonable theory of migration. *Transactions, Institute of British Geographers, New Series,* **3**, 179–201.

Hyrenius, H. and I. Adolfson 1964. *A fertility simulation model.* Demographic Institute, University of Goteborg, Sweden.

Illsley, R. and D. Gill 1968. Changing trends in illegitimacy. *Social Science and Medicine* **2**(4), 415–33.

India, 1980. *Evaluation of birth and death registration in India, 1961–71.* Occasional paper no. 1 of 1980, Office of the Registrar General, New Delhi.

International Bank for Reconstruction and Development 1972. *Urbanization.* Sector working paper, World Bank, Washington, DC.

International Bank for Reconstruction and Development 1976. *World tables 1976.* Baltimore, Md: Johns Hopkins University Press.

Isserman, A. 1985. Economic–demographic modeling with endogenously determined birth and migration rates: theory and prospects. *Environment and Planning A* **17**, 24–45.

Jabukowski, M. 1977. The theory of demographic transition and studies on the spatial differentiation of population dynamics. *Geographica Polonica* **35**, 73–89.

Jain, A. K. and A. Adlakha 1982. Preliminary estimates of fertility decline in India during the 1970s. *Population and Development Review* **8**, 589–606.

Jones, H. 1975. A spatial analysis of human fertility in Scotland. *Scottish Geographical Magazine* **91**, 102–13.

Jones, H. 1977a. Fertility decline in Barbados: some spatial considerations. *Studies in Family Planning* **8**(6), 157–62.

Jones, H. 1977b. Metropolitan dominance and family planning in Barbados. *Social and Economic Studies* **26**, 327–38.

Joseph, G. 1975. A Markov analysis of age/sex differences in inter-regional migration in Great Britain. *Regional Studies* **9**, 69–78.

Joseph, G. 1977. Inter-regional population distribution and growth in Britain – a projection exercise. *Scottish Journal of Political Economy,* **XXI** (2), 159–69.

Kain, J. F. and W. C. Apgar 1977. *Simulation of the market effects of housing allowances.* Vol. II: *Baseline and policy simulations for Pittsburgh and Chicago.* Department of City and Regional Planning, Harvard University.

Kain, J. F., W. C. Apgar and J. R. Ginn 1978. *Simulation of the market effects of housing allowances.* Vol. III: *Description of the NBER simulation model.* Department of City and Regional Planning, Harvard University.

Kennett, S. 1980. Migration within and between the metropolitan economic labour areas of Britain. In *Regional demographic development,* J. N. Hobcraft and P. H. Rees (eds), 165–87. London: Croom Helm.

Keyfitz, N. 1977. *Understanding world models.* Research memorandum RM-77-18, International Institute for Applied Systems Analysis, Laxenburg, Austria.

Keyfitz, N. 1980. Do cities grow by natural increase or by migration? *Geographical Analysis* **12**, 142–56.

Keyfitz, N. and W. Flieger 1971. *Population: facts and methods of demography.* San Francisco: Freeman, Cooper.

Kirk, D. 1979. World population and birth rates: agreements and disagreements. *Population and Development Review* **5**, 387–403.

Knodel, J. 1974. *The decline of fertility in Germany, 1871–1939.* Princeton, NJ: Princeton University Press.

Knodel, J. 1982. Child mortality and reproductive behaviour in German village populations in the past: a micro-level analysis of the replacement effect. *Population Studies* **36**, 177–200.

Knox, P. 1981. Convergence and divergence in regional patterns of infant mortality in the United Kingdom from 1949–51 to 1970–72. *Social Science and Medicine* **150**, 323–28.

Kpedekpo, G. M. K. 1982. *Essentials of demographic analysis for Africa*. London: Heinemann.

Kreibich, V. 1979. Modelling car availability, modal split and trip distribution by Monte Carlo simulation: a short way to integrated models. *Transportation* **8**, 153–66.

Kussmaul, A. 1981. *Servants in husbandry in early modern England*. Cambridge: Cambridge University Press.

Land, K. C. and A. Rogers (eds) 1982. *Multidimensional mathematical demography*. New York: Academic Press.

Landry, A. 1934. *La révolution démographique: études et essais sur les problèmes de la population*. Paris: Sirey.

Langford, C. 1981. Fertility change in Sri Lanka since the War: an analysis of the experience of different districts. *Population Studies* **35**, 285–306.

Law, C. M. 1967. The growth of urban population in England and Wales, 1801–1911. *Transactions, Institute of British Geographers* **41**, 125–43.

Lawton, R. 1973. People and work. In *The UK space: resources, environment and the future,* J. W. House (ed.), 75–163. London: Weidenfeld & Nicolson.

League of Nations 1935. *League of Nations Statistical Yearbook, 1934–36*. Geneva: League of Nations Printers.

Ledent, J. 1978a. *Some methodological and empirical considerations in the construction of increment–decrement life tables*. Research memorandum RM-78-25, International Institute for Applied Systems Analysis, Laxenburg, Austria.

Ledent, J. 1978b. *The factors and magnitude of urbanization under unchanged fertility and mobility patterns*. Research memorandum RM-78-57. International Institute for Applied Systems Analysis, Laxenburg, Austria.

Ledent, J. 1980. Multistate life tables: movement versus transition perspectives. *Environment and Planning A* **12**, 533–62.

Ledent, J. 1981. Constructing multiregional life tables using place-of-birth specific migration data. In *Advances in multiregional demography,* A. Rogers (ed.). Research report RR-81-16, International Institute for Applied Systems Analysis, Laxenburg, Austria.

Ledent, J. 1982a. Rural–urban migration, urbanization, and economic development. *Economic Development and Cultural Change* **30**, 507–38.

Ledent, J. 1982b. Long-range regional population forecasting: specification of a minimal demoeconomic model, with a test for Tucson, Arizona. *Papers of the Regional Science Association* **49**, 37–67.

Ledent, J. 1985. Forecasting interregional migration using longitudinal data. In *Population and the economy: theory and models,* A. Isserman (ed.). Boston, Mass.: Kluwer-Nijhoff.

Ledent, J. and P. H. Rees 1980. *Choices in the construction of multiregional life tables*. Working paper 289, School of Geography, University of Leeds. Working paper 80-173, International Institute for Applied Systems Analysis, Laxenburg, Austria.

Ledent, J. and P. H. Rees, 1986. Life tables. In *Migration and settlement: a comparative study*, A. Rogers and F. Willekens (eds), Ch. 10, 385–418. Dordrecht, Netherlands: Reidel.

Ledent, J. with D. Courgeau 1982. *Migration and settlement: 15. France*. Research report RR-82-28. International Institute for Applied Systems Analysis, Laxenburg, Austria.

Ledermann, S. 1969. *Nouvelles tables-types de mortalité.* Cahier no. 53, Institut National d'Etudes Démographiques, Travaux et Documents. Paris: Presses Universitaires de France.

Lee, R. D. 1977. Methods and models for analyzing historical series of births, deaths and marriages. In *Population patterns in the past,* R. D. Lee (ed.), 337–70. New York: Academic Press.

Leibenstein, H. 1974. Socio-economic fertility theories and their relevance to population policy. *International Labour Review* **109**, 443–57.

Leibenstein, H. 1975. The economic theory of fertility decline. *Quarterly Journal of Economics* **89**, 1–31.

Leontief, W. 1951. *The structure of the American economy.* New York: Oxford University Press.

Leridon, H. and J. Menken (eds) 1979. *Natural fertility.* Liège: Ordina Editions for the International Union for the Scientific Study of Population.

Lesthaeghe, R. J. 1977. *The decline of Belgian fertility, 1800–1970.* Princeton, NJ: Princeton University Press.

Lesthaeghe, R. J., P. O. Ohadike, J. Kocher and H. J. Page 1981. Child-spacing and fertility in sub-Saharan Africa: an overview of the issues. In *Child-spacing in Tropical Africa,* H. J. Page and R. Lesthaeghe (eds), 3–23. London: Academic Press.

Lieber, S. R. 1978. Place utility and migration. *Geografiska Annaler* **60B**, 16–27.

Livi Bacci, M. 1977. *A history of Italian fertility during the last two centuries.* Princeton NJ: Princeton University Press.

Long, J. F. 1977. Prospects for a composite demographic–economic model of migration for subnational projections. In *Report of the Conference on Economic and Demographic Methods for Projecting Population.* Washington, DC: American Statistical Association.

Lotka, A. J. 1936. The geographic distribution of intrinsic natural increase in the United States and an examination of the relation between several measures of net reproductivity. *Journal of the American Statistical Association* **31**, 273–94.

Luptacik, M. and I. Schmoranz 1980. Demographic changes and economic consequences: demo-economic multiplier for Austria. *Empirical Economics* **5**, 55–67.

Madden, M. 1977. A population employment housing forecasting framework for Merseyside. In *Policy analysis for urban and regional planning,* R. Baxter (ed.). London: Planning and Transportation Research.

Madden, M. and P. W. J. Batey 1980. Achieving consistency in demographic–economic forecasting. *Papers of the Regional Science Association* **44**, 91–108.

Madden, M. and P. W. J. Batey 1983. Linked population and economic models: some methodological issues in forecasting, analysis and policy optimization. *Journal of Regional Science* **23**, 141–64.

Madden, M., P. W. J. Batey and L. Worrall 1981. *A demographic economic forecasting framework for regional strategic planning.* Liverpool: Department of Civic Design, University of Liverpool.

Marcoux, A. 1971. La croissance de la population de la Tunisie, passe recent et perspectives. *Population,* Special Number, 105–23.

Martin Voorhees Associates and John Bates Services 1981. *Developing the migration component of the official subnational population projections.* Final report prepared for DPRP3 Division, Department of the Environment, Martin Voorhees Associates.

Masser, I. 1970. *A test of some models for predicting inter-metropolitan movement of population in England and Wales.* University working paper no. 9, Centre for Environment Studies, London.

Masser, I. 1972. *Analytical models for urban and regional planning.* Newton Abbot: David & Charles.

Masser, I. 1976. The design of spatial systems for internal migration analysis. *Regional Studies* **19**, 39–52.

Mauldin, W. P. 1978. Patterns of fertility decline in developing countries, 1950–75. *Studies in Family Planning* **9**, 75–84.

McFadden, D., S. Coslett, G. Duguay and W. Jung 1977. *Demographic data for policy analysis.* The Urban Travel Demand Forecasting Project, Phase 1, Final report series, Vol. 8. Institute for Transportation Studies, University of California, Berkeley.

McKeown, T. 1976. *The modern rise of population.* London: Edward Arnold.

Miernyk, W. H., E. R. Bonner, J. H. Chapman and K. Shellhammer 1967. *Impact of the space program on a local economy.* Morgantown, W. Va.: West Virginia University Library.

Mitchell, B. R. 1981. *European historical statistics, 1750–1975,* 2nd revised edn. London: Macmillan.

Mitchell, B. R. 1982. *International historical statistics: Africa and Asia.* London: Macmillan.

Miyazawa, K. 1976. *Input–output analysis and the structure of income distribution.* Berlin: Springer.

Moore, G. H. and J. Shiskin 1967. *Indicators of business expansions and contractions.* New York: Columbia University Press.

Mosher, W. D. 1980. The theory of change and response: an application to Puerto Rico, 1940 to 1970. *Population Studies* **34**, 45–58.

Murphy, M. and O. Sullivan 1983. *Housing tenure and fertility in post-war Britain.* Research paper no. 83-2, Centre for Population Studies, London.

Myrdal, G. 1957. *Economic theory and under-developed regions.* London: Methuen.

Nag, M. 1980. How modernization can also increase fertility. *Current Anthropology* **21**, 571–87.

Nair, P. S. 1982a. *Estimation of directional migration flows from limited data: methods and application.* Working paper no. 32, Netherlands Interuniversity Demographic Institute, Voorburg, The Netherlands.

Nair, P. S. 1982b. *India's population: a multiregional demographic analysis.* Working paper no. 35, Netherlands Interuniversity Demographic Institute, Voorburg, The Netherlands.

Nakamura, M. and A. O. Nakamura 1978. On microanalytic simulation and its application in population projection. *Journal of the Operational Society* **29**, 349–60.

Nelder, J. A. and R. W. M. Wedderburn 1972. Generalized linear models. *Journal of the Royal Statistical Society A* **135**, 370–84.

Notestein, F. W. 1945. Population: the long view. In *Food for the world*, T. W. Schulz (ed.), 36–57. Chicago, Ill.: Chicago University Press.

O'Connell, M. 1981. Regional fertility patterns in the United States: convergence or divergence? *International Regional Science Review* **6**(1), 1–14.

O'Dea, D. 1975. *Cyclical indicators for the postwar British economy.* Cambridge: Cambridge University Press.

Ogilvy, A. A. 1979. Migration – the influence of economic change. *Futures* **11**(5), 383–94.

Ogilvy, A. A. 1980. *Interregional migration since 1971: an appraisal of data from the National Health Service Central Register and Labour Force Surveys.* Occasional paper 16, Office of Population Censuses and Surveys, London.

Ogilvy, A. A. 1982. Population movements between the regions of Great Britain 1971–79. *Regional Studies* **16** (1), 65–73.

Olsson, G. 1965. Distance and human interaction. *Geografiska Annaler* **47B**, 3–43.

Omran, A. R. 1973. The fertility profile. In *Egypt: population, problems and prospects,* A.R. Omran (ed.). Chapel Hill, NC: Carolina Population Center.

Oosterhaven, J. 1981. *Interregional input–output analysis and Dutch regional settlement policy problems.* Aldershot: Gower.

OPCS (Office of Population Censuses and Surveys) 1973. *The Registrar General's statistical review of England and Wales for the year 1971.* London: HMSO.

OPCS 1975–77. *Census 1971. England and Wales. Migration Regional Report (10% sample). Yorkshire and Humberside region.* Parts I, II and III. London: HMSO.

OPCS 1975a. *Household composition tables, Part II (10% sample).* London: HMSO.

OPCS 1975b. *Household composition tables, Part III.* London: HMSO.

OPCS 1977a. *Mortality statistics. Area. 1975. England and Wales.* Series DH5, no. 2. London: HMSO.

OPCS 1977b. *Population estimates, 1975 (revised), 1976 (provisional). England and Wales.* Series PP1, no. 2. London: HMSO.

OPCS 1978a. *Mortality statistics. 1975. England and Wales.* Series DH1, no. 2. London: HMSO.

OPCS 1978b. *Birth statistics. 1975. England and Wales.* Series FM1, no. 2. London: HMSO.

OPCS 1978c. *Marriage and divorce statistics. 1975. England and Wales.* Series FM, no. 2. London: HMSO.

OPCS 1978d. *Census 1971. Great Britain. Migration tables (10% sample).* Areas as constituted on April 1 1974 for England and Wales and May 16 1975 for Scotland. London: HMSO.

OPCS 1981a. *Areal mortality.* London: HMSO.

OPCS 1981b. *Population projections. Area.* Series PP3, no. 4. London: HMSO.

OPCS 1983a. *Census 1981. Sex, age and marital status. Great Britain.* CEN81 SAM. London: HMSO.

OPCS 1983b. *Migration statistics.* Series MN, no. 8. London: HMSO.

OPCS 1984. Table 2. Population: national (estimates and projections). *Population Trends* **38**, 37.

OPCS, Census Division 1981. The first results of the 1981 Census of England and Wales. *Population Trends* **25**, 21–9.

OPCS, London and General Register Office, Edinburgh 1976. *Census 1971. Great Britain. Qualified Manpower Tables (10% sample).* London: HMSO.

OPCS, Immigrant Statistics Unit, Population Statistics Division 1978. Marriage and birth patterns among the New Commonwealth and Pakistani population. *Population Trends* **11**, 5–9.

OPCS, Population Statistics Division 1982. Recent population growth and the effect of the decline in births. *Population Trends* **27**, 18–25.

OPCS, Social Survey Division 1978. *The general household survey, 1975.* London: HMSO.

Orcutt, G. H., S. Caldwell and R. Wertheimer 1976. *Policy exploration through micro-simulation.* Washington DC: The Urban Institute.

Orcutt, G. H., M. Greenburger, A. Rivlin, and J. Korbel 1962. *Micro-analysis of socio-economic systems: a simulation study.* New York: Harper & Row.

Ordorica, M. and J. E. Potter 1981. *Evaluation of the Mexican fertility survey, 1976–77.* Scientific report, no. 21. World Fertility Survey, London.

Osborne, R. H. 1956. Internal migration in England and Wales 1951. *Advancement of Science* **12**, 425–34.

Overton, E. 1982. United Kingdom by population groups. In *Population change and social planning,* D. Eversley and W. Köllmann (eds), 20–61. London: Edward Arnold.

Page, H. J. and R. J. Lesthaeghe (eds) 1981. *Child spacing in Tropical Africa: traditions and change.* London: Academic Press.

Panel on Egypt 1982. *The estimation of recent trends in fertility and mortality in Egypt.* Report no. 9, Committee on Population and Demography, National Academy of Sciences, Washington, DC.

Philipov, D. and A. Rogers 1982. Multiregional population projections by place of previous residence. In *Multidimensional mathematical demography,* K. C. Land and A. Rogers (eds), 445–75. New York: Academic Press.

Pittenger, D. B. 1976. *Projecting state and local populations.* Cambridge, Mass.: Ballinger.

Plessis-Fraissard, M. 1976. *Households: a review of definitions, trends and forecasting methods.* Working paper 164, School of Geography, University of Leeds.

Plessis-Fraissard, M. 1979. *Migrants, accounts, spouses and households: an investigation.* Unpublished PhD thesis, School of Geography, University of Leeds.

Population Reference Bureau 1982. *World fertility chart.* Washington, DC: Population Reference Bureau.

Potter, J. E. 1977. Problems in using birth-history analysis to estimate trends in fertility. *Population Studies* **31**, 335–64.

Pressat, R. 1983. Premiers résultats du recensement de la Chine. *Population* **38**, 403–9.

Preston, S. H. 1976. *Mortality patterns in national populations.* New York: Academic Press.

Preston, S. H. (ed.) 1978. *The effects of infant and child mortality on fertility.* New York: Academic Press.

Preston, S. H. and E. van de Walle 1978. Urban French mortality in the nineteenth century. *Population Studies* **32**, 275–97.

Preston, S. H. and P. N. M. Bhat 1984. New evidence on fertility and mortality trends in India. *Population and Development Review* **10**, 481–503.

Rallu, J. 1983. Permanence des disparités régionales de la fécondité en Italie? *Population* **38** (1), 29–59.

Ram, S. and P. H. Rees 1985. *A spatial demographic analysis of the Indian population of Bradford.* Working paper 434, School of Geography, University of Leeds.

Ravenstein, E. G. 1876. Birth places and migration. *Geographical Magazine,* **3**, 173–7, 201–6, 229–33.

Ravenstein, E. G. 1885. The laws of migration. *Journal of the Royal Statistical Society* **48**, 167–235.

Razi, Z. 1980. *Life, marriage and death in a medieval parish: economy, society and demography in Halesowen, 1220–1400.* Cambridge: Cambridge University Press.

Rees, P. H. 1977. The measurement of migration from census data and other sources. *Environment and Planning A* **9**, 247–272.

Rees, P. H. 1979a. *Migration and settlement: 1. United Kingdom.* Research report RR-79-3, Institute for Applied Systems Analysis, Laxenburg, Austria.

Rees, P. H. 1979b. Regional projection models and accounting methods. *Journal of the Royal Statistical Society, Series A* **142**, 223–55.

Rees, P. H. 1981a. *Accounts based models for multiregional population analysis: methods, program and user's manual.* Working paper 295, School of Geography, University of Leeds.

Rees, P. H. 1981b. Population geography. In *Quantitative geography: a British view,* N. Wrigley and R. J. Bennett (eds), Ch. 29. London: Routledge & Kegan Paul.

Rees, P. H. 1983. Multiregional mathematical demography: themes and issues. *Environment and Planning A* **15**, 1571–83.

Rees, P. H. 1984a. *Spatial population analysis using movement data and accounting methods: theory, models, the 'MOVE' program and examples.* Working paper 404/computer manual 23, School of Geography, University of Leeds. Working paper no. 50, Netherlands Interuniversity Demographic Institute Vorburg, Netherlands.

Rees, P. H. 1984b. *Forecasting the population of India and subnational areas with minimal information.* Working paper 389, School of Geography, University of Leeds.

Rees, P. H. 1985. Does it really matter which migration data you use in a population model? Working paper 383, School of Geography, University of Leeds. In *Contemporary studies of migration,* P. E. White and G. A. van der Knaap (eds). 1985, 55–77. Norwich: Geobooks.

Rees, P. H. and J. C. H. Stillwell 1984. An integrated model of migration flows and population change for a system of UK metropolitan and non-metropolitan regions: a framework. In *Migration and mobility,* A. J. Boyce (ed.), 317–53. London: Taylor & Francis.

Rees, P. H. and F. Willekens 1981. *Data bases and accounting frameworks for IIASA's Comparative Migration and Settlement Study.* Collaborative paper CP-81-39, International Institute for Applied Systems Analysis, Laxenburg, Austria.

Rees, P. H. and A. G. Wilson 1977. *Spatial population analysis.* London: Edward Arnold.

Reyes, F. 1981. *Evaluation of the Republic of the Philippines Fertility Survey 1978.* Scientific report no. 19, World Fertility Survey, London.

Rhind, D. 1984. The future of the census. Talk given at *Results of the 1981 Census,* a joint conference of the Population Geography Study Group of the Institute of British Geographers, the Regional Science Association and the British Society for Population Studies, University of Sheffield, 20–22 September 1984.

Richardson, H. 1972. *Input–output and regional economics.* London: Weidenfeld & Nicolson.

Ridley, J. C. and M. C. Sheps 1966. An analytic simulation model for human reproduction with demographic and biological components. *Population Studies* **19**, 297–310.

Rikkinen, K. 1979. *Migration and settlement: 2. Finland.* Research report RR-79-2, International Institute for Applied Systems Analysis, Laxenburg, Austria.

Rogers, A. 1968. *Matrix analysis of inter-regional population growth and distribution.* Berkeley and Los Angeles: University of California Press.

Rogers, A. 1975. *Introduction to multiregional mathematical demography.* New York: Wiley.

Rogers, A. 1976. Shrinking large-scale population projection models by aggregation and decomposition. *Environment and Planning A* **8**, 515–41.

Rogers, A. 1982. *Parameterized multistate population dynamics.* Working paper WP-82-125, International Institute for Applied Systems Analysis, Laxenburg, Austria.

Rogers, A. 1985 *Regional population projection models,* Beverly Hills: Sage Publications.

Rogers, A. 1986. Population projections. In *Migration and settlement: a multiregional comparative study,* A. Rogers and F. Willekens (eds), 211–263. Dordrecht, Netherlands: Reidel.

Rogers, A. and L. Castro 1981. *Model migration schedules.* Research report RR-81-30, International Institute for Applied Systems Analysis, Laxenburg, Austria.

Rogers, A. and L. Castro 1982. Model migration schedules in multistate demographic analysis: the case of migration. In *Multistate mathematical demography,* K. C. Land and A. Rogers (eds), 113–54. New York: Academic Press.

Rogers, A. and J. Ledent 1976. Increment–decrement life tables: a comment. *Demography* 13, 287–90.

Rogers, A. and F. Planck 1984. *Parameterized multistate population projections.* Working paper 84-1, Population Program, Institute of Behavioral Science, University of Colorado, Boulder, Colorado.

Rogers, A. and F. Willekens (eds) 1986. *Migration and settlement: a comparative study.* Dordrecht, Netherlands: Reidel.

Rogers, A., R. Raquillet and L. Castro 1978. Model migration schedules and their applications. *Environment and Planning A* 10, 475–502.

Romaniuk, A. 1980. Increase in natural fertility during the early stages of modernization: evidence from an African case study, Zaire. *Population Studies* 34, 293–310.

Russell, J. C. 1948. *British medieval population.* Albuquerque, N. Mex.: New Mexico University Press.

Sadler, P., B. Archer and C. Owen 1970. *Regional income multipliers: the Anglesey study.* Bangor occasional papers in economics 1. Bangor: University of Wales Press.

Schinnar, A. P. 1976. A multidimensional accounting model for demographic and economic planning interactions. *Environment and Planning A* 8, 455–75.

Schinnar, A. P. 1977. An eco-demographic accounting-type multiplier analysis of Hungary. *Environment and Planning A* 9, 373–84.

Shannon, C. E. 1948. A mathematical theory of communication. *Bell System Technical Journal* 27, 379–423, 623–56.

Shorter, E., J. Knodel and E. van de Walle 1971. The decline of non-marital fertility in Europe, 1880–1940. *Population Studies* 25, 375–93.

Shorter, F. C. and M. Macura 1982. *Trends in fertility and mortality in Turkey, 1935–1975.* Report no. 8, Committee on Population and Demography, National Academy of Sciences, Washington, DC.

Shryock, H. S. and J. S. Siegel 1976. *The methods and materials of demography,* 2nd edn (condensed by E. G. Stockwell). London: Academic Press.

Sjaastad, L. A. 1962. The costs and returns of human migration. *Journal of Political Economy* 70 (Supplement), 80–93.

Somermeijer, W. H. 1971. Multi-polar human flow models. *Papers of the Regional Science Association* XXVI, 131–44.

Spengler, J. J. 1966. Values and fertility analysis. *Demography* 3, 109–30.

Spohr, H. 1974. Population projection with special regard to the distribution by marital status: results and applications of a matrix model. In *Population forecasting,* R. Campbell (ed.). London: Planning and Transportation Research.

Sri Lanka 1979. *The statistical pocket book of the Democratic Socialist Republic of Sri Lanka.* Colombo: Government Printers.

Srinivasan, K., S. J. Jejeebhoy, R. A. Easterlin and E. M. Crimmins 1984. Factors affecting fertility control in India: a cross-sectional study. *Population and Development Review* **10**, 273–96.

Stillwell, J. C. H. 1975. *Models of interregional migration: a review.* Working paper 100, School of Geography, University of Leeds.

Stillwell, J. C. H. 1978. Inter-zonal migration: some historical tests of spatial interaction models. *Environment and Planning A* **10**, 1187–200.

Stillwell, J. C. H. 1979. *Migration in England and Wales: a study of inter-area patterns, accounts, models and projections.* Unpublished PhD thesis, School of Geography, University of Leeds.

Stone, P. A. 1970. *Urban development in Britain,* Vol. 1: Population trends and housing. Economic and Social Studies XXVI, National Institute of Economic and Social Research. Cambridge: Cambridge University Press.

Stone, R. 1971. *Demographic accounting and model building.* Paris: Organization for Economic Cooperation and Development.

Sun, T. H. and Y. L. Soong 1979. On its way to zero growth: fertility transition in Taiwan, Republic of China. In *Fertility transition of the East Asian populations,* L.-J. Cho and K. Kobayashi (eds), 117–48. Honolulu: University Press of Hawaii.

Taeuber, I. B. 1958. *The population of Japan.* Princeton, NJ: Princeton University Press.

Teitelbaum, M. S. 1984. *The British fertility decline: demographic transition in the crucible of the industrial revolution.* Princeton, NJ: Princeton University Press.

Thailand 1980. *The statistical pocket book of Thailand.* Bangkok: Government Press.

Thomas, I. 1980. *Population growth.* London: Macmillan.

Thompson, W. S. 1929. Population. *American Journal of Sociology* **34**, 959–75.

Tsubouchi, Y. 1970. Changes in fertility in Japan by region. *Demography* **7**, 121–34.

United Nations 1949. *Demographic yearbook, 1948.* New York: United Nations.

United Nations 1955a. *Age and sex patterns of mortality: model life tables for underdeveloped countries.* Population studies no. 42, Department of International Economic and Social Affairs, Bureau of Social Affairs. New York: United Nations.

United Nations 1955b. *Demographic yearbook, 1954.* New York: United Nations.

United Nations 1956. *Demographic yearbook, 1955.* New York: United Nations.

United Nations 1964. *Demographic yearbook, 1963.* New York: United Nations.

United Nations 1966. *Demographic yearbook, 1965.* New York: United Nations.

United Nations 1967. *Methods of estimating basic demographic measures from incomplete data.* Populations studies no. 59. Department of International Economic and Social Affairs, Bureau of Social Affairs. New York: United Nations.

United Nations 1973. *The determinants and consequences of population trends.* 2 vols. New York: United Nations.

United Nations 1976. *Demographic yearbook, 1975.* New York: United Nations.

United Nations 1977. *Levels and trends of fertility throughout the world, 1950–70.* New York: United Nations.

United Nations 1978. *Statistics of internal migrations: a technical report*. Studies in methods, series F, no. 23. New York: United Nations.

United Nations 1980a. *World population trends and policies: 1979 monitoring report, Volume 1, Population trends*. Population studies no. 70. Department of International Economic and Social Affairs. New York: United Nations.

United Nations 1980b. *Demographic yearbook, 1979*. New York: United Nations.

United Nations 1980c. *Patterns of urban and rural population growth*. Department of International Economic and Social Affairs. New York: United Nations.

United Nations 1981a. *World population prospects as assessed in 1980*. Population studies no. 78, Department of International Economic and Social Affairs. New York: United Nations.

United Nations 1981b. *Statistical yearbook for Asia and the Pacific, 1981*. Economic and Social Commission for Asia and the Pacific. Bangkok: United Nations.

United Nations 1981c. *Demographic yearbook, 1980*. New York: United Nations.

United Nations 1982a. *Model life tables for developing countries*. Population studies no. 77, Department of International Economic and Social Affairs, New York: United Nations.

United Nations 1982b. *Levels and trends of mortality since 1950*. Department of International Economic and Social Affairs. New York: United Nations.

United Nations 1983. *Demographic yearbook, 1983*. New York: United Nations.

Vallin, J. 1971. Limitation des naissances en Tunisie. *Population,* Special Number 181–204.

van de Walle, E. 1973. La mortalité de départements francais ruraux au xixe siècle. In *Hommage à Marcel Reinhard. Sur la population francaise du XVIIIe et au XIXe siècles,* J. Dupâquier (ed.), 581–9. Paris: Societé de Démographie Historique.

van de Walle, E. 1974. *The female population of France in the nineteenth century: a reconstruction of 82 départements*. Princeton, NJ: Princeton University Press.

van de Walle, E. 1978. Alone in Europe: the French fertility decline until 1850. In *Historical studies of changing fertility,* C. Tilly (ed.), 257–88. Princeton, NJ: Princeton University Press.

van de Walle, E. 1979. France. In *European demography and economic growth,* W. R. Lee (ed.), 123–43. London: Croom Helm.

van de Walle, E. 1980. Motivation and technology in the decline of French fertility. In *Family and sexuality in French History,* R. Wheaton and T.K. Hareven (eds), 135–78. Philadelphia, Pa.: University of Pennsylvania Press.

van de Walle, E. and J. Knodel 1980. Europe's fertility transition: new evidence and lessons for today's developing world. *Population Bulletin* 34(6), 2–43.

van der Erf, R., H. Gordijn and K. Prins 1983. Gemeentegrenswijzigingen en demografische statistieken. (Municipal boundary changes and demographic statistics.) *Stedebouw en Volkshuisvesting* 64 (1), 20–5.

van der Knaap, G. A. and W. F. Sleegers 1982. *De structuur van migratiestromen in Nederland. De stadsgewestelijke migratie in de periode 1967–1978. (The structure of migration patterns in the Netherlands. The migration between and within daily urban systems in the period 1967–1978.)* Report no. 2, Economisch Geografisch Instituut, Erasmus Universiteit, Rotterdam.

van Engen, E. H. and G. A. van der Knaap 1980. *De structuur van migratiestromen in Nederland, de vergelijkbaarheid van gemeentelijke demografische gegevens over de periode 1950–1978. (The structure of migration flows in the Netherlands; comparability of municipal data over the period 1950–1978.)* Research report series C, no. 80–1, Economisch Geografisch Instituut, Rotterdam.

Vinovskis, M. A. (ed.) 1979. *Studies in American historical demography.* New York: Academic Press.

Visaria, P. and L. Visaria 1981. India's population: second and growing. *Population Bulletin* **36** (4), 1–55.

Weeden, R. 1973. *Inter-regional migration models and their application to Great Britain.* Regional papers II, National Institute of Economic and Social Research. Cambridge: Cambridge University Press.

Wegener, M. 1982. A multi-level economic–demographic model for the Dortmund region. *Sistemi Urbani* **4**, 371–401.

Wegener, M. 1983. A simulation study of movement in the Dortmund housing market. *Tijdschrift voor Economische en Sociale Geografie* **74**, 267–81.

Welsh Office 1979. *Migration into, out of and within Wales in the 1966–71 period.* Welsh Office occasional paper no. 4. Cardiff: HMSO.

Willekens, F. 1977. *The recovery of detailed migration patterns from aggregate data: an entropy maximizing approach.* Research memorandum RM-77-58, International Institute for Applied Systems Analysis, Laxenburg, Austria.

Willekens, F. 1983. Specification and calibration of spatial interaction models. *Tijdschrift voor Economische en Sociale Geografie* **74**, 239–52.

Willekens, F. 1984. *Comparability of migration. Utopia or reality?* Working paper no. 47, Netherlands Interuniversity Demographic Institute, Voorburg, The Netherlands.

Willekens, F. and N. Baydar 1983a. *Multidimensional forecasting: a systems approach.* Working paper no. 40, Netherlands Interuniversity Demographic Institute, Voorburg, The Netherlands.

Willekens, F. and N. Baydar 1983b. *Hybrid log-linear models.* Working paper no. 41, Netherlands Interuniversity Demographic Institute, Voorburg, The Netherlands.

Willekens, F. and N. Baydar 1983c. *Forecasting place-to-place migration with generalized linear models: an application to urbanization in the Netherlands.* Working paper no. 42, Netherlands Interuniversity Demographic Institute, Voorburg, The Netherlands.

Willekens, F. and P. Drewe 1984. A multiregional model for regional demographic projection. In *Demographic research and spatial policy,* H. ter Heide and F. J. Willekens (eds), pp. 309–34. London: Academic Press.

Willekens, F., A. Por and R. Raquillet 1979. *Entropy, multiproportional and quadratic techniques for inferring detailed migration patterns from aggregate data: mathematical theories, algorithms, applications and computer programs.* Working paper WP-79-88, International Institute for Applied Systems Analysis, Laxenburg, Austria.

Willekens, F., A. Por and R. Raquillet 1981. Entropy, multiproportional and quadratic techniques for inferring detailed migration patterns from aggregate data. In *Advances in multiregional demography,* A. Rogers, (ed.), 83–124. Research report RR-81-6, International Institute for Applied Systems Analysis, Laxenburg, Austria.

Willekens, F. and A. Rogers 1978. *Spatial population analysis: methods and computer programs.* Research report RR-78-18, International Institute for Applied Systems Analysis, Laxenburg, Austria.

Willekens, F., I. Shah, J. M. Shah and P. Ramachandran 1982. Multi-state analysis of marital status life tables: theory and application. *Population Studies* **36**, 129–144.

Williamson, J. 1965. Regional income inequality and the process of national development: a description of the patterns. *Economic Development and Cultural Change* **13**, 3–84.

Wilson, A. G. 1974. *Urban and regional models in geography and planning.* London: Wiley.

Wilson, A. G. and C. Pownall 1976. A new representation of the urban system for modelling and for the study of micro-level interdependence. *Area* **8**, 246–54.

Wilson, M. 1978. A spatial analysis of human fertility in Scotland: re-appraisal and extension. *Scottish Geographical Magazine* **94**, 130–43.

Wolpert, J. 1969. The basis for stability of interregional transactions. *Geographical Analysis* **1**, 152–80.

Wolpert, J. and W. Yapa 1971. The time path of migration flows in Belgium 1954–1962. *Geographical Analysis* **3**, 157–64.

Woods, R. I. 1979. *Population analysis in geography.* London: Longman.

Woods, R. I. 1981. Spatio-temporal models of ethnic segregation and their implications for housing policy. *Environment and Planning A* **13**, 1415–33.

Woods, R. I. 1982a. *Theoretical population geography.* London: Longman.

Woods, R. I. 1982b. The structure of mortality in mid-nineteenth century England and Wales. *Journal of Historical Geography* **8**, 373–94.

Woods, R. I. 1984a. Spatial demography. In *Geography and population: approaches and applications,* J. I. Clarke (ed.), 43–50. Oxford: Pergamon.

Woods, R. I. 1984b. Social class variations in the decline of marital fertility in late nineteenth-century London. *Geografiska Annaler* **66B**, 29–38.

Woods, R. I. 1985. The effects of population redistribution on the level of mortality in nineteenth-century England and Wales. *Journal of Economic History* **45**, 645–51.

Woods, R. I. 1986. Malthus, Marx and population crises. In *A World in Crisis?* R. J. Johnston and P. J. Taylor (eds), 127–49. Oxford: Basil Blackwell.

Woods, R. I. and P. R. A. Hinde 1985. Nuptiality and age at marriage in nineteenth-century England. *Journal of Family History* **10**, 119–44.

Woods, R. I. and C. W. Smith 1983. The decline of marital fertility in the late nineteenth century: the case of England and Wales. *Population Studies* **37**, 207–25.

Woods, R. I. and J. H. Woodward (eds), 1984. *Urban disease and mortality in nineteenth-century England.* London: Batsford Academic.

World Bank 1982. *World development report, 1982.* London: Oxford University Press.

World Fertility Survey 1977. *Strategies for the analysis of World Fertility Survey data.* Basic Documentation Series, no. 9, International Statistical Institute, The Hague, The Netherlands.

World Fertility Survey 1981. *Trinidad and Tobago fertility survey, 1977.* 2 vols. Port of Spain, Trinidad: Central Statistical Office.

Wrigley, E. A. and R. S. Schofield 1981. *The population history of England, 1541–1871: a reconstruction.* London: Edward Arnold.

Xenos, C. 1976. *Fertility change in Mauritius and the impact of the family planning programme.* Unpublished PhD thesis, University of London.

Yu, Y. C. 1978. The demographic situation in China. *Population Studies* **32**, 427–47.

Yu, Y. C. 1979. The population policy of China. *Population Studies* **33**, 125–42.

Yuan Tien, H. 1983. *Induced fertility transition: impact of population planning and socioeconomic change in the People's Republic of China.* Paper presented at an International Workshop on the Single Child Family in China, Contemporary China Centre, Queen Elizabeth House, Oxford.

Zelinsky, W. 1971. The hypothesis of the mobility transition. *Geographical Review* **61**, 219–49.

Index

Aberdeen 64
accounting
  frameworks 133–43
accounts
  models 133–4
  movement 135–9
  transitions 143–5
Adegbola, O. 3, 330
Adlakha, A. 69
Adolfson, I. 252
Africa 1, 3, 10–13, 79, 84, 93, 301, 330
age
  stable distribution 364
  structure 261, 270
age-time
  estimation methods 309–12
  frameworks 305–12
  notation 307–8
  observation paths 127–8, 305–7
Aird, J. S. 71, 330
Akkerman, A. 122
Alberta 253
Alexander, S. 116, 132
Algeria 79
Alonso, W. 48
Andhra Pradesh 334–8, 340
Andorka, R. 53
Anhui 71
Apgar, W. C. 252
Arriaga, E. 371
Artle, R. 277
Asia 3, 11–12, 81, 84, 301, 343, 367–89
Asian Pacific
  definition 367
  projected population 367–71
  projected urbanization 367–71
  population estimates 368–9
  rates of growth 368–9
Askham, J. 64
Australia 10–11, 321

Baker, R. J. 220
Balakrishnan, T. 46
Balkaran, S. 78
Bangladesh 74
Banister, J. 330
Banks, J. A. 45

Barbados 50, 57
Barclay, G. W. 13, 354
Barras, R. 273
Batey, P. W. J. 97, 121, 123, 276–7, 278,
  281–2, 287, 295
Baydar, N. 97, 115, 123, 196, 204, 209,
  225, 228, 237
Beaumont, P. 275
Beaver, S. E. 46
Bedfordshire 59
Belgium 14, 29, 40
Bennett, R. J. 10
Berkshire 59, 64
Berry, B. 380
Bhat, P. N. M. 330, 333, 336, 338
Bihar 338, 340
birth rates
  international variations 9–13, 68–94
Blaikie, P. 55, 340
Blalock, H. M. 17
Bogue, D. J. 75
Bombay 93
Bombay State 69–70, 81–2, 85–8, 90, 93
Bongaarts, J. 13, 330
Bonsall, P. 253
Boonstra, O. W. A. 14–15, 18, 42
Borchert, J. G. 207
Bose, A. 340
Boulder 278
Bourgeois–Pichat, J. 1, 24
Bracken, I. 275
Bradford 305
Bradley, I. E. 283
Brass, W. 1, 3, 330, 353–4
Brazil 50
Breheny, M. J. 273, 275
Broadbent, T. A. 273
Bulatao, R. A. 19
Bulgaria 86–9, 91
Burns, A. 83

Cadwallader, M. 17
Cairo 93
Caldwell, J. C. 39, 47, 92, 330
Calot, G. 330
Cambodia 367–71, 373–5, 377–8, 383–8
Campbell, R. 116, 193

Canada 10–11, 132, 145, 253, 321
Cartwright, A. 263
Carvalho, J. A. M. 3, 50
Cassedy, J. H. 1
Cassen, R. H. 333–6
Castro, L. 165, 312
causal models 17–18, 40–3
Central Policy Review Staff 130
Central Statistical Office 117
Cespedes, Y. 78
Champion, A. 312
Chang, C. 80
Chen, P. 71
Chenery, H. 380–1
Chilver, C. 53
China 13, 68, 70–1, 83, 330, 367–71,
  373–9, 389
Cho, L.-J. 80
Clairin, R. 312
Clarke, M. 97, 119, 123, 248, 253, 260,
  262, 265, 268, 275
Cleland, J. 57, 68
Cleveland 59
Cliff, A. D. 10
closure methods
  external migration ignored 146, 154–9
  gross migration 146, 154–9
  mixed 148, 154–9
  net migration 146, 154–9
  world system 148, 154–9
Clwyd 292
Clydeside 137–40, 155–8, 167–70, 172–4,
  178–80, 183, 190–2
Coale, A. J. 3, 9, 13, 23, 26, 28, 29, 38,
  40, 51, 58–9, 71, 80–1, 92, 312,
  330–2, 337
Cochrane–Hill, S. 66
cohort survival
  multiregional model 141–3
Colombia 71–4, 77–8, 81, 85–7, 90, 92, 94
Colorado 278
components
  of change 101–5
Compton, P. 53, 58
Cook, N. D. 13
Coombes, M. 312
Cordey–Hayes, M. 196
Costa Rica 76–7, 80–1, 86–7, 90
Courgeau, D. 304, 320–1
Coward, J. 53
Craig, J. 126, 130, 163
Crook, N. 3
Cuba 80
Cullen, J. 1
Cyprus 80

data
  census transition 163–6
  files 152–3

last residence 99–100, 104–5
  movement 99–104
  transition 99–104
database
  creation of 344–65
  criterion 349–51
  framework 348–9
  generality 349
  Netherlands 206–9
  procedures 351–7
  Thailand 344–65
Davis, K. 1
death
  microsimulation model 263–5
death rates
  international variations 9–13
deconsolidation
  methods 309–12
de Kanter, J. 283, 292
Demeny, P. 3, 23, 312, 331–2, 337
demographic regimes 11–13, 23–6
demographic transition
  model 21–3
  theory 21–3, 36–9, 46–9
  in Trinidad and Tobago 54–8
  in West 21–44
Denmark 53
Department of Employment 260–2, 270–1,
  292
Department of the Environment 116, 161,
  163, 267
Desbarats, J. M. 19
Detroit 252
Devon 34
distance
  measures 213, 221
divorce
  microsimulation model 265–6
Doeve, W. L. J. 348, 351, 353–6, 366
Dominican Republic 74, 78
Drewe, P. 143
Duncan, O. D. 17
Dyson, T. 3, 69, 337–8, 340

East Anglia 155–8, 170, 172–4, 178–80,
  183, 190–2, 325–8
Easterlin, R. A. 130, 341
East Midlands Region 155–8, 172–4,
  178–80, 183, 186, 189–92, 325–8
Edwards, S. L. 163
Eire 53
Egypt 68–70, 79, 81–2, 85–7, 89–90, 93
El-Badry, M. A. 70
El Salvador 80–1, 83
Elias, P. 167
England 23–43, 45, 52–4, 58–65, 86–7, 91,
  120–1, 150, 161, 164, 167
Ermisch, J. 24, 64
ESCAP 77

Espenshade, T. J. 116
estimation
  definition 302–3
  demographic 301–43
  examples 323–41
  general principles 341–3
  methods 161–9, 301–43
  migration arrays 315–19
  spatial 312–15
Europe 9–12, 21, 23–4, 40, 51, 83–4,
  88–91, 203, 302
Eversley, D. 59
Eyler, J. M. 1

Farr, W. 1
Feinberg, S. E. 255
fertility
  Coale's indices 14, 26–33, 40–3, 58–64
  microsimulation model 263–5
Figueroa, B. 77
Fiji 76–7
Finland 53, 319
Flieger, W. 312
Flinn, M. W. 24
Fonaroff, L. 54
forecasting
  household 245–7
  Merseyside 291–5
  migration 239–41
  multiregional framework 2
  population 245–7
Fox, A. 45
frameworks
  accountancy 321–2
  spatial 312–15
  temporal 319–23
France 23–31, 86–8, 91, 145, 321
Frey, W. 116
Fuller, G. 50, 55

Gander, J. P. 283
General Register Office 258, 260
Germany 28, 40
Gilje, E. 116, 193
Gill, D. 58
Glamorgan 59, 64
Glasgow 137
Glass, D. V. 1, 24, 26, 31
Gleave, D. 161, 196
GLIM
  package 343
GLMs
  for modelling migration 220–8
  model specification 222–5
  parameter estimation 225–8
Goldblatt, P. 45
Goldman, N. 72, 74, 78
Goodstadt, L. F. 330
Gordon, I. 163

Gottfried, R. S. 24
Great Britain 53, 85, 93, 117–19, 124, 132,
  165, 167, 292
Greater London Council 116
Greenwood, M. J. 14–15, 18
Grigg, D. B. 13, 21
Gujarat 69–70, 338, 340
Guyana 76–8, 80, 86–7, 90, 94
Guzman, J. M. 78

Haines, M. R. 41
Hajnal, J. 13
Hammel, E. A. 253
Harewood, J. 55
Harsman, B. 98, 121, 254
Haryana 69, 338, 340
Hawaii 277
headship rates
  analysis 253–4
  method 119–21
  projected 120
Henin, R. A. 79
Hermalin, A. 45
Hetherington, M. F. 247
Hewings, G. J. D. 275
Hill, A. 81
Himachal Pradesh 338, 340
Hinde, P. R. A. 27, 43
Hirsch, W. Z. 277
Hobcraft, J. N. 57, 68, 71–4, 78
Hofsten, E. 24
Hollerbach, P. E. 80
Honduras 80
Hong Kong 367–71, 373–75, 377–8
household
  components of increase 118
  composition matrix 122
  consumption framework 278–86
  dynamics 245
  forecasting framework 286–8
  numbers 116–18, 121
  one person 118
  projection 119–22
  size 171, 262, 271
  structure 262
  type 271
Humberside 59, 64, 155–8, 163, 170,
  172–4, 178–80, 183, 190–2, 255–6,
  259–61, 325–8
Hunan 71
Hungary 53
Hyman, G. 161
Hyrenius, H. 252

IIASA 99, 125
Illsley, R. 58
immigration 59, 305, 320–1
India 1, 68–9, 81–2, 89, 93, 305, 323,
  329–41

crude birth rates 336
crude death rates 336
fertility 335−7
forecasting the population 330−2
mortality 333−5
socio-economic variables 339−41
spatial demography 329−41
survival rates 332
Indonesia 74, 80, 367−71, 373−5, 377−8, 383−9
information
demographic system 149−53
International Bank for Reconstruction and Development 380, 384−7
Ireland 27
Isle of Man 167−8
Isseramn, A. 123−4
Italy 28, 40

Jabukowski, M. 26
Jain, A. K. 69
Jamaica 76−7, 80−1, 85−90, 92
Japan 1, 51, 85−91, 367−71, 373−5, 377−80, 389
Jiangxi 71
Jones, H. 50, 53, 57
Jordan 76−7, 94
Joseph, G. 163, 193, 196

Kain, J. F. 250, 252
Karnataka 338, 340
Kennett, S. 163
Kenya 10, 79
Kerala 334−40
Keyfitz, N. 312, 367, 376
Khan, M. 50
Kirk, D. 68
Knodel, J. 9, 28−9, 39, 41
Knox, P. 48, 53
Kols, M. A. 71
Korea 74, 80, 367−71, 373−5, 377−8, 389
Kpedekpo, G. M. K. 3
Kreibich, V. 253
Kussmaul, A. 41

Lancashire 31
Land, K. C. 2
Landry, A. 21
Langford, C. 77
last migrations 129, 133
last residence
data 99−100, 104−5
Latin America 3, 10−12, 79−81, 83−4, 89−92, 301
Law, C. M. 37
Lawton, R. 59
League of Nations 80
Ledent, J. 99, 107−8, 112−13, 142, 242, 275, 320−1, 338−9, 376, 380−1

Ledermann, S. 353
Lee, R. D. 18−19
Leibenstein, H. 39
Leontief, W. 123, 275, 281, 295−6
Leridon, H. 27
Lesthaeghe, R. J. 13−15, 18, 42, 79, 330
Lieber, S. R. 19
life expectancy 21, 23−5, 28, 34−5, 113−14
Lincolnshire 59
linkages
economic-demographic 277−8
demographic-economic 278−9
Livi Bacci, M. 29
London 1, 31, 33, 37, 42, 59, 64, 116, 132, 155−8, 163, 170, 172−5, 176, 178−80, 183, 186, 189−92, 325−8
Long, J. F. 273
Lotka, A. J. 1
Lundström, H. 24
Luptacik, M. 275, 278

McFadden, D. 255
McKeown, T. 26
Macura, M. 81
Madden, M. 97, 121, 123, 276, 278, 281−2, 287, 292, 295
Madhya Pradesh 338, 340
Madras 93
Maharashtra 69−70, 338, 340
Malaysia 75, 76−7, 367−71, 373−5, 377−8, 383−8
Malthusian model 13, 25
Manchester 155−8, 170, 172−4, 178−80, 183, 190−2
Marcoux, A. 79
Markovian
assumption 113−14
Marksjo, B. 98, 121
marriage
microsimulation model 264−6
Martin Voorhees Associates and John Bates Services 116, 130, 161, 193
Masser, I. 116, 180, 289
Mauldin, W. P. 80
Mauritius 79, 86−9, 90, 93
Menken, J. 27
Merseyside 98, 121, 155−8, 170, 172−4, 178−80, 183, 186, 190−2, 276−95
Mexico 10, 76−7, 80, 86−7, 89−90
microsimulation
applications 252−3
comparative results 261−2
of demographic processes 245−72
of household dynamics 245−72
Middle East 10−11
Miernyk, W. H. 278
migration
age groups 188−9
age structure 175−7

analysis 160–244
analysis strategy 242–3
arrays, edges 317
arrays, estimation of 315–19
arrays, faces 317
changes 178–80
characteristics in UK 169–92
components 205, 207–20
explanation 13–14, 19
external UK 323–9
forecasting 203–44
interregional 160–202
laws 13
measures 129
methods of observing 128–9
microsimulation model 265, 267
model schedule 115, 163–6
Netherlands, major findings 243–4
over distance 180–6
projecting flows 196–7
projecting in rates 195–6
projecting levels 194–5
projecting out rates 195–6
projection 160–244
projection methods 194–7
rival net rates, Asian Pacific 373, 378
spatial patterns 169–75, 191–2
time-series 205–20
trends 186–92
Mitchell, B. R. 83
Mitchell, W. C. 83
Miyazawa, K. 278, 283
model
  Batey–Madden 278–86, 295–7
  closure 116
  conditional probability 196, 199
  demographic-economic 273–97
  growth factor 197, 199
  microsimulation 245–72
  multistate population 289–91
  of a metropolis 273–97
  of household dynamics 263–8
  simple rates 196, 198
  spatial interaction 181–6, 197, 200–1
modelling
  distribution component 233–9
  generation component 228–33
  input-output 276–8
  migration 192–201, 220–39
  multiregional framework 2
  system 123–4, 192–201
models
  accounts based 143–6
  backcast 143
  classification of input-output 277–8
  comprehensive 123
  constraints 145–6
  economic-demographic 123
  extrapolative 123

forecast 143
  generalized linear 203–44
  multiregional cohort survival 141–3
  total populations 145
Molho, I. 167
Moore, G. H. 83
Moore, M. 340
Morrison, W. I. 283, 292
Mosher, W. D. 80
movement
  data 99–104
  rates 105–6, 129, 133
multipliers 281–6
  demographic-economic 285
  economic production 289
  employment 284
  multisector 286
multistate
  analysis for Thailand 344–66
municipalities
  in Netherlands 203–44
Murphy, M. 63
Myrdal, G. 48

Nag, M. 68, 80
Nair, P. S. 338–9
Nakamura, A. O. 253
Nakamura, M. 253
natural increase
  Asian Pacific 373, 378
Nelder, J. A. 220, 228
Nepal 74, 78
Netherlands 14, 53, 98, 115, 124, 132, 143,
    196, 206–44, 278, 305, 323
New Commonwealth 59, 263
New Zealand 10–11
Nicaragua 80
Norfolk 59
North America 12, 29, 302
Northern Ireland 53, 137–8, 140, 150,
    155–8, 161, 164–6, 178–80, 183, 186,
    190–2, 325–8
Northern Region 155–8, 172–4, 178–80,
    183, 190–2, 325–8
North West Region 137–8, 140, 155–8,
    172–4, 178–80, 183, 190–2, 292,
    325–8
Norway 53, 86–8, 91
Notestein, F. W. 21, 37
Nottinghamshire 64
nuptiality
  effects on fertility 16, 41–3

O'Connell, M. 48, 52
O'Dea, D. 83–4
Ogilvy, A. A. 130, 167, 188
Olsson, G. 13–14, 18
Omram, A. R. 70
Oosterhaven, J. 278

OPCS 52–3, 116–17, 151, 160, 167, 258–61, 263–4, 266–7, 270, 292, 323, 325
Orcutt, G. H. 250, 252, 275
Ord, J. K. 10
Ordorica, M. 78
Orissa 338, 340
Osborne, R. H. 163
Overton, E. 58–9

Page, H. J. 13, 330
Pakistan 50, 59, 74, 263
Palmore, J. A. 75
Panama 76–7, 80
Panel on Egypt 70
pattern analysis
  fertility 9–20, 23–35, 38–44, 45–65
  migration 160–244
  mortality 25, 28, 34–7, 47–9
Pender, M. 163
Peru 13, 76–8
Philippines 74, 78, 367–71, 373–5, 377–8, 383–8
Philipov, D. 113–14
Pittenger, D. B. 203
Pittsburgh 252
Planck, F. 115, 121
Plessis-Fraissard, M. 118–21, 254, 258
Poland 53
population
  at risk 104
  flow concepts 304–5
  generation model 255–60
  generation of 254–62
  regional projection 126
  stationary 111–13
Portugal 86–7, 91
Population Reference Bureau 336
Potter, J. E. 77–8
Pownall, C. 250, 253
Pressat, R. 330
Preston, S. H. 20, 32, 40, 330, 333, 336, 338
Princeton European Fertility Project 9, 14
probabilities
  survival 110–11
  survivorship 110–11
probability
  joint distribution 255
  scheme 255–6
programs
  computer 153
projecting
  in-migration totals 195–6
  migration flows 195–6
  out-migration totals 195–6
projection, of migration 192–201
  composition of migration 197–200
  effects 154–9

experiments 154–9
projections
  accounting parameters for 133–41
  alternative, Asian Pacific 374–5, 377, 379
  birthplace-dependent 114
  birthplace-independent 114
  influence of accounts 133
  influence of aggregation 130–1
  influence of external migration 132–3
  input assumptions 130
  movement model 139–41
  regional population 126–59
  sources of variation 129–33
  United Nations 367–79
  urbanization 367–79
Puerto Rico 80–1, 85–7, 90, 94
Punjab 69, 338, 340

Rajasthan 338, 340
Rallu, J. 53
Ram, S. 305, 320–1
rates
  measurement of 105–11
  models B 115–16
  movement 105–6
  observed 115–16
  occurrence-capture 110
  P 108–12
  S 108–12
  survivorship 108–10
  transition 108–11
  use of 111–15
Ravenstein, E. G. 13, 163, 180
Razi, Z. 24
Rees, P. H. 2, 58, 97, 99, 104–5, 110, 112–13, 115, 119, 132–3, 135, 146, 150, 152, 160, 163–4, 193, 272, 274, 287, 304–5, 314–15, 320–1, 323, 330, 332, 334, 336–7, 339, 345, 351
register
  NHSCR 166–9
Reyes, F. 78
Rhind, D. 315, 342–3
Richardson, H. 282
Ridley, J. C. 252
Rikkinen, K. 319–20
Roberts, A. J. 273, 275
Rogers, A. 2, 99, 107–8, 113–16, 119, 121, 124, 130–1, 133, 142, 146, 154, 165, 175, 203, 274, 287, 312, 338–9, 345
Romaniuk, A. 79, 93
Russell, J. C. 24
Russia 27

Sadler, P. 277
St Louis 277
sampling
  synthetic 254–62
Scheele, S. 254

Schinnar, A. P. 275, 278
Schmoranz, I. 275, 278
Schofield, R. S. 13, 23–5, 37
Scotland 53, 137–8, 140, 150, 155–8, 161, 164, 167–70, 172–4, 178–80, 183, 190–2, 325–8
sex
   structure 261
Shannon, C. E. 255
Sheps, M. C. 252
Shiskin, J. 83
Shorter, E. 26
Shorter, F. C. 81
Shryock, H. S. 303
Siegel, J. S. 303
simulations
   computational issues 268–9
   numerical results 268–72
   sample size 268
   sources of error 269
Singapore 80, 367–71, 373–5, 377–8
Sjaastad, L. A. 14
Sleegers, W. F. 204
Smith, C. W. 19, 29
Snickars, F. 254
Somawat, G. 69
Somermeijer, W. H. 180
Somerset 34
Soong, Y. L. 80
South East Region 155–8, 168–70, 172–5, 178–80, 183, 189, 190–2, 325–8
South West Region 155–8, 170, 172–4, 178–80, 183, 189–92, 325–8
Spain 28, 86–7, 91
spatial demography
   defined 1
Spengler, J. J. 47
Spohr, H. 289–90
Sri Lanka 74, 76–7, 80, 85–7, 89–90, 93
Srinivasan, K. 330, 341
Staffordshire 31
stationary
   population analysis 111–13
Stillwell, J. C. H. 97, 115, 123, 150, 160, 163, 193, 313
Stone, P. A. 130
Stone, R. 2, 254, 274–5
Sullivan, O. 63
Sun, T. H. 80
Surinam 80
Sweden 13, 23–7, 86–7, 91, 121, 254
Switzerland 40
system
   demographic information 149–53
Syrquin, M. 380–1

Taeuber, I. B. 1
Teitelbaum, M. S. 29, 40
Taiwan 80, 83, 86–90, 93

Tamil Nadu 69, 81–2, 85–8, 90, 93–4, 338, 340
Thailand 74, 76–7, 80, 323, 343–71, 373–5, 377–8, 383–9
   births 360–1
   deaths 360–1
   migration 360–1
   population 360–1
   regional population structure 364
   regions 358
Thomas, I. 66
Thompson, W. S. 21
time-series
   analysis 205–20
   fertility 83–91
transition
   data 99–104
   matrix method 121
   rates 108–11, 129, 133
Trinidad and Tobago 45, 49–58, 80, 85–7, 90
Tsubouchi, Y. 51
Tunisia 79
Turkey 81
Tyne and Wear 155–8, 165–6, 168, 170, 172–4, 178–80, 183, 190–2

United Kingdom 53, 58, 98, 115, 121, 126, 128, 130, 132, 137, 146, 148–202, 301, 305, 313, 315, 320, 323–9, 331–2
   external migration 323–9
   internal migration 160–202
United Nations 3, 10, 11, 53, 73–4, 79–80, 92, 104, 333, 335–6, 343, 367–89
urbanization
   and development 380–8
   and per capita GNP 380–8
   dynamics 376–80
   effects on fertility 16
   effects on mortality 37
   projections 367
USA 10–11, 28, 48, 52–3, 80, 83, 85–91, 114, 131, 146, 252
USSR 10–11, 53, 81
Uttar Pradesh 334–40

Vallin, J. 79
van der Erf, R. 207
van der Knaap, G. A. 204, 207
van der Walle, E. 9, 28–30, 32, 34, 39
van der Woude, A. M. 14–15, 18, 42
van Engen, E. H. 207
Venezuela 80–1, 85–7, 90
Vietnam 367–71, 373–5, 377–8
Vinovskis, M. A. 13
Visaria, L. 331–2, 335–7
Visaria, P. 331–2, 335–7

Wales 23–43, 45, 52–4, 58–66, 86–7, 91, 120–1, 137–8, 140, 150, 155–8, 161, 163–4, 167, 172–4, 178–80, 183, 190–2, 325–8
Watkins, S. C. 9, 28, 40
Wedderburn, R. W. M. 228
Weeden, R. 180
Wegener, M. 253
Welsh Office 163
West Bengal 338, 340
West Midlands Region 59, 155–8, 170, 172–4, 178–80, 183, 186, 189–92, 325–8
Willekens, F. 97, 99, 104, 107, 115, 119, 121, 123, 132, 142–3, 151, 204, 209, 225, 228, 237, 239, 315, 338–9, 345
Williams, H. C. W. L. 248, 253, 262, 268
Williamson, J. 48
Wilson, A. G. 2, 104, 110, 135, 164, 181, 193, 253, 274, 287, 304, 345, 351
Wilson, M. 53
Wolpert, J. 204
Woods, R. I. 1, 3, 10, 14, 18–19, 21, 26–7, 29, 31, 35–7, 43, 48, 331, 334, 337–9
Woodward, J. H. 35
World Bank 336
World Fertility Survey 45–6, 57, 68, 71–80, 93
Wrigley, E. A. 13, 23–5, 37

Xenos, C. 79

Yapa, W. 204
Yorkshire 31, 59, 155–8, 163, 170, 172–4, 178–80, 183, 190–2, 254, 256, 259–61, 267–72, 305, 325–8
Yu, Y. C. 330
Yuan Tien, H. 71
Yugoslavia 53

Zaire 79, 93
Zelinsky, W. 48
zones
    metropolitan 161–3
    non-metropolitan 161–3